Based on a large-scale empirical study, this book is the most extensive analysis of citizen participation in American politics currently available. It provides both a new perspective on the ways in which citizens take part in political life and a new theoretical understanding of the role of participation in a democracy.

Topics of particular interest include the relationship between social class and political activity, the detailed comparison of the different ways in which blacks and whites take part in American political life, the impact of the decline of the small town and the growth of urban centers on political participation, and the extent to which participation hinders or furthers democracy.

"A masterful blend of painstaking empirical analysis. . . . A classic that should dominate its area for years to come."
  – PHILIP E. CONVERSE, *University of Michigan*

PARTICIPATION IN AMERICA

PARTICIPATION IN AMERICA

Political Democracy and Social Equality

Sidney Verba
Norman H. Nie
University of Chicago

Harper & Row, Publishers
New York   Evanston   San Francisco   London

PARTICIPATION IN AMERICA: POLITICAL DEMOCRACY AND SOCIAL EQUALITY
Copyright © 1972 by Sidney Verba and Norman H. Nie

STANDARD BOOK NUMBER: 06-046823-8
LIBRARY OF CONGRESS CATALOG CARD NUMBER: 72-80128

To Our Parents

Contents

Tables

Figures

Preface

The political scientist is called upon to pursue two somewhat different goals. Those who want political science to be a generalizing science enjoin him to try to confirm the existence of general processes of politics. This involves abstraction from any particular situation and the development of theories or models of a general sort. On the other hand, many call upon the political scientist to be "relevant," a word that is often used in silly ways but that can have a quite serious meaning—i.e., that one provide understanding of important political situations, in particular places, at particular times.

The debate sometimes sounds as if one must choose between the two positions. In fact, they are quite compatible—in theory if not always in practice. We have, in this book, attempted to pursue both goals: to say something about the processes of politics in general and something about American politics at the beginning of the 1970s in particular.

We consider two general political processes: that by which citizens come to participate in political life and that by which their participation affects the responsiveness of governmental leaders. This involves the explication of some general variables—measures of various forms of political participation, measures of social status, of political attitudes, of voluntary association memberships, of citizen policy preferences, of leader policy preferences, and the like—and statements about expected relationships among them. These variables form the building blocks of a model of the causes and consequences of participation applicable to any nation. How that model works in a particular nation depends on the specific values of the variables in that instance.

It is by entering these specific values as they existed in the United States in the late 1960s that we see how these processes work in that particular context. This is what makes our work relevant to contemporary American politics. As we shall see, the particular values these variables have in the United States—the distribution of voluntary association memberships or party affiliations across social statuses, the particular political beliefs that exist, their distribution in the population, and so forth—when entered into the more general model tell us a lot about why American politics takes the shape it does.

The next step would be to test these models in other settings. This we hope to do, for the present volume is part of a larger, cross-national study of political participation. Later works will consider a similar set of questions in other nations as well as questions from a comparative perspective.[1] But though part of a larger enterprise, this book is meant to stand alone and to contribute to an understanding of contemporary American politics, and, more generally, to an understanding of some problems and dilemmas in democratic government.

[1]Some publications reporting cross-national comparisons on these issues are: Sidney Verba, Norman H. Nie, and Jae-on Kim, *The Modes of Democratic Participation: A Cross-National Analysis* (Sage Professional Papers in Comparative Politics, no. 01-013, 1971); Sidney Verba, Bashiruddin Ahmed, and Anio Bhatt, *Caste, Race, and Politics: A Comparison of India and the United States* (Beverly Hills: Sage Publications, 1971); and Sidney Verba, "Cross-National Survey Research: The Problem of Credibility," in Ivan Vallier, ed., *Comparative Methods in Sociology: Essays on Trends and Applications* (Berkeley and Los Angeles, 1971), pp. 309-356. Some parts of Chapter 4 were first published in Verba, Nie, and Kim, *op. cit.,* and some parts of Chapter 10 were first published in Verba, Ahmed, and Bhatt, *op. cit.*

Acknowledgments

A large-scale empirical study of the sort we are reporting in this volume goes on for many years and involves many people. The years we would like to forget. The people we would like to remember.

To begin with, we owe a substantial debt to our colleagues in the Cross-National Program on Political and Social Change, of which the study of American participation is one component. The framework for the study and the research design developed in a collaborative context with these other scholars. And the study is much richer because of this contribution of non-American scholars. To be sure, they come to the study of America with presuppositions, but presuppositions different from those brought in by the U.S. contingent. The collaborators in this program included: Rajni Kothari and Bashiruddin Ahmed of the Centre for the Study of Developing Societies, Delhi; Hajime Ikeuchi, Joji Watanuki, and Jun-Ichi Kyogoku of the University of Tokyo; Ichiro Miyake of the University of

Kyoto; and Ulf Himmelstrand and Albert Imohiosen, formerly both of the University of Ibadan, currently of the University of Uppsala and the University of Lagos, respectively. Gabriel A. Almond played a key role in initiating the cross-national study. And Robert Somers was an important collaborator in many substantive and methodological aspects of the work. Charles Y. Glock helped in the design of the survey.

In our analysis of the data we were helped by many people, some of whom made substantial and independent contributions. First and foremost is Jae-on Kim, whose skill in data analysis and whose understanding of the assumptions underlying such analysis is matched only by his capacity for sustained work on a problem and his patience with excitable and sometimes disorganized colleagues. This book would not be here without him.

John R. Petrocik worked tirelessly on the design and execution of many of the analyses, often under considerable time pressure and in difficult working conditions. Susan B. Hansen contributed to our analyses in many ways, and in particular helped shape the techniques used to link citizens with their community leaders. Jean Jenkins programmed and helped design the cluster analysis of citizen activists. William C. Mitchell, C. Hadlai Hull, and Wilfred Hansen designed and wrote numerous computer programs used in our analyses. Glen Edwards supervised the coding of the data. In addition, we benefited from the help of Eugene Durman, William Goldman, David Lawrence, Kristi Andersen, Robert Bourgeois, Jaap Rozema, Rachel Kats, Janet Quint, Lawrence Rose, Barry Rundquist, Anton van Rosmalen, Goldie Shabad, Paula Stich, Fenny van Kleef, and Carol-Ann Lugtigheid.

Arlee Ellis at Stanford and Shirley Saldanha at Chicago were key to the organization of our efforts—they held the project together. Cynthia Miller, Lynn Schell, and Anne Leonidoff typed and retyped the chapters of this manuscript.

Several people read the manuscript and provided comments that led to important improvements. For this we are grateful to Philip E. Converse, Andrew Greeley, Kent Jennings, G. Bingham Powell, and Kenneth Prewitt.

Our work has been aided by a number of institutions. The first meeting out of which the research project emerged was held at the Center for Advanced Study in the Behavioral Sciences at Stanford, which was also the pleasant site for extended stays in the United States of some of our non-American collaborators. The Institute of Political Studies at Stanford University and the Institute of International Studies at the University of California at Berkeley jointly sponsored the study and provided many facilities. The Survey Research Center of the University of California at Berkeley supervised the fieldwork and conducted the coding of the data. The actual fieldwork was done by the National Opinion Research Center of the University of Chicago, which in the later stages of the project became the home for the writing and data analysis, and gave generously of its facilities.

The University of Alberta provided computer time and facilities for some of the early data analysis and the University of Leiden (The Netherlands) made a similar contribution in the concluding months of our work. Dale H. Bent and Christian Bay at the University of Alberta and Hans Daalder and Chris P. Haveman at the University of Leiden made these contributions possible.

The fieldwork for the study was generously supported by the Carnegie Corporation of New York. The Ford Foundation supported our parallel data-collection efforts in other countries. The Institute of International Studies at Berkeley contributed to the costs of the data coding, and the Committee on International Studies of the University of Chicago contributed to the data-analysis costs. Most of the data analysis was conducted under a grant from the National Science Foundation (grant GS 3155). A study of this sort costs a great deal of money. These institutions generously provided it. We spent it. We hope the results are worth it.

We would also like to express our appreciation to the Ford Foundation, the Fulbright Program, and the National Science Foundation for providing us with time off from our university duties to complete this book—the first provided Verba with a research fellowship for the academic year 1971-1972 and the latter two supported Nie during the same period.

To our wives, who bore the burden of our nights of watching the computer and our days of fidgeting over data analyses, we can only say we will never do it again—well, hardly ever.

SV
NN
Dec., 1972

Je participe
Tu participes
Il participe
Nous participons
Vous participez
Ils profitent

From a wall in Paris, 1972.

Chapter 1
Participation
and Democracy

Much of the current debate about the quality of American political life revolves around the question of participation. If democracy is interpreted as rule by the people, then the question of who participates in political decisions becomes the question of the nature of democracy in a society. Where few take part in decisions there is little democracy; the more participation there is in decisions, the more democracy there is. Such a definition of democracy is crude, because it says little about elections, or free speech, or guarantees of minority rights, or majority rule; yet it may get at the heart of the matter, since all other institutions associated with democracy can be related to the general question of who participates or is able to participate in political life.

Many of the questions raised about participation in American political life are normative ones: How much participation ought there to be? Who should participate? How should political leaders respond to the voice of the people? And in general, how adequate is American democracy, and how might it be improved? There are also empirical questions: How much participation is there in America? Who participates? How do citizens participate? How equally distributed among the citizenry are opportunities to participate? Who takes advantage of such opportunities? What are the processes by which citizens come to participate? And perhaps most important of all (and most difficult to answer), What are the consequences of citizen participation?

In this book we shall attempt to answer these empirical questions. In so doing, we hope to contribute to answers to the normative ones as well.

WHAT IS PARTICIPATION?

Political participation refers to those activities by private citizens that are more or less directly aimed at influencing the selection of governmental personnel and/or the actions they take. The definition is rough, but it is adequate for delimiting our sphere of interest. It indicates that we are basically interested in *political* participation; that is, in acts that aim at influencing *governmental* decisions. Actually, we are interested more abstractly in attempts to influence the authoritative allocations of values for a society, which may or may not take place through governmental decisions. But, like most political scientists who start out with such an abstract concern, we shall concentrate on governmental decisions as a close approximation of this more general process.

Our concept of participation is broader than some, narrower than others. It is a broad conception in that we are interested in a wide variety of ways citizens participate in relation to varied issues. In particular we wish to look beyond citizen participation in the electoral process—beyond voting and campaign activity—to various other ways citizens can be active. And we want to look beyond the question of why some citizens are active and others not. We want to raise the question of what difference it makes how many citizens are active and which citizens they are.

Our conception of participation is narrower than some in that we are interested in acts that aim at *influencing* the government, either by affecting the *choice* of government personnel or by affecting the *choices made by* government personnel. We are not dealing with what can be called "ceremonial" or "support" participation, where citizens "take part" by expressing support for the government, by marching in parades, by working hard in developmental projects, by participating in youth groups organized by the government, or by voting in ceremonial elections.

This distinction is important, especially in an era when so much attention is focused on the political mobilization of citizens in the "support" sense. This is what is meant by participation in many of the developing societies of the world and sometimes in the United States as well.[1] In contrast, the kind of

---

[1] James Townsend, for instance, in his book *Political Participation in Communist China* (Berkeley and Los Angeles: University of California Press, 1967), characterizes the Chinese style of political participation as stressing execution of party policies, the contact downward from cadre to mass, and as involving an insistence that "political action support the supreme, unified national interest as defined solely by the Communist Party" (Chapter 4). For good discussions of mobilized as opposed to democratic participation, see Aristide Zolberg, *Creating Political Order* (Chicago: Rand McNally, 1966) and John P. Nettl, *Political Mobilization: A Sociological Analysis of Methods and Concepts* (London: Faber, 1967).

In the United States, participation as a means of securing support for decisions of leaders rather than a means of influencing their decisions is often found in programs of participation in private organizations, particularly participation in management. On participation as a means of eliciting consent see Sidney Verba, *Small Groups and Political Behavior* (Princeton, N.J.: Princeton University Press, 1961), Chapters 6 and 7.

participation in which we are interested—perhaps it should be labeled *democratic participation*—works the other way. It emphasizes processes of influencing governmental policies, not carrying them out; it emphasizes a flow of influence upward from the masses; and, above all, it does not involve support for a preexisting unified national interest but is part of a process by which the national interest or interests are created.

Our focus is narrower in another way: We are interested in participatory *activities*. We do not include in our definition of participation, as some have, attitudes toward participation—citizens' sense of efficacy or civic norms. These psychological orientations may be important as sources of participation, but we are more interested in the actual behavior of citizens in attempting to influence the government.

Third, we have limited our attention largely to participation *vis-à-vis* the government. The argument has been made that effective participation depends upon opportunities to participate in other spheres—family, school, job, voluntary associations. A participatory polity may rest on a participatory society.[2] We do not quarrel with this assumption and, indeed, will present some evidence to support it when we look at the processes that bring citizens to participate. But we shall not attempt to describe and explain patterns of participation outside of those that are more narrowly *political*—i.e., aimed at affecting the government.

One last limitation in our focus: Our present concern is with activities "within the system"—ways of influencing politics that are generally recognized as legal and legitimate. This eliminates many of the tactics of political protest. The importance of these tactics has grown in recent years, at least for particular groups and particular interests. Our focus on "ordinary" political participation does not imply that these other means are unimportant or inappropriate. Indeed, some of the characteristics of ordinary participatory activities—especially the way particular modes of activity are distributed across the population and the consequences of that distribution—may help explain some of the reasons for the rise in alternative tactics. But the study of these other modes would be another book, not the one we have written.

WHY IS PARTICIPATION IMPORTANT?

The study of political participation is important for an understanding of American politics for several crucial reasons: In the first place, as already suggested, it is at the heart of democratic theory and at the heart of the democratic political formula in the United States.

[2] There are a number of reasons why scholars have stressed the importance of participation outside the directly political arena. For one thing, insofar as major decisions are made by private institutions, effective control by citizens over their own lives would require participation *vis-à-vis* these institutions. On this topic, see Carole Pateman, *Participation and Democratic Theory* (London: Cambridge University Press, 1970), Chapters 4 and 5. Furthermore, it is argued that opportunities to participate in the private sphere provide the training and skills needed to participate politically. This has been the position of such writers as G. D. H. Cole and is supported by evidence in Gabriel A. Almond and Sidney Verba, *The Civic Culture: Political Attitudes and Democracy in Five Nations* (Princeton, N.J.: Princeton University Press, 1963), Chapters 11 and 12. For a more elaborate theory on the relationship between authority patterns in the nongovernmental sphere and political democracy, see Harry Eckstein, *A Theory of Stable Democracy* (Princeton, N.J.: Center of International Studies, 1961).

Second, participation, when and if effective, has a particularly crucial relationship to all other social and political goals. It represents a process by which goals are set and means are chosen in relation to all sorts of social issues. Indeed, this is why it is crucial to democratic theory and to political systems in general. Through participation the goals of the society are set in a way that is assumed to maximize the allocation of benefits in a society to match the needs and desires of the populace. Participation is not committed to any social goals but is a technique for setting goals, choosing priorities, and deciding what resources to commit to goal attainment.

There is currently a debate among social scientists about the adequacy of participatory mechanisms in the United States as means for communicating the needs and interests of the citizens to the government. The debate is in part more about the adequacy of political science than political reality. The issue is whether and to what extent the study of political participation should be limited to the actual participatory situation in the United States (which leaves many observers gloomy), or whether scholars, who have greater vision, should consider alternative possibilities, such as new participatory opportunities, groups, and techniques.[3]

Even if one focuses on that which can be empirically studied—the current or past situation *vis-à-vis* participation—there is debate on the adequacy of the system of participation in the United States. There are two reasons why this system might be found inadequate for communicating the needs of the citizens and for setting social policy. One reason has to do with the extent to which the citizenry knows its own interests. More conservative critics of participatory mechanisms argue that citizens do not have the skill to calculate the consequences of their acts. Therefore, they may damage their own best (but unrecognized) long-run interests by short-range and ill-conceived demands.[4] More radical critics often agree that citizens do not know their own best interests, but this is because of a "mobilization of bias" whereby citizens are socialized to be unaware of their own interests and political capabilities.[5]

This critique of the adequacy of participatory mechanisms is hard to deal with empirically; and as Thompson points out, many theorists of participation assume that citizens are autonomous and the best judges of their own interests.[6] We shall not question this assumption either; rather we shall concentrate on the question of how effectively those interests and needs felt by citizens are communicated. We leave to others the question of whether those interests and needs result from biased socialization, from false con-

---

[3] The debate is endless. See the exchange between Jack Walker and Robert Dahl (Walker, "A Critique of the Elitist Theory of Democracy" and Dahl, "Further Reflections on 'The Elitist Theory of Democracy' "), *American Political Science Review*, Vol. 60 (June 1966), 285 ff. Two good general accounts are Dennis F. Thompson, *The Democratic Citizen* (London: Cambridge University Press, 1970) and Andrew MacFarland, *Power and Leadership in Pluralist Systems* (Stanford: Stanford University Press, 1969).

[4] Walter Lippman, in his many writings, has been an articulate spokesman for this position.

[5] See Peter Bachrach and Morton S. Baratz, "Decisions and Non-Decisions: An Analytic Framework," *American Political Science Review*, Vol. 57 (September 1963), pp. 632-642.

[6] Thompson, *The Democratic Citizen*, pp. 15-19.

sciousness, or from an inability to see long-range consequences. However, we shall attempt to distinguish between participation in circumstances in which citizens are likely to have a clear view of their own interests and circumstances in which they are not.

There is a second reason why participatory mechanisms in the United States might be considered inadequate. The interests of citizens might be inadequately communicated because, on the average, citizens are not active enough, or their interests might be unequally communicated because citizens are unequally active. This topic is more amenable to study. And though what exactly is adequate or inadequate is more normative than empirical, the question of how much participation there is and how equally it is distributed is empirical and well worth close study.

Participation is important not only because it communicates the citizen's needs and desires to the government, but because it has other, more direct benefits. Some have argued that it is, in itself, a prime source of satisfaction—satisfaction with the government and satisfaction with one's own role.[7] Furthermore, it has been viewed as an educational device through which "civic virtues" are learned. As John Stuart Mill, one of the many advocates of this position put it, "Among the foremost benefits of free government is that education of the intelligence and of the sentiments which is carried down to the very lowest ranks of the people when they are called to take part in acts which directly affect the great interests of the country."[8] Through participation, one learns responsibility.

In this sense, participation has more than instrumental value—it is an end in itself. Indeed, one can argue that under conditions of democratic norms one's self-esteem is seriously damaged if one has all decisions made for him and does not participate in those that affect his own life. From some perspectives, lack of ability to participate can imply lack of full membership within the system. The new demands for participation that have recently emerged in American society have both their instrumental (as means to other ends) and consummative (as ends in themselves) components.

WHAT IS THIS BOOK ABOUT?

We shall attempt to deal with some of these broad questions in relation to participation in American political life. Our main concern is with participation as an instrumental act by which citizens influence the government. Further, we wish to consider participation from the perspective of the functioning of the United States as a democratic polity, rather than from the point of view of the individual citizen as a participant. We are more interested in politics than in political psychology, more in the ways participation by citizens conditions the way political decisions are made than with the social and psychological reasons for individual citizen participation.

[7] See Almond and Verba, *The Civic Culture*, Chapter 9.
[8] J. S. Mill, *Considerations on Representative Government* (New York: Holt, 1873).

To deal with the "macro" questions about democratic politics, we shall have to raise some "micro" questions about the behavior of citizens and the sources of that behavior. Our goal is to understand how the preferences of the citizens are communicated upward to those who make governmental decisions. To understand this, we have to know why some citizens communicate their preferences and others do not. But rather than stopping with an answer to the question of why some are active and some are not, we will try to deal with the question of what difference it makes: What difference does it make in what those who make political decisions see as the preferences of the public, and what difference does it make in what they do about those preferences?

Our problem links micro- and macropolitics, for it deals with one of the most crucial questions of the relationship of the citizen to the state: How are the preferences of the citizens of a society aggregated into a social choice—i.e., into a governmental policy or a choice of governmental personnel? The question is made more complicated and more crucial by three considerations. In the first place, we are dealing, as we inevitably must in any complex social system, with citizens and groups of citizens who have diverse and conflicting interests. Second, we are interested in governmental decisions that are decisions for the entire system (for the entire nation if the national government, for the entire community if the local government). The combination of these first two points creates the fundamental political problem of how to make social policy out of a diversity of interests.

The third consideration is that we are dealing in the United States with a society with a democratic "political formula"—in Mosca's sense of the political formula as the rules that are supposed to govern a society. It is a formula that emphasizes popular control and government by the people. Politics ruled by more authoritarian political formulas can deal with the process of social choice out of diverse interests in a simpler manner: Elites do what they want. This of course is an oversimplification in that all societies will have (and probably need) some mechanisms for popular control. But the deviation is from central control in the direction of more dispersed control.

When one begins with a model of popular control, the tensions built into political decision-making come to the fore. These tensions derive from the difficulty in arriving at an authoritative social choice that is in some way responsive to the diversity of preferences within a complex and large social system. The problem can be seen from two perspectives: that of the decision-making system as a whole and that of the individual participant. If we think of decisions that affect the entire society—a major law, or a decision to go to war—it becomes clear that responsiveness is complicated indeed. On any particular issue, different segments of the public will have different views; some will have no position, others will have varied views held with varied intensity. And on such issues, there will be many other forces brought to bear over and above the preferences and participatory acts of the public: The governmental decision-makers have their own views and own preferences, the situation itself exerts pressures (as filtered through the perceptions of the decision-makers), resources are limited, previous decisions and commitments loom large, and so forth. What does it mean to talk of public participation under such circumstances? Elections, which simplify the participatory influence of the citizenry into a choice among candidates rather than a choice among policies, cannot reflect the distribution of preferences in a society, for the very reason that they simplify the range of policy preferences into a choice among a few candidates.

Consider the problem from the point of view of the individual participant. The one thing that is clear about his situation is that he is one small part of a very large whole. The voice of any particular citizen can have little measurable impact on such large social choices as the policies of the government or the outcome of an election. Nor can the result of such decisions or the policies of elected officials be expected to match the detailed preferences of more than a few citizens.

Thus, from the point of view of the system—or more precisely, from the point of view of those making choices that affect the society—choices cannot in any simple way be responsive to the participatory demands of the populace. This is true even if we assume that the only motivation of decision-makers is to respond to those demands. The other pressures under which they operate undercut this responsive capability even further. From the point of view of the individual participant, the problem is that he is but one among many citizens with varied preferences, and yet a single social choice must be made. Under such circumstances, he can expect but little voice, nor can he expect a set of policy outcomes that matches his preferences.

These considerations make clear that a study of participation and its effects cannot deal with the simple question of whether or not governmental officials are responsive to citizens, or even with the more complex question of how responsive they are. Responsiveness is not an either-or thing; nor can it be placed on a simple scale with leaders in some places more responsive than leaders elsewhere. Rather one must consider the question of whose preferences leaders respond to, and, most important, the mechanisms by which they become aware of these preferences and become motivated to act upon them. One of the main mechanisms by which leaders become aware of citizen preferences and become motivated to act on them is the system of political participation. This is the main subject of this book.

In this respect, we take a somewhat different approach from many of the works that have tried to relate citizen participation to the operation of the political system. For a number of other studies, the main problem has been how participation relates to the stability and survival of democratic polities. How does it affect the loyalty of citizens? What is the optimum amount of participation in a society? At what point does popular participation unleash antidemocratic forces? At what point does it unleash conflicts among groups that cannot be contained by peaceful politics? For these studies, the relevant consequences of participation are (on the micro level) the degree of satisfaction of the citizen, his feelings of loyalty, his attitudes toward opposing groups. On the macro level, the important consequences are conflict or its absence within society, and the stability or instability of the government and the society.[9]

These questions remain important and are by no means unrelated to the problems we shall pursue. But our main concern is not with whether participation increases or decreases the stability of democracies. Rather we are concerned with the way it affects the internal workings of democratic governments, with the effect participation has on what values are allocated to whom within the society. For us the relevant consequence of participation for the individual citizen is what he gets from the government. For the system as a whole the relevant consequence is how governmental benefits are allocated among citizens and among groups of citizens.

From this point of view, participation is of greatest interest to us as an instrumental activity whereby citizens influence (or try to influence) what the government does. We use a term as vague as *what the government does* rather than *decision-making* or *policy-making* because we want to encompass the widest possible range of governmental activities that might have some impact on the lives of the citizenry. We are interested in the "authoritative allocation of values in a society," to use David Easton's term, and in the fundamental political question of what determines that allocation.

Such a broad formulation would lead one to consider all aspects of politics. Our concern is somewhat narrower. We are interested in the impact on governmental actions of the activities of the citizens. There are, of course, many forces working on governmental officials, whether they are members of Congress or other legislative bodies, higher civil servants, or lower-level bureaucrats. These include the characteristics they bring to their jobs, their attitudes and values as to what ought to be done, the specific requirements of their roles, the legal prescriptions they must follow, the demands placed on them by other governmental officials, and so forth. Our focus is on what we call the *participation input:* the set of pressures that derive from the participatory activities of citizens who are not part of the official structure. One can imagine in the crudest terms that the governmental official is influenced by forces of the following kinds:

We shall study the impact of the forces from the left—the participation input. This should warn the reader that our simplification of the problem is a great simplification indeed. It leaves out much of what determines what officials do. We do this with no regrets because the problem left to us is large

[9]See for instance, Almond and Verba, *The Civic Culture,* Chapter 15; Eckstein, *A Theory of Stable Democracy;* and Seymour M. Lipset, *Political Man* (Garden City, N.Y.: Doubleday, 1960), Chapter 3.

enough. And in explicating the impact of participation we may learn quite a bit about the overall matrix of forces affecting the governmental official. At the end of this book we shall consider some of the other forces that affect governmental officials, a consideration that will help put the material on the role of participation into context.

In short, we start with a very broad question: Why are values allocated the way they are in the United States? But we move to a narrower one: What impact does public participation have on this? To deal with this latter question we shall have to deal with three still narrower questions:

1. What is the nature of the participation input—i.e., what does the set of citizen activities facing the public official look like?

2. What are the forces that determine the size and shape of the participation input—i.e., why is there the amount and kind of participation that there is in the United States?

3. What are the consequences of the participation input—i.e., how does it affect the allocation of values?

These three questions are the main thread that ties this book together.

The following diagram summarizes the simple structure of the book. Because these three questions form the main themes of the book, we can present our overall approach in terms of them. The faintly outlined box reminds us that there is much left out of our scheme.

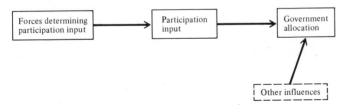

The Participation Input

Our first concern will be to characterize and analyze the "shape" of the participation input in America. The problem appears at first glance to be a simple empirical one: What citizens engage in what activities with what frequency? Such a question can be answered by presenting the results of a survey of the American population in which citizens were asked to describe their participatory activities. We shall present such results. But in order to make such results meaningful—or even to design such a survey—it is necessary first to consider the logic of participation itself.

If, as we assume (and will attempt later to test), participation has some impact on what the government does, what are the characteristics of the participation input that would shape that impact? There are three components of the participation input that, we believe, are relevant in this respect: How much participation is there, what kind is it, and from what segments of the society does it come?

How much participation?   This is the simplest component of the participation input. We assume that the more citizen participation there is, the more likely it is to affect the behavior of the government though, as we shall see, the relationship between the amount of participation and the response of the government is not all that simple. The amount of participation has two dimensions: the amount of political activity and the number of political activists. Often these two dimensions are merged. Thus when one considers voting participation, the amount of activity and the number of activists are one and the same: If there is a 30 percent turnout for an election, there is said to be little voting activity and few voters; if turnout is 80 percent, there is said to be much voting activity and many activists. But the amount of activity and the number of activists are one and the same in relation to voting simply because each citizen has, in a particular election, a strict limit on the amount of activity he can engage in. One man, one vote.

When one considers most other forms of political activity (efforts expended in a campaign, letters written to newspapers or Congressmen, and organizational activity), it is clear that the amount of activity (how many doorbells are rung, how many letters are sent, how many organizational meetings there are) is partially independent of the number of activists. There may be a given amount of activity coming from a small proportion of the population or from a large proportion. It is our assumption that the impact of participation depends both on how much there is and how many activists there are.

How can citizens influence the government?   As we pointed out, we have taken a narrower view than some as to what participation is. We are interested in activity aimed at influencing the government, not activity aimed at supporting the government or psychological orientations to participation. On the other hand, our view is broad, since we are interested in all the ways the citizen can exert that influence. Such a broad scope leads to concern with the alternative ways in which the citizen can influence the government. Our assumption is that the citizen has available a wide repertory of activities, and that these activities differ in terms of the type of impact that they can have on the government. Some citizen activities have major effects on the overall direction of governmental policy. The votes of citizens in a Presidential election are a major force in shaping the direction of the nation for a four-year period—though in such circumstances the vote of the single individual is of very marginal importance. Other citizen activities may affect only some narrow decision of a local government, or of a particular bureau or official. These activities, though much narrower in the scope of their impact, are important to consider if one wants to gauge the overall impact of participation. They may be of great importance to the citizen or citizens who are participating, though their results are not felt by others. And in such cases the individual participators may be much more potent.

Involved here is a classic issue of the interests citizens bring, and should bring, into politics via their participation: Do they participate *vis-à-vis* broad social issues or to obtain some narrow benefit? For many earlier theorists of citizen participation, such participation would have deleterious consequences for the public good if citizens brought into politics their own selfish interests rather than the interests of the broader community. As James Bryce wrote, capable citizens should have "honesty enough to seek the general interest rather than try to secure their own interest at the expense of the community."[10] Participation, according to men like Bryce, Tocqueville, or J. S. Mill, would train citizens in the civic virtue of considering the common good rather than their own narrow good. With "virtuous" citizens participating, public policy would be better, because such participants bring wisdom and a wider range of views.

A more modern view is that participation can lead to better public policy even if citizens bring their own narrow and selfish interests into politics. Through such "selfish" participation, the government is informed of these interests and pressured to respond. In this way it produces public goods more closely attuned to citizen needs than it would if there were no participation.[11]

The distinction is a difficult one to draw precisely. Sophisticated citizens can phrase the most narrow interest as public virtue and, indeed, it might take a philosopher-king to tell one from the other. But the distinction is important. Citizens participate vis-à-vis issues that reflect their own relatively narrow interests; they also participate vis-à-vis issues that affect the whole society. Whether they participate more virtuously in one sphere than another is uncertain, nor is it clear where they contribute most wisdom. But, as we shall show, participation on broad social issues and participation on narrow "selfish" ones are both significant parts of the participatory system in America. And each affects, in different ways, the government's allocation of benefits to citizens. We shall focus on both.

We shall explicate this distinction more fully in Part I where we deal with the alternative modes of citizen participation. The important point here is that the alternative activities available to citizens can produce different kinds of outcomes. Thus, if we want to see how participation affects the government, we must be aware of what kind of participation is involved. This will take us beyond the electoral system: beyond voting and campaign activity, on which much of the study of participation has focused. It will also lead to a reconsideration of the important question of the rationality of participation. For us, participation is a means to an end, an activity whereby citizens attempt to affect governmental activities in ways that will benefit them. But the citizen's ability to do that may depend upon the type of participatory activity

---

[10] James Bryce, *The Hindrance to Good Citizenship* (New Haven, Conn.: Yale University Press, 1910), p. 11. See also Mill, *Considerations on Representative Government*. Rousseau was particularly opposed to bringing into politics the views of organized groups. Citizen participation should bring in the wisdom of men interested in the common good. On the other hand, organized groups would interfere with the general good. See Judith N. Shklar, *Men and Citizens: Rousseau's Social Theory* (London: Cambridge University Press, 1969), p. 93.

[11] This is one of the presuppositions of much of the interest group literature. Out of the clash of special interests will come an overall policy best suited to the needs of the nation. For a recent critique of this position, see Theodore Lowi, *The End of Liberalism* (New York: Norton, 1969).

in which he is engaged and the particular change in governmental activities he desires. As we shall see, to raise the question of citizen rationality in relation to his activity as a voter is to raise that question for a circumstance where the means-ends calculations of rational behavior are most difficult. If we consider a wider range of activities, the question of the extent to which citizens can be rational political actors may take on another cast.

From whom does the participation come?   The last, and perhaps most crucial, component of the participatory input has to do with who is participating. This question differs from the question raised as to the number of political activists in America. There we were simply interested in whether a large or a small percentage of the population was active. Here we are interested in the ways the activist segment of the public differs from the rest of the population. Are they a representative sample of the population or do they come disproportionately from particular social groups?

The answer is, of course, crucial in terms of the effect that participation will have on governmental policy. If participants come proportionately from all parts of society, from upper- and lower-income groups, from blacks and whites, from city and country dwellers, then political leaders who respond to participation will be responding to an accurate representation of the needs, desires, and preferences of the public at large. If, as our not surprising findings will show, the participants are by no means representative of the public as a whole but come disproportionately from particular—especially upper-status— groups, then participation works differently.

Political participation has often been justified as a means by which social or economic inequalities can be reduced. Those of lower status—workers, poor farmers, new immigrants—would use their political influence associated with participation to induce the government to carry out policies beneficial to them. This belief leads to pressure for an equalization in the opportunities to participate and the removal of legal restraints to that participation. Yet the opening of opportunity does not equalize participation rates. All may receive equal access to participation in a formal sense—suffrage is universal, the right to petition is guaranteed to all, all can join in campaign activity. But the fact remains that participation is voluntary. Some will take more advantage of opportunities than others.[12] Most studies of participation, including our own, demonstrate that it is just those with higher income, higher education, and higher-status occupations who participate. There are many reasons for this, such as greater resources, skill, and psychological commitment, many of which we will discuss. But for whatever reason they participate more, the result is that those who may need governmental assistance the least participate the most—i.e., those already at the top of the stratification hierarchy are likely to be the most active.

This relationship between social stratification and participation is the main

---

[12]On this general issue, see Reinhard Bendix, *Nation-Building and Citizenship* (New York: Wiley, 1964).

continuing theme throughout our book. We will deal with the reasons for, and the consequences of, the relationship. Our purpose in the section of our volume dedicated to explicating the shape of the participation input is simply to demonstrate that such a relationship exists; that the participants in fact come from the more advantaged portions of the society. In this, our research will confirm the findings of others. But we hope to go beyond others in several ways. In the first place, our elaboration of the ways citizens can participate will provide us with a more variegated view of the composition of the participant population, for those who participate in politics in certain ways differ somewhat in social composition from those who participate in other ways. Second, we want to deal extensively with the reasons why the participants represent a specific segment of the population. And last, we want to consider explicitly the consequences of this. The second and third tasks represent the second and third themes of this book.

The Forces Determining the Participation Input

Our second theme is the set of forces that shape the participation input. For this, we consider the participation input to be the dependent variable and ask: Why do some people participate while others do not, and why do they participate in the ways they do? There are, of course, many answers. Some citizens have needs and problems that lead them to participate; others do not. Some citizens have the resources needed for participation (skills, time, and money); others do not. Some have attitudes conducive to participation: they believe it is effective, that politics is important, and that participation is a civic duty. Other citizens do not have these attitudes: they believe that participation is useless, that politics is unimportant, and that one ought to keep out of such affairs. Some citizens are in social circumstances where those around them expect them to participate; others are not. Some citizens live in circumstances where participation is made easy by institutional structures; others live in circumstances where they are surrounded by institutions that inhibit participation. All these forces working together lead some individuals to participate and others to stay home.

Our approach to this complex multiplicity of sources for participation derives from our concern with the relationship between participation and social stratification. We shall begin by considering why the participant population comes disproportionately from the upper-status groups of society. We will do this by proposing and testing a simple model of the process by which citizens come to participate—a model we call our *standard socioeconomic* model of participation. According to this model, the social status of an individual—his job, education, and income—determines to a large extent how much he participates. It does this through the intervening effects of a variety of "civic attitudes" conducive to participation: attitudes such as a sense of efficacy, of psychological involvement in politics, and a feeling of obligation to participate.

As we shall see, this model works. A good deal of the variance in how much and in what ways people participate is explained by their social-status characteristics, mediated by the intervening effect of their civic attitudes. However, the model does not tell the entire story. There are other social characteristics that cause deviations from the participation input that one would have if only the socioeconomic-status model were operating; there are other relevant political attitudes, not just the "civic" ones; and there are the intervening effects of particular social circumstances and particular institutions.

The standard socioeconomic model gives us a base line from which we look for deviations due to these other forces. These other forces lead some individuals to participate more than one would expect, given their socioeconomic characteristics, and others to participate less. This approach allows us to consider the impact of a variety of characteristics on the likelihood that an individual will participate: his position in the life cycle, his race, the organizations with which he is affiliated, his party affiliation, the nature of the community in which he lives, and his political beliefs.

Much of this analysis will involve asking a series of micropolitical questions, all having to do with the circumstances under which one individual decides to participate while another does not. But our major focus remains the macropolitical problem in two ways. In the first place, one set of circumstances affecting participation involves the environment in which the citizen lives: the kinds of organizational structures he has been exposed to and the kind of community within which he lives. Second, we are interested less in the individual decision to participate per se than in the effect this has on the shape of the participation input.

We start with the standard socioeconomic model because it tells us why the participant population is so heavily skewed in the direction of those with upper-social status, and we are interested in these additional social circumstances, attitudes, and social and political structures because they modify the workings of the standard socioeconomic model. The standard socioeconomic model, if it represented the sum of the forces leading to participation, would result in a participation input highly skewed in the direction of upper-status groups. Those with higher status would develop attitudes that make them the most participatory. The additional factors we shall consider change the participation input from what it would be if the only forces that were working were the socioeconomic ones. Some of these additional characteristics lead to a less skewed participation input—i.e., they represent forces that lead lower-status people to participate more than one would predict on the basis of their social status. In some cases they may accelerate the effects of the socioeconomic model—i.e., the characteristics represent forces that increase the participation of upper-status people. And in some cases the additional characteristics affect the rate of participation but do not do so differentially among social status groups.

Thus, when we consider such social circumstances as being self-consciously aware of one's group membership (e.g., of being a black American), or of belonging to such social institutions as voluntary associations and political parties, we will ask two questions: (1) Do these circumstances or these institutions raise or lower the likelihood that an individual will participate? And (2), What effects, if any, do they have on the difference in the rate of participation between upper- and lower-status citizens? Do they operate to accelerate the workings of the socioeconomic model so that the participatory gap between upper- and lower-status citizens increases, or do they operate to reduce the gap? This will enable us to look at such important attitudinal characteristics of the American population as group consciousness among blacks and such important institutions as private voluntary associations or political parties in terms of the extent to which they help to equalize the participation rate among citizens at different social levels or to increase the difference in participation rates.

The Consequences of Participation

The last theme of our book is the consequences of participation. As pointed out earlier, we assume that the participation input—the amount of participation, the kind of participation, and the social groups from whom the participation comes—makes a difference in governmental actions. And such, of course, has been the assumption among most students of participation. But most studies have focused on the causes of participation, not directly on the consequences. There are many good reasons for this, not the least of which is the difficulty in measuring governmental performance and the greater difficulty in connecting that performance to the participation of the citizenry.

We will attempt to make such a connection between participation and performance in the last section of the book. In the first place we shall attempt this hypothetically. We know, or will know by the time we reach that section, that the participation input is heavily skewed in the direction of upper-status citizens. But this would make a difference in what was communicated to political leaders only if this participant population also had preferences for policies or demands for governmental services that differed from those of their more quiescent fellow-citizens. Thus we will consider the question of the extent to which the participant population, when it participates, presents to the political leaders an image of public preferences different from that which exists in the public as a whole.

This question is the first step in understanding how participatory mechanisms connect the citizen and the government. If political leaders attend to the participant population, to what extent will they become aware of a set of problems different from that faced by the nonparticipant part of the population, and to what extent will they hear preferences for policies different from those in the population as a whole? The answer is crucial for understanding what kind of impact participation will have on governmental policy. As we shall see, the participants differ substantially from the nonparticipants in the problems they consider salient and in the solutions they prefer.

In addition we shall consider some differences between the two political parties in the ways they channel citizen preferences into the government.

Our last task will be to look more directly at the question of the consequences of participation. We gathered data on the attitudes and behavior of local political leaders in the same communities where we interviewed ordinary citizens. Using these data and using the community as the unit of analysis, we create a measure of the "concurrence" of political leaders with the citizens in their community—i.e., the degree to which citizens and local leaders agree on policy priorities in the community. Our major question then becomes: What effect does the participation of the citizens in the community have on the degree to which leaders concur with citizens?

The question, as our previous discussion should have made clear, is by no means a simple one. The "participation of the citizens" is a complex phenomenon. The participation input consists not only of an amount of participation but of various kinds, and the origins of that participation in different social groups. We want to see whether the type of participation, as well as the amount, makes a difference in the concurrence between citizens and political leaders. We also want to see how much it matters who participates, particularly since we will have shown that the participants are by no means representative of the citizenry as a whole.

The last point suggests that we must differentiate among various forms of leader concurrence: in particular, between leader concurrence with the population as a whole and leader concurrence with various segments of the population. For instance, does participation lead to greater concurrence with the participators or with all citizens? In other words, are the only beneficiaries of participation those who participate, or do all citizens in a community—the active and the inactive—benefit from the activity of the participants? The relationship between participation in the community and the concurrence of leaders with citizens is not likely to be a simple one whereby the more participation there is, the more leaders will agree with the citizens of their communities. But it is a domain wherein one can expect an orderly if somewhat more complex set of relationships. The parts of our book that precede this last section will suggest a number of more precise hypotheses about the shape of that relationship. With this discussion of the consequences of participation, we hope to place political participation into the context of the functioning of democratic political systems.

A NOTE ON METHOD

This book is based on a large-scale survey of the American public conducted in 1967. Survey research is, we believe, the only research technique that could have provided us with a body of data as rich, detailed, and systematic. But, as many have pointed out, survey techniques have limitations. Two of the most important are that they tend to use the individual as the unit of analysis and that they study one point in time. And these, of course, are serious limitations when one wants to study political participation from a macropolitical perspective in an era of rapid political change. We cannot completely overcome these limitations, but we have tried to overcome some of them by enriching our study beyond the limitations of standard survey research. We do this in the following ways:

Survey results as aggregates.   In part we try to overcome the focus of survey research on the individual citizen by the simple expedient of considering our survey results in the aggregate. If, on the individual level we know which citizens are likely to participate, we also know, on the aggregate level, what the resulting participant population will look like.

The context of individual activity.   Along with our interviews with individual citizens, we gathered information on a variety of characteristics of the communities in which they live. These additional data allow us to deal with the impact of environment on the political behavior of the individual citizen. By augmenting a standard national-survey sample with 1,000 additional interviews in 65 target communities with populations of 50,000 and under, we are able to execute analyses where the individual or the community in which he lives is the unit of analysis. In this way, as well, we go beyond the individualistic focus of much survey research. (See Appendix A for a more detailed description of the sample.)

The linkage between citizens and leaders.   Just as we gathered information on the characteristics of the communities within which our sample fell, we also gathered information on the attitudes and behavior of a set of local political leaders in these same communities. These data allow us to consider patterns of linkage between citizen and leader. Rather than stopping with a consideration of the activities citizens engage in, we can also consider how leaders respond to such activities.[13]

Extension of our data over time.   To add a time dimension to our study—in order to test some of our hypotheses with data over time and in order to see how the particular moment of our study might differ from other points in time—we have used a series of other survey studies (those conducted over the past twenty years by the Survey Research Center of the University of Michigan) to consider some of our main findings in an historical perspective.

AN OUTLINE OF THIS BOOK
The outline of the book will follow the themes just explicated. In presenting the outline, we can also present a schematic summary of those themes.

Part I: The Participation Input
As pointed out, the participation input consists of three major components: *how much* participation there is (and how it is distributed among the citizens), *what kind* of activity there is, and *from whom* that activity comes.

[13]This approach to participation, combining material from several different levels, was influenced by Stein Rokkan's seminal paper, "The Comparative Study of Political Participation: Notes Towards a Perspective on Current Research," in Austin Ranney, ed., *Essays in the Behavioral Study of Politics* (Urbana, Ill.: University of Illinois Press, 1962). Our debt to that essay is apparent throughout this volume.

The Participation Input

How much participation?

Of what sort?

By whom?

Chapter 2 will deal with the first component of the participation input: how much participation there is in America and how widely distributed it is throughout the population.

In Chapters 3 and 4 we will consider the second component: What kind of citizen activity is there? Chapter 3 will argue that there are ways in which citizens can participate that differ in terms of the kinds of governmental actions they can affect, as well as in several other significant ways. And we will explicate our reasons for focusing on four particular modes of participation in the light of some general considerations about participation and its relationship to the political process.

Following that, we will attempt in Chapter 4 to demonstrate that the four modes of participation represent a structure of political acts consistent with the pattern of activity engaged in by citizens. And we will isolate sets of citizens who specialize in one or another mode of activity, and in this manner develop a typology of political actors somewhat more elaborate than that usually employed. Our data will enable us to estimate how many of the various types of actors actually exist.

Chapter 5 will provide us with an opportunity to validate the differences among the various types of political activists. We will do this by showing that these different types of activists have different orientations to politics and that these orientations are consistent with what one would expect, given our discussion of the different modes of activity in Chapter 3.

In Chapter 6, we will complete our characterization of the participation input by dealing with the question of who participates. In that chapter we will present a demographic profile for each of the types of political activists and compare that profile with that of the population as a whole. This will tell us the extent to which the participant population is representative of the population as a whole, or whether it deviates from that population in significant ways. In Chapter 7, we will reconsider the subject of the rationality of political participation in the light of the alternative ways in which citizens can participate.

Part II: The Process of Politicization.

In Part II we will consider the forces shaping the participation input. By raising the question of why citizens participate—and participate in the particular ways in which they do—we raise the question of why the participation input takes the shape that it does. The components of that process are summarized in the following diagram:

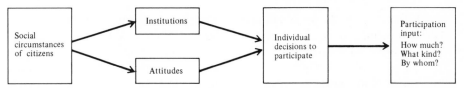

The individual's decision to participate and how to participate depends on his social circumstances—the set of social characteristics that defines his "life space," where he lives, what he does for a living, his education, his race, and so forth. These social circumstances generate sets of attitudes conducive to or inhibitory of political participation. How and how much he participates will also be affected by the institutional structures within which he finds himself. All of these forces lead him to a decision to participate or not, and the sum of the individual decisions to participate that derive from these forces present us with the participation input.

This diagram is but a framework for considering the forces that lead to participation, and an empty framework at that, since we have not specified which social circumstances or attitudes or social structures are relevant and which are not.

We will flesh out the framework by inserting into the diagram a "basic" set of social circumstances and attitudes that lead to participation. These are what we have called the standard socioeconomic model of the process by which individuals come to participate. According to this model, social status determines to a large extent the amount to which he participates. And it does so through the intervening effect of a variety of "civic" attitudes conducive to such participation—attitudes such as a sense of efficacy, of psychological involvement in politics, of an obligation to participate, and so on. When the model "works," upper-status individuals are more likely to decide to participate, and the resulting participation input is heavily weighted in their favor.

The Standard Socioeconomic Model

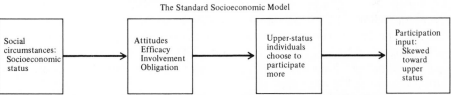

The standard socioeconomic status model of politicization is presented in Chapter 8. It will thereafter be used as a base line. In studying the impact on participation of other forces, we shall look at the way they lead to deviations from the amount of participation that one would expect from an individual with a particular social status. The additional factors will be considered in Chapters 9-14.

In Chapter 9, "Participation and the Life Cycle," we refer essentially to the set of changes in political participation that come with aging and movement through the various stages of the life cycle. We shall see how these relate to the amount of participation predicted by the standard socioeconomic status model. In Chapter 10, we consider the difference in the participatory rates of blacks and whites over and above the difference one would expect on the basis of the relative socioeconomic statuses of the two groups. If there are lower participation rates among black Americans (as we shall see there are), is this due to their lower average social status or, in some way, to their being black? And we will consider the impact on the participation gap between blacks and whites of the sense of group identity that has developed among black Americans.

The next three chapters continue the analysis of the processes that lead to participation by considering how the workings of the socioeconomic model are modified by various institutional frameworks within which the citizen may find himself: voluntary associations, political parties, and the local community.

One social structure central to studies of democratic participation has been the voluntary association, and this is the subject of Chapter 11. It has been found to be an institution that increases the likelihood that citizens will participate. In considering the relationship between voluntary associations and the standard socioeconomic model, we will ask if voluntary associations have an independent effect on the participation of their members over and above the fact that organizational members are generally of higher social status. If organizational affiliation does have an independent effect, we will ask how it modifies the workings of the socioeconomic model. Further questions discussed in this chapter are, Does organizational affiliation lead lower-status individuals to participate more than they ordinarily would? Or does such affiliation accelerate the workings of the socioeconomic status model by adding an increment of participation to those upper-status individuals already participating?

In Chapter 12 we consider how party affiliation affects the participation rate of the citizen—again in terms of the way party affiliation leads to deviations from the "normal" socioeconomic model. Does party affiliation provide a means whereby lower-status individuals increase their participation beyond what one would expect given their status? Does it increase or decrease the participation gap between upper- and lower-status citizens? These questions are proposed in Chapter 12.

How does the structure of the community within which the citizen lives affect his likelihood of participation? We will deal with this question in Chapter 13 largely from the point of view of the size and complexity of the community. In so doing, we will try to disentangle a complex set of relationships. The larger and more complex the community, the more difficult it may be for the citizen to participate effectively. But the larger and more complex the community, the more likely its residents are to have those personal characteristics—higher education, higher status jobs—that make them more capable of effective participation. We will consider how these contradictory tendencies affect participation.

In Chapter 14, we will consider some of the forces influencing participation from an historical perspective, using data from other studies to trace the evolving relationship among social status, the life cycle, race, and participation over the past twenty years. This analysis will help to confirm the existence of some of the patterns we find in our cross-sectional data.

Figure 1-1 presents the more elaborate model of the process leading to participation, as reflected in the various chapters of Part II.

Part III: The Consequences of Participation.

In Part III, we consider the results of participation. Chapter 15 considers the consequences of participation from the point of view of the preferences that are communicated by the participant population in contrast with the preferences of those who are inactive. The main question here is, Would it make any difference if government leaders paid attention to the participants rather than to the population as a whole?

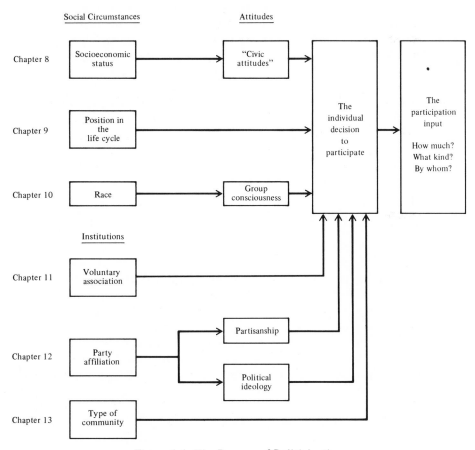

Figure 1-1. The Process of Politicization

In Chapter 16 we will pursue this problem by dealing with the reasons why it *does* make a difference—that is, why the preferences of the participants differ from those of the inactive citizens. In particular, we will consider some differences between the two parties in the way in which they act as channels for preferences.

In Chapters 17, 18, and 19 we consider the effects of participation more directly. In Chapter 17 we develop a measure of "concurrence" between citizens and leaders. We use our sample of communities as units of analysis to ask what effect participation has on concurrence. In Chapter 18 we will test some hypotheses as to the impact on leader concurrence with citizens of the amount of participation in the community, of the type of participation, and of the social groups that participate. In short, we will attempt in Chapter 18 to test the effects of the various components of the participation input. And we will consider the ways in which leaders can be responsive—in what way, on what topics, and to whom? In Chapter 19 we will ask how the nature of the community and the modes of participation affect type of response.

In sum, the overall structure of our argument, and of the book, leads us to consider first what participation is; we then back up to see what causes it; and then move ahead to its consequences. The structure looks like this:

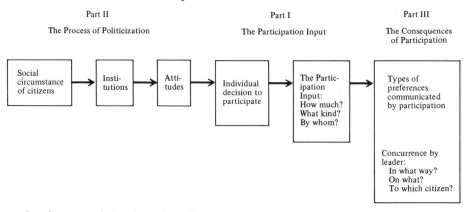

In short, we intend to describe how much and what kind of participation there is in the United States, and what groups that participation comes from. We then turn to what leads to that participation, and then look at some consequences of participation. None of these tasks is simple, and our outline above may be unclear about how we shall deal with one part or another of our scheme. But to explicate further any of the sections of the book would require the presentation of the whole book. And it is to that task that we now turn.

Part I
THE PARTICIPATION
INPUT

In this section we consider:
How much participation there is in America
The ways in which citizens participate
From whom the participation comes

Chapter 2
Citizen Participation:
How Much?
How Widespread?

How much participation is there in America? And how concentrated is that participation: that is, does it come from a small activist stratum or from a fairly broad segment of the population? The discussion of these two questions among students of American politics has a long and rather inconclusive history. When Tocqueville examined America in the early nineteenth century, he was struck by the high rate of mass participation compared with that elsewhere. He commented: "In some countries the inhabitants seem unwilling to avail themselves of the political privileges which the law gives them; ... but if an American were condemned to confine his activity to his own affairs, he would be robbed of one-half of his existence ... ."[1] And recent empirical studies of political participation that have taken a comparative perspective have also found that levels of political activity in the United States (with the

[1] Alexis de Tocqueville, *Democracy in America* (New York: Knopf, 1945), Vol. 1, p. 250.

exception of voter turnout) are quite high when compared with rates in other industrial societies.[2]

On the other hand, students of American politics have often commented on the low level of political participation in America. They suggest (backed by considerable empirical evidence) that elections, particularly those not involving the selection of a president, are determined by only a small fraction of the eligible voters, and that even fewer citizens engage in other types of political activity such as participating in election campaigns or contacting their elected representatives.[3]

The two questions—how much? and how widespread?—are partially interrelated. Where the activity of each citizen is strictly limited—as it is when we consider voting in a particular election—the amount of activity and the number of activists are one and the same. But where the amount of activity of each citizen can vary—a citizen can write no letter, one letter, or ten letters to his Congressman—the amount of activity and the degree to which that activity comes from a wide range of citizens are not the same. Of course, even in this case there is some relationship between amount of activity and the degree to which it is widespread. The more the overall amount of political activity, the more likely is it to come from a broad segment of the population. Nevertheless, it is important to separate the questions, for one can have the same amount of activity coming in one case from a small, activist portion of the population while the bulk of the citizens are quiescent, and in another case coming from a wider range of citizens, though in lesser amount from each. The ten letters can come from one citizen or from ten. And, of course, it makes a difference.

Over the last several decades, investigations of political participation using survey techniques have amassed a great deal of information on the level and distribution of political participation in the United States. Many of these data are confined to electoral participation and come from the excellent series of election studies by the Survey Research Center at the University of Michigan. Most of the data on other (i.e., nonelectoral) types of participation exist in bits and pieces from a number of different studies; but this information, together with the data from the voting studies, has begun to form a rather standard and accepted picture of the structure of political participation in this country—a

[2] For comparative data, see Gabriel A. Almond and Sidney Verba, *The Civic Culture;* Sidney Verba, Norman H. Nie, and Jae-on Kim, *The Modes of Democratic Participation: A Cross-National Comparison* (Beverly Hills: Sage Publications, 1971); and Norman H. Nie, G. Bingham Powell, and Kenneth Prewitt, "Social Structure and Political Participation," *American Political Science Review,* vol. 63 (June and September, 1969), pp. 361-378, 808-832.

[3] This theme appears throughout the empirical literature on political behavior. See, for just a few of many examples, Lester Milbrath, *Political Participation* (Chicago: Rand McNally, 1965); Robert Dahl, *Who Governs? Democracy and Power in an American City* (New Haven, Conn.: Yale University Press, 1961); and Angus Campbell et al., *The American Voter* (New York: Wiley, 1960), Chapter 4. The same theme is found in earlier commentators. See James Bryce, *The American Commonwealth* (New York: Macmillan, 1910), Vol. 2, pp. 291-293, where he expresses amazement at the lack of concern with political matters even among the educated classes in America.

picture of low levels of citizen participation and the concentration of political activity in the hands of a small portion of the citizens.[4]

Data from the Survey Research Center election studies indicate, for example, that fewer than one citizen in three attempts to influence the voting decisions of others, and this figure has remained constant over the past four Presidential elections. Less than 10 percent attend political meetings or rallies during an election, about 8 percent donate money, and no more than 5 percent of the citizenry belong to political parties or partisan organizations.[5] Furthermore, it is often the same citizens who attend meetings, donate money, belong to partisan organizations, and are otherwise active in the elections.

These data are, of course, restricted to electoral participation within a given Presidential election, but other types of political activity with longer time referents suggest only slightly higher rates of participation. Almond and Verba find, for example, that less than 28 percent of the citizenry have ever attempted in any way to influence the outcome of a governmental decision in their local community, and fewer than 16 percent have made similar influence attempts at the national level.[6] Secondary analysis of their data has also demonstrated that the various activities are highly correlated, indicating that many of the same citizens participate across the range of activities.[7]

Investigators have also found a cumulative pattern in political participation. They find that citizens who engage in the more infrequent and costly acts of participation also perform those activities that are more widespread in the population. Conversely, they have found that citizens who fail to participate in those activities that are more frequent and require the commitment of less time and energy are far less likely to be among those who perform the less frequent variety of participatory acts.

In the now classic study of the 1952 and 1956 Presidential election, *The American Voter,* Campbell et al. suggest the following concerning the level of participation in this country: "For most Americans voting is the sole act of participation in politics. Moreover since the groups in our samples who did report engaging in these activities are widely overlapping, the percentages cannot be added together to reach an estimate of the total number who were active."[8] In reference to participation rates in New Haven, Robert Dahl

[4] An early study using survey data came to the conclusion that "the figures on political participation are so low as to give support to the conclusion that in America the few act politically for the many." Julian Woodward and Elmo Roper, "Political Activity of American Citizens," *American Political Science Review,* vol. 44 (December 1950), pp. 872-885.

[5] These data are compiled from the Survey Research Center *Election Study Codebook* for the Presidential elections of 1960 and 1964. The data for the 1956 Presidential election are presented in Campbell et al., *The American Voter,* p. 51.

[6] Gabriel A. Almond and Sidney Verba, *Five-Nation Study Codebook,* distributed by Inter-University Consortium for Political Research, Survey Research Center, University of Michigan.

[7] Nie, Powell, and Prewitt, "Social Structure and Political Participation."

[8] Campbell et al., *The American Voter,* pp. 50-51. The percentages they refer to that cannot be added due to great amounts of overlap are: membership in political organizations (3%); contributing money (10%); attending meetings or rallies (7%); any other campaign work (3%).

summarizes his findings on both electoral and nonelectoral participation, findings he feels are typical of many American communities:

> During the last decade the number of non-voters has varied from a quarter to a half in some mayoralty elections. Even those who vote rarely do more, and the more active the form of participation, the fewer the citizens who participate. Only a *tiny minority* of the registered voters undertakes the more vigorous kinds of campaign participation. . . . It might be thought that citizens participate more actively outside campaigns and elections . . . but just as with campaign activity, most people do very little beyond merely talking with their friends.[9]

Robert Lane comments on the intercorrelated cumulative structure of participation:

> If a person electioneers he is *almost certain* to attend party meetings.
> If a person attends meetings he is *almost certain* to be among those who contact public officers and other political leaders.
> If a person contacts public officers and leaders he is *almost certain* to be a member of some politically oriented (though not strictly political) association.
> If a person is a member of such an association he is *almost certain* to be a voter.
> . . .
> [In other words] there is a "latent structure" pattern in most populations such that those who perform certain less frequent political acts are *almost certain* to perform *all* [italics his] the more frequent acts.[10]

Finally, Lester Milbrath, in a comprehensive review of the research findings from a large number of studies of political activity in the United States, summarizes the level, structure, and distribution of political participation in the following way:

> Only about 4 or 5% are active in a party, campaign, and attend meetings. About 10% make monetary contributions, about 13% contact public officials, and about 15% display a button or sticker. Around 25 or 30% try to proselytize others to vote a certain way, and from 40 to 70% vote in any given election . . . there seems to be a hierarchy of political involvement, in that persons at a given level of involvement tend to perform many of the same acts, including those performed by persons at lower levels of involvement. . . .

He concludes:

> About one-third of the American adult population can be characterized as politically apathetic or passive; in most cases they are unaware, literally, of the political part of the world around them. Another 60% play largely spectator roles; they watch, they cheer, they vote, but they do not do battle . . . the percentage of gladiators does not exceed 5 to 7%.[11]

In contrast, then, with the impressions of America as an "activist" society, these works seem to be in agreement that, aside from the vote, there is relatively little political activity in America, and most of what there is is concentrated in the hands of a small activist group.

[9]Dahl, *Who Governs?* pp. 276-277 (italics ours).
[10]Robert E. Lane, *Political Life: Why People Get Involved in Politics* (Glencoe, Ill.: Free Press, 1959) pp. 93-94 (italics ours except where otherwise indicated).
[11]Milbrath, *Political Participation,* pp. 16, 21

There are a number of reasons why participation may appear high to some and low to others. One obvious reason is that definitions vary. Insofar as one expands one's definition of participation to include such psychological states as political interest or such activity as media attention or political discussion, one finds more activity. The more narrowly one limits the scope of what one considers participation, the smaller the amount one will find.[12]

In part the difference in perception of the amount of participation may depend on the standard used. If one expects participation to be high, the same amount looks much smaller than if one expects the ordinary citizen to be relatively passive. If one uses as a benchmark data from other countries, participation in America looks relatively high. But even here it may depend on how broad a scope one gives to one's definition of participation. In comparative terms, Americans do not vote as frequently as do others elsewhere (though the explanation of that probably lies more in restrictive regulations than lack of interest), but in certain kinds of nonelectoral activity they participate quite a bit more.[13] Another reasonable benchmark for political activity in America at any point in time is some other point in time. (In Chapter 14 we will consider participation rates as they have changed historically.)

In some sense the high vs. low debate has no answer, and the data we present in this chapter will certainly not provide one. We will present data on a wide range of activities, and the reader can judge whether the rates are high or low. We will, however, present one benchmark for comparison, and this from within the United States. We will consider the rate of activity in voluntary associations to see how participation in that sphere compares with that in politics. Our data, on the other hand, will be a bit more conclusive on the question of the clustering of participation—that is, whether whatever participation exists is all in the hands of a few.

Our definition of participation is, as we pointed out in the previous chapter, narrower than some and broader than others. It is narrower in that we consider as acts of participation only those activities aimed at influencing the government in some way. We do not include psychological orientations or such acts as political discussion and media attention. On the other hand, we have a broad view of the ways one can influence the government—both inside and outside the electoral sphere.

Table 2-1 presents the proportion of adult Americans performing each of twelve acts of political participation. Items originally containing more than two categories have been dichotomized for this presentation, and the division points can be inferred from the brief descriptions given in the table. The items are presented in descending order according to the proportion of

---

[12]Similarly, the amount of participation one finds may depend on the time frame one uses. For instance, 19% of our respondents report attending a political rally or meeting "in the last three years," whereas only 8% reported such activity in response to a similar question in a University of Michigan Survey Research Center Study about "the current election year" (Campbell et al., *The American Voter*, p. 51). Similar data emerge from the later election studies.

[13]See the references in footnote 2.

respondents engaging in them. The acts of participation presented in this table cover the entire spectrum of political activity as we defined it in Chapter 1.[14]

Regular voting in Presidential elections is the only political activity (of our measures) that a majority of American citizens report performing. Approximately 72 percent of those who were old enough to vote in both the 1960 and 1964 Presidential elections claim to have done so.[15] About 47 percent of the citizens interviewed report that they always vote in local elections. Although there seems to be some overreporting in these figures (as there almost always is in post-hoc replies to survey questions on voting), the order of magnitude seems roughly correct. Voting, both local and national, is the only political act presented in Table 2-1 in which over a third of the American citizenry claim to engage.

Slightly under 32 percent of the citizens interviewed claim to be active members of organizations involved in community affairs. This is the most frequent type of political activity other than voting.[16] Similar results derive from asking the respondents whether they had ever worked with others in their local community in an attempt to solve some local problem. Approximately 30 percent of the citizens replied positively.

About 28 percent of those interviewed report that they sometimes attempt to persuade others how to vote, and slightly over a quarter (26 percent) claim ever to have worked actively for a political party or candidate during an election. These two campaign activities are the last two acts in Table 2-1 which more than 20 percent of the citizens report performing.

Slightly less than 20 percent report ever having initiated a contact with a local government leader about some issue or problem, and about 19 percent report having attended at least one political meeting or rally in the past three years. Just under 18 percent report initiating contacts with state and national governmental officials on some issue. We are now down to those activities reported by less than 15 percent of the adult population. Fourteen percent report working to form a group or organization to attempt to deal with a community problem, and some 13 percent have given money, at one time or another, to a political party or candidate. Finally, a little over 8 percent report current memberships in political clubs and organizations.

[14] The exact question wording, coding categories, and frequency distributions for all the participation items reported in Table 2-1 are presented in Appendix B.1. The percentages reported throughout this book are based on the weighted N of 3,095 cases, though the exact number of cases may vary slightly from table to table because of missing data. Normally the number of cases is not reported in the body of the table. Appendices B.1, C, and D contain the major independent and dependent variables utilized in the analysis along with the unweighted number of cases, the weighted number of cases, and the percentages (based on the weighted N) for each category of the variable. The reader wishing to do test statistics therefore can reconstruct frequencies on the basis of the information in the relevant table and in these appendices. In those few instances where tables refer to specific subpopulations, the number of cases is presented so that full information is available in every instance.

[15] This figure clearly reflects some overreporting. The harder aggregate statistics indicate turnout rates of 64% in 1960 and 62% in 1964. Part of the overreporting may be due to the regularly observed phenomenon of overreporting in post-hoc survey questions asking respondents whether they voted or not. For reports on the validity of responses to voting questions, see Aage R. Clausen, "Response Validity: Vote Report," *Public Opinion Quarterly*, vol. 32 (Winter 1968-69), pp. 588-606.

[16] See footnote *b* to Table 2-1 for the exact meaning of this item.

Table 2-1

Percentage Engaging in Twelve Different Acts of Political Participation

Type of political participation	Percentage
1. Report regularly voting in Presidential elections[a]	72
2. Report always voting in local elections	47
3. Active in at least one organization involved in community problems[b]	32
4. Have worked with others in trying to solve some community problems	30
5. Have attempted to persuade others to vote as they were	28
6. Have ever actively worked for a party or candidates during an election	26
7. Have ever contacted a local government official about some issue or problem	20
8. Have attended at least one political meeting or rally in last three years	19
9. Have ever contacted a state or national government official about some issue or problem	18
10. Have ever formed a group or organization to attempt to solve some local community problem	14
11. Have ever given money to a party or candidate during an election campaign	13
12. Presently a member of a political club or organization	8

Number of Cases: weighted   3,095
unweighted 2,549

[a]Composite variable created from reports of voting in 1960 and 1964 Presidential elections. Percentage is equal to those who report they have voted in both elections.

[b]This variable is a composite index where the proportion presented above is equal to the proportion of those in the sample who are active in at least one voluntary association that, they report, takes an active role in attempting to solve community problems. The procedure utilized was as follows: Each respondent was asked whether he was a member of fifteen types of voluntary associations. For each affirmative answer he was then asked whether he regularly attended meetings or otherwise took a leadership role in the organization. If yes, he was considered an active member. If he was an active member and if he reported that the organization regularly attempted to solve community problems, he was considered to have performed this type of political act. Appendix B.1 provides more detailed information on the construction of this index, and all questions on organizational membership and involvement. Membership in expressly *political* clubs or organizations was excluded from this index.

It is quite clear from these frequency distributions that most acts of political participation are performed by only a small segment of the citizenry. Six of the twelve activities measured are performed by fewer than 20 percent of the citizens, and only Presidential and local voting have frequencies of performance significantly greater than 30 percent. Voting in Presidential elections is the only participatory act out of our rather extensive list of activities that is performed by a majority of those interviewed.

When the data from this table are compared to the data from previous studies, some interesting, if minor, differences appear. On most measures of partisan or electoral activity (voting excluded), we find a much higher proportion of participators than those uncovered by the Survey Research Center voting studies. Most of these differences are, however, explained by the different time frames used in the studies. Whereas we are interested in rates of participation over a longer period, the voting studies were concerned with activity in a single Presidential election. When a longer period is used, we find that a number of citizens actively participate in some elections but not in others. These differences are in no way surprising, but neither are they totally devoid of significance for the problem of estimating levels and distributions of participation. These relatively large discrepancies suggest that active political involvement is not sustained, and that a significant number of citizens move in and out of active political participation in the electoral process.[17]

Taken as a whole, however, these data are in substantial agreement with the data from other studies. In fact, Milbrath's summary description of the level of participation in the United States (with a minor adjustment of a few of the percentages) easily could have been written as a summary of the data presented in Table 2-1.

From the perspective of the simple frequency distributions such as those recorded in Table 2-1, as well as similar distributions from previous studies, the level of political participation across a wide variety of activities seems quite low and can be summarized in the following way:

1. Few, if any, types of political activity beyond the act of voting are performed by more than a third of the American citizenry.

2. Activities that require the investment of more than trivial amounts of time and energy as well as those that have a short time referent (such as a single election) tend to be performed by no more than 10 to 15 percent of the citizens.

3. Less demanding activities as well as those with longer time referents (i.e., longer than a single election campaign) are performed by between 15 and 30 percent of the citizenry.

CONCENTRATION OF ACTIVITY

Analysis of a series of simple frequency distributions can take us only so far. In fact, this type of data often hides more than it reveals, for it does not give us information on the overlap or distribution of the various activities. For six out of the twelve activities on Table 2-1, the participation rate is less than 20 percent, and four of the remaining six activities are performed by less than 33 percent of the citizens. The temptation is to interpret these data to mean that 70 to 80 percent of the citizenry engage in no activity beyond voting, while 20 to 30 percent perform all of the more active types of participation. But it would also be consistent with the data if each of the various activities

---

[17]The one or two other discrepancies are trivial, and are caused by minor variations in the structure and context of the questions. Our measure of membership in political organizations, for example, simply contained a broader definition of political organizations than the one employed in the voting studies.

were performed by a different 20-30 percent of the citizenry, and everybody were in some way active. In short, any meaningful analysis of the level of political activity must determine whether these infrequent acts of political participation are concentrated in the hands of a few or dispersed through a wide segment of the American citizenry.

Consider for a moment the different types of political systems that would emerge out of two polar situations—each compatible with the frequency distributions presented in Table 2-1. In the first situation a majority of the citizens would vote, and some of these voters might also engage in one or another of the more frequent types of political activity. But all other activity— the more difficult acts—would be engaged in by a small number of activists. In the opposite situation there would be the same overall amount of political activity in the society, but it would not be nearly so concentrated in the hands of a given group of citizens. There would undoubtedly still be a small group of politically apathetic citizens, and another group of citizens might engage in more activity than the average, but the vast majority of citizens would engage in one, two, or three activities in addition to voting. Some would initiate contacts with governmental leaders; others would contribute money to political causes; yet other citizens might concentrate their efforts on working with others to solve community problems. In this type of society the distinction between gladiators and spectators would be less sharp. Many citizens would be active in one way or another.

Which of these pictures comes closer to describing the participatory structure in the United States? How many citizens are totally apathetic? How many engage in at least some activity? And what proportion of our citizenry is extremely active in politics? Figure 2-1 presents data relevant to these issues. On it we have placed the proportion of citizens engaging in zero to ten of the political activities presented in Table 2-1 with the exception of voting. No activity in this set is performed by as many as one-third of the citizens. The range of frequency of performance of these activities is between 8 and 32 percent. Whereas this might suggest that two-thirds of our respondents engage in none of these acts, we find that, in fact, less than a third of the sample reports engaging in no such act. Sixty-nine percent of our respondents report engaging in at least one of these acts, and almost half our sample (47 percent) report engaging in two or more. Acts of participation are not clustered in a limited set of citizens—at least not in as limited a set as would be possible given the proportions engaging in any one of the acts in Figure 2-1.

A more stringent test of the distribution of political participation in American society is presented in Figure 2-2. Here we display the proportions of citizens engaging in the six least frequent types of political activities: those acts of participation performed by fewer than 20 percent of the citizens. The frequency of performance of the individual acts ranges from 20 percent (contacting local governmental officials) down to 8 percent (membership in political organizations), and the average act in this group is performed by

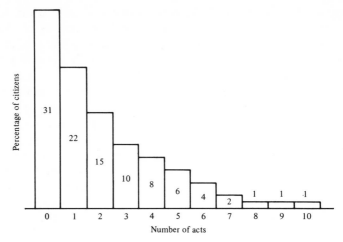

Figure 2-1. Number of Political Acts Other than Voting

approximately 15 percent of the citizens. Most of these political activities have considerable costs attached to them. Contacting governmental officials, forming groups and organizations to tackle community problems, donating money, and membership in political groups are all activities that require the commitment of time and energy, often in considerable amount.

Again these data would be compatible with a situation in which about 80 percent of our sample engaged in none of these activities and this type of activity was in the hands of 20 percent of the population. But as Figure 2-2 indicates, these acts are somewhat more widespread—47 percent of our sample report having engaged in one or more of them.

The data presented in Figures 2-1 and 2-2 indicate a wider spread of participation through the citizenry than the initial simple frequency distributions suggest. Why does this description of the concentration of participation differ from others found in the literature? The answer involves the problem of interpreting simple frequency distributions of individual items of participation. The data have been approached with certain assumptions. The first is that all types of political participation are highly intercorrelated and that the same group of citizens participates in all the activities. This assumption is not totally incorrect, for there is a considerable intercorrelation among participatory acts.[18] Our own data confirm these relationships, and in the following chapter we will present these findings. The problem, however, is one of degree. The data from a series of frequency distributions often seem to be interpreted as if the correlations were nearly perfect rather than merely substantial. The spread of political activity across the population demonstrated in Figures 2-1 and 2-2 reveals that the correlations are quite moderate.

---

[18]Campbell et al. (*The American Voter*); Berelson, Lazarsfeld, and McPhee (*Voting*); Nie, Powell, and Prewitt ("Social Structure and Political Participation"); and Milbrath (*Political Participation*) are but a few of those who have reported high intercorrelations among various types of political activity.

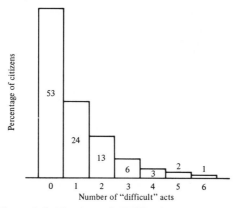

Figure 2-2. Number of "Difficult" Political Acts

The second assumption that often appears in the literature is that there is a patterned hierarchical structure to political activity whereby citizens who engage in the more infrequent and costly acts of participation always perform the more common varieties as well. The converse is also assumed to be true—citizens who do not perform the most common types of participation do not engage in the more infrequent types. This assumption is also consistent with the evidence, including some we will present in the following chapter.[19] But here again, as with the correlation among activities, statistical tendencies have been converted into absolutes and then applied as a description of American political reality.

If one approaches data such as those presented in Table 2-1 with these two assumptions, it is easy to see how one can read the data as describing a small activist stratum and a large inactive mass. However, when the assumptions underlying this description are tested, they turn out to be only partially true. Figure 2-3 provides a useful test of these assumptions. We present the data for several sets of political activities and illustrate the pattern of overlap one would find under several different sets of assumptions, including the two just cited. We can then compare these hypothetical patterns with reality.

Let us begin with the first set of circle diagrams in the upper portion of the figure, Example 1. The extreme left margin of the figure gives the proportion of citizens in our sample who have contacted governmental leaders (either local, state, or national officials) and the proportion who have worked with some group or organization in their locality in an attempt to solve some community problem. The data indicate that about 30 percent of the citizenry report having engaged in each of these activities. The circles labeled (a), (b), and (c) contain the proportion of the citizenry who would perform each, both,

[19]Milbrath (*Political Participation*) and Matthews and Prothro [Donald R. Matthews and James W. Prothro, *Negroes and the New Southern Politics* (New York: Harcourt, 1962)] have actually employed cumulative scales of political participation in their studies, while Lane, as previously cited, has discussed the cumulative structure of participation in great detail.

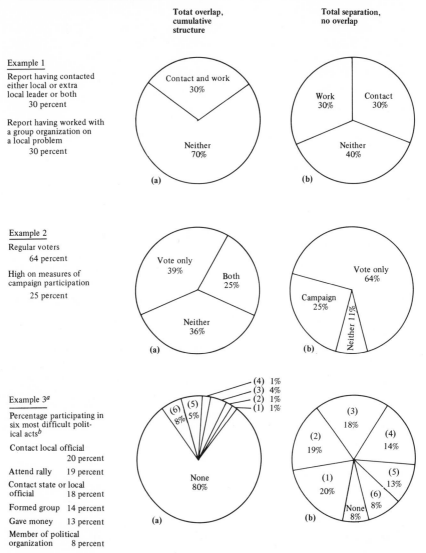

Example 1

Report having contacted either local or extra local leader or both
        30 percent

Report having worked with a group organization on a local problem
        30 percent

Example 2

Regular voters
        64 percent

High on measures of campaign participation
        25 percent

Example 3[a]

Percentage participating in six most difficult political acts[b]

Contact local official
                20 percent

Attend rally   19 percent

Contact state or local official   18 percent

Formed group   14 percent

Gave money   13 percent

Member of political organization   8 percent

[a] The numbers in parentheses on the circle diagrams in this example refer to the number of acts performed.
[b] These are the same activities presented in Figure 2-2.

Figure 2-3. The Overlap Among Activities: Hypothetical and Real Data

or neither of the activities under various assumptions concerning the relationship among political activities.

Circle (a) presents the distribution that would occur if the two assumptions discussed—high correlation and cumulative structure—were true. These assumptions predict that the same 30 percent of the citizens would perform each

Random overlap,
random structure

Actual data

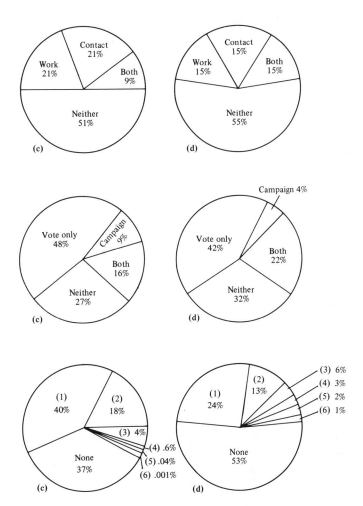

of the acts, leaving 70 percent who have performed neither.[20] Circle (b) presents the opposite situation, that those who performed one activity would

[20] Actual data would, of course, never be this clear, for even if the assumption were correct, various types of measurement error would produce trivial amounts of overlap or slippage—a few citizens would report contacting but not working with organizations and vice versa. Nevertheless, the distributions would, by and large, correspond to those presented in Circle (a).

not perform the other. This pattern would indicate a situation of total specialization of political activity. Under these circumstances, 30 percent of the citizenry would contact political leaders, a different 30 percent would work with others on community problems, and the remaining 40 percent would engage in neither type of activity.

Circle (c) presents the proportion of citizens who would perform these two activities if the likelihood of their overlap were random. In the case of random distribution, 21 percent of the citizens would have contacted governmental leaders, 21 percent would have worked with groups or organizations on local problems, 9 percent would have engaged in both, and 51 percent would have performed neither of the activities.

Circle (d) presents the *actual* overlapping distributions of these two activities. The distributions clearly indicate that the actual data fall in between the total overlap predicted in (a) and the random one predicted in (c). The predictions of Circle (b), on the other hand (the case of total specialization of activity), least fit the data. On the whole, this analysis indicates that the random prediction of Circle (c) is a closer approximation of reality than the cumulative prediction of Circle (a), which assumes a total overlap. This is particularly true if we are concerned with predicting the percentage who engage in neither political activity. Only four percentage points separate the random prediction from the actual proportion engaging in neither activity, whereas fifteen percentage points separate the actual distributions from those predicted by total correlation. Nevertheless, we should not overlook the fact that participation in either of the acts does considerably raise the probabilities of participating in the other act.

This first example tells us something about the degree of correlation among political activities, but because each of the acts is performed by the same proportion of citizens it does not provide us with the information required to evaluate the assumption concerning the hierarchical pattern in political activity, whereby those performing "difficult" acts always perform easy ones. Example 2 in Figure 2-3, however, provides us with both types of information on two modes of participation (voting and campaign activity) that have often been viewed as part of a single cumulative continuum of electoral participation. The frequencies are given on the left of the circle diagram. Sixty-four percent of the sample of citizens have been classified as regular voters.[21] Twenty-five percent of the citizens have been classified as high participators in electoral campaigns by means of a composite index composed of five items.[22]

[21]We have created a single voting variable out of the two voting items originally presented in Table 2-1 (p. 31). To be counted as a regular voter, the respondent had to report that he usually, if not always, voted in local elections and voted in both of the Presidential elections. About 64% of the citizens were classified as regular voters by this method. Close to half of those who were classified as nonvoters report at least some voting in either local and/or Presidential elections, but we have chosen to classify them as nonvoters. See Appendix C for exact wording.

[22]In order for a citizen to be classified as one of the 25% who are high on campaign activity, he must have reported that he often or always attempted to persuade others to vote as he intended to vote, plus he must have performed one or more of the following four more active forms of campaign activity: (1) attending at least one

The circle diagrams in Example 2 parallel exactly those in Example 1. Circle (a) represents the expected pattern under perfect overlap and cumulative structure, (b) represents total specialization, (c) gives the probabilities of overlap if the two acts were randomly distributed, and (d) presents the actual data. In the situation in Circle (a), all 25 percent of the citizens who were active enough to be classified as campaign activists would also be regular voters. Because no campaign activists would be found among the nonvoters, 36 percent of the citizens would have engaged in neither regular voting nor campaigning. In Circle (b) we see the "specialization" assumption. None of the 25 percent who are campaign activists would vote, and only 11 percent would do nothing. Last, if the relationship between these two types of activities were random or chance, 9 percent of the citizens would be campaign activists who do not vote, 48 percent would vote only, and 16 percent would vote and campaign [Circle (c)]. A comparison between the hypothetical distributions and the actual data in Circle (d) supports the following points:

1. The specialization assumption is way off.
2. A cumulative structure does appear to exist. Random overlap would predict 9 percent of the population active in campaigns, but nonvoting. The actual distribution reveals only 4 percent falling into this activity pattern. Those who are active in campaigns usually vote.
3. There is clearly a correlation among the activities. Chance predicts that only 16 percent would engage in both activities—the actual data indicate that 22 percent perform both.
4. The actual pattern again falls between the assumption of randomness [Circle (c)] and that of cumulative overlap, though in this case it is closer to cumulative overlap than was Example 1. It may be that the overlap assumptions fit activities within the electoral sphere better than they fit the relations among more diverse activities.

Example 3 provides by far the most interesting case. Here we compare the three hypothetical patterns with actual data in relation to the six least frequent and most costly forms of participation measured. The simple frequency distributions of the six acts appear in the left margin. Circle (a) again presents the distribution in a situation of total correlation and perfect cumulative structure. If these assumptions were true, 80 percent of the citizenry would have engaged in none of these six acts, whereas 20 percent would have participated in one or more of them. Eight percent would have participated in all six, 5 percent in five of the acts, 1 percent in four out of the six acts, and so forth. Circle (b) presents the opposite situation: total specialization of activity. In this case, 8 percent of the citizens would have engaged in no activity, and each remaining activity would be performed by a different group of citizens. Circle (c) represents the distribution of the population according to the number of acts

---

political meeting or rally in the past three to four years, (2) contributing money to a party or candidate, (3) doing other types of work for a party or candidate in the last few years, and/or (4) belonging to a political club or organization.

performed, if their distribution were ruled by chance—i.e., if the activities were uncorrelated and unstructured. Circle (d) presents the actual proportion of citizens performing varying numbers of the six activities.

On the one hand, it is quite clear that the random distribution is a much closer approximation of reality than the one that assumes total cumulation. On the other hand, it is equally evident that the distributions are not random and that there is considerable correlation among the items. Total cumulation predicts that 80 percent of the citizenry will be inactive. Random overlap predicts that only 37 percent will engage in no activity. The actual data indicate that some 53 percent have performed none of the six acts. At the most active extreme, the differences are equally dramatic. Chance overlap would expect .6 percent to have performed four acts, .04 percent to have performed five of the six acts, and a minuscule .001 percent to have performed all six acts—a total of less than seven-tenths of 1 percent performing four or more acts. But the data indicate that almost 6 percent of the citizens have engaged in four or more of the six activities. Acts of political participation are, therefore, much more correlated and concentrated than chance would predict, but much more widely distributed than the assumption of full cumulation would lead us to believe.

In short, researchers simply may have overestimated the degree of structure in and the amount of correlation among the varieties of participatory acts when interpreting simple frequency distributions. In so doing, they may have seriously underestimated the amount of political participation in America and its degree of dispersion. We are not arguing that rates of participation are high or that the distribution of political activity is equal across the population, for the data simply do not merit such interpretation. The limited amount of political activity and the tendency of participation to be concentrated among some citizens are quite evident in our analysis. (And indeed much of the rest of this volume will be spent discussing the reasons and consequences.) What we have encountered, however, is a slightly different picture of participation— one in which the overall level of political activity seems somewhat higher, the distribution not quite so concentrated, and the cumulative structure not quite so pronounced as has been previously believed.

ESTABLISHING A BASE FOR EVALUATION

The analysis has not yet provided us with a base line for evaluating levels of political activity, and without such guidelines it is difficult, if not impossible, to give any real meaning to the amounts of participation uncovered. After all is said and done, we still really cannot say whether participation is high or low, adequate or inadequate. One way of providing a base line is to compare rates of participation in this country with rates in others. As mentioned, when such comparisons are made, participation in the United States seems fairly high, particularly when it comes to participation outside of the electoral sphere.[23]

[23] See Verba, Nie, and Kim, *The Modes of Democratic Participation,* p. 36, for a preliminary report of data along these lines. See also Almond and Verba, *The Civic Culture.*

To provide a somewhat different kind of base line, we will compare the rate of political activity with another kind of activity, that in voluntary associations. The comparison is useful because the two types of activity—that in politics and that in voluntary associations—are similar in several important respects. First, participation in organizations, like political participation, is largely voluntary. Second, both take place within the context of formally organized social collectivities. And third, the comparisons are useful simply because participation in voluntary associations is a common form of activity with which most of us are familiar, and it therefore provides us with an opportunity to turn abstract numbers into a concrete (if intuitive) understanding of the amounts of activity for which they stand.[24]

Each of the respondents in our sample was asked about his membership and activity in sixteen separate types of voluntary associations ranging from labor unions to recreational groups to religious organizations and covering the spectrum of organized social activity in this society.[25] Sixty-two percent of those interviewed report some membership, but about a third of the 62 percent who are members are inactive. Thus about 40 percent of the population claim to be active members of one or more organization. These figures are not as high as those for political participation. Sixty-nine percent of the citizenry have engaged in one or more acts of participation, excluding voting. Forty-seven percent have participated in two such acts. If we compare rates of performance in the six most costly types of participatory acts (as presented in Figure 2-2) with rates of active membership in all types of voluntary associations (Table 2-2), the comparisons are even clearer. Only 40 percent of the citizens are active members of one or more organizations, while almost 47 percent engage in one or more of the active types of participation.[26]

In addition, membership in political organizations, while not high (only 8 percent belong), is not so low either when compared with other types of organizations. Membership in political organizations rank fifth out of sixteen in frequency. Only labor unions, school service groups such as the PTA, fraternal orders, and sporting groups have more members than political clubs and organizations. Furthermore, when one examines rates of active membership in these sixteen types of organizations, political groups are one of only four types that have a rate of active membership exceeding 65 percent. That is, although labor unions and sports groups have more members than political organizations, a much larger proportion of their members are inactive.

Low rates of activity in one sector of social life do not automatically make

[24] These comparisons are not without their problems, for there are as many differences as similarities in these two types of activities. Political participation, for example, has multiple forms, but as a rule it is aimed at a single institution—the government. A citizen votes, contacts, campaigns, joins political organizations, etc.—all of these acts refer to the government. In organizational participation, membership is a single mode but can be addressed at an almost unlimited variety of types of organizations—hobby groups, service organizations, professional associations, etc. The significance of such differences for our analysis of course remains unknown.

[25] However, simple membership in a church congregation was not considered as a membership in a voluntary association. Rather we counted church-related groups such as "sisterhoods," Knights of Columbus, and so forth.

[26] Though we measure political acts over several years and organizational membership at one point in time, we do not think this biases the results in favor of finding more political than organizational activity. Memberships at one point in time probably represent a cumulation over a long period.

Table 2-2

Membership and Activity Rates in Sixteen Types of Organizations

Type of organization	Percentage reporting membership	Rank	Percentage of members active	Rank
Labor unions	17	1	37	16
School service groups, such as PTA or school alumni groups	17	2	60	7
Fraternal groups, such as Elks, Eagles, Masons, and their women's auxiliaries	15	3	65	5
Sports clubs	12	4	53	10
Political groups, such as Democratic or Republican clubs, and political action groups, such as voter's leagues	8	5	66	4
Veteran's groups such as the American Legion	7	6	48	14
Youth groups, such as Boy Scouts and Girl Scouts	7	7	88	1
Miscellaneous groups not covered	7	8	50	12
Professional or academic societies, such as American Dental Association, Phi Beta Kappa	7	9	57	8
Church-related groups, such as women's auxiliary, Bible groups[a]	6	10	80	2
Service clubs, such as Lions, Rotary, Zenta, Junior Chamber of Commerce	6	11	78	3
Hobby or garden clubs, such as stamp or coin clubs, flower clubs, pet clubs	5	12	42	15
Farm organizations, such as Farmer's Union, Farm Bureau, Grange	4	13	49	13
Literary, art, discussion or study clubs, such as book-review clubs, theater groups	4	14	56	9
School fraternities and sororities, such as Sigma Chi, Delta Gamma	3	15	63	6
Nationality groups, such as Sons of Norway, Hibernian Society	2	16	52	11

[a]This does not include church membership but rather associations emerging around the church or religion.

rates in other areas (which have slightly higher rates) high. However, these data do provide us with a little more perspective for an evaluation of the level of participation. The level of political activity is low insofar as many citizens engage in no participation at all (from 17 to 31 percent depending upon whether one includes voting), but by the same yardstick, levels of other analogous types of social participation appear to be even lower. If, as Dahl suggests, "politics is a remote, alien, and unrewarding activity ... [which] lies for most people at the outer periphery of attention, interest and activity,"[27] the same must be said of most other forms of voluntary social participation.

This chapter is only a bare outline of the picture of political participation in our society. Much more needs to be filled in. We have found that the rate of political activity is perhaps higher than has been believed. However, while a majority of American citizens engage in a number of political activities, there is also a significant proportion who perform little or no activity and a small group who are extremely active.

We have also found that the correlations among political activities do not result in the unidimensional and cumulative structure that others have suggested. This finding accords well with our multidimensional view of participation outlined in Chapter 1. We turn therefore to a more systematic investigation of the interrelationships among political activities in our search for the dimensions of political involvement.

[27] Dahl, *Who Governs?*, p. 279.

Chapter 3
The Modes of Participation:
An Overview

Most studies of participation have, we believe, paid little attention to the question of the alternative ways in which citizens can participate. The reason for this was suggested in the previous chapter. Most studies have been of participation within the context of electoral politics. Thus participation has come to be defined as voting and perhaps as voting plus some additional campaign activity. Further, the assumption has often been that participation is a unidimensional phenomenon. Participatory acts vary in terms of their difficulty; they can otherwise be thought of as interchangeable. What counts is the amount of participation engaged in by a citizen, not the type of act in which he engages. Berelson, Lazersfeld, and McPhee argue, for instance, that "almost all measures of political involvement and participation are highly correlated with one another and for analytical purposes, interchangeable."[1] Others such as Lane and Milbrath argue for a hierarchy of political acts such

---

[1] Bernard Berelson, Paul F. Lazarsfeld, and William N. McPhee, *Voting* (Chicago: University of Chicago Press, 1954), p. 24.

that the citizen who engages in the most difficult act is almost certain to engage in the easier ones.[2]

Our view differs. We wish to look beyond the vote as a means of activity and beyond the electoral system. Nor do we consider participation a unidimensional phenomenon. In short, the citizenry is not divided simply into more or less active citizens. Rather there are many types of activists engaging in different acts, with different motives, and different consequences.

Political acts differ in what they *can get the citizen:* Some types of activity supply little more than the gratification from taking part; other political acts can lead to more specific and concrete payoffs. Political acts differ in what they *get the citizen into:* Some activity is likely to bring him into open conflict with others; some is not. And political acts differ in what *it takes to get into them:* Some activity calls for initiative, time, resources, skill; some does not.

Citizens also differ among themselves in similar ways. There are different things that they want to get from the government. The number of interests that citizens have are many and almost infinitely varied. Citizens also differ in the situations they are willing to get into when they participate. Some citizens are willing, even eager, for the conflict of politics, whereas others avoid controversy and contention. And of course citizens differ in what they are willing and able to put into politics: Some have a lot of initiative, resources, skill; others do not.

Our analysis of how citizens participate has several purposes. One is to show how the various political activities mesh with the various circumstances and characteristics of citizens. Such an analysis will indicate the richness of citizen-government interactions, a richness lost if one limits one's attention to citizen participation within the rigidly defined mold of the electoral process, where the ways a citizen can be active are limited as are the interests that can be expressed. An analysis of how citizens participate will also allow us to reconsider the question of the citizen as rational political actor. This question has usually been raised *vis-à-vis* the citizen as voter. Is it rational for him to vote at all, and if he votes, does he cast his vote rationally? But when we consider a wide range of citizen activities—which allows us to consider the important question of how the choice of act relates to the citizen's interests— the question of his rationality is seen in a new light. We shall return to this theme in Chapter 7. Our analysis of how citizens participate and how this fits into their structure of needs and interests sets the stage for the rest of the book, where we deal with the processes by which citizens come to participate and with the consequences of that participation. For both the process of coming to participate and the consequences differ depending on the kind of act involved.

PARTICIPATION MODES

Let us turn to a closer consideration of how citizens can participate. First, we shall introduce several alternative modes of activity with which citizens can

[2] Lane, *Political Life,* pp. 93-94 and Milbrath, *Political Participation,* pp. 19 and 22.

participate in politics. In this chapter we shall attempt to explicate the systematic way these modes of activity differ. In the following chapters of this section, we shall attempt to verify that these modes of activity are significantly different by showing that specific political acts cluster together into a structure of participation consistent with our expectations about these modes; that one can identify specific citizens who specialize in one mode rather than another; and that these citizens differ from each other in their political orientations in ways consistent with our understanding of the differences among the modes of political activity.

Let us begin with some concrete political acts, classified into modes of activity, and follow this by a consideration of the general ways in which they differ. This makes sense, for to begin with an abstract set of categories might lead to a set of potential types of activity for which there were no empirical examples. Our raw material is the set of thirteen specific political activities whose frequencies we reported in Chapter 2. This set of acts by no means exhausts the activities in which citizens engage, but it covers most of those activities ordinarily carried on by citizens.

We asked about these thirteen acts because we believed they could be grouped into four modes of activity. The choice of the first two types of act, voting and campaign activity, needs little justification because although it is our argument that citizens do not participate only through the electoral process, that process certainly represents the major way in which citizens can regularly influence government performance.

The first type of act within the electoral process is, of course, the vote. Voting is the most widespread and regularized political activity, and in terms of the overall impact of the citizenry on governmental performance it may be the single most important act. Our questions on voting in local elections and in the 1960 and 1964 Presidential elections tap this activity.

The next set of participatory activities is associated with voting. It encompasses those other activities that take place during elections—campaign activities such as working for a party or candidate, attending meetings, contributing money, and trying to convince others how they should vote. These activities differ from the actual act of voting in that they represent ways in which an individual can increase his influence over the electoral process by influencing the votes of others, the selection of candidates, and/or the formation of campaign issues.

Voting and campaign activity are thus two of the major ways in which individuals can participate in politics. To find the other means of participation, we looked first for that kind of activity most different from the electoral situation. The vote represents a massive involvement of most citizens at scheduled times. Both voting and campaign activity take place in response to elections whose content and timing are set for the citizen, and in which the substantive issues are controlled by candidates and officials. At the other extreme are those instances in which individuals with particular concerns initiate contacts with government officials. Here we have the individual *vis-à-vis* the government or some small segment of the government. He acts alone; and *he* determines the timing, target, and substance of the act of participation. This type of participation, which we call citizen-initiated contacts, represents a third type of political activity. It is indexed by our questions on contacts with local and extra-local officials.

Finally we are interested in another regularly utilized mode of participation outside of the electoral process. This fourth type of activity involves group or organizational activity by citizens to deal with social and political problems. In this case the individual does not act alone as he does in citizen-initiated contacts but rather joins with others to influence the actions of government. However, like citizen-initiated contacts and unlike electoral participation, cooperative group activity is initiated by private citizens and may take place at any time and in relation to any type of issue or problem of concern to the group. This mode of activity is tapped by our question on working with a local group to deal with a community problem, helping to form such a group, and by our index of the number of active memberships reported by the respondent in organizations that are, in turn, active in community affairs.

Thus we suggest that there are four broad modes of political participation that are used, in ordinary circumstances, by citizens: voting, campaign activity, citizen-initiated contacts, and cooperative participation. And each of these modes of activity can be engaged in through a variety of specific acts. This does not exhaust the totality of available political acts, but it covers a wide and significant set.

These four modes of participation represent a significant set of activities because they encompass a number of alternative ways in which the citizen can attempt to influence the government. To see this we can consider some general dimensions along which citizen acts can be arrayed. These dimensions derive from some general consideration of the problems associated with participation. The first has to do with the *type of influence* exerted over leaders by the political act, the second with the *scope of the outcome* that can be expected from the act, the third with the *amount of conflict* in which such acts involve the participant, and the fourth with the *amount of initiative* needed to engage in the act. Let us consider each of these.

The Type of Influence

Political acts can influence governmental leaders in several ways: They can exert pressure or they can communicate information about the preferences of citizens, or both. Acts vary in how much pressure they exert—i.e., in how much the political leader is induced to comply in order to avoid some negative consequence. They also vary in how much information they convey about the preferences of citizens. Though how much pressure and/or information a particular type of activity will convey depends on the particular circumstances surrounding the act (who is active *vis-à-vis* what official), we can make some rough distinctions among the four types of political acts in these terms. Voting should be generally high in pressure (especially if leaders want reelection) but relatively low in information (the vote not conveying much about the preferences of the voter). Campaign activity is also likely to be high in exerting pressure for the same reason that voting is. But it may convey more information than the vote does simply because the campaign activists are a more visible group with whom candidates interact. Cooperative activity is likely to convey more information about preferences than either of the electoral modes because citizens organize around specific problems. But the degree to which such activities exert pressure may depend on how many and which citizens are cooperating. Last, citizen-initiated contacts convey a lot of information about the preferences of the particular participant making the contact, but the degree of pressure is likely to be lower on the average, simply because only one citizen is involved. In sum, the situation is as follows:

Act	Type of Influence
Voting	High pressure/low information
Campaign activity	High pressure/low to high information
Cooperative activity	Low to high pressure/high information
Citizen-initiated contacts	Low pressure/high information

We will discuss this distinction further in Chapter 7, when we consider the alternative message-carrying capabilities of political acts more closely. We will return to it in the concluding section of our book, where we consider the consequences of political activity. As we shall see at that time, the type of influence involved has a major effect on the way leaders respond to citizen activities.

For the rest of this chapter and the next few chapters, however, we will put this distinction aside. It deals with how citizen acts influence leaders—the subject of Part III. The other three dimensions of participation we are about to introduce deal with the factors that might motivate a citizen to be active in one way rather than another. For this reason we think they are more important in understanding why citizens choose one mode of activity rather than another.

The Scope of the Outcome

Most political science analysis has focused on policies that have a collective impact and that affect the entire society or large segments of it. The outcome of an election affects all citizens, voter and nonvoter alike. A tax reform bill or a governmental decision on foreign policy has a collective impact on all citizens. It has been argued that this is the essence of governmental activity—that the outcome of such activity cannot be decomposed.[3] For the citizen-participator, this has important implications. He cannot use the power or

[3]See Mancur Olson, *The Logic of Collective Action* (Cambridge, Mass.: Harvard University Press, 1965). Our discussion draws on his analysis.

influence of his participatory acts to obtain specific goods consumed by him alone. Coleman argues, for instance, that the political power of the citizen differs from the economic power of money in that the former cannot be used to obtain divisible goods but must be used to influence major social outcomes—such as an election—when many others are active as well. Thus the influence of any individual is likely to be small.[4]

But governments do not make decisions only about broad social policies. Often they make decisions that will affect only a particular citizen or his immediate family. For example, the government issues a zoning variance to an individual so that he can enlarge his home, provides a license, grants an exemption from the army because of a family hardship, removes an unsightly telephone pole, offers agricultural assistance, or agrees to provide a better water supply to a given home. These activities usually represent specific applications of general policies. If the application is fully automatic—the clerk sells a license or a postage stamp to anyone who has the money—it is not an activity of interest to us. It makes little sense to talk of participating to influence the government in such cases. But much application of policy is not automatic and does not affect all citizens in a particular category. Rather, a specific outcome may depend on specific interaction between a citizen and a government official. Rather than being automatic, the way in which governmental policy is applied to a citizen may depend on the citizen's knowledge, skill, and activity—that is, on the effectiveness of his participation.

Thus, rather than thinking of all governmental activity as having a collective impact, one might distinguish among such activities in terms of their scope—i.e., the number of citizens affected. This is clearly a problem of degree and not a simple dichotomy. Neither extreme—all affected equally or only one person affected—is ever reached. The purely particularized outcome, where all the cost or benefit goes to one person or a very few people, is nonexistent in relation to governmental decisions. Conversely, the impact of governmental outcomes on citizens is rarely equal across all members of the society. But the distinction as a matter of degree is useful if we want to understand why citizens choose to be active in one way rather than another and the consequences of their activity.

In terms of the citizen's power and the importance of the outcome, there is a significant difference between these two situations. When it comes to major outcomes with broad collective impact, the influence of the individual citizen is likely to be small because so many others also will be active and interested. This does not mean, however, that the citizenry as a whole has little voice. In some cases, as in the electoral process, the voice of the citizenry as a whole is decisive. And even when not institutionalized through elections, the public has other means to influence broad decisions. When it comes to narrower decisions, the single citizen or small group may indeed have a decisive voice;

[4] James S. Coleman, "Political Money," *American Political Science Review*, vol. 65 (March 1971), pp. 1074-1087.

at least their intervention can have a measureable effect on the outcome. One can see whether one's complaint on a narrow matter was heeded; one cannot easily weigh one's contribution to an election victory. Thus the ordinary citizen can have little individual influence on collective decisions, but the set of citizens may have major influence. On the narrow decisions, the individual citizen may have a major voice, but the rest of the citizenry may have none because they are uninvolved in the issue.

In terms of the impact of collective and narrow decisions, the situation is the same. The broad collective decisions have an impact on all; looked at from the point of view of the sum of all citizens, they are important outcomes. But for any single citizen, the impact may be more or less intense. The life of the ordinary citizen may change a lot, a little, or not at all when one party succeeds another into office. When it comes to the narrow decisions that affect only a few, the situation is reversed. The impact of the decision on the collectivity as a whole is minimal. But the impact on the citizen who feels its effect is likely to be large indeed.

Social scientists have tended to focus on the larger collective decisions, as is evidenced by the focus of political science on elections, or on citizen impact on foreign policy, or on major domestic policies. And such focus is appropriate because these are important decisions. But the narrower decisions deserve closer study in terms of who can influence them, and how benefits are allocated through them. For the individual involved, such interactions with the government are important indeed. And though any single one of these interactions may seem trivial from the perspective of the allocation of benefits within the larger society, the total set of such narrow decisions represents an important component of social policy.

In short, any full consideration of the citizen as political actor—how he acts and why he acts as he does—will involve consideration of citizen activity with narrow and broad goals. Thus our prime dimension of participation has to do with whether the participatory act is intended to and can in fact influence a particularized outcome, a collective outcome, or both.

The Conflict Dimension

As pointed out in the introduction, political participation inevitably raises questions of the generation and reconciliation of conflict in a society. Insofar as governmental benefits are limited, activity by one group to obtain something for itself may injure the interests of others. And institutions that further public participation may serve to exacerbate such conflict. They make it legitimate to express claims and counterclaims and they bring these competing claims into the open.

But one can make distinctions among participatory activities in terms of the extent to which conflict with others is involved. Some political activities are engaged in against other participants: one set of participants tries to gain some beneficial outcome at the expense of another. In other cases, participants seek some beneficial outcome under circumstances where there are no "counterparticipants"; their gain does not imply clear losses for others. Despite the finiteness of the government budget, participation to influence the government can go on with little conflict.

Again, the distinction is not a clear dichotomy. No benefit for an individual or group is costless for others (as our colleagues in economics at the University of Chicago tell us, "There is no such thing as a free lunch"). But participatory situations clearly differ in the extent to which the situation is a zero-sum conflict with winners and losers rather than an attempt by one group to influence policy with no clear opposition.

It is likely that the conflict dimension is related to the scope of the potential outcome. The wider the impact of the outcome, the more likely is it that there will be opposing groups active in relation to it. If the governmental outcome that the participants seek has a narrow impact that has a noticeable effect on the participants alone and affecting others only indirectly, this increases the likelihood that the participatory situation would involve just one set of participants attempting to achieve one particular policy outcome.

Initiative Required

To the dimensions of potential outcome and conflict we add that of the initiative required to engage in the act. This dimension is similar to (indeed taps one component of) the "difficulty of the act" criterion that has been the usual one in the literature. We are interested in the amount of time and effort needed for an act of participation, but more so in how much initiative is needed by the individual in choosing when to act and how to act.[5]

THE DIMENSIONS AND MODES OF ACTIVITY

These three distinctions among types of political acts, when combined in different ways, produce what one can consider alternative systems by which the citizenry influences the government. Much of our analysis of politics has involved the study of situations in which large groups of collaborating citizens oppose each other in relation to some outcome affecting the entire collectivity. Party competition for control over governmental offices is the prototype, but this also describes other clashes over major governmental policies that affect many citizens. At the other extreme are those citizen-government interactions in which the citizen acts alone. The outcome affects only him, and he is not directly opposed by any other citizen.

The usefulness of these dimensions can be seen in relation to the four modes of political activity mentioned; these four modes differ from each other in terms of these dimensions and this will structure what activity an individual chooses.

---

[5] For an interesting set of dimensions of participation, parallel in part our own but different in other ways, see Robert Friedman, *Participation in Democracy: A Theory of Democracy and Democratic Socialization*, unpublished Ph.D. dissertation, Princeton University, 1972.

Citizen-Initiated Contacts

The most distinctive characteristic of citizen-initiated contacts concerns the scope of the outcome. Only this mode of participation can reasonably be expected to result in a particularized benefit. The individual participant takes the initiative in contacting a government official and, most important, he decides what to contact about. The "choosing of the agenda" by the citizen-contactor—something that is possible for contacting activity only—is crucial for two reasons. First, it ensures that the subject matter of the participatory act is salient and important to the individual, and second, it makes possible particularization of the subject matter to the individual. Under such circumstances, he may still contact about some general social problem—he may write his Congressman about the war in Vietnam or complain to a local governmental official about some general failure in performance—but he may also contact about some particular problem affecting only himself or his family.

The potential-outcome dimension is most crucial for distinguishing citizen-initiated contacts from other acts. On the conflict dimension, we assume that such contacts do not usually involve direct conflict with other citizens. Furthermore, because the individual chooses the occasion to participate, as well as the subject matter and the official to contact, such activity requires quite a bit of initiative on the part of the contactor.

Voting

The vote is in some ways the polar opposite of the citizen-initiated contact. The citizen does not choose the occasion to vote as he chooses the occasion to contact; nor does he set the agenda of the participatory act. He chooses neither the candidates nor the issues. Under such circumstances, one cannot expect particularized outcomes, relevant only to the individual. In fact, the citizen may participate with little or no outcome in mind. There is evidence, for instance, that a prime motivation for voting is the gratification of the act itself—not some expected outcome.[6] Relatively little initiative is needed to vote in comparison with what is needed for the other activities. Voting, furthermore, as part of the electoral process, is a conflictual activity that does pit one group of citizens against another (at least where elections are competitive).

Campaign Activity

Campaign activity, like voting, produces collective outcomes. And it involves the citizen in conflictual situations. But some initiative is required of the citizen; campaign activity is clearly a more difficult political act than mere voting. However, it is unclear how much initiative is needed to be active in campaigning—more than is needed for voting certainly, but perhaps less than is needed for contacting. The fact that the campaigner works along with others means that he may become active on the initiative of others.

---

[6] Almond and Verba, for instance, found the most frequent reason given for voting in the United States was that citizens received a sense of gratification from it. See Almond and Verba, *The Civic Culture*, pp. 107-108.

Cooperative Activity

When a citizen cooperates with others—either in informal groups or in formal organizations—it reduces the likelihood that the political activity will be aimed at some benefit particularized to him alone. Thus cooperative activity is more likely to be relevant to outcomes of a somewhat collective nature, though the outcome may affect a group in the society rather than the entire collectivity. It is somewhat less clear whether such cooperative activity is likely to take place in a situation of conflict with other groups. Conflict is more likely to be involved in cooperative activity than in citizen-initiated contacts because the stakes are usually higher, but it is less likely to be involved than in the electoral situation.

Indeed, there may be several different types of cooperative activity. Much of such activity involves the mobilization of community energies to achieve relatively noncontroversial goals: People join to support a bond issue for a new hospital, they cooperate to strengthen the PTA, they act jointly to improve community services. Of course, bitter conflict can break out in relation to any of these actions, but it usually does not because the activities are not aimed at any opposition group. On the other hand, cooperation among citizens may involve a greater commitment to a politics of conflict, particularly if the group is a deprived minority and the attainment of what they want requires that they move others who are perceived as hostile.

Our assumption—supported by data to be presented—is that most of such cooperative activity takes place in relatively nonconflictual settings. Groups act for what they perceive as a benefit for their group or for the community as a whole, and in neither case are they likely to be directly opposed by other citizens pushing an opposite policy.[7]

Cooperative activity probably requires some initiative, though the amount of such initiative depends on whether the individual helped form such a cooperative group or just joined it.

The characteristics of the four modes of activity in relation to the three dimensions of participation are summarized in Table 3-1, in which we can see that each of the four modes of activity shares some characteristics with one or another mode, but that each has a unique combination of characteristics across the dimensions. Voting is unique in requiring less initiative than the other acts; citizen-initiated contacts are unique in that such contacts can produce particularized benefits; campaign and cooperative activity, though similar in having collective outcomes and requiring initiative, differ in the degree to which they involve the citizen in conflictual situations.

---

[7]Cooperative activity can, however, take many forms. In some cases it can involve minority groups acting to obtain some benefit under conditions of great conflict. Cooperative activity, furthermore, often appears to be on the border of politics. Much of it involves citizens working directly on community problems with only indirect intervention of the government. But, because it does affect how values are allocated in a community, we have considered it a highly political activity.

Table 3-1

The Four Modes of Participation and the Dimensions of Participation

Modes of activity	Conflict dimension	Scope of outcome	Initiative required
Electoral activity — Voting	Conflictual	Collective outcome	Little
Campaign activity	Conflictual	Collective outcome	Some
Nonelectoral activity — Cooperative activity	Usually nonconflictual	Collective outcome	Some or a lot
Citizen-initiated contacts	Nonconflictual	Collective or particularized outcome	A lot

CONCLUSION

The modes of political activity, because of the way they relate to the dimensions of participation, are meaningfully different ways in which the individual citizen tries to influence his government. They fit closely what we have considered alternative systems of citizen-government interaction. Most political analyses have focused on the citizen as a voter. In this process, the citizen acts as one of a large number of citizens in relation to a major collective outcome—the selection of governmental personnel. His own influence is relatively low. Not only does he have relatively little effect on the outcome, but he does not choose the alternatives with which he is faced. At the other extreme is the citizen-initiated contact, in which the citizen contacts an official on some problem. The problem may be very narrow, a situation made possible by the fact that the citizen "chooses the agenda" of the participatory act. Though the outcome may have little measurable impact on the overall system, the outcome may be very important for him. And, unlike the situation in relation to voting, his own activity may make a major difference. Furthermore, the set of these dispersed contacts may represent a major allocative mechanism in society. In between, we have cooperative activity, not as particularized as contacting but more precisely related to citizen problems than elections. It represents a major way groups of citizens press claims on the government. Last, we have campaign activity, whereby citizens may obtain a greater degree of control over electoral outcomes than via mere voting.

Distinguishing among these modes of participation, of course, complicates the study of political participation, but it is a useful complication. Most studies that have looked for the causes or consequences of participation have made no such distinctions. However, if these modes of activity are different in the ways we suggest, it may be that the conditions that lead to participation differ from one mode to another. Interests, motivations, resources, opportunities may lead different groups into different kinds of activity, or perhaps some groups may be blocked from one mode or another. Similarly, the consequences of participation, in terms of the way in which the government allocates benefits through its activity, may differ depending upon which mode of activity the citizen has chosen. These are the kinds of questions we wish to explore and for which the distinctions among the modes of activity have been drawn.

Thus far we have attempted to justify our focus on four modes of participation in terms of the difference in the way in which they relate the individual to his government. We shall now attempt to demonstrate, in several ways, that this way of dividing up the universe of participation has some empirical justification in the data themselves. In Chapter 4 we shall ask whether the modes of activity we have specified are consistent with an empirical structure of participatory acts found within our data, and whether we can identify particular citizens who engage in one mode of activity rather than another. And in Chapter 5 we will look at some of the psychological correlates of the various modes of activity to see if the orientations that one would expect to be associated with each mode—given our discussion in this chapter—are indeed so associated. Each of these three exercises will represent a further attempt to validate the distinctions that we have made and will shed light on the nature of participation. In Chapter 6 we will see whether social groups differ, not only in the amount of their activity, but in the kind of activities as well. In Chapter 7 we will discuss the issue of citizen rationality, arguing that the citizen may look more rational than is sometimes thought when one considers the various ways he can be active.

Chapter 4
The Modes of Participation:
An Empirical Analysis

Our argument that the four modes of political participation represent different "systems" by which the citizen can influence the government has been based on an analysis of the "logic" of the modes of activity—what outcomes they can influence, how much they involve the individual in conflict, and how much initiative they require. In this chapter we shall try to validate these arguments by examining the empirical relationships among various political acts.

Each mode of activity can be carried out using a variety of specific acts: One can be active in campaigns by ringing doorbells, contributing money to a party, or trying to persuade others how to vote. One can be active in the "contacting mode" by contacting local and/or national officials and by contacting by mail and/or in person. If political acts are *not* "interchangeable," if there is, as we argue, a multidimensionality to political participation, then the citizen who engages in one specific act within one of the modes should be more likely to engage in other acts within that mode than he is to engage in acts in another mode. This follows from the logic of the participation modes. If the modes differ in the problems for which they are relevant, in the extent to which they involve the citizen in conflict, and in the initiative they require, then those citizens with particular kinds of problems, or attitudes toward conflict, or different amounts of initiative should be found concentrating their activity in particular modes.

Because we are examining the ways various political acts cluster together and because we shall depend in part on factor analysis, the *deus ex machina* of the social sciences, (where the *machina* is an IBM 360) it is important to be clear on what we are *not* doing. We are not looking to see what clusterings among political acts we find. Rather we are looking to see whether the clustering we expect to find, given our analysis of the alternative characteristics of the modes of activity, is indeed found.

In designing our questionnaire, we attempted to gather several independent measures for each of the four hypothesized modes of political activity. We queried respondents as to whether they had voted in the 1964 Presidential election and in the 1960 Presidential election, and we had them report the frequency of their voting in local elections. We asked five different questions about their involvement in campaign and political party activity: membership in political clubs, attendance at meetings and rallies, donation of money, work for a party, and attempts to persuade others to vote one way rather than another. We also asked them to report on their cooperative political activities: whether they had ever formed a group to deal with a social problem or had worked with an existing group. We also derived a measure of their cooperative activity based on their number of active memberships in organizations that are directly concerned with public issues and problems. Finally, each citizen was asked whether he had initiated a contact with a local government leader and whether he had initiated such a contact with an official of the state or national government. (The proportions reporting that they engaged in each type of activity were presented in Table 2-1.[1])

Our detailed analysis of the structure of participation begins with Table 4-1 giving the simple correlation coefficients among these thirteen political activities.[2] On the average, the correlations are quite moderate. The mean of all coefficients is .25, and only one in five is greater than .30. However, each of the 72 coefficients reported in Table 4-1 is positive and statistically significant.[3] Thus the acts are not completely separate or uncorrelated. Performance of any individual political act increases the probabilities of per-

---

[1] Complete question wording for the thirteen participation items is to be found in Appendix B.1.

[2] For a discussion of the use of parametric linear statistics with ordinal data, see Appendix G.

[3] In general, tests of statistical significance are not applied in the analysis reported in this volume when the cross-section sample is the unit of analysis. Because our sample is a very large one, almost every relationship is statistically significant. For example, in a random sample of 2,000 cases (our unweighted sample is 2,549) a conservative estimate of statistical significance indicates that any coefficient of greater than .04 is significant at the .05 level. A coefficient of greater than .06 is significant at the .001 level.

In Chapters 13, 19, and 20, where the community rather than the individual becomes the unit of analysis, we will employ tests of statistical significance. Such tests are important in these instances because the number of cases on which these analyses are based is much smaller, varying between 65 and 110.

Table 4-1

Pearson r Simple Correlation Matrix Among Thirteen Political Activities

Participation variable	1	2	3	4	5	6	7	8	9	10	11	12	13
Persuade others how to vote	—	.47	.35	.27	.27	.21	.19	.24	.24	.23	.22	.24	.23
Actively work for party or candidate		—	.50	.36	.46	.19	.19	.27	.31	.24	.27	.26	.22
Attend political meeting or rally			—	.37	.45	.20	.18	.25	.23	.24	.30	.25	.21
Contribute money to party or candidate				—	.36	.17	.17	.20	.21	.12	.24	.20	.20
Membership in political clubs					—	.14	.13	.18	.22	.22	.29	.17	.19
Voted in 1964 Presidential election						—	.71	.64	.18	.10	.19	.13	.14
Voted in 1960 Presidential election							—	.60	.17	.09	.18	.11	.12
Frequency of voting in local elections								—	.22	.14	.23	.17	.18
Work with others on local problem									—	.38	.34	.29	.23
Form a group to work on local problems										—	.28	.22	.19
Active membership in community problem-solving organizations											—	.26	.27
Contact local officials												—	.23
Contact state and national officials													—

Group labels:
- Columns 1–5: Campaign activity
- Columns 6–8: Voting
- Columns 9–11: Cooperative activity
- Columns 12–13: Contacting

forming each and every other act. In this sense, the data are compatible with a weak "unitary" model of participation in which citizens have general propensities to be active or passive. On the other hand, the correlations vary substantially: they range from a very weak .10, between forming a group to solve a community problem and voting in the 1960 Presidential election, to a quite substantial .71 between the two measures of Presidential voting.

The matrix in Table 4-1 has been ordered by the four modes of activity. The boxed clusters contain the correlations between activities of a given type or mode, and the correlations outside the boxes present the coefficients between acts of different types. The correlations cluster into the hypothesized types of activity. The average correlation within the clusters is about .45. The average for those outside of the clusters is less than .20.

The first cluster contains the five campaign activities and has a mean correlation of .38. This is about three times the average correlation between campaign activities and variables outside the cluster.[4] The second cluster, consisting of the three voting activities, stands out. The average correlation among these three acts is .66, and their range is quite small, between .60 and .71. It is also important to note that the correlations between the voting items and the other acts are among the weakest in the matrix. We shall discuss the meaning of this finding in a few pages.

The pattern in the third cluster—the three group-based activities—is similar to the one for electoral participation, with an average coefficient within the cluster of .34. The identifiability of the fourth type of participation—contacting government officials—is more problematic. Their relationship to each other is about average, and they do not seem to stand apart from the other types of activities. Indeed, contacting a local official is most closely related to cooperating with others in a local problem; contacting an extralocal official is most closely related to being an active member of an organization engaged in solving community problems. This poses a puzzle in relation to our assumptions, a puzzle to which we shall return.

The data suggest, then, that although all political activities are intercorrelated, the correlations between acts within the same mode are generally higher than those across different modes of activity and, therefore, that citizens tend to concentrate their activity by mode. Consider, for instance, the following example: "Forming a group to work on a local problem" and "contributing money to a party or candidate" are both relatively infrequent acts; the former performed by 14 percent of the citizenry, the latter by 13 percent. Despite the similarity in the proportions engaging in these two specific acts, each act is more closely related to other acts within its own mode— including acts performed by many more people—than the two acts are related to each other. "Forming a group" and "contributing campaign money"

---

[4] By "three times the average correlation" we mean that the average amount of variation that one campaign act has in common with another (the square of the correlation) is over 14 percent, while activities outside of this and the other clusters account, on the average, for only 4 percent of their mutual variation.

correlate at .12. "Forming a group" correlates much more closely with the other cooperative acts, though the latter are much more frequent acts; and "contributing money" has a similar closeness of relationship to such more frequent acts as "persuading others how to vote" or "attending a political rally."

However, the correlation matrix leaves unanswered several questions about the clustering of political activities. We cannot tell yet whether the correlation among these thirteen variables can be best explained by a single underlying factor or by the four factors anticipated by our arguments. Nor do we know for sure whether or not we have isolated the only or even the most significant clusters in the matrix; for there may be other clusterings that are hidden by our ordering of the activities. Finally, we have the problem of contacting; the correlation matrix does not provide much evidence for considering these acts to be a distinct mode of participation.

To deal with these issues, we shall turn to factor analysis. Several characteristics of factor-analytic techniques make them ideally suited to our purposes. First, methods of factoring can reduce a large number of individual variables (in this case the thirteen acts of participation) into a smaller number of underlying dimensions or factors based upon the most significant clusterings among the variables. And unlike the clusters in the correlation matrix, the dimensions are located by a theory-blind empirical method. The results of the factor analysis can then be compared with the dimensions we expected to find on the basis of our theory. Second, factoring methods can help us determine the relative importance of the various dimensions in the total pattern of political participation. Finally, factor analysis contains procedures for determining the relationships among the dimensions it uncovers so that we can begin to learn something about the ways in which citizens combine activities across, as well as within, dimensions of activity.[5]

A FACTOR ANALYSIS OF THE STRUCTURE OF PARTICIPATION

There is a large variety of factor-analytic models, most of which require two analytically different steps. In the first step, often known as the extraction of factors, one looks for a possible reduction of dimensions—the correlations among a large number of individual variables may be adequately explained in terms of smaller numbers of underlying dimensions. In the second step, one usually rotates the result of the first step to a more stable and a simpler structure. The rotated structure is usually presented in the published papers. In our analysis, however, we will report the results for both steps because each tells us something slightly different about the nature of the relationship among these variables.

---

[5]Factor analysis has received much criticism as a technique for dimensional analysis. We try to validate our results in several ways in Appendix E. We include there a replication of this analysis, using Guttman-Lingoes Smallest Space Analysis.

Principal-Component Solution

Principal-component analysis is a relatively straightforward way of transforming a large set of variables into a smaller group of "principal components" that are orthogonal (uncorrelated) to each other.[6] The first component represents the single best summary of the linear relationships exhibited in the data. When a set of variables are all positively correlated—as are our thirteen political activities—the first component tends to represent a general dimension. Subsequent components tend to be bipolar, with one set of variables loading positively and others negatively. These subsequent components highlight contrasts in the relationship among the acts that remain after one has accounted for the general underlying dimension.[7]

Table 4-2 presents the results of a principal-component analysis and reports the first four factors extracted.[8] The numbers running down the column under each component are the "factor loadings" of each participation variable on that component, and can range from $+1.0$ to -1.0, indicating positive or negative relationships of more or less strength.[9] Consider the first principal factor or component. Each of the thirteen political activities displays a positive and fairly similar association to this composite variable. This suggests that it is meaningful to talk of a common dimension that can be described as a propensity for political activity or a prime "activeness" component. And the

[6] The principal component analysis has three variants that are usually referred to as *principal components, principal axes,* or *principal factors.* The three variants differ only in the scaling of the composite variables (factors or components): a principal axis is usually standardized to have a mean of zero and a variance equal to the total variance it accounts for; a principal component is the same as a principal axis except that its mean is not standardized to zero; a principal factor is normalized to have a zero mean and unit variance. [See Rozeboom, *Foundations of the Theory of Prediction* (Homewood, Ill.: Dorsey, 1966).] However, much confusion exists in actual usage. Because the scaling factors do not change the general line of our argument, we shall use the terms *factor* and *component* interchangeably in this section of the chapter.

[7] The first factor or component is that combination of the variables that accounts for more variance in the data as a whole than does any other possible linear combination. The second factor or component is the best linear combination of variables that is orthogonal to the first, i.e., that linear combination of variables that accounts for the largest amount of residual variance after the effect of the first component has been removed. Subsequent components are defined in identical manners where each new component is extracted on the residual variance left after the effects of all previous factors or components have been removed. The patterns displayed in principal component solutions are indicative of the nature of the characteristics that bind some of the variables together and that distinguish one subset of variables from another. The initial unrotated solution does not attempt to arrange the variables according to clusters and therefore does not usually permit us to name the components.

[8] The customary way of deciding the number of significant components or factors to be extracted is to retain components with "eigenvalues" greater than or equal to 1.0. However, there is less than total agreement on the appropriateness of the criterion. For a fuller description of the rationale behind the eigenvalue criterion, see Henry F. Kaiser, "The Application of Electronic Computers in Factor Analysis," *Educational and Psychological Measurement,* vol. 20 (1960), pp. 141-157. For reasons for not blindly following the criterion, see Raymond F. Cattell, "Factor Analysis: An Introduction to Essentials." *Biometrics,* vol. 21, (1965), pp. 190-215, 405-435. The last component we have falls slightly below this general criterion. However, we retained four components first because our hypothesis anticipated four significant dimensions and the fourth component was both interpretable and had an eigenvalue fairly close to the 1.0 cutoff point. The reason we stop after the fourth component, on the other hand, was because the remaining components were not only much smaller, but also uninterpretable.

[9] The square of these loadings is equal to the percentage of variance in the variable explained by the component. The farthest right column in the table presents the amount of total variance in each one of the concrete variables which is accounted for by the first four principal components. These numbers, termed *communalities,* are the sum of the squared loadings in each row. The percentage of total variance presented at the bottom of the table indicates how much of the total variance among the variables is accounted for by each of the components. This figure is equal to the sum of the squared loadings on all variables in each of the columns.

Table 4-2

Initial Principal-Factor Matrix (unrotated) of the Thirteen Participatory Acts

Participation variable	Component 1	Component 2	Component 3	Component 4	Communalities
Persuade others how to vote	.59	-.15	-.14	.09	.40
Actively work for party or candidate	.68	-.25	-.30	-.09	.63
Attend political meeting or rally	.65	-.23	-.32	-.10	.59
Contribute money to party or candidate	.54	-.17	-.36	.17	.48
Membership in political clubs	.58	-.29	-.36	-.18	.58
Voted in 1964 Presidential election	.55	.71	.01	-.02	.81
Voted in 1960 Presidential election	.53	.71	.01	-.04	.79
Frequency of voting in local elections	.60	.59	.01	-.02	.72
Work with others on local problem	.55	-.17	.47	-.22	.60
Form group to work on local problems	.45	-.26	.47	-.46	.70
Active membership in community problem-solving organizations	.56	-.16	.28	-.00	.41
Contact local officials	.47	-.19	.32	.33	.47
Contact state and national officials	.45	-.15	.25	.64	.70
Percentage of total variance	31	14	9	7	.61
Eigenvalue	4.05	1.79	1.15	.87	

various political acts are interchangeable as indicators of that dimension. To this extent these data are not inconsistent with a view that participation is unidimensional. This activity dimension explains between 20 and 40 percent of the variance in each of the acts, and it accounts for almost one-third (31 percent) of the total variance among the thirteen variables. On the other hand, the first dimension by no means describes all of the patterned structure among the political activities. The subsequent three components account together for as large a portion of the total variance among the activities as does the first component, and they clearly indicate some significant contrasts in the data unaccounted for by the general dimension.

The second component unambiguously points to the uniqueness of voting when compared to other political acts. Here we see that the three voting variables (the two Presidential voting measures and frequency of voting in local elections) display high positive loadings ranging from .6 to .7, whereas all the other ten activities have weak negative loadings. We can say, therefore, that once the degree of activity has been removed, the most salient distinction among the political acts is whether they measure voting or some other form of participation.

On the third component, we find that all of the nonelectoral activities (both contacting and the cooperative activities) display moderate and consistent positive loadings, whereas the five campaign activities have somewhat smaller but consistent negative loadings. This component suggests that even after general level of activity and the uniqueness of voting have been removed, there remains a significant distinction between campaign activity and nonelectoral modes of participation. This third component accounts for approximately 9 percent of the total variance in the 13 activities and over a sixth of the common variance explainable by the four components.

Both forms of electoral participation, voting as well as campaign activities, have loadings near zero on the fourth and final component. This component appears to separate the two forms of nonelectoral participation. Two of the three cooperative activities load negatively, while citizen-initiated contacts (both local and outside of the community) have relatively strong positive loadings. The interpretation of this final component should, however, be considered more tentative than those attributed to the previous ones, for we are dealing here with much more refined patterns of residual variation, and the configuration of loadings is not as clear as those in the earlier components.[10]

The Rotated-Factor Solution

The rotated-factor solution provides us with even more information on the ways citizens concentrate their political activity. The rotational method we

---

[10] This component is the only one of the four with an eigenvalue of less than 1.0. It is, however, not far below this cutoff point, being .87. The logic for including this component is spelled out in some detail in footnote 8 of this chapter.

employ rearranges the initial or unrotated factors into an equal number of clusters of variables, each representing more or less identifiable dimensions.[11] The loading of the individual acts on the various factors can be compared with the pattern our previous discussion led us to expect. The pattern in the rotated-factor matrix presented in Table 4-3 strikingly matches our expectations. Each of the four expected modes of activity constitutes a separate factor. The specific activities display high loadings on the appropriate factor and near-zero loadings on the other three. From left to right, the five campaign activities form the first factor, the three voting measures the second, the three group-based activities the third, and the two indicators of citizen-initiated contacts form the fourth factor. With only one or two minor deviations, virtually all of the variance in each variable is accounted for by only one factor. In every instance the activities have their highest loadings on the expected factor.

The "structure" we have found is quite consistent with our expectations as to how specific acts relate to more general modes of activity. The dimensions we used to distinguish among the modes of activity—the problem it can be used for, the relationship to conflict, and the initiative required—are long-term characteristics of individuals. This led us to expect the pattern of relationship among the specific acts that we find: if someone engages in one activity in a certain mode, he tends to engage in other activities within that mode.

A CLOSER LOOK AT CONTACTING

The preceding analysis still leaves some puzzles, particularly in relation to contacting. Contacting did not stand out as clearly in our correlation matrix as did the other clusters of political acts. The simple correlation among the contacting items was much weaker than those among acts in the voting, campaigning, or cooperative modes. Also, the contrast between contacting and cooperative activity was the weakest in the principal-component analysis.

We decided to look at this more closely, for there are theoretical reasons for this lack of distinction between contacting and cooperative acts. One of our major dimensions of political participation involved the scope of the outcome of the act, in particular, whether the act could lead to a particularized benefit relevant to the individual and his family or to a more general social policy affecting large groups or the entire collectivity. This led us to consider contacting to be a unique mode of activity. Only through contacting can the

---

[11] We have chosen to use an "oblique" rather than one of the more common "orthogonal" rotational methods because the correlations among the various acts (reported in Table 4-1) show *all* of the participatory activities to be positively correlated. Under such conditions it would be totally unrealistic to expect to find or to attempt to locate orthogonal (uncorrelated) factors. However, the choice among the various available oblique solutions was less simple. We ultimately chose the "binormamin" rotational technique first introduced hy Kaiser and Dickman. For a detailed discussion of this method see Harry H. Harman, *Modern Factor Analysis* (Chicago: University of Chicago Press, 1967). While the decision to use this particular rotational method was not arbitrary, we should emphasize, for readers unfamiliar with the details ot factor analysis, that there is no agreed-upon best oblique rotational method. We experimented with three different methods. All yielded rotated solutions substantively identical to the binormamin solution reported in Table 4-3. The rotational solutions differed only in the amount of correlations among the factors. The binormamin solution was ultimately selected because we felt it yielded the truest picture of the actual degree of angle (amount of correlation) among the factors.

Table 4-3

Binormamin Rotated-Pattern Matrix for the Thirteen Participation Variables[a]

Participation variable	Campaign activity	Voting	Cooperative activity	Contacting
Persuade others how to vote	.53	.15	.14	.27
Actively work for party or candidate	.75	.11	.20	.11
Attend political meeting or rally	.74	.12	.17	.08
Contribute money to party or candidate	.64	.10	−.07	.23
Membership in political clubs	.74	.04	.18	−.03
Voted in 1964 Presidential election	.11	.89	.06	.06
Voted in 1960 Presidential election	.10	.88	.05	.04
Frequency of voting in local elections	.18	.81	.12	.11
Work with others on local problem	.15	.13	.71	.23
Form group to work on local problem	.14	.02	.82	.01
Active membership in community problem-solving organizations	.25	.14	.47	.34
Contact local officials	.15	.06	.28	.60
Contact state and national officials	.15	.07	.04	.82

[a]In oblique rotations there are actually two different matrices—"pattern" and "structure." To save space, we will present only the former throughout this chapter, for the two display the same clusterings. Technically, the pattern matrix represents standardized regression weights of factors on each variable, whereas the structure matrix represents the correlations between each variable and each factor.

individual "set the agenda" for his political act, and this, in turn, is a necessary condition for the attainment of particularized benefits. But though contacting is unique in that it can be used to obtain particularized benefits, it need not be so used. Contacts can relate to wider problems. This suggested that we ought to distinguish more directly between contacts that are aimed at particularized benefits and those that are aimed at general social benefits.

Whenever citizens reported a contact with either an official in the local community or one at some higher level of government, we asked about the subject matter of the contact. Each contact was coded into one of two categories, depending on the breadth of its referent: (1) particularized contacts, in which the issue pertains only to the individual or his family; and (2) contacts pertaining to broader social issues, in which the referent is a group or category of citizens, or the entire community or society. This empirical distinction corresponds closely to our theoretical distinction between particularized and collective outcomes.

Some examples will make the distinctions between these two types of contact clear.

Contacts with Particularized Referents

Here we group all contacts in which the issue refers only to the respondent or his immediate family, and in which a government decision responsive to that contact would presumably have little or no direct impact on others in the society. To be coded in this category, the contact had to refer specifically to the individual himself or to those immediately around him, such as his family. Some examples taken directly from the responses are: enlisting the aid of a Congressman to bring a son home from Peace Corps service when his younger brother died, asking the state commissioner of insurance to help in the collection of an unpaid hospitalization claim, petitioning a state senator to intervene with the county social-service administration to reverse a decision on eligibility for disability benefits, urging a local councilman to pressure the Department of Streets to extend a sidewalk to a newly built home, and asking a precinctman about a patronage job.

Contacts with Broad Referents

Contacts in this category refer to issues or problems that are more public in nature in which government actions would affect a significant segment of the population, if not the entire community or society. Though the examples here vary in scope of referent, they all refer to public issues rather than to private interests. Examples of contacts in which the referent is a subgroup of the population include prices received by farmers, housing for Negro families, state aid to Catholic schools, and salaries for secondary-school teachers. Examples of broader issues, affecting the community or society, include a letter to a senator about the war in Vietnam or the test-ban treaty, a visit to a mayor concerning the need for a recreation center for young people, and a letter to the President urging action on a pending Civil Rights Act.

Approximately one-third of all citizen-initiated contacts with government officials in the community or outside it are about particularized problems. The remaining 65 percent of citizen contacts on both governmental levels relate to broader social issues. Using this distinction, we characterize our respondents on four new variables: whether or not they contacted (1) a local leader about an individualized problem, (2) a local leader about a group or community problem, (3) a state or national leader about a personalized problem, or (4) a state or national leader about a group or society problem.

These transformed variables, along with the other eleven political activities, were then subjected to a new principal component analysis. This is presented in Table 4-4. The pattern is quite interesting when compared with the first principal component analysis reported in Table 4-2. As in the earlier analysis, we find all acts of participation, including the two items measuring contact on a broad community or social issue, related to the first overall dimension of participation. However, there is one striking deviation from this pattern: The two items measuring contact on a particularized problem have close to zero loadings on this general measure of participation. Whereas all other acts of participation are related to a general "political activeness" dimension, we have now isolated a type of participation that apparently has no relationship to the general dimension of political activity.[12]

This new pattern is consistent with our discussion of the dimension of the scope of the outcome of participation. Most modes of activity relate to general social problems and their solution. Actions affecting elections (voting and campaigning), cooperative activity, and contacts with officials on a social matter have this in common. But particularized contact has no general goal, which may explain why almost all types of political activity are somewhat intercorrelated except for such contacts. The rather unusual position of particularized contacts reinforces the importance of the "scope of outcome" dimension of political participation. Contacting on a narrow personal issue

[12] One of the assumptions of factor analysis is that variables are independently measured. In constructing new variables, we therefore tried to eliminate autocorrelation. The respondents were allowed to answer positively for both personal and social problems on each level. However, there is some danger of autocorrelation because we allowed at most three contacts on the local or extralocal levels. It is difficult, though not impossible (because of the way we built the variables), for respondents to be coded positively on both particularized and more general contacts. Thus there may be some artificial negative correlation between the two types of contacting, making it unlikely that particularized contacts would load highly on a component on which more general contacts also loaded. To control for this, we ran the factor analysis twice more, once putting in only the measures of contact with social referents, and once doing the opposite. In the first analysis, the two contact measures on broader issues displayed a pattern that was virtually identical to the one presented in Table 4-4. Citizen-initiated contacts about broader social issues—like all of the other eleven activities—are related to the general activity dimension of political participation. In the second analysis, the two citizen-initiated contacts about particularistic issues had almost no relationship to other forms of participation, even when the possible contaminating effects of other types of contact were removed.

A detailed examination of the correlation matrix shows that the two measures of particularized contacting are not correlated strongly. The fact that they stand out as a separate factor reflects more of their lack of relation to other variables than of their strong internal association. The negative loadings of the contacting variables on the opposite factor is likely an artifact of our creation of the variables, as is the weakness of the correlations among the two particularized variables themselves.

Table 4-4
Principal Components of Fifteen Participatory Acts

Participation variable	Component 1	Component 2	Component 3	Component 4	Communalities
Persuade others how to vote	.59	–.15	–.10	–.11	.39
Actively work for party or candidate	.68	–.25	–.26	–.16	.62
Attend political meeting or rally	.65	–.22	–.31	–.13	.58
Contribute money to party or candidate	.54	–.16	–.33	–.19	.46
Membership in political clubs	.58	–.28	–.29	–.20	.54
Voted in 1964 Presidential election	.55	.71	.02	–.00	.81
Voted in 1960 Presidential election	.53	.71	.03	–.03	.79
Frequency of voting in local elections	.60	.60	.02	.01	.72
Work with others on local problem	.55	–.17	.35	.31	.55
Form a group to work on local problems	.46	–.26	.35	.35	.52
Active membership in community problem-solving organizations	.56	–.16	.24	.16	.42
Contact local leaders—social referent	.48	.02	.37	.01	.42
Contact state or national leaders—social referent	.42	–.03	.35	–.15	.34
Contact local leaders—personalized referent	.07	–.22	–.39	.58	.49
Contact state or national leaders—personalized referent	.14	–.15	–.34	.60	.50
Percentage of total variance	27	12	8	7	54
Eigenvalue	4.1	1.8	1.2	1.1	

stands at one extreme of that dimension,[13] and it has no relationship to general political activity. This is a very distinctive type of political participation, a type we might somewhat paradoxically call *parochial participation*—borrowing the term from Almond and Verba, who use it to identify citizens who lack any positive orientation toward public life.[14]

The other three components are also quite clear. On the second component reported in Table 4-4 we see a clear contrast between voting and the other political acts. Again, voting stands out as a quite distinctive mode of activity. The next component is most interesting: on it we find positively loaded the three acts that represent cooperative activity, but we find equally strong loadings for the two items measuring contacting with a social referent. These are two sets of acts we had considered to be in different modes. And they are different in terms of the nature of the act—contacting being an individual act directed at a political leader, cooperative activity involving other citizens. But they have much in common in terms of our overall dimensions of political activity: the scope of their potential outcome is broad, they involve little conflict, and they require some initiative. In this sense, the acts are quite similar to each other. And on the third component, we see that this mode of activity that combines cooperative activity and contacting on a social issue contrasts equally strongly both with campaign activity and with particularized contacting. It is clearly a mode of activity quite different from either of those.

The last component is in some sense the mirror image of the first principal component. On it, particularized contacting stands out in contrast to all other acts.

In short, the second principal-component analysis, in which we divide contacting into two types of acts, provides a somewhat different set of activity modes: voting and campaign activity remain clearly identifiable (voting on the second principal component, campaign activity by its unique combination of strong loadings on the first component and negative ones on the third). But two new modes of activity appear. One is *personalized contacting,* a mode that stands out from all the rest. The other is a combination of cooperative activity and contacting on a social issue, which, for the sake of convenience, we can label *communal activity.* Communal activity is composed of all the acts of participation that aim at influencing broader social issues in the community or society, and that take place in a participatory setting devoid of the counter-participants that characterize electoral involvement.

From one perspective, these four modes of activity appear less clear than the first fourfold distinction, for now two different kinds of act load on a single

[13] This does not mean that all of those who initiate particularized contacts are necessarily preoccupied with government as a mechanism for solving their own problems, for if this were the case, the loadings for these variables would be highly negative rather than zero. The near-zero loadings suggest that this type of activity simply has no relationship to the generalized orientation toward broader social and political issues.

[14] Almond and Verba, *The Civic Culture,* Chapter 1.

factor, and a single kind of act—contacting—loads on two separate factors. However, from a theoretical perspective, these activity clusters are clearer than before and consistent with our argument concerning the importance of the potential scope of the outcome of a political act. Insofar as different acts are used to influence similar types of issues, we find that the acts cluster together. Citizens who are concerned about certain types of broad social issues, who maintain a predisposition for participatory settings devoid of counterpartici-pants, and who are willing to exert considerable amounts of participatory initiative are likely, these findings suggest, to perform *all* of the acts that share these characteristics. By the same token, when the same concrete act (e.g., contacting) is utilized in relation to different types of issues, we find that they load on separate factors. In this way our findings here are precisely what would be predicted from our earlier theoretical perspective on the distinctions among the various modes of activity. Contacts on both general and particu-larized issues are similar types of activity in certain respects—they are engaged in alone and require initiative—but that similarity seems less important than the difference in goals.

The Second Rotated-Factor Solution

We can make the new structure of the participation items even clearer by presenting a rotated factor solution, using again the binormanin rotation. The result of this analysis, including the two forms of contacting, is reported in Table 4-5. One can only describe it as a remarkably clear and "clean" result. It provides striking confirmation of the structure expected on the basis of our reconsideration of the contacting variable. Four modes are identifiable, and each constitutes a separate factor. The first is clearly campaign activity, the second voting, the third our new communal activity factor, and the fourth isolates particularized contacting. In each case the expected items load positively and strongly, while all other items have loadings close to zero or negative loadings. The third factor, communal activity, is worth noting: social contacting and cooperative activities all load positively and fairly strongly. Every other variable is negative or close to zero. This mode, combining activities we had originally separated, is distinctive as well.

Thus, the progression of our ideas on political participation can be summarized as follows: Our initial conception led us to anticipate four modes of participation—voting, campaigning, cooperative activities, and citizen-initiated contacts. However, a closer look at the data suggested that citizen-initiated contacts differ depending upon the scope of the potential outcome of the political act. Personalized contacts were found to be distinct from other acts of political participation. Furthermore, the new factor analysis containing the distinction between personalized and social contacts revealed a clustering of two dimensions—cooperative acts and contacts on social matters—which we labeled a "communal activity dimension."

Initial Conception	Refinement	Empirical Clustering
1. Campaigning ⟶	1. Campaigning ⟶	1. Campaigning
2. Voting ⟶	2. Voting ⟶	2. Voting
3. Cooperative acts ⟶	3. Cooperative acts ⟶	3. Communal acts
4. Citizen-initiated ⟷ contacts	4. Contacts on social issues	4. Personalized contacts
	5. Personalized contacts	

If we reconsider Table 3-1, p. 55, in which we related the particular modes of activity to the several dimensions of participation, we can see the way our new set of modes fits closely to the pattern reported there and, indeed, gives it a somewhat clearer structure. Table 4-6 shows the new set of relationships. Voting and campaign activity do not change, of course, in their relationship to the dimensions of participation. Communal activity has the same relationship to those dimensions as cooperative activity had. In other words, citizen-initiated contacts on a social issue are relatively nonconflictual, have a collective goal, and require considerable initiative. These were the characteristics of cooperative acts. Last, particularized contacting differs from contacting on a more general issue in that the goal is clearly not collective. Thus the ambiguity between the two types of contacting in relation to the dimension of the scope of the outcome is cleared up.

Both analyses of the "structure" of participation—before and after the reconsideration of contacting—produced interesting results.[15] In some sense, the revision of our original expectations in the second analysis leads to a result closer to the expectations we should have had on the basis of our consideration of the logic of participation. The second analysis stresses the importance of the nature of the outcome for distinguishing among political acts. And it lends support to our contention that participation may be a quite rational act for the average citizen, an act whose rationality becomes clear only when one considers the possibility that different acts can lead to different outcomes.

The unique position of particularized contacting suggests that we have found a mode of political activity that is not "political" in the ordinary sense of the word, which is why we consider it to be, somewhat paradoxically, parochial participation. Its goal is narrow and involves none of the broader issues involved in most political activity. The data suggest that there may be something unique about people who engage in such activities, particularly those who engage only in those activities. What may hold the other modes of activity together is that all involve some political consciousness, some aware-

---

[15] The four new modes of participation differ in relation to the dimension of "type of influence" discussed in Chapter 3 in roughly the same way as do the original four modes. Our assumption is that the relationship would look like this:
Voting: high pressure/low information
Campaign activity: high pressure/low to high information
Communal activity: low to high pressure/high information
Particularized contacting: low pressure/high information

Table 4-5

Binormamin Rotated-Pattern Matrix of the Participation Variables Including Both Forms of Contacting: United States

Participation variable	Campaign activity	Voting	Cooperative activity and social contacting	Particularized contacting
Persuade others how to vote	.54	.05	.11	-.03
Actively work for party or candidate	.79	-.02	-.00	.02
Attend political meeting or rally	.79	-.01	-.05	.08
Contribute money to party or candidate	.74	.01	-.16	.04
Membership in political clubs	.80	-.09	-.09	-.00
Voted in 1964 Presidential election	-.02	.91	-.02	-.01
Voted in 1960 Presidential election	-.03	.90	-.03	-.02
Frequency of voting in local elections	.05	.81	.05	.02
Work with others on local problem	-.05	.04	.75	.06
Form a group to work on local problems	-.09	-.08	.77	.10
Active membership in community problem-solving organizations	.12	.05	.56	.01
Contact local leaders—social referent	.08	-.02	.60	.19
Contact state or national leaders—social referent	.11	.03	.44	-.31
Contact local leaders—personalized referent	.01	.02	-.03	.70
Contact state or national leaders—personalized referent	.03	-.01	.08	.70

Table 4-6

The Four Modes of Participation and the Dimensions of Participation: A Reconsideration

Modes of activity		Conflict dimension	Scope of outcome	Initiative required
Electoral activity	Voting	Conflictual	Collective outcome	Little
Electoral activity	Campaign activity	Conflictual	Collective outcome	Some
Nonelectoral activity	Communal activity	Usually non-conflictual	Collective outcome	Some or a lot
Nonelectoral activity	Particularized contacts	Nonconflictual	Particularized contacts	A lot

ness of and concern about issues that transcend the individual's most narrow life space. But parochial participation can take place in the absence of such general concern with political matters. We shall test this hypothesis.

In short we have found two different ways of dividing the universe of political participation. These ways are both meaningful. For most purposes, the second structure is relevant—i.e., where particularized contacts are separated from other contacts and social contacts and cooperative acts form a communal mode of activity. This structure consistently distinguishes among the acts in terms of the scope of their outcome. But occasionally there will be purposes for which the initial classification, in which contacting is kept together, is more relevant. This will be the case (as we shall see when we compare black and white participation) when the nature of the act—taking the initiative to contact an official personally—is more significant than the scope of the outcome.

FROM TYPES OF PARTICIPATION TO TYPES OF PARTICIPATORS

We began this chapter with a criticism of the tendency to divide the American public into types of political actors based solely on the amount of participation. Our analysis of the nature of participation suggests that there are not merely gladiators, spectators, and apathetics (to use Milbrath's metaphor). Rather, activists differ among themselves in *how* they engage in political life. Thus far, however, we have not determined the degree to which citizens actually specialize in one or another mode of participation. Can we in fact locate citizens who concentrate on one type of activity to the exclusion of others?

Full answers to questions of what types of participators exist and how they combine activity across the four modes are beyond the scope of the factor analytic methods we have been employing. Factor analytic and correlational techniques are directed to the classification of *variables* and not to the classification of *people*. We shall turn to other analytic techniques (namely cluster analysis) in order to seek out types of participators. We can, however, begin our search for types of participators by looking more closely at the results of our factor analysis. The correlations among the factors should provide good indications of the extent to which there is specialization in one mode or another as well as the way particular modes of activity are likely to be combined with one another.

Table 4-7 presents the correlations among the four factor scales constructed on the basis of the final oblique rotated-factor solution presented in Table 4-5.[16] In addition, the table displays the correlations between each of the modes and a summary index of participation that will be employed throughout the remainder of this book as the primary indicator of the total amount of participation performed.[17] The latter correlations tell us how strongly each of the modes is related to what we have previously termed the prime-activity component.

The correlations among the four modes of activity indicate a considerable amount of independence among the modes—only one correlation can be considered strong, the remainder being either very weak or moderate. The coefficients also vary greatly from one pair to another.

Campaign and communal activity are the most closely related, even though there is a considerable amount of independence. (The square of the correlation between these two modes of activity indicates that each activity predicts a little more than a quarter of the variance in the other.) And both modes, it should be added, are strongly related to the overall activity index—much more so than either of the two remaining modes. In short, campaign and communal activity appear to form the most common core of political activism insofar as such a core exists.

Voting is much more weakly related to communal and campaign activity than the latter two are to each other. This is particularly striking when one remembers that both campaign activity and voting are activities within the same electoral process. Equally intriguing from this perspective is the fact that the size of the correlation between voting and communal activity is virtually

---

[16] The factor scales of the four modes of participation on which the correlations reported in Table 4-7 are based were constructed using the factor scale score coefficient matrix (which is a product of the binormamin rotation). However, in the computation of the scale scores, only the coefficients from the variables central to each of the factors were included. The weights for the other residual variables were disregarded. The items used in each of the factor scales correspond to those included within the boxes under each factor in Table 4-5. Details of this scale construction technique as well as distributional descriptions of the scales are presented in Appendix B.2.

[17] The overall participation index was constructed from a higher-order factor analysis of the four factor scales. This overall index is thus based on a single common-factor model that assumes that the main thing the participation variables have in common is a reflection of degree of activeness. The summary index then measures only this component of each of the modes of activity. Appendix B.2 presents data bearing on the fit of this assumption and provides information on the technique of higher-order factor scale construction and on the distributional characteristics of this summary measure of participation. The correlations between the summary participation index and the modes of activity are actually the loadings of the four variables on the higher-order factor.

Table 4-7

The Correlations Among the Four Modes of Participation

	Campaign activity	Communal activity	Voting	Particularized contacting
Campaign activity	—	.52	.31	.10
Communal activity		—	.28	.06
Voting			—	.06
Particularized contacting				—
Overall index of participation	.88	.79	.48	.15

as large as that between voting and campaign activity. Voting also displays a much weaker, though still very substantial, relationship to the summary participation index. Furthermore, particularized contacting has hardly any correlation with any of the other modes or with the general activity index.

The patterns of correlation revealed in Table 4-7 are consistent with our earlier arguments concerning the general structure of participation as well as with our discussions of the differing nature of each of the modes of activity. The overall weakness of the correlations substantiates our contention that the modes are to a considerable degree performed by different individuals. On the other hand, the fact that voting, campaign, and communal activity maintain some positive correlation with one another coincides with our previous contention that these three acts share a common motivational base—presumably, some concern for issues beyond the individual's immediate life space.

That campaign and communal activity form the most common core of participation is not surprising. The two modes differ on the conflict dimension, but they are alike on the other two main characteristics of political acts: they both require initiative and are the major ways by which citizens attempt to influence political outcomes of broad scope. It should be remembered, however, that campaign and communal activity are by no means the same. Many individuals perform one without performing the other.

The considerable separation of voting from these activities, and its lesser relationship to the general activity index, are consistent with the uniqueness of voting in terms of the much lower amount of initiative required. However, the fact that voting maintains some relationship to campaign and communal activity and to the summary index of participation suggests that, for some citizens at least, voting is also predicated on a concern for broader social issues.

We have already written much commentary on the absence of relationship between particularized contacting and other forms of participation. The findings here simply substantiate the earlier ones, providing a more direct test of the almost complete separation of contacting on personal matters from the other modes of participation, a separateness that we contend stems from the uniquely particularized scope of the outcomes that are the subject matter of these contacts.

To this point we have been focusing on modes of activity and not directly on participant types. Now we want to look at the citizens themselves. What types of participants are to be found when one considers not only how active citizens are but the ways in which they are active? More specifically, can one locate *sets of citizens* whose overall patterns of political activism (in terms of both the amount and kind of activity they perform) fit with the expectations that emerge from our analysis of the dimensions of participation? It will be useful to see how successful we can be at this endeavor. In the first place, it would further validate our analysis of participation if we found groups of citizens with patterns of activity consistent with our expectations. Second, it will be descriptively interesting to see what types of participators exist and what proportion of the citizenry falls in each type. We may in this way be able to offer a richer classification of citizen participators—one that takes into account both the amount and kinds of activities citizens perform. Last, it will be useful to have isolated such sets of citizens when we try to deal more fully with the question of why different citizens engage in different kinds of political activity.

For this purpose, we turn to cluster analysis, a technique that typologizes people, not variables. Like factor analysis, clustering techniques tend to be "brutally empirical." The former arranges sets of variables into groups; the latter takes a set of individuals characterized by a given set of variables and arranges the individuals into clusters based on similarity to each other across the variables that define them. As with our use of factor analysis, the atheoretical nature of the clustering technique is particularly useful because of the theoretically derived expectations we have as to the results:

1. If our analysis of the structure of participation is correct, we should find relatively "good" clustering—i.e., a fairly high proportion of the population should fall into a relatively small number of clusters or types of participators that are internally homogeneous and distinct from other clusters.

2. The clusters that emerge from the analysis should resemble those that our previous discussion would lead one to expect. Our factor analysis indicated that the modes correlate with each other and there is an underlying dimension of activism to which all modes, save personalized contacting, relate. Therefore, just as it is an oversimplification to typologize individuals solely on the basis of their amount of participation, so is it a mistake to think of them as arrayed on four unrelated modes of political activity.

But what types of participators are there in America? What we have learned about the four modes of participation, their relationship to each other and to the prime activity dimension, as well as the way all these findings fit with our arguments about the motivational characteristics of the modes, lead us to expect the following six types:

1. *The totally inactive.* Given the central importance of the prime activity dimension and its strong relationship to three of the four modes of activism, we anticipate finding some citizens who engage in no or, at most, negligible amounts of political activity.

2. *The totally active.* Similarly, the general dimension of participation suggests that there will be some citizens who do everything. However, the fact that particularized contacting has no relation to the general dimension of activity suggests that these complete activists may or may not engage in such contacts. But they will be active in voting, campaigning, and communal activity.

3. *The voting specialists.* The facts that voting is the only political act requiring relatively little initiative, that it is the most widespread political act, and that it forms the most distinctive factor (in that the individual indicators are very highly correlated with each other and have little relationship to other activities) suggest that we will find citizens who vote with considerable regularity but engage in no other form of participation.

4. *The parochial activists.* The characteristics of particularized contacting suggest that we should find a group whose activity is limited to this mode of participation. This is indicated by the lack of correlation between particularized contacting and all other modes of activity, including the prime activity dimension. There should be some citizens who combine particularized contacting with other acts, but there should also be others who perform only this act. Those who limit their activity to particularized contacting would be particularly interesting. They would be quite active *vis-à-vis* the government (contacting requires considerable initiative), but active only in terms of relatively narrow problems affecting their own lives. We could, therefore, label such citizens *parochial activists.* [18]

5. *The communalists.* The distinctions between communal activity and campaign activity—their different relationship to conflict, their sharp contrast on the principal component analysis, and the fact that they form separate dimensions on our rotated-factor analysis—lead us to expect some citizens who will specialize in the former while being inactive in the latter. They will be high in communal activity while being relatively low in campaign activity. They are likely also to be fairly regular voters, because voting is a relatively easy act that has been shown to have some positive correlation with communal activity. Communalists may or may not be active in particularized contacting, and whether or not a communalist reports making such a contact would not seem to be a particularly salient characteristic of his participatory pattern given his involvement in publicly oriented activity.

6. *The campaigners.* The logic that leads us to expect communalists leads us to expect campaign activists as well. These would be characterized by their

[18] Parochial activists may or may not vote—though we do not expect them to be very regular voters. Occasional voting would, however, not be inconsistent with this pattern of activity.

high degree of campaign activity coupled with low amounts of communal activity. They would probably vote with great regularity but their degree of particularized contacting would be uncertain.

Table 4-8 summarizes the participatory characteristics of the six types of participators we expect to find. A plus signifies that we expect a given type of participant to be highly active on a particular mode of activity, a minus that they will be inactive, and a zero that we have no expectation in either direction. A glance at Table 4-8 will make clear that there are *many other* possible patterns of activity beyond the six we have specified. The question is: To what extent do the respondents in our sample of the American citizenry have patterns of activity that fall into this particular set of patterns?

Table 4-8

Expectations Concerning Six Types of Participants and Their Predicted Activity Patterns

Type of Actor	Voting	Campaign activity	Communal activity	Particularized contacting
Inactive	−	−	−	−
Voting specialist	+	−	−	−
Parochial activist	0	−	−	+
Communalist	+	−	+	0
Campaigner	+	+	−	0
Complete activist	+	+	+	0

Clustering techniques are difficult with large bodies of data and have rarely been applied to data of the sort we have. And our analyses went through several stages. In Appendix F we present a description of the hierarchical clustering technique used. Here we shall present the final result. That result is quite encouraging. We were able successfully to categorize a large proportion (93 percent of our sample) into six types that were quite homogeneous internally and quite similar to our expectations. The results make clear that one can rank citizens in terms of how active they are, but among activists one also finds citizens who specialize in one mode of activity rather than another. In Table 4-9 we present the six groups that emerged from our cluster analysis. For each group we indicate its mean score on a standardized scale for each of the four modes of participation. Looking at the scores for each group, we see that each has a distinct pattern, and the patterns closely fit our expectations. The groups have been labeled accordingly. The result is, we believe, a more refined profile of the American citizenry as participants than has heretofore appeared.

Table 4-9

Participatory Profiles of the American Citizenry[a]

	Scores on participation scales for				
Groups produced by cluster analysis	Voting	Campaign activity	Communal activity	Particularized contacting	Percent of sample in type
1. Inactive	37	9	3	0	22
2. Voting specialists	94	5	3	0	21
3. Parochial participants	73	13	3	100	4
4. Communalists	92	16	69	12	20
5. Campaigners	95	70	16	13	15
6. Complete activists	98	93	92	15	11
					93
Unclassifiable					7
					100%
Population means on the participation scales	76	29	28	14	

[a]See Appendix F for details.

The Inactives (22%)

A little over a fifth of the citizenry takes almost no part in political life. They are not active in campaigns; they do not become involved in the communal activities of their villages, towns, or cities; nor do they initiate particularized contacts with governmental officials. Most don't vote; the rest vote only occasionally. This substantial number of Americans makes no participatory input.

The Voting Specialists (21%)

This group comprises another fifth of the population. In many ways they are like the inactives. They do not participate in campaigns or communal activity, nor do they make particularized contacts. But all of these citizens report having voted in both the Presidential elections about which we asked and all report that they either always or almost always vote in local elections. The regularity with which they vote contrasted with the fact that they attempt to influence the action of government in no other way makes it appropriate to consider them "voting specialists." Though this group is fairly large, it is not as large as many analyses of American politics lead one to expect. It is not true that most Americans vote and do nothing else. There is a substantial number of voting specialists, but they are far from a majority.

The Parochial Participants (4%)

Though the parochial participants represent a small proportion of the population, they are a most interesting group. They engage in neither communal nor campaign activity, and are about average as voters. However, *all* report making particularized contacts. Thus, they are citizens who do engage in an activity that requires initiative, but their interests in government activity appear to be limited to the ways that activity affects their personal lives.

The Communalists (20%)

The communalists are defined by their high level of communal activity and low level of campaign activity. All perform at least two of the five demanding communal acts but almost no campaign activity. They are a fairly sizable group. One out of every five citizens displays this pattern of participation—a most interesting pattern that combines willingness to be quite active in the affairs of one's community, while staying out of the relatively conflictual realm of campaigning.

The Campaigners (15%)

This group is the mirror-image of the communalists. These citizens engage in almost no communal activity but are most active in political campaigns. They appear to prefer the contest of elections while leaving less conflictual communal activities for others. Indeed, the contrast between the communalists and the campaigners is one of the best pieces of evidence we have for the multidimensionality of participation. The two groups perform about the same overall amount of activity, but their profiles of activity are sharply different. Each specializes in one mode to the exclusion of the others. The campaigners are not as numerous as the communalists, but they are a fairly substantial proportion of the population.

The Complete Activists (11%)

The complete activists engage in all types of activity with great frequency. How active they are becomes clear when they are compared to the communalists and campaigners. Not only do they combine both campaign and communal participation but they are considerably more active on each mode than either of the groups that specialize in the respective acts. About one in ten Americans falls in this most active segment.

CONCLUSIONS

In this chapter we have isolated four distinct modes of participation. With the exception of the refinement obtained by separating citizen-initiated contacts according to the scope of their outcomes, the modes we have discovered are precisely those we predicted at the outset. What is more, this refinement did not alter our view of participation but brought the empirical clusters of activity even closer to our theoretical conceptions. We also found sets of citizens who concentrate or specialize their activity within the modes, as well as some who are generally active and others who are inactive. In short, the analysis in this chapter substantiates our multidimensional view of participation in a manner highly consistent with our theoretical arguments about the logic of participation.

Our analysis provides us with a useful and more refined typology of political actors. In Chapter 5 we shall see that the various types of activists differ in the ways they orient themselves to politics—they have different interests and attitudes about politics and they differ in how they view their roles. These differences in orientation will help confirm that the sets of citizen-groups in our typology are indeed significantly different.

Chapter 5
The Types of Participators:
Their Orientations to Politics

Our justification for focusing on four different modes of participation has been that these modes constitute distinctive channels of participation, permitting citizens to exercise different kinds of influences over different types of issues. But thus far the empirical evidence that these modes of activity meaningfully partition the universe of participatory acts has been based solely on an analysis of the relationships among the acts themselves. We have shown that specific acts combine with each other into meaningful modes, and that we can locate concrete types of participators who specialize in one mode of activity or another. In this chapter we want to go a step further in validating these distinctions and provide other evidence that the types of participators we have isolated differ in other meaningful ways beyond their distinct activity patterns. We shall attempt to do this by demonstrating that our six types of activists differ in their orientations to politics, and more important, that the differences in their orientations are consistent with what one would expect given the characteristics of their political activity.

We shall use several basic sets of political orientations.[1]

General Psychological Involvement in Politics

We refer here to a simple but important political orientation: the extent to which the individual expresses an interest in and is attentive to political matters. This attitude is indexed by a series of questions on the extent to which the respondent is interested in politics and public affairs, discusses such matters, and is attentive to them in the media. This orientation is a crucial political one, giving us some indication of the extent to which the respondent is concerned with and pays attention to matters outside of his routine daily life.[2] It thus taps the public-private distinction among the modes. And within modes that are applicable to broad social issues it should also differentiate between those requiring greater and lesser amounts of initiative.

Skill and Competence

We refer to the extent to which the citizen believes himself to be effective in politics and the extent to which he gives objective evidence of some political skill. The former, which we can call his sense of efficacy, is indexed by a series of questions on the extent to which the respondent thinks he could—if he wanted to—influence governmental decisions.[3] The more objective measure of his skill is indexed by a series of questions measuring the extent of his information about politics. Skill and competence should relate primarily to the degree of initiative an act requires. Unlike psychological involvement, it should not differentiate on the public-private dimension.

Involvement in Conflict and Cleavage

We use three different measures to index the extent to which the respondent is oriented to the conflictual aspects of politics.

Partisan Affiliation   The main institution around which political conflict in the United States is structured is the political party. And the degree to which an individual identifies himself with one of the two parties is one of our

---

[1] For a fuller description of the items and scales used in this chapter, see Appendix B.3.1.

[2] The concept of psychological involvement in politics dates back to the earliest studies of political behavior. For a review of the central concept of involvement or psychological commitment to politics and some of the most important measurements of this variable, see John P. Robinson, Jerrold G. Rusk, and Kendra B. Head, *Measures of Political Attitudes* (Ann Arbor, Mich.: Survey Research Center, University of Michigan, 1968), p. 456.

[3] The empirical measures of political efficacy date back at least to some of the earlier works on voting behavior. See, for example, Angus Campbell, Gerald Gurin, and Warren E. Miller, *The Voter Decides* (Evanston, Ill.: Row Peterson, 1954); Berelson, Lazarsfeld, and McPhee, *Voting;* and Kenneth Prewitt, "Political Efficacy," *International Encyclopedia of the Social Sciences,* vol. 12, pp. 225-227. For the most extensive discussion of the relationship of efficacy to voting behavior, see Campbell et al., *The American Voter.* Almond and Verba, *The Civic Culture,* has an extensive discussion of the relationship of efficacy to a variety of orientations and behaviors (though these authors term efficacy *subjective competence*). For an extensive review of the research findings concerning the relationship between efficacy and participation, see Milbrath, *Political Participation.*

For an intensive cross-national comparison of political efficacy or competence that utilizes the data from the five-nation study in Almond and Verba's *The Civic Culture,* see E. N. Muller, "Cross-National Dimensions of Political Competence," *American Political Science Review,* vol. 64 (Summer 1970), pp. 792-809.

indicators of the degree to which he is involved in political conflict. Party affiliation, of course, is a more multifaceted phenomenon reflecting a long-term and often habitual commitment. Nevertheless we believe that it also reflects a willingness to join one side or the other in a political controversy. However, this particular measure may more reliably identify those who avoid conflict than it identifies those who are heavily involved in it—i.e., those who are nonpartisan are likely to have made a positive commitment to avoid conflict while those who are partisan may be so for various reasons.[4]

Taking Sides in Community Conflict   Our second measure of the respondent's involvement in conflict is more direct. We asked respondents quite simply if there was conflict within their community and whether they usually took sides in such conflicts. Those respondents who saw conflict and took sides in it were considered to be high in their involvement in conflict; the others were low.[5]

Issue Extremity   This is a measure of the extent to which the respondent holds sets of issue positions that are consistent and at the extremes of the issue spectrum. The position itself could be on the left or the right.

The three sets of items that tap the involvement of the citizen in conflict or cleavage—his partisanship, his willingness to take sides in community conflict, and the extremity of his policy positions—represent a mixed and heterogeneous set of measures. For that reason we have kept them separate, and have not combined them into a single scale of "conflict orientation." However, to some extent they all tap the degree to which the citizen is involved in aspects of politics in which one citizen is pitted against another.

The conflict orientations then should distinguish between acts that involve counterparticipants and those that do not. However, this orientation should also bear some relationship to the public-private distinction; i.e., strong conflict orientations would probably not characterize those who concentrate on particularized outcomes. Finally, within acts involving counterparticipants we would expect most conflict orientations to increase along with the amount of initiative required to perform the activity.

[4] There is an exceedingly large literature on the concept of partisan identity and its measurement. This variable, defined as a psychological characteristic of citizens independent of their voting record, is largely developed by those involved in the national voting studies at the Survey Research Center, University of Michigan. Some works that define and utilize this concept are Campbell, Gurin, and Miller, *The Voter Decides;* Campbell et al., *The American Voter;* and Angus Campbell et al., *Elections and the Political Order* (New York: Wiley, 1966). For some interesting cross-national comparisons of party identity, see Almond and Verba, *The Civic Culture.* For an extended discussion of the historical development of the concept of partisan identity and its role in theories about American political behavior, see Kenneth Prewitt and Norman H. Nie, "The SRC Election Studies: An Evaluation," *British Journal of Politics,* vol. 1(1971). Other uses of the concept are discussed in Philip E. Converse, "Of Time and Partisan Stability," *Comparative Political Studies,* vol. 2 (July 1969), pp. 139-171.

[5] Almost all the orientations we have introduced up to this point have been explored in some depth in previous studies. However, general willingness to take sides in conflict situations has not been an attitude that has received much attention in previous studies. There have been a few studies, however, that approximate our definition of orientation toward conflict. Almond and Verba's investigation of intense and hostile partisanship is in many ways parallel to our usage, though more limited in that it deals only with conflict surrounding political parties. G. Bingham Powell's study of conflict in an Austrian community, *Social Fragmentation and Political Hostility: An Austrian Case Study,* (Stanford, Calif.: Stanford University Press, 1970), also deals with conflict orientation in a somewhat similar manner, as does Lester W. Milbrath, "Predispositions Toward Political Conflict," *Western Political Quarterly,* vol. 21 (March 1968), pp. 5-18.

Civic Mindedness

The last political orientation which we list here is the degree to which the respondent considers himself to be a contributor to the welfare of the community as a whole. We consider this a measure of the extent to which the citizen views himself as a "civic" being, one who gives time and effort to the needs and problems of his community. Civic-mindedness taps at least two of the distinctions among the modes of activity. First, it bears directly on the scope of the outcome, for those who concentrate on acts used exclusively for the pursuit of particularized benefits would surely not be expected to feel that they make a particularly large contribution to the overall community welfare. Second, it has an equally obvious relationship to the conflict dimensions, for acts aimed at nonconflictual public goals are much more likely to be viewed by those who perform them as contributing to the welfare of the "whole" community than acts performed in a more conflictual setting.

The four sets of political orientations are, of course, not the only ones that could be tapped. But they are particularly relevant to us because of the way we expect them to relate to the various modes of participation and the types of citizens who concentrate on them. The expectations as to those relationships can be summarized as follows.

The Inactives   For those citizens who engage in no political activity, our expectations are quite clear. They should have little or no psychological involvement in politics, little or no skill and competence, they should be indifferent to matters of political cleavage and conflict, and they should have little sense of contribution to the community.

The Voting Specialists   The major characteristic of the voting specialists, which sets them apart from other activists, is that they limit themselves to activity requiring little initiative. Thus one would not expect them to be either high in psychological involvement or particularly skilled and competent. The fact that the occasion for their vote is presented to them with no requirement that they take much initiative means that they can participate in politics without any great involvement or any great sense of their own power. In voting they do take sides in a political conflict, but not in a very active way. Thus one would expect them to be fairly high in partisanship (and this also because partisan affiliation is an important habitual attachment for many voters), but not particularly likely to take sides in community conflict or to have extreme issue positions. And last, they are not particularly likely to have a strong sense of contribution to the community.

The Parochial Participants   Their activity pattern is characterized by the relatively high level of initiative required for their activity coupled with the narrow scope of its referent. This suggests that they should combine some skill and competence (needed for them to be able to act) with an absence of psychological involvement in political matters. We would not expect them to be particularly involved in conflict and cleavage, or to be civic-minded.

The Communalists   They engage in activity requiring a high degree of initiative—activity that seems to involve general communal goals rather than overt conflict among contending parties. Thus we expect them to be high in their psychological involvement in politics, in their skill and competence, and in their sense of community contribution. They ought to be particularly low in their involvement in conflict and cleavage.

The Campaigners   These citizens engage in activity with as broad an outcome as that of the communalists and should therefore be similar in having a fairly high degree of psychological involvement in politics. They ought also to be fairly high in their degree of skill and competence, but the fact that their activity may not require as much initiative as that of the communalists (because partisans can easily work through established party groups) means that they may have lower levels of skill and competence than the communalists. The largest contrast with the communalists ought to be in terms of their involvement in cleavage and conflict. Furthermore, this fact ought to lower the extent to which they have a sense of general contribution to the community.

The Complete Activists   Because they combine all modes of activity, we expect them to be the mirror image of the inactivists: they should be high in psychological involvement, skill and competence, involvement in conflict and cleavage, and in sense of civic contribution.

These expectations of the orientations and characteristics of each of the types of participators are summarized in Table 5-1. What is important from our point of view is that we expect a unique combination of orientations for each type of activist. If this turns out to be the case, it will provide additional support for our contention that these are significantly different modes of activity. And this particularly will be the case if we find significant differences between sets of activists whose overall level of activity is similar though the type of activity differs. Furthermore, the particular pattern of orientation found will increase our understanding of the nature of these alternative modes of activity.

In Table 5-2 we present some data relevant to this question. The figures in the cells are the mean scores on scales measuring the various orientations, the scales having been standardized so that each has a mean of 0 and a standard deviation of 1.0. For some orientations there is a large difference in the mean scores across the activist types, for others there is less—psychological involvement and efficacy varying greatly, while issue extremity varies only slightly. But for each of the orientations, the pattern is consistent with that predicted in Table 5-1. The inactives are low on all the orientations, the complete activists high, and the other types of activists pattern as expected.

We can make the alternative patterns clearer if we present an orientational profile for each of the types of political activists. To do this we have restandardized the variance of the orientations across the six types of participators so that each orientation has the same discriminatory power. This

Table 5-1

The Six Types of Participators: The Main Characteristics of Their Activity Pattern and Some Expected Orientations

Type of participator	Main characteristics of activity pattern	Psychological involvement	Skill and competence		Some expected orientations			Civic-mindedness
					Involvement in conflict and cleavage			
			Efficacy	Information	Partisanship	Take sides in conflict	Issue extremity	
Inactives	No activity	Low	Low	Low	Low	Low	Low	Low
Voting specialists	Act requiring little initiative but performed against counterparticipants	Low	Low	Low	High	Low	Low	Low
Parochial participants	Act requiring initiative but with a narrow, personal outcome. Probably little conflict involved.	Low	High	High	Low	Low	Low	Low
Communalists	Act requiring initiative, and with a broad social outcome, but relatively nonconflictual.	High	High	High	Low	Low	Low	High
Partisan activists	Act requiring moderate initiative; broad social outcome; relatively conflictual.	High	Medium/High	Medium/High	High	High	High	Low/Medium
Complete activists	All activities	High	High	High	High	High	High	High

Table 5-2

The Orientations of the Six Types of Participation

| | | | | Orientations | | | |
| | | Skill and competence | | | Involvement in conflict and cleavage | | |
Type of participator	Psychological involvement	Efficacy	Information	Partisanship	Take sides in conflict	Issue extremity	Civic-mindedness
Inactives	-.53	-.67	-.56	-.22	-.28	-.04	-.21
Voting specialists	-.31	-.44	-.05	+.11	-.12	-.01	-.16
Parochial participants	-.20	-.16	+.13	-.08	+.02	0	-.25
Communalists	+.20	+.70	+.33	-.18	+.03	-.10	+.31
Partisan activists	+.32	+.32	+.17	+.38	+.16	+.10	-.03
Complete activists	+.84	+1.21	+.73	+.40	+.60	+.19	+.46

gives each orientation equal prominence in the profiles even though the data in Table 5-2 make it quite clear that some orientations discriminate among the types of actors much more strongly than do others.[6]

In Figures 5-1 and 5-2 we present these orientational profiles. The horizontal lines on each figure represent the mean position for the population as a whole in relation to a particular orientation. The bars above and below the horizontal line indicate the extent to which a particular type of actor deviates from the population as a whole on that orientation, either in a positive or negative direction. Thus each figure presents to us the particular profile of orientations to politics characteristic of each of our types of political actors.

The Inactives   [Figure 5-1(a)].The orientational profile of the inactives provides us with a good base line for comparison with other activists. As expected, the citizens who engage in no political activity are also psychologically detached from politics. They are well below the mean on all orientations, being less likely than the average citizen to be psychologically involved, to have skill and competence, to be involved in conflict, or to have a sense of civic contribution.

The Voting Specialists   [Figure 5-1(b)].The voting specialists are just what their name implies—they never or rarely miss voting in an election, but that exhausts their political activity. They are not active in campaigns or in communal activity, nor do they contact officials on personal problems. This limitation of their activity to the political act that requires the least initiative is reflected in their profile of orientations. They are lower than the average citizen in psychological involvement and efficacy, though not so low as the inactives. They are slightly lower than average in information and lower than average in their sense of contributing to the community.

The most interesting aspect of their orientations has to do with their involvement in conflict and cleavage. They are quite a bit higher than the average citizen in the degree of their partisanship, but lower in their likelihood

[6] This was done because similar absolute differences among the orientations are not always equally salient characteristics, as when some orientations, such as efficacy, have a range of 1.97 across the six types, whereas civic-mindedness has a range of only .69. Finding, for example, that parochial participants fall 25 points below the population on efficacy may be a much less significant characteristic of the parochial participants than the fact that they are 25 points below the population on civic-mindedness. On efficacy they represent the third lowest group, but are much higher than the two groups below them, whereas they are far below any other type of participator in their level of civic-mindedness. The procedure for obtaining these standardized scores was as follows:

1. The means for all six types of participators on a given orientation were used to compute a new mean, ignoring the fact that there are different numbers of citizens in each of the groups. That is, the new mean is simply the sum of the actual means (reported in Table 5-1) divided by 6.

2. We then obtained the standard deviation of this mean. The sum of squares for this standard deviation was simply the squared sum of the differences between this new mean and the original group means.

3. Each type of participator was assigned a new standardized score for the orientation by the standard z score formula of

$$\text{Score} = \frac{X - \bar{X}}{SD}$$

where: X is the original group mean of the ith group
   $\bar{X}$ is the new mean for the six groups (i.e., the result of step 1 above)
   SD is the standard deviation around the new mean (i.e., the result of step 2)

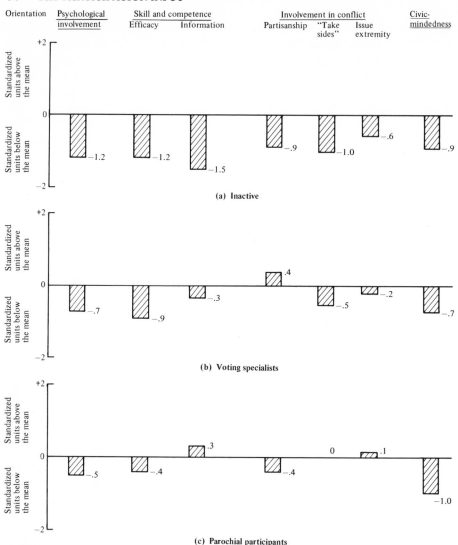

Figure 5-1. Orientational Profiles: Inactives, Voting Specialists, and Parochial Participants

to take sides in community conflict and in their issue extremity. This combination of heightened partisanship with avoidance of conflict in community matters and an absence of issue extremity confirms our view of the voting specialists as citizens whose activity is confined to what requires least initiative and whose general psychological involvement in politics is quite low, but whose activities are guided by habitual attachment to their political party.

The Parochial Participants   [Figure 5-1(c)].The orientational profile of the parochial participants is in good accord with our expectations. These citizens are lower than any other group—including the inactives—in their sense of contributing to the community, thus underscoring the extent to which their political activity is focused on the narrow problems of their own personal lives. This is paralleled by a low level of psychological involvement, a relative absence of partisanship, and a somewhat lower than average level on the other measures of involvement in conflict and cleavage.

Our expectation had been that, despite their relative paucity of political consciousness, the parochial participants would be moderately high in skill and competence because these are needed for the kind of activity in which they engage. Our expectations are fulfilled only in part. Parochial participants do have somewhat more information than the average citizen; in fact, they have almost as high a score on the information index as the campaigners. And their level of information stands out given their low profile in other respects. On the other hand, they feel somewhat less efficacious than is average. They are, however, more efficacious than regular voters, a fact consistent with our expectations. It may be that our measures of efficacy focus too heavily on the respondent's perceived sense of ability to influence *public* issues.[7]

The Communalists   [Figure 5-2(a)].With the communalists we come to the first group high in overall level of political activity. This is reflected in their pattern of orientations. They are above average in their psychological involvement in politics, and well above average in their sense of efficacy, in their level of information, and in their sense of contributing to the community. On the latter characteristic they are particularly outstanding, and besides the complete activists they are the only group above average in this respect.

Equally striking in their profile of orientations (and consistent with our expectations) is the communalists' relatively low level of involvement in conflict and cleavage. They are much less likely than the average citizen to be partisan, their low scores on the measure of partisanship are matched only by the scores of the inactives, a group with whom the communalists have little else in common. They are less extreme on their issue positions than any other group, and are at the population average in their likelihood of taking sides in community disputes—but that puts them lower than any activist group in this respect. In short, the organizational profile of the communalists is consistent with our characterization of the kind of activity in which they engage: relatively nonconflictual, and aimed at the attainment of broad community goals.[8]

The Campaign Activists   [Figure 5-2(b)].The contrast between the campaign activists and the communalists is quite sharp. The groups are similar in their

---

[7] One fact that leads us to believe that this may be the case is that the parochial participants believe that they can get officials to aid them more often in the solution of personal problems than of public ones, a pattern opposite that of the other types of activists.

[8] From some points of view, these communalists might not only seem nonpartisan but nonpolitical as well. They appear to be people who are active in the public life of the community but who stay out of politics—as the latter word is ordinarily used. However, from the point of view of "who gets what" in the community, such activity is important, and the political role—in a broader sense of "political"—of these people is crucial.

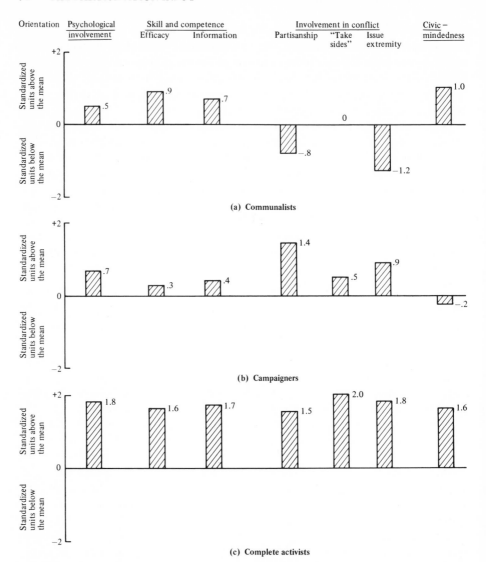

Figure 5-2. Orientational Profiles: Communalists, Campaigners, and Complete Activists

degree of psychological involvement in politics, but from then on the profiles diverge. The campaign activists are somewhat more informed and feel somewhat more efficacious than the average citizen, but they are not as outstanding in this respect as are the communalists, a fact consistent with our belief that communal activity requires more initiative than campaign activity. The campaigners are the opposite of the communalists in terms of their involvement in conflict and cleavage. That they are more likely than the average citizen to have a strong partisan affiliation is, of course, to be expected, but it is striking that they are also more likely to take sides in community conflict and to have relatively extreme issue positions. Also, they differ from the communalists in having a lower than average sense of contribution to the community at large.

The contrast between the communalists and the campaigners in terms of orientations is consistent with the contrasts we drew between the two groups in terms of their patterns of activity. The campaign activists are involved in the more conflictual aspects of politics and have orientations to match. The communalists avoid conflictual activity, and their orientations are consistent with this. The communalists have a sense of contribution to the community at large that the campaigners lack. Yet, as we have pointed out before, the communalists and the campaign activists are relatively equal in terms of their overall level of activity. Thus, the orientational data are consistent with our argument that equally active citizens may differ substantially in the pattern and in the meaning of their activity.

The Complete Activists   [Figure 5-2(c)].Little need be said about this group. They are the mirror image of the inactives: high on all orientations. They have the most psychological involvement, the highest sense of efficacy, and the most information. They are involved in conflict and cleavage as are the campaign activists, but they also have a sense of contribution to the community at large. Their "complete" activity is matched by a "complete" set of orientations supporting that activity.

SUMMARY

Our orientational data clearly support our arguments that citizens differ not only in how much activity they engage in but also in the type of activity, and that this difference in type represents significant variations in the ways citizens attempt to influence government and the types of issues that lead them to become active.

The inactives are citizens who do not participate in politics and seem uninterested in participating. At the other extreme are the complete activists, whose orientations reflect their total involvement in politics. In between there are a variety of types of participants who perform different amounts and types of activities. There are the parochial participants, who perform the difficult act of contacting public officials but confine the focus of their contacts to particularized problems. Their rather high levels of information provide them with the ability to use the government for private benefits while their preoccupation with this type of problem is reflected in their almost total lack of more general political involvement or sense of civic contribution.

The communalists are quite different, even though they often perform the same type of activity as the parochial activists—contacting. The communalists carry on numerous community and civic activities, but at the same time they avoid electoral politics. These citizens combine skill and competence with a strong commitment to politics and public affairs, a striking sense of civic-mindedness, and a hesitancy to become involved in situations of political conflict. The campaigners, in contrast, are heavily involved in conflict and cleavage, less concerned with the civic problems of the community than with the ongoing social policy debate and the electoral process. Finally, there are the voting specialists, whose peculiar pattern of political participation seems to emanate from their unusually strong attachments to political parties, which they maintain (unlike the partisans) without high levels of concern for politics or its issues.

It is clear from the data in this chapter that our various types of activists not only act differently, they think differently.

Chapter 6
Who Are the Activists?

In Part I we are explicating some modes of citizen participation. And we have shown that one can identify sets of citizens who concentrate their activity in one mode or another—as well as citizens who are generally inactive or generally active. In this chapter we will present some data on the social composition of the various types of activists.

The reader will remember that at the beginning of Part I we raised three questions, the answers to which would give us a rather complete description of the participation input: How much activity? What kind of activity? And by whom? We have dealt with the amount and kind. In this chapter we will deal with the last question—by whom? The data here are descriptively important, for they define fairly clearly the participators in American political life.

The data are important for another reason. They set the stage for a more extended discussion in Part II of the forces that shape the participation input and, in Part III, of the consequences of participation. One of our major concerns is with the extent to which political participation comes disproportionately from particular social groups, in particular from various upper-status groups. If this is the case, we will wish to deal with two further questions: Why is it in fact the case? And what are the consequences in terms of governmental actions of this asymmetry? In this chapter we will simply demonstrate that there is indeed overrepresentation of particular groups among the participants, and that the overrepresentation is clearest *vis-à-vis* groups with upper social status.

Our approach will be to estimate the extent to which various social categories—better-educated, blacks, women, Catholics, etc.—are over- or underrepresented in each activist type. The measure of over- and underrepresentation is simply a ratio of the proportion of a particular social category found in a particular activist type to the proportion of that social category in the population as a whole. Thus citizens under thirty represent about 16 percent of our sample. If we find that they form only 8 percent of the communalists, we would consider them underrepresented by 50 percent in that group, and give communalists a score of —50 in relation to young citizens. If, on the other hand, they were 24 percent of the communalists, we would assign a score of +50, reflecting their overrepresentation.[1]

The reader ought to remember that the overrepresentation of a particular social category in one of the activist types does not necessarily mean that most or all of that activist type comes from the particular social category. Those with professional and other high-level occupations, for instance, have an overrepresentation score of +56 among the complete activists—i.e., they are much more likely to be in that group than one would expect, given their proportion in the population. But because professionals and other high occupations are a relatively small part of our sample (17 percent), they make up less than one-fourth of the complete activists.

In Figures 6-1 through 6-3 we present the data on the representation of various types of citizens in the several activist groups. We deal with citizens of various social classes—based on education and income—and also differentiate citizens by sex, age, race, religion, and place of residence. Other categorizations could be used, but these will give a clear and complete enough picture. In one sense the data speak for themselves; it will be quite clear which social categories are over- or underrepresented in which activist groups. We will, therefore, simply point to the features that most distinguish each of the types

---

[1] The formal definition of the ratio of over- and underrepresentation for any given social group within any given population is

$$PR = \frac{X_i - Y_i}{X_i} \times 100$$

where: PR = ratio of over- or underrepresentation.

X_i = the percentage of the entire population in the social group.

Y_i = the proportion of the same social group within a given category of participators.

The reader should note that the amount of under- and overrepresentation is a function of both the number of percentage points and the size of the group. For example, a 7-percentage-point difference in the proportion of blacks in the general population and within some type of participator represents an enormous disproportion because blacks constitute only 13 percent of the population. A similar difference for females, who constitute a little over 50 percent of the population, produces much less disproportion.

of activists. In another way, of course, the data do not speak for themselves. There are unanswered questions as to why one finds the patterns one does, questions that require a more multivariate approach in which a variety of social characteristics are considered simultaneously. We shall turn to that task in Part II.

Let us now consider the demographic profiles of the various activist groups. In Figure 6-1 we consider the inactives and the voting specialists.

The Inactives   [Figure 6-1(a)].This figure clearly illustrates the most important point to be made in this chapter—a point that is already well documented in the literature.[2] Those citizens with lower social status—low levels of education or income—are greatly overrepresented among those who are politically inactive, while the upper-status groups are underrepresented among the inactives. This is clearly seen in the top two sections of Figure 6-1(a) where the data on education and income are presented. To take a concrete example, consider the data on education. Citizens with no high-school education formed 28 percent of our sample, but they are 43 percent of the inactives, leading to an overrepresentation score of +45. And similar results would have obtained if we had used a measure of occupational status.

Additional patterns of over- and underrepresentation can also be discerned: men are somewhat underrepresented among the inactives, women somewhat overrepresented. Young people are quite a bit more likely to be inactive, as, to a lesser extent, are those over sixty-five, while those in the middle years are somewhat less likely to be in this group. Blacks are substantially overrepresented among the inactives, whites a bit underrepresented. There is some difference between Protestants and Catholics, with the latter less likely to be inactive. And as far as place of residence goes, the inactives tend slightly to come from small towns.

The passive citizen, thus, comes disproportionately from these groups: with lower social status, blacks, the young, and, to a lesser extent, women, Protestants, and those who live in small towns.

Voting Specialists   [Figure 6-1(b)]. In some respects voting specialists resemble the inactives. They come disproportionately from lower-education and income groups, though the disproportion is not so great as with the inactives. College-educated citizens or those with high incomes are quite underrepresented among those who limit their activity to voting. In addition, voting specialists come disproportionately from older citizens, Catholics, big-city dwellers, and, to a small extent, women.

Parochial Participants   [Figure 6-2(a)]. This group shows the least variation across educational or income categories of any participation type. Parochial participators come from throughout the social spectrum. However, college-educated citizens and those in our top income bracket are underrepresented.

---

[2] For a survey of the literature documenting the generality of this finding, see Milbrath, *Political Participation*, especially Chapters 3 and 5.

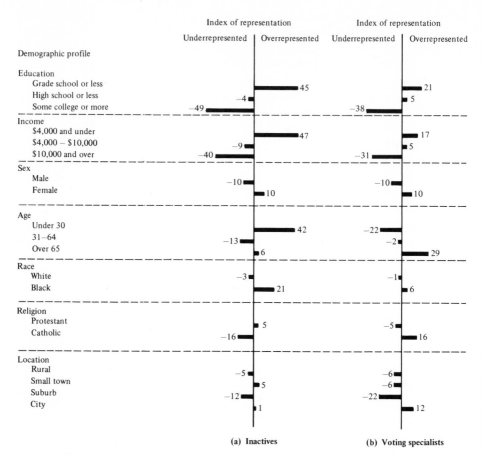

Figure 6-1. Demographic Profile of Inactives and Voting Specialists

Young citizens are likely to be in this category as are Catholics and those who live in suburbs and large cities. But blacks are underrepresented (an apparent contradiction, considering that they are more likely to be in cities and less likely to have high status—an apparent contradiction to which we shall return).

The Communalists   [Figure 6-2(b)]. Here we begin to see a pattern opposite of that among the inactives, the voting specialists, and the parochial participants. With the communalists, the upper-status groups are overrepresented and the lower-status ones underrepresented. Communalists come disproportionately from those with college education and with high incomes. They are unlikely to be black. Catholics are underrepresented in this group, Protestants a bit overrepresented. Communal activity is also related to location—people from rural areas and the suburbs are quite a bit overrepresented, while city dwellers are underrepresented.

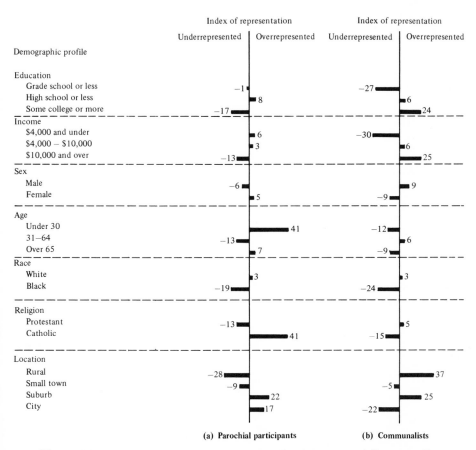

Index of representation

Underrepresented | Overrepresented   Underrepresented | Overrepresented

Demographic profile

Education
  Grade school or less   −1
  High school or less   8
  Some college or more   −17

Income
  $4,000 and under   6
  $4,000 − $10,000   3
  $10,000 and over   −13

Sex
  Male   −6
  Female   5

Age
  Under 30   41
  31−64   −13
  Over 65   7

Race
  White   3
  Black   −19

Religion
  Protestant   −13
  Catholic   41

Location
  Rural   −28
  Small town   −9
  Suburb   22
  City   17

Index of representation (right panel):

Education
  Grade school or less   −27
  High school or less   6
  Some college or more   24

Income
  $4,000 and under   −30
  $4,000 − $10,000   6
  $10,000 and over   25

Sex
  Male   9
  Female   −9

Age
  Under 30   −12
  31−64   6
  Over 65   −9

Race
  White   3
  Black   −24

Religion
  Protestant   5
  Catholic   −15

Location
  Rural   37
  Small town   −5
  Suburb   25
  City   −22

(a) Parochial participants   (b) Communalists

Figure 6-2. Demographic Profile of Parochial Participants and Communalists

The Partisan Activists.   [Figure 6-3(a)]. As has previously been the case, the partisan activists are an interesting contrast to the communalists. They are similar to communalists in the tendency for upper-income and education groups to be overrepresented and lower-status groups underrepresented, though the situation is a bit less extreme in relation to education than that found among the communalists. But in several interesting ways, the partisans contrast with the communalists. Catholics are overrepresented among the partisans, whereas they were underrepresented among the communalists. And whereas communalists came disproportionately from rural areas and suburbs and were underrepresented in cities, the opposite is true of partisan activists.

The Complete Activists.   [Figure 6-3(b)]. They are a most distinctive group. They are largely the reverse of the inactives and come from upper-status groups. And the degree of overrepresentation of those at the top of the status hierarchy is striking. In addition, complete activists come disproportionately from those in the middle age groups and from small towns. Catholics are somewhat less likely to be complete activists, and there is a small (but quite small) tendency for blacks and women to be underrepresented among the complete activists.

The overall pattern across the various types of actors is fairly clear. We can see from which groups the participation input comes. The following points emerge from the data:

1. Participants come disproportionately from upper-status groups. This is clearest if one compares the inactives with the complete activists.

2. Aside from the complete activists, the groups in which upper-status citizens are most overrepresented are the communalists and the partisan activists. Thus the more difficult activities are engaged in heavily by upper-status citizens.

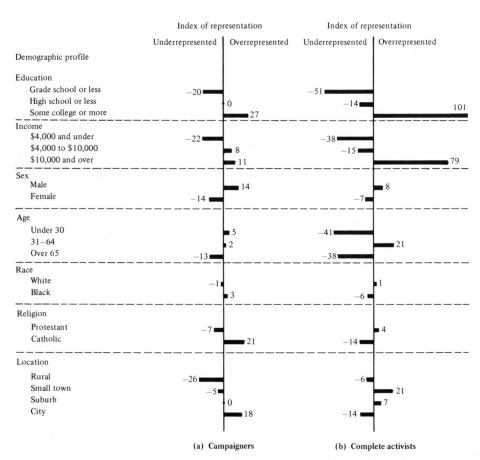

Figure 6-3. Demographic Profile of Campaigners and Complete Activists

3. Those who limit their activity to voting come disproportionately from lower-status groups.

4. Parochial participants come from all parts of the status hierarchy, though upper-status citizens are somewhat less likely to limit themselves to this activity.

5. Men are somewhat overrepresented in the more activist groups, but not to a very great degree.

6. Blacks tend to be overrepresented in the inactivist category, and they are especially disadvantaged when it comes to communal activity and particularized contacting. On the other hand, they participate fairly proportionately in electoral politics, both as voting specialists and partisan activists. Though blacks are quite a bit more likely to be inactive, their degree of underrepresentation among the most active is not great. This asymmetry suggests that blacks are more likely to stay completely out of politics than are whites, but once they become involved they may participate at high levels.

7. Some interesting differences among the types of activists appear that are not linked to social status. Though both communalists and partisan activists come from similar status backgrounds, the former are much less likely to be Catholic, the latter much more likely. Catholics are also overrepresented among the voting specialists. In short, one sees a difference in political style between Protestants and Catholics, with the latter more likely to be involved in partisan activity.

8. Location plays a part, particularly *vis-à-vis* communal activists and those who work in electoral politics. The former are more likely to be found in rural areas and suburbs than in cities. In cities, on the other hand, electoral activists—both partisans and voting specialists—are more likely to be found.

These findings have been presented with little discussion. They deserve more and will receive it, for they form the basis of much of the rest of this book. The major theme running through the next two sections is the relationship between social status and participation. We have made clear that there is such a relationship, and we can now consider its roots, some ways it can be modified by other social structures, and some of its consequences.

In addition, the findings provide a number of specific puzzles that we shall look at more closely. To what extent are some of the other patterns—the lower participation of blacks, the higher participation of suburbanites—merely the spurious reflection of the close relationship of social status and participation? The same can be asked about the patterns associated with age or religion. Why are blacks so underrepresented in communal activity and particularized contacting? Does the type of community one lives in have—as the data suggest but do not quite demonstrate—an independent effect on how active a citizen is? These are questions we will turn to in Part II.

Chapter 7
The Rationality
of Political Activity:
A Reconsideration

The alternative modes of political activity, we have argued, represent different ways by which the citizen influences his government. This argument is supported by the findings reported in Chapter 5 that different sets of orientations accompany the various types of activity. We can carry this argument a step further by considering more closely what it is that citizens expect to obtain—or can reasonably expect to obtain—from their participation; and how this differs from one mode to another. Participation is, to us, most importantly an instrumental activity through which citizens attempt to influence the government to act in ways the citizens prefer. But the alternative modes can produce different types of governmental response. In this chapter we look beyond our data to other studies to see how this is the case.

The problem relates to the current debate about the rationality of political activity.[1] It is not our purpose to enter the complexities of that debate, but

[1] There is a wide literature on this subject. Some of the most important works are: Angus Campbell, et al., *The American Voter*, Chapter 10; Philip E. Converse, "The Nature of Belief Systems in Mass Publics," in David E. Apter (ed.), *Ideology and Discontent* (New York: Free Press, 1964), pp. 206-261; Herbert McClosky,

102

some of the considerations involved highlight differences among our various modes of activity. And, in turn, the problem of rationality looks somewhat different when one has expanded one's notion of political activity beyond the electoral context. In particular, we can go beyond the question of whether it is rational to vote and whether citizens choose candidates rationally to the question of how the choice among alternative political activities relates to citizen needs and preferences.

The debate centers around the question: When citizens participate, do they do so rationally? For a citizen to do so, he must know what he wants in terms of a governmental response (i.e., know what policy he wishes the government to pursue or know what benefit he wishes the government to provide), he must know what action is likely to increase the chances of the government providing what he wants, and he must act accordingly, taking into account the cost of that activity in relation to other uses of his time and effort. The citizen "inputs" some act of participation in the expectation that the government will "output" what he wants. If the former is appropriate to the latter—i.e., his participation increases the likelihood that the government will perform as he desires—the citizen is behaving rationally.

The clarity of the citizen's expectation is important. If one is really talking of governmental response to a citizen, the citizen's action must carry a message about his desires precise enough for the government to know how to respond to it. The citizen, in turn, must be able to tell, at least to some minimal degree, if the action of the government is responsive. To put it another way, an act of participation involves an hypothesis on the part of the participant that his act will lead to a desired response by the government. But for the act to be rationally instrumental, it must involve a *testable* hypothesis—i.e., the participant must be able to tell whether he has had any success. This suggests that the citizen's ability to act rationally in politics may depend on the nature of the political act, particularly on two of the dimensions we used to characterize political acts—the type of influence they exert (pressure or informational) and the scope of the outcome they can influence.

Most of the debate on the citizen as rational actor has dealt with him in his role as voter. And voters in general do not much measure up to the standards of rationality.

For one thing, the public has little information on which candidate takes which position during an election. In fact, they may know almost nothing about candidates. Miller and Stokes indicate that about half of their sample had heard or read nothing about either Congressional candidate in their district and that only 25 percent had read anything at all about both

"Consensus and Ideology in American Politics," *American Political Science Review,* vol. 58 (June 1964), pp. 361-382; V. O. Key, Jr., *The Responsible Electorate* (Cambridge, Mass.: Harvard University Press, 1966); Michael J. Shapiro, "Rational Political-Man: A Synthesis of Economic and Social-Psychological Perspectives," *American Political Science Review,* vol. 63 (December 1969), pp. 1106-1119; and William H. Riker and Peter C. Ordeshook, "A Theory of the Calculus of Voting," *American Political Science Review,* vol. 62 (March 1968), pp. 25-42.

candidates, still probably putting them a long way from having the information needed to make the kind of rational choice we have been discussing.[2] And in an earlier study, it was found that less than half the public knew which party controlled the Congress—certainly a useful bit of information if one is to evaluate a candidate's potential performance.[3]

In addition, it appears that few citizens know what they want. They do not have clear and consistent positions on the important issues of the day. Attitudes on public issues are lightly held, and answers to survey questions on specific issues facing the nation often appear to have a random quality.[4] Nor do citizens have clear and consistent sets of issue positions. The absence of clear structure in citizen attitudes on the issues of elections is confirmed by Campbell, et al. in their analysis in *The American Voter* of the "level of conceptualization" of voters.[5] Very few respondents (3.5 percent of voters) could be considered to have a political ideology of a clear sort (and even these people provide fairly vague notions of their political ideology if one reads the examples of answers). The kind of abstract conceptualization that could give structure to the electoral choice is almost completely missing. When citizens vote, they are more likely to be influenced by candidate images or by their traditional party affiliation than they are by the issue positions of the candidates or parties.

More recent attempts to find issue-voting (behavior consistent with our definition of rational participation) have found only a trace more of it than the authors of the classic analysis in *The American Voter* did. In some elections one finds more issue-voting than was found in 1956 by Campbell, et al., in *The American Voter,* but still not much.[6] If respondents self-select the issues upon which to evaluate the parties, issue-partisanship (the perception of which party will more likely take the action you want on the issues most salient to you) predicts the vote better than when the issue is presented to the respondent by the researcher. But it still predicts the vote less well than does candidate image or party affiliation. And, as we shall argue, the procedure of allowing the respondent to choose the issue is quite unrealistic.[7]

RATIONALITY AND CONTACTING

But voting is only one mode of activity. These data on the relative lack of instrumental orientation toward the vote contrast sharply with our data on citizen-initiated contacts. Our respondents were asked about contacts that

[2] Warren Miller and Donald E. Stokes, "Constituency Influences on Congress," in Campbell et al., *Elections and the Political Order,* p. 366.

[3] See Robert E. Lane and David O. Sears, *Public Opinion* (Englewood Cliffs, N.J.: Prentice-Hall, 1964), p. 61.

[4] Converse, "The Nature of Belief Systems in Mass Publics."

[5] Campbell et al., *The American Voter,* Chapter 10.

[6] Key, *The Responsible Electorate,* and Philip E. Converse, Warren E. Miller, Jerrold G. Rusk, and Arthur C. Wolfe, "Continuity and Change in American Politics: Parties and Issues in the 1968 Election," *American Political Science Review,* vol. 63 (December 1969), pp. 1083-1105.

[7] See David E. Repass, "Issue Salience and Party Choice," *American Political Science Review,* vol. 65 (June 1971), pp. 389-400.

they initiated with government officials within and/or outside of the community. If they had initiated a contact, they were asked to identify the official and also to tell us the nature of the problem.

As one reads the answers to these questions one is struck by how relatively precise and instrumental the responses are. About one-third of all contacts, as we have noted, were on problems particularized to the individual or his family; the rest are more general in referent. As one could expect, the former type of contact involves requests for specific benefits and is clearly instrumental activity: the citizen knows what he wants and acts to obtain it. But even when the subject matter of the contact is a broader problem involving the entire community or the entire society, the problems tend to be fairly clear and specific. Citizens specify a problem area and a solution. And the choice of official to contact usually is quite appropriate: citizen-initiated contacts about school matters go to school officials or other relevant local officials, contacts about more general legislative matters go to state legislators or Congressmen, contacts about the war in Vietnam go to one's Senator, Congressman, or perhaps the President. This is not to argue a fantastically high level of sophistication about channels of influence among the citizenry. Rather, the data simply illustrate a circumstance in which citizens act politically with specific goals in mind and in ways that are quite appropriate for the achievement of those goals.

The main reason for this, we believe, is that in contacting, the citizen takes the initiative: he decides when to contact, whom to contact, and the subject matter of that contact. This is not to imply that the situation is totally unstructured for him and that he simply acts as he wants when the spirit moves him. He is constrained to act in certain ways by the channels available for contacting the government and he may be motivated to raise one particular problem or issue rather than another by governmental action or inaction in particular areas. But the agenda is set by the individual and quite freely chosen by him. Of the vast number of programs in which the government is engaged, he chooses one about which to complain; of the vast number of ways in which government activity impinges on his own life, he focuses on one for attention; of the vast number of things the government is not doing that might affect the individual, he brings up one for discussion. This choosing of the agenda by the individual is the main characteristic that differentiates citizen-initiated contacts from other modes of participation.

This choice guarantees that the issue of the participatory act is salient and important to the respondent. As many have pointed out, the personal "agendas" of citizens are fantastically varied. Each citizen has his own particular set of problems and concerns. These are usually close to his own life space, involving job, family, house. Or, if what concerns him is more general—war, high prices, the quality of schools, traffic problems, property taxes—there remains an almost infinite variety of personal sets of public issues.

A contact initiated by the citizen can be tailored to his specific set of problems. That this indeed seems to happen can be illustrated by one small piece of data. In addition to the questions on the subject matter of their contacts to officials, our respondents were asked to tell us the most important problems they faced in their personal and family lives and the most important problems that they saw facing the community. There were no constraints on the problems that could be mentioned, and the answers range widely. The answers to the question on the citizen's contact and the problems he perceived were coded into several hundred categories. Almost as many categories were necessary for coding the "contact" questions as for coding the "perceived problems" questions, despite the fact that many fewer respondents were answering contact questions. (About a third of our respondents had contacted an official, while almost everyone could name a personal or community problem.) What this indicates is that citizen-initiated contacting brings into the political system a set of concerns roughly as wide as the set of concerns that the citizenry faces.

RATIONALITY AND VOTING

The situation facing the voter is sharply different. He does not choose the occasion to vote, nor does he choose the agenda; he doesn't choose the issues that divide the candidates, nor does he usually have much voice in choosing the candidates themselves. And given the fact that his own agenda is quite individual and may contain many and varied issues, it is unreasonable to expect that there will be a voting choice tailored to his own particular policy preferences at the moment. It is even more unreasonable to expect that the questions posed to him by interviewers about his views on the issues—issues he has not chosen—will elicit responses that will then clearly predict the vote.[8] His vote can only be a rather blunt instrument under these circumstances; it cannot have the sharpness and precision of the statements that accompany citizen-initiated contacts.

Given the lack of fit between the concerns of the individual and issues of the election, it is not surprising that issue-oriented voting is rare. Even if the citizen were motivated to vote on issues, the election usually offers an uncongenial setting. Given the multiplicity of issues in an election, there must be some way for the individual to simplify the choice situation into a meaningful dichotomy so that he can vote with a clear outcome in mind. This simplification of the choice situation can come about in one of two ways: the individual must have a clear and well-structured ideology and the parties must offer him a choice congruent with the ideology, or there must be some "overriding" issue in the election, and the parties must offer a clear alternative

[8] Repass, "Issue Salience and Party Choice," shows that one can better predict the vote if one uses attitude position on the issue that the respondent chooses as most salient to him. But, though this removes some artificiality in political science research on voting by giving freer rein to the problems the respondent himself considers important, it adds a new artificiality. Our contention is that it is unrealistic for the individual to be allowed to choose the agenda of the election, for indeed the issues are not posed by him but by the parties and the candidates.

on that issue. An ideology allows a clear choice in a multi-issue situation, since such a belief system places individual issues into some overall structure. One then chooses a party in terms of its agreement with that ideology. But there is no need to spend time on this possibility, for there is little evidence that voters think in such ideological terms. Even if they did, the American parties would not offer them clear alternatives in those terms.

In the absence of an ideology that clearly sums up all issues and provides a general choice for the individual between the two political parties, the election can allow instrumental voting of a precise sort if there is an overriding issue. In this case, the individual believes that there is a single issue in the campaign compared with which other issues are minor and that one of the voting alternatives clearly is preferable to the others in relation to that issue. Under these circumstances, an individual can vote with the hope that his vote will increase the likelihood of a direct instrumental gratification—i.e., that his favorite party or candidate will win and carry out the policy he prefers in connection with the overriding issue.

But is this possible in the voting choice? It is certainly possible but unlikely. For one thing, such overriding issues do not often appear, and, second, the choice on the issue may not be clear. Actually, at the time we were conducting our study, there was an issue that seemed to be overriding—this was the issue of Vietnam. Our questionnaire contained a number of questions on it. In response to a completely open-ended question 66 percent of our sample said that the war in Vietnam was the most important problem facing the nation (74 percent if one takes into account the first and second most important problem), and many others simply referred to war. Ninety-one percent said that they worried about Vietnam.[9]

It would be hard to find a national issue upon which there was a greater focus of attention. But does this issue fit our criteria of an overriding one? Are individuals willing to vote on that issue alone and do they perceive a clear choice? In two additional surveys conducted closer to the 1968 election, respondents were asked how much importance they would give to a candidate's stand on Vietnam. In February, 1968, 18 percent of a sample said that Vietnam would be more important than any other issue in making up their minds, and an additional 72 percent said that Vietnam would be important but that other issues would be important too. Only 4 percent said that the stand of the candidate on Vietnam would not be important. (Parallel data in June, 1968, are 12 percent, 83 percent, and 6 percent respectively.)[10] At least for the group that says it will be the most important issue for them, the war in

[9] The data on Vietnam are from a series of studies of attitudes on that issue conducted by Richard A. Brody, Jerome Laulicht, Benjamin I. Page, and Sidney Verba. For some reports on these data see, Brody, Page, Verba, and Laulicht, "Vietnam, the Urban Crisis and the 1968 Election," paper delivered at the annual meeting of the American Sociological Association, San Francisco, September, 1969; Brody and Page, "Policy Voting and the Electoral Process: The Vietnam War Issue," paper delivered at the 1971 annual meeting of the American Political Science Association, Chicago, September, 1971; and Milton J. Rosenberg, Sidney Verba, and Philip Converse, *Vietnam and the Silent Majority* (New York: Harper and Row, 1970).

[10] See Brody, Page, Verba and Laulicht, "Vietnam, the Urban Crisis and the 1968 Election."

Vietnam fulfilled the first criterion for an overriding issue. But they are still a small part of our sample.

And what of the second criterion: that the individual is offered a choice on the issues by the political parties? Whether the parties did offer a choice on the issue is a question that can be answered in many ways. Let us look at the question from the point of view of the voter: Did *he* see a choice? A few survey results are relevant. In our survey in 1967 (in which 65 percent said that Vietnam was the most important issue facing the country), 66 percent agreed with the statement that it would make no difference which party was in power as far as Vietnam was concerned. (Eleven percent disagreed slightly with that statement, and 11 percent disagreed strongly.)

More telling, perhaps, is the public's perception of the position of the candidates on the issue. In a study of the 1968 election (by Brody, Page, Laulicht, and Verba), respondents were asked to place various candidates on a seven-position "hawk-dove" scale based on where they thought the candidate stood on the Vietnam issue. Most citizens saw little or no difference between the candidates. The average perception of the position of the candidates placed Nixon at 4.4 on the scale, Humphrey at 4.1 (i.e., on the average, Humphrey was seen as a touch more dovish than Nixon, but only a touch). In contrast, citizens placed George Wallace at 6.5. Looked at another way, over half (57 percent) of the citizens who assigned a place to both major party candidates placed them in the same position or within one scale point of each other.[11]

The data strongly suggest that the candidates were not perceived by the public as offering widely divergent alternatives on the subject of Vietnam. In addition, there is evidence that as the election campaign progressed, the issue became less and less important, perhaps because the two candidates most similar on Vietnam were chosen.[12] And an intensive analysis (by Brody and Page) of the public speeches of the two candidates shows a combination of convergence and vagueness—both of which make issue-voting difficult.[13] The specific case of Vietnam does not demonstrate that an overriding issue might not emerge in some election. But the relatively stringent criteria that would have to be met before one could say that the individual was voting with a specific policy outcome in mind suggest that the situation will be rare. And, of course, we are familiar with the general tendency of election campaigns to blur political issues.[14]

---

[11] Brody and Page, "Policy Voting and the Electoral Process."

[12] Brody, Page, Verba and Laulicht, "Vietnam, the Urban Crisis and the 1968 Election."

[13] Brody and Page, "Policy Voting and the Electoral Process."

[14] That individuals do not approach the vote with a clear perception of alternatives ought not to be taken to imply that citizens are somehow failing in their obligations to have such clear perceptions. The obvious point is that they receive precious little help from the parties or candidates for this. See Stanley Kelley, Jr., *Political Campaigning: Problems in Creating an Informed Electorate,* (Washington: Brookings, 1960). As he puts it:

Contemporary campaign discussion is often of such a character that it is unlikely to help voters much in their efforts to arrive at a wise choice of public officials. It may, in fact, have quite the reverse effect. Campaign propagandists obscure the real differences between candidates and parties by distortion, by evasiveness, and by talking generalities. (p. 80)

This is not to argue that voting on the basis of ideology or clear issue-perception is impossible. Quite the contrary. In our view, the reason why such voting is rare lies within the nature of the collective decision made during an election, not in the incompetence or "irrationality" of the voter. Given a candidate who makes a strong ideological appeal—that is, takes a strong and consistent position on a large number of issues—one might find more voters responding in those terms. Or given a candidate who taps some deeply felt and widely shared issue, one might find more voters voting instrumentally with a fairly precise goal in mind. Thus, Field and Anderson, in their comparison of the 1964 election with the data reported on the 1956 election in *The American Voter,* find that there is more reference to ideological terms in the 1964 Johnson-Goldwater race. References to explicit ideology rise from 9 percent in 1956 (they use a somewhat different definition of this than do the authors of *The American Voter*) to 16 percent in the 1960 to 24 percent in the 1964 election.[15] The rise in frequency of ideological references in 1960 suggests that the base year of 1956 in *The American Voter* may have been a year of abnormally low levels of political controversy. But even the level of ideological reference found in 1964—and we are really dealing here with such general political terms as *liberal* and *conservative*—is hardly impressive given the type of political appeal made by Goldwater. Nevertheless, the difference between 1964 and 1956 does suggest that the nature of the choice situation—as exemplified by the two Presidential candidates—structures the type of response available.

More relevant to our argument is the 1968 election, in which the Survey Research Center found, among those who voted for George Wallace, clear goal orientation consistent with the appeal that Wallace had been making.[16] In contrast to the appeal of Goldwater in 1964, in which there was some response in general ideological terms, Wallace's appeal was in terms of a specific set of overriding issues (race, crime, the urban crisis) of great salience to a group of voters and on which the candidate was taking a strong and clear position. As the Survey Research Center analysts correctly point out, this example indicates that issue-oriented voting is possible, given the right set of issues that are deeply felt and salient to a group, as were the race and urban issues in 1968. But the fact that this type of instrumental voting appears in relation to a third-party candidate and for only a small segment of the population indicates that this is not yet the mainstream orientation of the American public to the voting choice.

Anyone who examines the course of discussion in campaigns can hardly fail to conclude that it is often as well designed to subvert as to facilitate rational voting behavior. What candidates say frequently lacks relevance to any decision voters face, exposes differences in the views of candidates imperfectly, and is filled with evasions, ambiguities and distortions. (p. 51)

On this general subject, see also Anthony Downs, *An Economic Theory of Democracy* (New York: Harper & Row, 1957).

[15] John O. Field and Ronald E. Anderson, "Ideology and the Public's Conceptualization of the 1964 Election," *Public Opinion Quarterly,* vol. 33 (Fall 1969), pp. 380-398.

[16] Converse, et al., "Continuity and Change in American Politics."

The difficulty in using the vote to satisfy the specific desires of citizens can be seen quite clearly if we compare the responses reported in *The American Voter* where respondents favored a party or candidate because of some expectation of a specific beneficial outcome with the responses we received on the subject matter of citizen contacts.

Two differences seem to stand out. In relation to contacts, the individual seems to be looking forward: He is asking for some future benefit from the government. In relation to the vote, he is likely to be looking backward, even when he is focused on a specific instrumental goal. Thus *The American Voter* authors refer to the frequent appearance among "nature of the times" respondents of comments about promises that have not been kept. And the one woman quoted who mentions a specific particularized reason for favoring one party over another refers to "the good wages my husband makes."[17] V. O. Key, Jr., who makes the strongest argument for the rationality of the voter (in our terms, for his ability to make choices with a specific political outcome in mind) makes that argument in terms of the ability of the voter to make rational evaluations of past performance rather than clear demands for future performance.[18]

The second reason why expectations of specific gratification in response to one's vote differ from such expectations in response to citizen-initiated contacts is that, in some sense, such expectations are appropriate in the latter case and inappropriate in the former. The individual who contacts the government with a salient and specific outcome in mind engages in more reasonable behavior than does the individual who sees the election as related to the particular specific problem that is most salient to him at the time. (Though, as the Wallace campaign reminds us, candidates—probably third-party candidates—can sometimes tap such issues.)

This may explain why the type of answers we quote as to the subject matter of citizen-initiated contacts—answers we consider to indicate some precise understanding of political needs—are the type that, when they appeared in answer to the question of what one likes about the parties or candidates in *The American Voter,* were coded in one of the lowest categories in terms of conceptualization; the "nature of the times" category. The point is that the individual can select the agenda of a contact, and he does so in the context of the specific problems that are troubling him at the time. However, in relation to the vote, one of two things may happen: on the one hand, he may respond to the agenda as offered to him in the election, but he will do so in vague terms (as when he gives general or group-oriented answers to open ended questions) or in inconsistent and changeable terms (as when he answers questions on specific issues) because the agenda presented to him is not of his choosing and does not reflect the problems he faces most immediately. On the other hand, if he does respond to the election in terms of his own salient and specific problem, his response is inappropriate because the election rarely revolves

---

[17] Campbell, et al., *The American Voter,* p. 244.
[18] Key, *The Responsible Electorate,* p. 61.

around that problem at all or, if it does, it will certainly not revolve around that problem alone. Or one can look at this from the point of view of our distinction between pressure and information as means of influencing the government. The voting situation is an uncongenial one for conveying specific citizen preferences because there is no way to cram that information into the vote, whereas one can express precise information when one contacts a leader.

In the light of these considerations, it is no wonder that issue orientations have no larger role in the voting choice. Nor is it any wonder that those who attempt to develop a calculus from which one can infer that it is reasonable for a citizen to bother to vote—given the small impact he can have on the election—have had to turn to variables such as the gratification one receives from fulfilling a civic duty.[19] This preserves the rationality of the vote—if it makes you feel good, it's rational to do it—but it hardly makes voting an instrumental act aimed at obtaining some beneficial governmental action. And mere habit may play a role in voting turnout. As our data in Chapter 5 indicated, voting specialists are characterized by habitual attachment to a political party and relatively little emotional concern with the issues. As we shall show later, the likelihood of voting can be partially explained simply by the length of time one has been an eligible voter, a fact consistent with an habitual basis of voting. Last, one of the prime characteristics of voting—the ease of the act and the lack of initiative required—makes it likelier that citizens will vote even if they see no specific gain from the outcome.

The difference between citizen-initiated contacts and voting support our contention that contact mechanisms and electoral mechanisms represent different systems for relating citizens to the government. Both elections and citizen-initiated contacts represent simplifying mechanisms whereby individual preferences are converted into social choice, i.e., mechanisms whereby the vast multiplicity of demands and needs that citizens have can be communicated to the government and allocations of societal resources can be made relevant to these needs and demands. But the voting and contact mechanisms work in different ways. In the election, we are dealing with social choice for the entire society. The preferences of citizens are simplified by being channeled into a limited number of choices: a choice among a few parties, or between those parties and abstention. Under such circumstances, the individual is unlikely to find a voting choice that allows him to make an instrumental decision relevant to the specific set of salient problems that face him at the time of the election—problems that our data (and the data of others) tell us are likely to be highly particularized, involving the health of the individual, his economic situation, and the condition of his neighborhood, as well as more public issues.[20] It is unlikely that a candidate will stand for the specific set of goals the individual has or even that the set of problems that concern him most will become the subject of the election.

[19] Riker and Ordeshook, "A Theory of the Calculus of Voting."
[20] See Hadley Cantril, *The Pattern of Human Concerns* (New Brunswick, N.J.: Rutgers University Press, 1965).

The problem is not specific to the American two-party system. The fact that electoral choice in the United States is often reduced to that between two political parties intensifies both the simplification of the choice and its incongruence with the specific set of problems facing the individual. If there were more parties offering more specific programs, the individual could tailor his voting choice somewhat more to his own specific salient needs and problems. (And it is not accidental that the best example of issue-oriented voting—Wallace in 1968—involves a third-party candidate.) But that does not solve the problem of social choice. The more parties, the more an individual may find one party that comes close to his particular set of preferences. But the choice means less in terms of influencing governmental policy, because the party elected will be a minority party and will have to form some coalition with other parties to enter a government.[21] It is not the number of parties, but the making of a social choice for the whole society that leads to the distance between the vote and the particular salient preferences of the individual.

Citizen-initiated contacts represent an alternative way of simplifying social choice. This is done by decomposing the choice to the individual level. These contacts often deal with particularized problems; in many cases the response to a contact would have major impact on the individual without affecting the overall allocation of societal benefits in more than marginal ways. But the sum total of all such contacts and the myriad responses to them do represent a mechanism for social allocation without the clear necessity of general social choice. By decomposing social choice to a vast number of specific interactions with the government, the structure of citizen-initiated contacts may represent an important means of achieving instrumental goals from the government, goals that are close to the most salient problems felt by the individual.

The contrast between the vote and citizen-initiated contacts leads to further comment on the American public. Research on political beliefs has led to the conclusions that the American public rarely approaches political matters with a clear and well-defined perception of the issues, that the public is ill-informed, its political beliefs lightly held and quickly changeable, its view of political matters vague and distant, and that politics and political controversy lack salience, i.e., the individual is more likely to be concerned with his own narrow day-to-day problems than with the issues that excite the few politically involved and sophisticated citizens. This view of the American public has usually been derived from studies of political matters in which, to use our phraseology, the agenda has been set for the individual by others. (Sometimes the agenda is set by the researcher who comes to the respondent with fixed-alternative questions about political matters the researcher considers important.) This view also derives from studies of electoral choice, in which individuals are not found to have a clear issue-oriented view of the meaning of the election. It derives from studies of attitudes on foreign policy, in which

---

[21] The classic political science debate over forms of electoral system, particularly the choice between proportional representation and single-member district systems, is relevant here. See also Downs, *An Economic Theory of Democracy*.

the individual is found to know and care little about the foreign-policy choices of the government; and it derives from studies of the consistency and stability of attitudes on major public issues when the individual is asked to take sides on some such issue.[22] For this realm of politics, the view of the public is accurate and relevant.

Our only objection is to a tendency to consider such a position representative of the sum of the citizen's relations with the government. Our data on the content of citizen-initiated contacts show a citizenry involved with the government in ways that are highly salient to them, on issues that they define, and through channels that seem appropriate. What we are suggesting is that on matters of the politics of everyday life, citizens know what they want.[23]

Furthermore, we ought to make clear that in contrasting voting and citizen-initiated contacts, we do not intend to praise the latter as a means of participation and criticize the former. Quite the contrary. A system based on individual contacts would allow adequate citizen control over the government only if access to those contacts were equally available for all and, more important, if there were no significant "macro" policy issues that had to be decided. As some data to be presented later will show, the former condition does not hold. Access to contacting is not as widespread as access to the vote. And the latter condition does not hold either. Social policy has to be made. Particularized contacts can be effective for the individual contactor but they are inadequate as a guide to more general social policy.

The point is that if one wants to maximize popular control over governmental activities that affect the lives of citizens, both types of mechanisms—the contacting and the electoral—are needed. Because governmental policies are almost always quite general, their application to a specific individual in a specific situation involves particular adjustments or decisions made by low-level government officials. Insofar as this is the case, the ability of the citizen to make himself heard on such a matter—by contacting the officials— represents an important aspect of citizen control. Though such contacts may be important in filling the policy gaps and in adjusting policy to the individual, effective citizen control over governmental policy would be limited indeed if citizens related to their government only as isolated individuals concerned with their narrow parochial problems. The larger political questions would remain outside popular control. Therefore, though electoral mechanisms remain crude, they are the most effective for these purposes.

Thus, despite much of what we have said, the vote remains probably a most effective means for citizen control over leaders. Even if the individual voter has little power over the election outcome, the set of all voters is powerful

[22] See Converse, "The Nature of Belief Systems in Mass Publics"; Campbell, et. al., *The American Voter;* McClosky, "Consensus and Ideology in American Politics"; and Gabriel A. Almond, *The American People and Foreign Policy* (New York: Harcourt, 1950).

[23] This is consistent with the finding that individuals manifest issue positions with more consistency on local issues and on specific issues than on general political issues. Luttbeg finds that the mass-elite distinction in terms of consistency of attitudes found on national issues does not apply to more local ones. See Norman Luttbeg,"The Structure of Beliefs among Leaders and the Public," *Public Opinion Quarterly,* vol. 32 (Fall 1968), pp. 398-410.

indeed. But the comparison of voting with citizen-initiated contacting helps us comprehend why it remains such an inadequate mechanism for citizen control, an inadequacy that may lie less in the incapacities of the citizenry than in the nature of the electoral mechanism itself.

Indeed, as we shall demonstrate in Chapter 19, voting *in combination with other acts* is a most potent political force. Other acts have, as we suggested, more information-carrying capacity. On the other hand, votes are most powerful in applying pressure on leaders. When the two coexist—pressure plus information—participation is, as we shall see, most effective. Even if the vote can carry little information, voting can make governmental leaders more sensitive to other more informative messages coming from citizens.

THE RATIONALITY OF COMMUNAL AND CAMPAIGN ACTIVITY

For the purposes of illustrating the differences in the ways the modes of activity relate the citizen to his government, the contrast between voting and citizen-initiated contacts is the most important and illuminating. We can fill out the picture by looking briefly at communal and campaign activity.

Much of what has been said about contacting can also be said about communal activity. Indeed, one of the component acts of the communal mode of participation involves contacting officials on a social issue. In these cases, the citizen acts, as we have suggested, with fairly specific goals and with fairly good selectivity in terms of the officials chosen for contact. The other component of communal participation involves activity in cooperation with others—informal cooperation with friends, neighbors, fellow-workers or other citizens of similar interest—or activity through formally organized groups. Such activity is particularly widespread in America. Over a century ago, Tocqueville commented on the distinctive amount of such activity in the United States. And recent data on participation in a variety of nations suggest that participation through cooperation with others is the mode of activity for which the rate in the United States far exceeds rates found elsewhere.[24]

Insofar as citizens are cooperating with others in attempting to influence governmental policy, one would not expect that the average citizen can set the agenda as freely as he can when he is contacting on his own, for he has to consider the views of the others with whom he cooperates. Nevertheless, such group-oriented activity should resemble contacting more than it does activity in the electoral process in terms of its ability to satisfy the most direct instrumental needs of the citizen. Citizens tend to become involved in groups that deal with problems salient to them. The problems are not as particular as the problems brought by those who contact on personal and family matters; they may indeed be general social problems of the community. But the citizen will choose to become involved in relation to problems that touch him. Parents become active in school groups; sportsmen in groups concerned with recrea-

[24] See Almond and Verba, *The Civic Culture,* Chapter 7; and Verba, Nie, and Kim, *The Modes of Democratic Participation,* p. 36.

tional facilities. The cooperation may involve informal relations among like-minded citizens, but the very term *like-minded* makes clear that the participants will be those for whom the problem is salient. Or the cooperation may involve activity through formal organizations, but citizens tend to join organizations that relate to things they consider important.

In this sense, communal activity (and, in particular, those activities carried on in cooperation with others) may combine some of the advantages of contacting with those of voting. Communal activity engaged in concert with one's fellows can deal with fairly specific problems that are high on the agenda of citizens—problems that affect some specific group to which they belong or problems that affect the community as a whole. In this sense they have the specificity and information-carrying capacity of contacting. On the other hand, the fact that citizens are joining together to act politically increases the potential influence that they can have, especially when the issue involved is broader than those associated with particularized contacting.[25] Whether these activities are those of formally organized interest groups or of informal groupings of citizens coming together for a specific purpose, they form an important part of the participatory system in the United States.

Last, we can consider campaign activity. The campaign activist is, in some sense, in the same position as the voter. He may have somewhat more control over the agenda of the election—he may be active in nominations and in issue selection—but it is unlikely that the average campaign activist has much voice in these matters either. But because campaign participation requires more time, effort, and initiative than voting, it is hard to see it as motivated solely by habit or sense of civic obligation.

How then does the campaign activist get instrumental benefits? Is it rational for him to be active? Several answers are possible. In the first place, campaign activists do differ from ordinary voters in having clearer issue orientations. As our data in Chapter 5 made clear, campaign activists score higher on the scale of issue extremity than any other type of political actor, except the complete activists.[26] In addition to their stronger and more consistent issue positions, they tend to have a better developed ideological view of the differences between the parties than do ordinary citizens.[27] Thus, in terms of their own orientations to politics, campaign activists may be better equipped than the average citizen to vote "instrumentally." They are more likely to have clear and consistent policy views and to see policy differences between the parties. Yet, these activists may also be blocked from successfully pursuing

---

[25] The vast literature on pressure groups in America is relevant here. Stein Rokkan makes one of the best and most explicit cases for the importance of group activity as a means of filling in the gaps left by electoral competition. See his chapter on Norway in Robert A. Dahl (ed.), *Political Oppositions in Western Democracies* (New Haven, Conn.: Yale University Press, 1966).

[26] See Chapter 5, Figure 5-2. See also Herbert McClosky, Paul J. Hoffmann, and Rosemary O'Hara, "Issue Conflict and Consensus among Party Leaders and Followers," *American Political Science Review*, vol. 54 (June 1960), pp. 406-427.

[27] Dwaine Marvick and Charles R. Nixon, "Recruitment Contrasts in Rival Campaign Groups," in Marvick (ed.), *Political Decision Makers: Recruitment and Performance* (New York: Free Press, 1961), pp. 193-217.

instrumental goals within the electoral process by the same thing that blocks voters: They do not control the agenda of the election and therefore that agenda is unlikely to match their own.

What happens under such circumstances? There are no national data on this subject, but Eldersveld's data on party workers in Detroit are most revealing in the light of our discussion of elections and instrumental gratification. He finds that for lower-echelon party workers (which is what most of our campaign activists are), one must distinguish between the motivations for initial involvement in partisan activity and the motives for remaining active.

> ... while grass roots workers may have been recruited under the guise of the "voluntaristic-idealistic-impersonal task-oriented" concept of party work, ... these precinct leaders in large numbers change motivational direction during their careers. Many become disillusioned; the majority articulated personal demands, needs and satisfactions to be derived from party activity. In reality this means that the majority of precinct leaders changed their motivational relationship to the party. ... They either became disillusioned, or they conceptualized their relationship in terms of social friendship satisfactions (66 percent of the Democrats, 49 percent of the Republicans), a desire to be "in the know" and gain prestige in the neighborhood (4 percent of the Democrats, 6 percent of the Republicans), or they saw other personalized satisfaction such as the enjoyment of the "fun and excitement" of a campaign (6 percent of the Democrats, 4 percent of the Republicans).[28]

In short, then, party activists may join parties because of some instrumental goal, a belief that they can influence governmental policy in some desired direction. However, over time, these goals become less important and side benefits become more important. On the lower levels, these side benefits tend to be social in nature (one enjoys party work, meets others, etc.), while on the upper level they are both social and material (one makes business connections, etc.). This finding is consistent with our findings on the high issue orientation of partisan activists and with our view of the electoral process as a relatively uncongenial setting for participation oriented toward dealing with issues one considers important. It may be that the ineffectiveness of the electoral mechanism for satisfying specific policy goals means that activists either adopt alternative goals that do not depend on governmental responsiveness, or drop out. We will return to this subject in Chapter 12, where we will present contrasting data on the two parties.

THE PARTICIPATION INPUT: A SUMMARY OF PART I

In Part I we have attempted to analyze and describe the participation input: How much participation is there, of what kind, and from what people? In this chapter we have attempted to demonstrate that the alternative modes of participation do in fact differ in the kinds of benefits that citizens can

[28] See Samuel J. Eldersveld, *Political Parties: A Behavioral Analysis* (Chicago: Rand McNally, 1964) pp. 290-292. A study of the incentives for the maintenance of activism among precinct party officials in North Carolina and Massachusetts found a similar stress on personal satisfactions. See Lewis Bowman, Dennis Ippolito, and William Donaldson, "Incentives for the Maintenance of Grassroots Political Activism," *Midwest Journal of Political Science*, vol 13 (February 1969) pp. 126-139. Marvick and Nixon, "Recruitment Contrasts in

reasonably expect from them. For some modes of participation, means-ends calculations are more difficult than for others, but when one looks across the range of alternative activities open to the citizen one may find a greater degree of instrumental and rational activity than is sometimes assumed. And where one finds rather ill-developed means-ends calculations—as in relation to voting—the source may lie in the nature of the electoral system itself at least as much as it lies in the incapacity of the average voter.

It may be useful now to tie together what we have found about the participation input. Table 7-1 summarizes a good deal of what we have found. In Column A we list the six types of participants that we have found to fit the patterns of activity of American citizens, and we give the proportion of the population that falls into each of these types. In Column B we characterize their respective patterns of activity, and in Column C we indicate how these activities fit our theoretical dimensions of participation. In Column D we give the main characteristics of each group in terms of political orientations, a pattern of orientations that, we believe, confirms the meaningfulness of the distinctions we make among the types of political actors. In Column E we indicate the social composition of the various activist groups. In short, one can tell from Table 7-1 how many people are active in America, the ways in which they are active (and in particular, the all-important question of the types of outcome their activity can influence), and their social characteristics.

The participation input summarized in Table 7-1 suggests a quite variegated pattern of participation in the United States, not a mere division of the population into several different activity levels. This is not simply to say that there are many different kinds of activities open to citizens. Rather the data reported in Part I support a stronger conclusion: that there are several different *systems* of participation in the United States.

There are several justifications for this stronger conclusion. In the first place, we have found that the various political acts in which citizens can engage form meaningful patterns and constitute particular modes of activity. Second, we have found that there are groups of citizens who "specialize" in one mode of activity or another. It is true that there are some citizens who engage in all modes of activity and some who do nothing, but substantial numbers of citizens limit their activity fairly closely to one mode or another. Third, we found that the alternative types of activists have distinct patterns of orientation to politics that are consistent with our analysis of the implications of the various ways citizens can participate. And, last and probably most important, we have shown that the alternative patterns of activity relate the citizen to his government in different ways: They can influence different kinds of governmental decisions, and they allow the participant to exercise more or less influence over the result of his participatory attempt.

Rival Campaign Groups," find a greater stress on concern for public issues as a reason for party activism among their sample in Los Angeles, but their question may be such as to engender "official justifications." However, they also find a heavy stress on social gains from party activity. On this subject, see also Robert Salisbury, "The Urban Party Organization Member," *Public Opinion Quarterly*, vol. 29 (Winter 1965-66), pp. 550-564.

Table 7-1

The Participation Input: A Summary

A Type of participant	*B* Pattern of activity	*C* Theoretical dimensions of activity pattern	*D* Leading orientations	*E* Main social characteristics
The inactives (22%)	No activity		Totally uninvolved, no interest, skill, sense of competence, or concern with conflict.	Lower socioeconomic levels and blacks are overrepresented, as are older and younger citizens (but not middle-aged ones) and women.
The voting specialists (21%)	They vote regularly, but do nothing else.	Broad collective outcomes, counterparticipants, and low initiative.	Strong partisan identity but otherwise relatively uninvolved and with low skills and competence.	Lower socioeconomic levels are overrepresented. Older citizens are overrepresented, as are those in big cities. Underrepresented in rural areas.
The parochial participants (4%)	They contact officials on particularized problems and are otherwise inactive.	Particularized outcomes, no conflict, and high initiative.	Some political skill (information) but otherwise no political involvement.	Lower socioeconomic groups are overrepresented, but blacks are underrepresented. Catholic rather than Protestant. Big cities rather than small towns.

118

The communalists (20%)	They contact officials on broad social issues and engage in co-operative activity. Vote fairly regularly, but avoid election campaigns.	Collective outcomes (but may be narrower than those of elections), high initiative, and relatively no conflict.	High sense of community contribution, involvement in politics, skill and competence. Nonpartisan and avoid conflict.	Upper socioeconomic levels very overrepresented, blacks underrepresented. Protestant rather than Catholic. Overrepresented in rural areas and small towns; underrepresented in big cities.
The campaigners (15%)	Heavily active in campaigns and vote regularly.	Broad collective outcomes, moderate to high initiative, and relatively conflictual.	Politically involved, relatively skilled and competent, partisan and involved in conflict, but little sense of community contribution.	Overrepresentation of upper-status groups. Blacks and particularly Catholics overrepresented. Big-city and suburbs rather than small towns and rural areas.
The complete activists (11%)	Active in all ways.	All characteristics of all acts.	Involved in politics in all ways, highly skilled and competent.	Heavy overrepresentation of upper-status groups. Old and young underrepresented.
(7% of sample unclassified).				

What Are the Alternative Systems of Participation?

First, there is the system of particularized contacting, a channel of participation that permits citizens to seek a variety of decomposable benefits from the government—benefits that aid only them. Through this system of participation, the individual citizen may seek some government service or may seek to stop some government activity that is impinging on his life. This system of participation does not touch on the great issues of policy, and perhaps for that reason little attention has been paid to it. But the government affects our lives in so many small ways that this would appear to be a critical channel, and if it were closed to some groups, they would be severely deprived. Indeed, life would be much more difficult even in the most democratic society if there were no means available to obtain minor adjustments and dispensations from general government policy, especially when that policy is made on such a grand scale and at places so distant from the lives it affects.

Particularized contacting is an activity carried on by all sorts of citizens—by some who are active in other ways, by some who are not. This reflects the fact that such activity deals with myriad specific problems affecting all sorts of people. Those citizens who limit their activity to particularized contacting are a special type. We have labeled them *parochial participants,* for though they have the skill and initiative to engage in fairly difficult activity, they show no involvement in political life in the broader sense.

Next we have uncovered the communalist system of participation, whereby citizens alone or, more often with others, attempt to deal with the more general problems of their communities or of particular groups. The problems are not so narrow as those dealt with via particularized contacting, but they are nevertheless problems that are specifically pertinent to the individuals or groups active in this way. The activity also seems to be relatively nonconflictual, either because the goal is some general benefit to the community or because it is some benefit to the specific group of activists but is not seen by others as affecting them negatively. Much of this activity seems to consist of mobilizing community resources or one's fellow citizens to deal directly with community problems or to induce the government to do so.

The communalists' attitudes fit their activity: They have a high sense of contribution to the community and a general involvement in politics, but they seem to avoid conflict. As we have suggested, activity of this sort is found more frequently in the United States than in a variety of other countries—a fifth of the U.S. citizenry concentrate on this form of participation. However, data presented in Chapter 13 suggest that such activity flourishes under conditions that may be disappearing in America. If so, the system of political participation in the United States will lose an important and distinctive component.

The third and fourth modes of participation with which we have dealt involve the electoral system. One way citizens take part is via an active role in the campaign process. Our data show that almost a third of the citizenry participate in some way in this process, and that over 15 percent concentrate on this form of political involvement. When we add this 15 percent to the even larger number of communalists, we see two vigorous, yet separate, systems whereby private citizens can and do attempt to influence the direction of our political life. But campaign activity differs from communal activity because the issues of the former are less specific to the participants and because they involve more conflict.

The last mode of activity is voting. We find a substantial proportion of citizens (21 percent) who limit their activity to this—but it is not nearly so large a group as other studies have suggested. And although we have found the vote to be a rather limited mode of engagement, there would appear to be few other available mechanisms whereby the preferences of all citizens can simultaneously be taken into account, giving them some control over the selection of leadership. Furthermore, some data to be presented in Chapter 19 will indicate that although voting may have minimal effectiveness as a channel for communicating the specific needs and desires of a particular participant, when aggregated across all citizens and especially when combined with other activities conveying more information, it remains a most powerful system for insuring the responsiveness of elites.

Each of the modes of participation is distinctive and each, therefore, forms an important component of the overall system of participation in the United States. It is a rich and complex system. But it is also a system for which all the components are not equally accessible to all citizens. This became clear in Chapter 6, where we considered the question of who the participators are. As that chapter indicated, and as Table 7-1 summarizes, some social groups have more access to the various modes of activity than others. In the next two sections of our book we will deal with the reasons for and the consequences of this fact.

Part II
THE PROCESS
OF POLITICIZATION

In this section we shall consider the processes that lead some citizens to participate while others remain inactive. This, in turn, shapes the participation input. We begin by considering a "standard socioeconomic" model of politicization whereby the forces leading citizens to participate involve their social status mediated by a set of "civic" attitudes. The rest of the section deals with other social and psychological influences that modify the workings of the standard socioeconomic model. Of particular interest to us is the extent to which these other forces lead to a reduction or an increase in the participatory disparity between lower- and upper-status citizens.

Chapter 8
Social Status and Political Participation: The Standard Model

In Chapter 6 we completed our characterization of the participation input by considering the question, from whom does the participation come? The specification of the alternative ways in which citizens can participate leads to a more variegated answer than would be the case if we had a simple hierarchy on which some citizens are active, and others are not. But, in its broadest outline, the data clearly confirm a generalization that is already well established in the literature: Citizens of higher social and economic status participate more in politics. This generalization has been confirmed many times in many nations. And it generally holds true whether one uses level of education, income, or occupation as the measure of social status.[1] In addition, studies of political development have found a close relationship—most often using aggregate data on the national level—between the rate of political participation and such measures as median education, income per capita, and proportion in white-collar employ.[2]

---

[1] For a summary of the literature that makes this point, see Milbrath, *Political Participation*, pp. 114-128.

[2] This was, of course, one of the major findings of Lipset in *Political Man*, Chapter 3. Others using more refined techniques of analysis have tended to find the same results. See, for instance, Phillips Cutright, "National

125

There are many explanations for this relationship—the higher-status individual has a greater stake in politics, he has greater skills, more resources, greater awareness of political matter, he is exposed to more communications about politics, he interacts with others who participate.

Most explanations of the relationship between socioeconomic status and participation contain the following basic components:

Socioeconomic Status   ————————————▶ Civic Attitudes ————————————▶   Participation

Individuals of higher social status develop such civic orientations as concern for politics, information, and feelings of efficacy, and these orientations in turn lead to participation. It is not our purpose in this chapter to quarrel with this model. As we shall shortly demonstrate, it fits the data from our study fairly well. But we consider the workings of the simple socioeconomic model to be just the beginning of our understanding of the processes that bring individuals to participate. For us, the socioeconomic model presents a base line. We shall begin by considering how much of the variance in political participation is explained by this simple socioeconomic model. Then we will turn to other social, psychological, and structural characteristics to see how they affect this base-line model. Thus we do not reject the socioeconomic model, but rather wish to see what other forces are at work affecting participation in America.

Our acceptance of the model is, however, qualified in one other way. Our previous analysis of the differences between those citizens who are active in one mode of activity rather than another suggests that it may be a great oversimplification to fit one model of the process by which individuals come to participate to the various modes of activity. What leads a citizen to engage in one type of activity may differ from what leads him to another. This general theme will be carried with us as we look at the socioeconomic forces associated with participation and at the other forces that lead to deviations from the socioeconomic model. The impact of socioeconomic status may differ across the acts, as may the impact of other social and psychological factors.

There are two main reasons why it is important to focus on the workings of the socioeconomic model and on the forces that lead to deviations from it. The first reason is that such an exploration will tell us much about the social circumstances that are conducive to political activity as well as the psychological characteristics that lead citizens to be active. Such an exploration takes us a long way toward an answer to the question of why some citizens participate while others do not. Second, we are interested in the processes that lead people to participate because of the consequences of those processes. The process that is operating—the one by which citizens of higher socioeconomic status come

Political Development: Social and Economic Correlates," in Nelson W. Polsby, Robert A. Dentler, and Paul A. Smith (eds.), *Politics and Social Life* (Boston: Houghton Mifflin, 1963), pp. 569-582; Donald J. McCrone and Charles F. Cnudde, "Toward a Communications Theory of Democratic Political Development: A Causal Model," *American Political Science Review*, vol. 61 (March 1967), pp. 72-79. For an attempt to integrate the findings at the individual level of analysis with those from the national aggregate data studies, see Nie, Powell, and Prewitt, "Social Structure and Political Participation."

to participate, or some other social process (i.e., some additional social or psychological characteristic affecting participation)—determines who winds up in the participant population. If the socioeconomic model "works" and there are no additional forces that cause deviations from it, the result is that citizens of upper social status participate more than those of lower social status. The consequences of such a situation would, of course, be significant in terms of the governmental response to participation. The participation input would come disproportionately from one stratum of society. It would mean that those who might most need beneficial output from the government—the poor and the ill-educated, for instance—would participate less than those already better endowed with those social and economic benefits. Therefore, the consequences of participation for social and economic equality might differ substantially if what brought individuals to participate were high socioeconomic status rather than some other force.

At the end of this chapter we will list some of these other social and psychological forces that lead to deviations from the simple working of the socioeconomic model, and in following chapters we will consider these forces more closely. But one point must be made here: The working of the socioeconomic model leads to "overparticipation" by those of upper social and economic status. The fact that there are other forces working that affect participation—such as race and racial identity, organizational affiliation, and the nature of the community—does not necessarily mean that the resultant participant population is less skewed in the direction of upper social-status citizens. Some forces may work to moderate the "bias" of the socioeconomic model, others may exacerbate it, and still others may change the amount of one form of participation or another without affecting the relative distribution of participation across the several socioeconomic strata. We shall explore these variations as we move through this section, but first we will examine the simple model we mentioned.

SOME MEASURES OF PARTICIPATION

In this chapter—indeed in the rest of this book—we shall be dealing with the forces that lead to participation and with the consequences of that participation. To facilitate that analysis it will be useful to have some standard measures of participation, so that we can compare citizens in terms of how much they participate under varying conditions and gauge the impact of various social and psychological characteristics on citizen activity. One way we have done and will continue to do this is through the use of our typology of activists.

However, much of the following analysis will involve the simultaneous consideration of multiple factors that influence participation. For this, we need more flexible measures. Thus we shall use several standard scales of participation. Because these will be used throughout the book, it is useful to introduce them here and explain their meaning. We shall be using five standard participation scales: one for overall participation and one for each of the four basic modes of participation—voting, campaign activity, communal activity, and particularized contacting. The scales are basically those introduced in Chapter 4.

To ease the comparison among the various scales, we have standardized them. On each scale the mean of the population is 0. Positive numbers mean that an individual scores above the average for all citizens. Negative numbers mean that he participates less, not that he has "negative" participation. The scale is graduated so that a score of 100 means that an individual participates to an amount one standard deviation above the mean of the population as a whole, —100 that he participates one standard deviation below the mean. We call the points on the scale *participation units.* A citizen might participate at a rate of 50 participation units above the mean on overall participation. Or a particular category of citizens might score, on the average, 80 participation units below the mean on voting participation.[3]

To give the reader some notion of the concrete meaning of the standard participation scale, we refer him to Figure 8-1, where we present the scale for overall participation, which can run from a low of —96 to a high of +415. The mean score for the population as a whole is zero. The asymmetry in the scale, with a greater proportion of the population below the mean than above it, is a reflection of the distribution of political activity. There were more totally inactive respondents than there were citizens active in every form of participation. This fact is also reflected in the distance between the mean for the population, which is 0, and the median, which is —28. The "superactivist" deviates, therefore, more from the norm of the population than does the inactive.[4]

On the standard scale we have indicated where various kinds of citizens might fall. By looking at the profiles of the citizens who would fall at various points on the scale, the reader can obtain some sense of the concrete referent of the scale. The citizen who performs all fifteen acts with the greatest possible frequency receives a score of 415. There was only one such individual in the entire sample. A little less than 5 percent receive the lowest possible score of —96. There is a vast number of types of citizens one might locate between these extremes. On Figure 8-1 we locate the scores of the six types of activists isolated by the cluster analysis in Chapter 4. The complete activist, for instance, who votes regularly and is active in three or four campaign activities as well as

---

[3] Appendix B.2 describes the construction of these scales and presents their intercorrelations. Since factor scales are already standardized with means of 0 and standard deviations of 1, we simply multiplied the scores by 100 for purposes of visual display.

[4] The lowest possible score would be received by the citizen who gave negative answers on all fifteen participation items we asked—he never voted, never contacted, and so forth. The highest score would require positive answers to all questions about activities, as well as answers that fell in the highest category in terms of frequency of that act. Since there are more citizens vho receive the absolutely low score than who receive the top scores (5% of the respondents are at the —96 point on the scale, while, in fact, only one individual in our entire sample actually received the highest score), the lowest point represents less deviation from the population as a whole than does the upper score. To put it another way, using the measures we have, a citizen is more likely to be totally inactive than to be superactive.

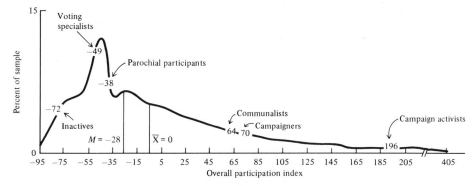

Figure 8-1. Standard Scale of Overall Participation: Distributional Characteristics and Relation to Participant Types

in three or four communal acts, has a mean on this scale of 196. The campaigner and the communalist have scores around 70. These last two groups are over two-thirds of a standard deviation above the mean for the population as a whole and 100 points above the median.

The parochial participants, the voting specialists, and the inactives are all below both the mean and the median. There is, incidentally, a substantive point worth noting here, one that confirms our earlier analysis of the spread of participation in the United States. It is not the case, as many argue, that the average American votes and does nothing else. The voting specialist, even though he appears at the polls regularly for both national and local elections, is still participating half a standard deviation below the population mean and about one-quarter of a standard deviation below the median. Note, however, the visible peak in the participation scale, which indicates that a significant portion of the population does limit its activity to regular voting.

Similar standard scales have been developed for each of the modes of activity. The citizen scoring highest on the scale is the one who did everything possible (as we measure it) in relation to that mode of activity; the citizen scoring lowest does nothing in relation to that mode. For easier comparison, the scales are all standardized so that the mean is zero and the standard deviation is 100.[5]

SOCIOECONOMIC STATUS AND PARTICIPATION

We can now begin to use the various participation scales. The first use will be to show the extent to which the data fit the standard socioeconomic model

[5] In the following table, we report the ranges for the four scales as well as for the overall participation scale. The scales differ from each other in the minimum and maximum values that can be achieved. This is due to the differences among the acts in whether the modal activity lies above or below the mean. The voting scale differs from the others in that it has a much narrower range than the other scales. This reflects reality: since voting is so widespread and since the opportunities to vote are clearly limited by the number of elections, one can not deviate from the average citizen very much in a more active direction. However, since most people vote at least

of the process by which citizens come to participate. In doing this we do not decompose the components of socioeconomic status to ask what the relative contribution to participation is of education or income or occupation. Rather, we want to give some indication of the extent to which socioeconomic status, broadly defined, relates to participation and the degree to which the standard socioeconomic model fits the data.

The data in Figure 8-2 make clear that the relationship between socioeconomic position and political activity is quite close. For our standard participation measure of overall participation we plot the relationship with a scale of socioeconomic status based on a combined measure of the educational level of the respondent, and the occupation and income of the head of household.[6] We divide the "SES" scale into sixths. The relationship between socioeconomic status and overall participation is linear and fairly strong. Those in the lowest sixth of the socioeconomic scale have an average score of —46 on the overall participation scale; those in the top sixth have a score of 66. In other words, those in the lower sixth on socioeconomic status score about half a standard deviation below the mean of the population on overall participation, while those in the upper sixth score on the average about two-thirds of a standard deviation above the mean.

Our major concern is with the way the relationship between socioeconomic status and participation affects the composition of the participation input—i.e., who participates. We can observe this more directly by looking at the way the social composition changes as one moves from those least active to those most active. In Figure 8-3 we divide the population into sixths using our overall participation scale, and indicate the status composition of each participation level—i.e., what proportion comes from the top, middle, and lower thirds of our socioeconomic scales. (Figure 8-3, in other words, is merely a more descriptive way of looking at the data reported in Figure 8-2. Rather than looking at the various status groups and asking how active they are, we look at the various activity groups and ask about the status distribution within these activity groups.) The data make clear how skewed the participant

---

occasionally, one can much more readily deviate in a negative direction from the population as a whole. The other acts are more open at the top—one can participate more frequently—and since there are many who are inactive in the nonvoting modes, one does not deviate from the population that much if one is inactive in these modes. (See Appendix B.2 for further discussion.)

Range of Standard Participation Scores

	Lowest	Median	Mean	Highest
Voting scale	−225	36	0	71
Campaign scale	−66	−42	0	409
Communal scale	−75	−47	0	500
Particularized contact scale	−33	−33	0	505
Overall participation scale	−96	−28	0	415

[6] Appendix B.2 gives the exact items from which the SES index was built and describes the scale construction technique.

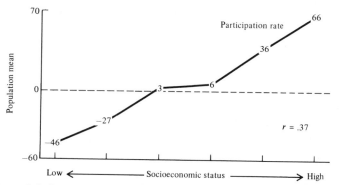

Figure 8-2. Socioeconomic Status and the Overall Participation Scale

population is in the direction of upper-status citizens. Among the most active citizens, 57 percent come from the top third of the status hierarchy and only 14 percent come from the lower third. At the other end of the activity continuum we find that among the least active citizens only 10 percent come from the upper-status group, but 59 percent come from the lower. This figure, of course, merely tells us what was clear in Chapter 6 when we described the social composition of our various types of activists. But it is worth repeating that finding here in relation to our new standardized scale of participation. It also shows quite descriptively that a relationship that looks moderate from some perspectives (the correlation between our SES and participation scales is, after all, only .37) is in fact a quite striking one from the point of view of what it implies about the composition of a population.

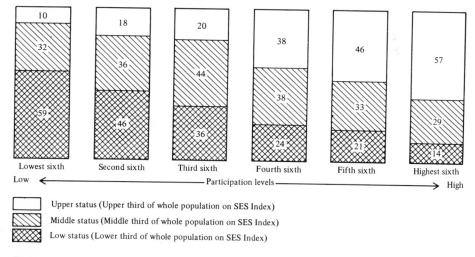

Figure 8-3. Status Composition at Varying Levels of Participation (Numbers on bars refer to the percentage of each participation group coming from a particular socioeconomic status group.)

We can now turn to the separate modes of participation to see how they relate to status. Here we notice some differences (Figure 8-4). Campaign activity, communal activity, and voting are quite strongly associated with socioeconomic status: r's of .30, .33, and .27 respectively. Particularized contacting, however, offers a sharp contrast with the other modes of participation. There is little relationship between socioeconomic status and particularized contact (r .07). At the extremes one finds a difference. Those in the lowest socioeconomic category are least likely to contact government officials on a particularized problem and those in the upper category most likely. But the predominant pattern is one of relatively little relationship between this mode of activity and socioeconomic status.

The data thus conform with the data of others in indicating that those of higher status participate more. But our refinement of the measure of participation indicates that there are differences in the extent to which this generalization applies to the alternative modes of participation. It applies most strongly and clearly to the two modes of activity that are oriented toward general problems and that represent a higher level of difficulty—campaigning and communal activity. It applies a little less strongly to voting, and hardly at all to particularized contacting.

The United States is often contrasted with other countries as being a society where class and status matter relatively little in political life. But in regard to

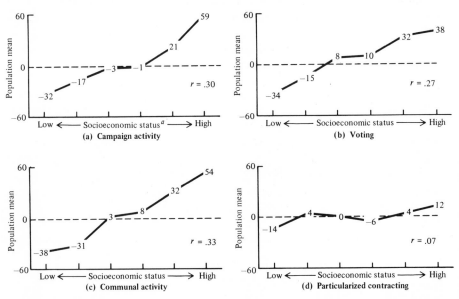

Figure 8-4. Mean Participation Rates of Six Status Groups on the Standard Participation Scales

the relationship between social status and political participation, the United States clearly has a class-biased pattern. Indeed, as we shall show in our concluding chapter, the U.S. pattern shows more class bias than almost all other countries for which comparable data exist.

THE PROCESS OF POLITICIZATION

What is it that links higher socioeconomic status with political participation? As indicated, many connective links have been suggested. Some depend on the social environment of upper-status citizens: They are more likely to be members of organizations, and they are more likely to be surrounded by others who are participating. Some connecting links depend on the availability of resources and skills: Upper-status citizens have the time, the money, and the knowledge to be effective in politics. Other connecting links depend on the psychological characteristics of upper-status citizens: They are more likely to be concerned with general political problems, and they are more likely to feel efficacious.

It is likely that all these intervening characteristics play some role in connecting social status with participation, but we would like to postpone for a while our consideration of some of these characteristics—in particular the role played by organizational affiliation and the nature of the social environment in which citizens of different social statuses live—because they deserve closer analysis. Here we want to present the intervening components of the simple "base-line" model that we already set forth—the general set of civic orientations that have been found to accompany higher social status and that in turn are associated with political participation.

The civic orientations are those that were found in Chapter 5 to characterize the highly participant: psychological involvement in politics (measured by a variety of items dealing with expressed interest in and attention to political matters), a sense of political efficacy, information about politics, and a sense of contribution to the community. These four orientations differ somewhat, but can be considered a single set of civic orientations.[7] They have no policy or partisan content, but rather measure the extent to which the citizen is involved in politics, feels competent to act politically, has a sense of community responsibility, and has the information needed for political activity.

In Figure 8-5 we present a simple path model of the relationship between socioeconomic status and our overall activity score as mediated through the civic orientations. The coefficient on the line between socioeconomic status and the civic orientations is the path coefficient (equivalent in this case to a simple r) between SES and the orientations. The coefficient on the line from the civic orientations to the measure of overall activity is the path coefficient after the

---

[7] The four civic-orientation scales used in Chapter 5 were subjected to a factor analysis and then combined on the basis of their loadings on the first principal components. Each of the four orientations has a loading of .5 or higher on the first principal component and they provide us with a very nice summary index of general civic-orientations for the purposes of this rather simple analysis.

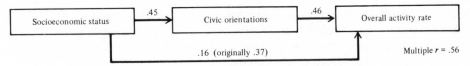

Figure 8-5. The Process of Politicization: Overall Activity Rate

effect of socioeconomic status has been removed. The coefficient on the line from SES directly to activity is the direct (residual) effect of SES on activity that remains after the indirect effect via the orientations has been removed. And we add, on the line between SES and activity, the original direct relationship of SES and activity before the intervening effects of the civic attitudes have been removed.[8]

Socioeconomic status relates strongly to the civic orientations (.45), and the link between the latter and activity is similarly strong (.46). It is clear that civic orientations play a major role in connecting socioeconomic status with political activity. The original relationship of socioeconomic status to the overall scale of participation was .37. It is much reduced—to .16—when one removes the influence on participation that is mediated by civic orientations. In other words, the data are fairly consistent with a model whereby higher socioeconomic status increases political participation by increasing the civic orientations—involvement, efficacy, skills—of citizens.

This model obviously needs and deserves further elaboration. Above all, one would want to look more closely at the differences among the various orientations we have used as well as differences in the role of the various components of our index of socioeconomic status. We shall do neither here, for neither is necessary for our argument. The several orientations play somewhat different roles (as, for instance, we show in Chapter 5), and a full understanding of the psychological roots of activity would require that we distinguish among them. For our purpose it is sufficient that the set of orientations lead generally to political activity.[9]

Similarly, one could disentangle the role of education, occupation, and income. Such analysis would be fruitful, but once again, for our purposes what counts is that citizens of upper status—using any of these measures or all combined—participate more than do those of lower status. We are interested in what other social forces increase or decrease this participation disparity between upper- and lower-status citizens as well as the consequences of this.

[8] For further discussions of path analysis, see Otis Dudley Duncan, "Contingencies in Constructing Causal Models," in Edgar F. Borgatta (ed.), *Sociological Methodology* (San Francisco: Jossey-Bass, 1969), pp. 74-112; Duncan, "Path Analysis: Sociological Examples," *American Journal of Sociology*, vol. 72 (July 1966), pp. 1-16; Kenneth C. Land, "Principles of Path Analysis," in Borgatta (ed.), *Sociological Methodology*, pp. 3-37; and Jae-on Kim, "Path Analysis and Causal Interpretation in Survey Analysis," 1971, unpublished manuscript. The line between socioeconomic status and civic-orientation is the simple *r* between the two measures. All other numbers in the figures are path coefficients except for the original simple *r* between SES and activity, which is parenthesized.

[9] For examples of differentiation among such orientations see Nie, Powell, and Prewitt, "Social Structure and Political Participation," and Verba, Nie, and Kim, *The Modes of Democratic Participation: A Cross-National Comparison.*

For that purpose, the simple model forms a most useful beginning.

Figure 8-6 presents similar path models for the four modes of participation. In each case the relationship between socioeconomic status and the civic orientations remain identical because the same variables are involved and they are entered first into the model. For campaign and communal activity, the total pattern is almost identical to that for overall activity. The path to participation that runs from socioeconomic status through civic orientations is a strong one. In each case the originally rather strong direct relationship between socioeconomic status and activity is greatly reduced when one removes the effects on activity that are mediated by the civic orientations. The pattern for voting is similar, although the relationship of the orientations to voting is somewhat less, as is the multiple r for socioeconomic status and the orientations. But for particularized contact we see a contrast. The standard socioeconomic model does not explain why citizens engage in these activities, a finding consistent with our earlier findings that these are activities carried out by citizens from across the socioeconomic spectrum and that they are not dependent on a more general psychological involvement in politics. Not only does particularized contacting produce different benefits, it derives from a process quite different from the one that leads to other activities.

In short, the standard socioeconomic model works very well for our overall measure of activity and for campaign and communal activity. It works less

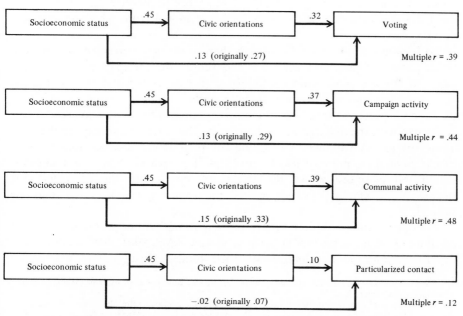

Figure 8-6. The Process of Politicization: The Several Modes

well—but quite well nevertheless—for voting.[10] It does not work for particularized contacting. The last obvious point: Though the model fits the data, the
combination of socioeconomic status and the intervening attitudes by no
means explains all the variance in participation. Other factors may be
operating.

THE STANDARD SES MODEL AS A BASE LINE

Our purpose in the rest of this section is to look at a variety of other factors
that affect the rate of participation of citizens: position in the life cycle, race,
membership in voluntary associations and political parties, and the nature of
the community. These alternative factors can be thought of as modifying the
working of the standard socioeconomic model. Some of the factors may
"accelerate" the workings of the model. By this we mean that they lead to an
even greater disparity in participation between upper- and lower-status
citizens than would exist if only our "standard" model were operating. Others
may modify the working of the model by diminishing the participation
distance between the various social levels.

We shall be interested in seeing the impact of each factor on participation
over and above the socioeconomic characteristics of the individual. If we are
to understand the relationship of race, or organizations, or place of residence
to participation, we shall have to correct or control for the confounding effects
of socioeconomic status. This is so because blacks differ systematically from
whites in socioeconomic status as do organizational members from nonmembers and residents of one community from those in another. In this sense we
use the socioeconomic model as a base-line model from which to consider
deviations.

To facilitate this, we shall introduce here some new corrected measures of
participation. These measures are the scores on the participation scales
adjusted for the score one would expect for an individual of a particular
socioeconomic status. The uncorrected standard scale of participation allows
us to compare, for instance, the participation rate of the average black
American with the average white American. The corrected version of the scale
allows us to ask whether, controlling for their lower socioeconomic status,
blacks participate more or less than whites. The answer to the latter question
would tell us more about the effects of race. Both the corrected and
uncorrected scales are useful, and in the following chapters we shall use
both.[11]

In establishing a base-line rate of participation that one would expect from
an individual at a particular socioeconomic level, and then dealing with
deviations from the base line, we do not assume a causal priortiy priority for

---

[10] We shall see why the standard SES model works less well for voting when we examine the impact of party
attachments in Chapter 12.

[11] We will employ this corrected measure of participation controlling for the effects of social class
throughout the book. Appendix B.3 explains how this measure was built and Appendix G.2 describes some of
the general methodological issues involved in the type of correction method we utilize.

social class over other social characteristics. Rather we are dealing with a complex of forces that operate simultaneously. Our explication of the socioeconomic forces first, followed by the introduction of others, is a useful way of obtaining some order out of a complicated reality. And because the socioeconomic forces are powerful ones, because they may confound relations of other variables to participation, and because the extent to which they operate to bring citizens to participate affects the composition of the participant population, the strategy of considering deviations from that base line should prove useful.

Chapter 9
Participation
and the Life Cycle

We can begin our consideration of other factors—beyond those we specified in the standard socioeconomic model—by considering the way participation is affected by the stage of life of the citizen. Most studies of political participation have found a distinctive curve of participation associated with age or, as we prefer to consider it, position in the life cycle. In the early years after a citizen reaches voting age, participation rates are generally low. Then they rise during the middle years and decline in later years.[1] Our data display a similar pattern, as seen in Figure 9-1. We present there the scores of various age groups on our overall scale of participation and our scale for voting. The pattern of increase from the twenties to the forties followed by a decline is clearly in evidence.[2]

---

[1] See Milbrath, *Political Participation*, pp. 134-135, for citations for this finding.

[2] The data for campaign and communal participation form a pattern almost identical to that for overall participation. In order to ease presentation, we can use the overall measure as a surrogate for both these modes of participation in this chapter. Particularized contacting, on the other hand, does not vary in frequency across the life cycle. Citizens of all ages are equally likely to engage in such activities, a situation consistent with the contingent and narrow nature of the problems associated with such contacting—problems that can appear at

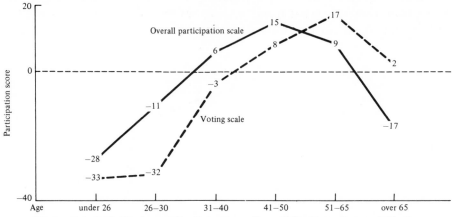

Figure 9-1. Life Cycle and Participation: Overall Participation and Voting

The usual explanation for this pattern is based on what we might call the problems of "start-up" and "slow-down." In the early years one has the problem of "start-up." Individuals are still unsettled; they are likely to be residentially and occupationally mobile. They have yet to develop the stake in the politics of a particular locality that comes with extended residence, with home ownership, with children in school, and the like. In addition, they face the specific legal obstacles to voting associated with short residence. In later years, the problem is one of "slow-down." Old age brings with it sociological withdrawal as individuals retire from active employment. And it brings as well physical infirmities and fatigue that lower the rate of political activity. And at both ends of the life cycle, a psychological factor enters this "start-up/slow-down" explanation. Early in life, interest and involvement in politics are lower in part because exposure to political life has not existed for long and in part because the initiation of many aspects of one's life—starting an occupation, a family—it is the dominant concern. And in later life, interest and involvement in politics fall off as a concomitant of aging.

The Problem of Slow-down

The explanation of the rise and fall in participation rates through the life cycle is certainly plausible. But our consideration of the role of socioeconomic factors in participation suggests some caution. Consider the data in Figure 9-2. There we present the proportion of respondents in the upper half of our socioeconomic status scale among the several age groups. The pattern is

---

any point in the life cycle, including old age. We shall present the data on voting rates separately in this chapter. Voting displays a pattern similar to campaign and communal activity. But much of the evidence for the cycle of participation comes from voting studies, and the voting data we shall present form an interesting contrast with these earlier findings.

remarkably like that found for participation. The proportion in the upper half of the scale rises somewhat from the twenties through the forties, and then declines, falling off particularly sharply after age sixty-five.

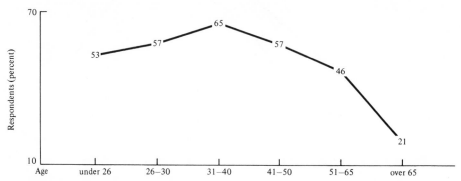

Figure 9-2. Percentage of Respondents in Upper Half of SES Scale at Different Age Levels

Figure 9-2 ought not to be taken to imply that socioeconomic status fluctuates. Status is more stable than that. Rather, what it reflects are two types of variation with age in the components of socioeconomic status. One is the variation in income that accompanies passage through the life cycle: Income rises in the earlier years, peaks in the middle years, and declines when citizens retire. The second reason for the variation of status with age has to do with changes in the distribution of educational attainments over time, with the older citizens being, on the average, less educated. Does this association of age with education and income help explain the rise and fall of participation through the life-cycle?

To test for this possibility, we can use our corrected measure of political participation because this measure will correct for differences in these status variables as we move across the age categories. These data are presented in Figure 9-3. There we see the participation scores at various age levels adjusted for the differences in the status composition of each age group. (In our analysis we shall usually "correct" for three status variables—income, education, and occupation. For the age analysis we do not correct for occupation, because of ambiguity in occupational status among the youngest and oldest groups due to part-time jobs, first jobs, and retirement.) In Figure 9-3(a) we present the data on overall participation and in 9-3(b) on voting—in each instance repeating the uncorrected data from Figure 9-1 for comparison.

Because we will be using this mode of data presentation often, it may be useful to digress a bit to explicate what Figure 9-3 shows. The figures plotted

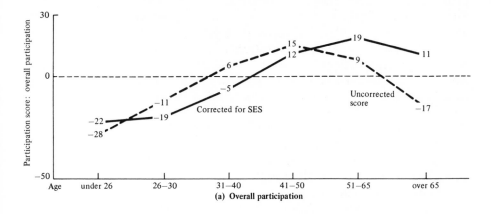

(a) Overall participation

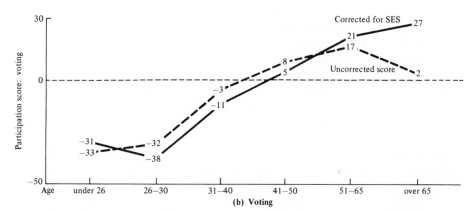

(b) Voting

Figure 9-3. Life Cycle and Participation: Corrected for Socioeconomic Status

on the dotted line are the actual participation scores for each age group. On the solid line we plot the "corrected" score.[3] This is the participation score of the group after one has removed all linear differences in participation stemming from an individual's educational attainment and income. With this corrected measure we can see the relationship between age and participation without the effects of the status differences among the age groups.

Three types of information can be derived from a figure such as Figure 9-3:

1. One can consider the shape of the relationship between the independent

---

[3] For details on how we correct, see Appendix G. For the specific corrected participation scale, see Appendix B.2.

variable (in this case, age) and participation before and after the correction. The uncorrected data show the actual relationship between the independent and dependent variables; the corrected data indicate the relationship when status differences are held constant. If there were no independent relationship between age and participation (independent of the status variables for which we are correcting), the corrected line would be flat. In short, all age groups would have a score of zero on our standardized measure, and there would be no difference in participation across the age groups over and above what results from differences in socioeconomic levels. We see from the data in Figure 9-3(a) that there is a tendency for the line to flatten, indicating that *some* of the difference among age groups derives from differences in socioeconomic status. But the line does not flatten completely, indicating that there remain age-related effects.

2. One can examine shifts in particular groups. Does a particular group's participation score go up or down when one corrects for some other variable such as socioeconomic status? If the score goes up (relative to the uncorrected measure), it means that one reason the group's participation is low derives from socioeconomic status. Correct for that, and the group participation score goes up. An example is seen in Figure 9-3(a) for the oldest age group. Their participation score rises from —17 to 11, indicating that their original low score was due in part to their status characteristics, not to their age. If a group's score goes down when one corrects for socioeconomic status, it means that one of the reasons it was participating as *much* as it was on the uncorrected score was its socioeconomic status.

3. One can compare groups with each other (or with the population as a whole) on the uncorrected and on the corrected scores. If, on the uncorrected score, one group scores higher than another, it simply means that it participates more. If it scores higher than the population mean (which is standardized at zero) it indicates that it participates more than the average citizen. Because the population mean is always set at zero on our standard participation scales, one can easily interpret positive and negative scores; the former indicating a group that is more active than average, the latter a group that is less active than average. An example is the youngest age group, with its uncorrected score of —28, indicating that it is less active than average.

The interpretation of differences in the corrected scores is analogous. If a group participates more than another on a corrected score, it means it is more active than the other group, over and above any differences between them due to socioeconomic status. If a group participates more than the population mean on the corrected score, it indicates that that group is more active than average even after one has taken into account its socioeconomic level. As an example, consider the youngest age group again. Their score of —22 on the corrected participation scale means that they participate less than one would have predicted given their income and education. They can be considered "underparticipators."

To return to our substantive question: To what degree are differences in participation across age groups a reflection of differences among them in status characteristics? Compare the corrected and uncorrected scores in Figure 9-3. When we use the corrected scores, the decline in participation found in the older group almost disappears on the overall participation measure [Figure 9-3(a)] and it disappears completely for voting participation [Figure 9-3(b)]. On the left side of the curve, however, the upward slope reflecting the increase from the twenties and thirties to the forties remains.

The data suggest that the lower level of political participation found among older citizens may not reflect a slowing down associated with aging. Rather they suggest that older people simply have, on the average, lower levels of education and income and their lower rates of activity result from that fact. But the data do not yet dispose of the slow-down explanation for declining participation rates in later years because the lower average socioeconomic status found among older people may derive from two different sources. On the one hand, the older respondents in our sample were raised in an earlier era, when education was less available, when occupational statuses tended to be lower, and when, concomitantly, incomes were lower. They are from a poorer and less well-trained generation. If their lower participation rate simply reflects this difference, then the elimination of the downturn in participation that is found when we control for socioeconomic status represents the removal of a spurious effect. We have found that slow-down does not take place.

On the other hand, part of the socioeconomic status measure does not remain fully fixed throughout an individual's life. Specifically, income often declines sharply as citizens age and retire. Insofar as the decline in participation during the later years results from this changeable component of socioeconomic status, our analysis represents less a refutation of the slow-down explanation than an explication of the reason for the slow-down.

This point is crucial in understanding how aging relates to participation. If the lower level of participation found among older people derives from the fact that they are of a generation that has always had, on the average, sociological characteristics that would put them lower on our status scale, this means that our data imply no decline in participation. And there is no need for a slow-down explanation. The lower rate of participation among older people is what one would expect at any stage of the life cycle from a group with that distribution of status characteristics and we can assume that the older citizens participated at low levels throughout their lives. If, on the other hand, the lower participation rate derives directly from a drop in these status characteristics that comes with aging, it suggests that we are indeed observing a decline in participation with age.

Fortunately, we can distinguish between the two situations. Our measure of socioeconomic status used on Figure 9-3 has two components—income and education. The former, as we pointed out, can fluctuate with age. Citizens' incomes usually decline, but an individual's educational attainment is usually fixed early in life and does not fall off in later years. Consider then the life-cycle curves of measures of participation corrected separately for the educational status of the respondent and for income rather than for those two together. Figure 9-4(a) reports data for overall participation; Figure 9-4(b) for voting. To make the situation clearer we have added to Figures 9-4(a) and 9-4(b) the data on the uncorrected participation scores (from Figure 9-1), but have entered the data only for the three oldest groups. As can be seen, correcting for income alone straightens the participation line for voting in relation to older citizens; there is no drop-off, and it reduces the drop-off for overall participation. Correcting for education alone leaves a downturn in both overall and voting participation rates among the older group. But here as well the downturn is much less than in the uncorrected data.

The data suggest that there is some validity to each of the explanations of why correcting for socioeconomic status reduces the downturn in participation

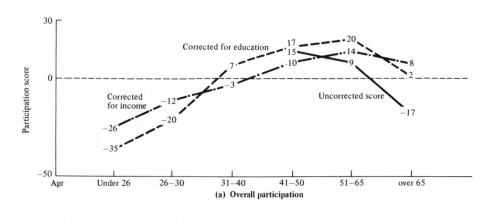

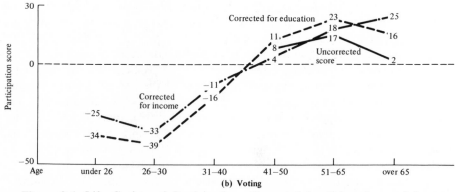

Figure 9-4. Life Cycle and Participation: Corrected for Education and Income Separately

in later years. The fact that correcting for income straightens the line more than does correcting for education, suggests that one reason for the decline in participation is that it accompanies a decline in economic circumstances. But the income measure may also reflect the generally lower status that those older members of our sample have always had, because they come from an earlier generation. Education, on the other hand, reflects only the latter characteristic: the lower status associated with the generation of the older citizens. Though a correction for education does not reduce the downturn as much, it does reduce it considerably for overall participation, while for voting it almost disappears. And insofar as a correction for education reduces that downturn, it suggests that what has appeared to be a slow-down in participation really reflects the different distribution of status characteristics at different age levels.

In short, the data support the conclusion that there is indeed a genuine slow-down in later years. But the slow-down has been exaggerated by failure to consider the relationship of age to the educational composition of the populace. And for voting—as the correction for education alone makes clear—there is hardly any genuine slow-down at all.

The Problem of Start-up

We have shown that, correcting for socioeconomic status, there is evidence for less of a slow-down in participation late in life than has been suggested. But even after such correction, there remains evidence for an increase in participation when one compares those in their twenties with those in their thirties and forties. Suppose, however, we create a new measure of participation from which we have removed the effect of a characteristic associated with the phenomenon of start-up—length of residence in the community. Citizens who have lived for a shorter time in the community are, in general, less politically active. This has several sources: Voting is limited by residence requirements; new residents may not have established a stake in the community. They may not have developed the affiliational and interpersonal resources for participation, and they have other demands on their time. All this characterizes younger citizens and could account for their lower participation rate.[4] Removing these effects should, if the start-up explanations have validity, raise the level of participation of younger citizens to levels more comparable to those of older ones.

[4] Comparing the various age groups, we find, as expected, that younger citizens are more likely to be short-term residents in the community.

	Age					
	Under 26	26-30	31-40	41-50	51-65	66+
Proportion living less than 3 years in community	45%	36%	24%	15%	8%	10%

In Figures 9-5(a) and 9-5(b) we compare the uncorrected participation data with the data for a measure of participation corrected for the length of residence of the individual in the community. In Figure 9-5(a) we do this for overall participation and in 9-5(b) for voting. In each case we also reproduce the uncorrected scores for the youngest three age groups. For both the overall measure of participation and for voting, adding a correction for the start-up characteristic of residence length raises the participation level of the younger citizens. But there still remains an increase in overall participation in the early years, and, for voting, a decline followed by an increase.

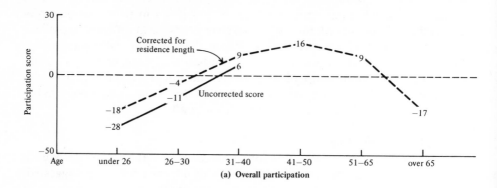

(a) Overall participation

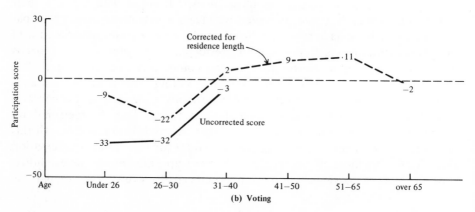

(b) Voting

Figure 9-5. Life Cycle and Participation: Corrected for Length of Residence in Community

Thus, by correcting our measure of participation for socioeconomic status or for residence length, we greatly change the shape of the curve of participation across the life cycle. Just as correcting for socioeconomic status eliminates a good deal of the downturn apparent in later life, correcting for the start-up characteristic of residence length reduces the difference between the youngest age groups and the somewhat older ones. At neither end of the age distribution is the lower level of activity completely removed, but it is reduced considerably.

But it ought to be made clear that our ability to "straighten the line" of participation in later years by correcting for socioeconomic status and our ability to do the same for the early years by correcting for start-up characteristics have different interpretations. In the former case, we believe that correcting for socioeconomic status—especially when we do it for a status characteristic like education, which does not change over time—involves eliminating a spurious relationship between age and participation. We have shown that participation declines less than previously thought. In the latter case, where we correct for start-up characteristics—characteristics that do change during the life cycle as residence length grows and younger people obtain active employment—we have explicated why there is a slow start-up into politics rather than demonstrating that the slow start is unreal.

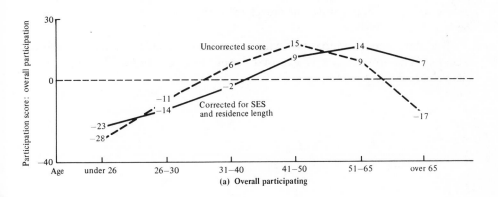

(a) Overall participating

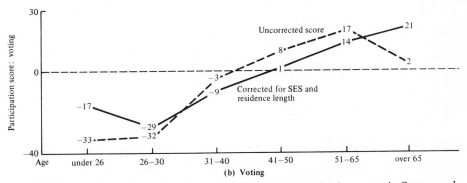

(b) Voting

Figure 9-6. Life Cycle and Participation: Corrected for Socioeconomic Status and Residence Length

SUMMARY

The overall result of our data manipulations can be seen in Figure 9-6. There we compare the original shape of the relationship between age and participation—for overall participation and for voting—with the shape that emerges after we correct for both socioeconomic status (education and income) and length of residence in the community. What was originally a pattern of steady increase throughout the life cycle followed by a sharp decline in later years becomes a somewhat more gradual increase in participation throughout the life cycle. For overall participation there is a decline in activity rate for those citizens over sixty-six, but a relatively minor decline compared with the original data. And for voting, there is no decline even among the oldest group. (There is, however, a slight decline in voting rate between the youngest age group and the next—for reasons that are obscure to us.)

We can look at the data another way. Before we correct for the confounding effects of residence length and socioeconomic status, we see that the peak decade for overall political activity comes when the citizen is in his forties. After correcting for these, we find that the peak decade is in the fifties. For voting, the peak activity period moves from the fifties and early sixties to the period after sixty-six.

The data seem compatible with a gradual learning model of political activity. The longer one is exposed to politics, the more likely one is to participate.[5]

---

[5] We had expected differences between men and women in the way the life-cycle interacts with political participation rates. But when the same type of analysis was conducted for men and women separately, no such difference was found.

Chapter 10
Blacks, Whites, and Participation

One cannot consider participation in American politics without considering the problem from the point of view of the difference between blacks and whites. If political participation is, as we have argued, the major mechanism by which citizens in a society express their wishes and place demands on the government, the relationship of this mechanism to one of the major social cleavages should be crucial indeed. It is particularly crucial because of the importance of political participation to deprived groups. There are many ways deprived groups can seek to overcome that deprivation. They may strive as individuals to advance, or they may work as a group. They may seek advancement through social and economic channels, or they may pursue political and governmental paths to advancement. Insofar as they take the political or governmental path, they are more likely to be effective if they act as a group rather than as individuals—that is, an individual may move ahead in the economy under the proper circumstances, but numbers and organization are more important for advancement through political mechanisms. The use of the political path, the attempt to achieve advancement through pressures on government for beneficial decisions that then facilitate economic and social advance, represents a major way the racial differences in the society may be overcome. How black Americans use that path is the subject of this chapter.

The consideration of racial differences in participation is also important from the point of view of our general model of political participation. In the first place, it allows us to look more closely at the role of participation as an instrument used by individuals and groups to obtain governmental benefits. Such benefits are, of course, most needed by groups living under conditions of severe deprivation. Second, it will allow us to test some of the differences that we have suggested exist among the various modes of participation. Certain modes of participation may be more useful or more easily available to severely deprived groups than others. And last, it allows us to consider again the workings of the standard socioeconomic model as well as the forces that lead to deviation from it.

Consider the question of the instrumental use of political participation by deprived groups. The issue has to do with the relationship between political participation and social and economic equality. Through political participation, deprived groups can obtain beneficial governmental output—welfare legislation, antidiscrimination legislation, specific allocations—that may, over time, make them equal in social and economic ways. For this to happen though, the political system has to be more open to such groups than the economic and the social systems. The deprived group uses its access to politics as a way of opening social and economic channels of advancement. However, there is one thing wrong with this approach to overcoming deprivation: those social and economic deprivations—lower levels of education, lower status occupations, inadequate income—that political participation is supposed to be used to overcome impede political participation. As Chapter 8 made clear, political participation is predominantly the activity of the wealthier, better educated citizens with higher-status occupations. Those who need the beneficial outcomes of participation the least—who are already advantaged in social and economic terms—participate the most.

If a deprived group is to use political participation to its advantage, it must participate in politics more than one would ordinarily expect, given its level of education, income, or occupation. It must somehow bypass the processes that lead those with higher social status to participate more and those with lower status to participate less—the processes summarized in our standard socioeconomic model. There are a variety of ways of bypassing this process, but the one we are most interested in, in relation to American blacks, is the development of self-conscious awareness of one's group membership. The growth of this self-awareness among black Americans was one of the leading changes in American politics in the 1950s and 1960s.[1] Its significance is that

---

[1] See Joel D. Aberbach and Jack L. Walker, "The Meanings of Black Power: A Comparison of White and Black Interpretations of a Political Slogan," *American Political Science Review*, vol. 64 (June 1970), pp. 367-389. "Black power," they point out, is most likely to mean "racial unity" or a "fair share for Blacks," not "Black rule over Whites" as whites most frequently believe. For other data on a rising sense of self-awareness among American blacks, see William J. Brink and Louis Harris, *Black and White: A Study of U.S. Racial Attitudes Today* (New York: Simon and Schuster, 1967); and Gary Marx, *Protest and Prejudice: A Study of Belief in the Black Community* (New York: Harper & Row, 1967).

such group consciousness may substitute for the higher social status that impels citizens into political participation. It may represent an alternative mechanism for mobilizing citizens to political activity.

If the group-consciousness mechanism of mobilization to political activity is operating, one would expect that members of such a group would participate more than one would predict on the basis of their social and economic characteristics; that such participation would be most pronounced among those who were most aware of their deprived status; and that, within the deprived group, such general status characteristics as education would have less of an impact on participation than they have among the more advantaged white group.[2]

To begin with, though, we can state our problem in more concrete terms by looking simply at the differences between blacks and whites in terms of their proportional representation among the various types of participators in the typology. This is reported in Table 10-1. (These data also appeared in Chapter 6.) The most severe difference is in the inactivist category, where blacks have an overrepresentation score of $+21$. Black overrepresentation in the inactivist category contrasts with their underrepresentation among the parochial participators and the communalists. They are more or less proportionally represented in the categories associated with elections—among the voters and the campaign activists. One of the interesting facets of the pattern of participation among blacks is that although they are severely *overrepresented* among the inactives, they are not severely *underrepresented* among the complete activists. There is an asymmetry in their level of activity. Many more blacks fall in the inactive category than one would expect from their percentage in the population as a whole, but among the complete activists they are represented fairly proportionately. Blacks, Table 10-1 suggests, participate less than whites, but not substantially less. And they participate roughly equally with whites in the electoral process. Last, when they participate they can be quite active. These points are substantially correct but will require some important modification as we look more closely at black-white differences in participation. To that task we now turn.

SOCIOECONOMIC STATUS, RACE, AND PARTICIPATION

Can black Americans use participatory mechanisms as a means of overcoming their deprived status in social and economic terms? To answer the question one has to look at the relationship among three characteristics: race, socioeconomic status, and rates of political participation. The relationship is a complicated one, not only statistically but substantively. The problem is complex because of the number of ways these three characteristics relate to our problem. Socioeconomic status is, in some sense, the key characteristic. It is, of course, closely related to race. Blacks in American society are likely to

---

[2] For an elaboration of this model as well as several other models of the process of mobilization to political participation, see Sidney Verba, Bashiruddhin Ahmed, and Anil Bhatt, *Caste, Race, and Politics: A Comparative Study of India and the United States* (Beverly Hills, Calif.: Sage Publications, 1971). This work compares the political activity of American blacks with that of Harijans (untouchables) in India. Data confirming this model appear in that publication as well as in Marvin E. Olsen, "Social and Political Participation of Blacks," *American Sociological Review*, vol. 35 (August 1970), pp. 682-697.

Table 10-1

Political Actor Typology by Race

	Over- or underrepresentation of blacks in the participation types
Inactive	+.21
Voting specialist	+.05
Parochial participant	−.19
Communalist	−.24
Partisan	+.03
Complete activist	−.06

(For the measure of over- and underrepresentation, see p. 96, footnote 1.)

be in lower-status jobs than whites, to have less education, and to have lower incomes. These characteristics, in turn, inhibit the rate of political activity of citizens. On the other hand, it is the redress of the deprivation in social and economic terms that is likely to be the goal of black participation. We can handle the problem best by looking at it in several different ways: first by comparing the relationship of race to socioeconomic stratification with the relationship of race to political stratification, and second by looking at the relationship among all three sets of characteristics.

If a deprived group such as the American blacks is to use the political system to redress deprivation in the socioeconomic system, the former system must be more "open" than the latter. They must achieve political equality on the road to socioeconomic equality. There are a number of reasons why one would expect that opportunities for political participation would be more open than opportunities for jobs, income, or education. Equalitarian values are probably more generally held in relation to politics than in relation to other areas, and such values are more easily enforced in the political than in the social and economic arenas. Furthermore, the advantages the deprived groups have in terms of numbers and potential organization are particularly relevant in politics.

But is access to political participation in fact more equal than access to social or economic benefits? Such a question allows no precise answer. One of the reasons is that one is comparing different hierarchies measured by different variables. How many dollars of income is a vote worth? Votes or other acts of participation are opportunities to acquire other benefits, but how much they bring is uncertain. Nevertheless, because our concern is for the relative position of the deprived and the dominant groups, we can offer an answer to the question asked in a relative way. We cannot ask whether blacks are better off in the political arena than in the economic—that would require comparing votes with dollars. But we can ask whether the difference between blacks and whites is greater in one arena than in another. Specifically, we can ask whether the *degree of association* between racial status and economic status is greater than that between racial status and political participation.

To compare the socioeconomic and the political spheres, we can use the standardized scales of socioeconomic status and of political participation that we have used in various analyses so far. Though there are complex measurement difficulties, each scale gives a fairly good indication of whether one individual receives more of the social and economic benefits of the society than another, and whether one individual participates more in the political life of his society than another. Our hypothesis is that there is greater association between race and socioeconomic status than between race and political participation. In Figure 10-1(a) and 10-1(b) we divide the population into six equal parts based on position within the socioeconomic hierarchy or the political-participation hierarchy. The division is arbitrary—we do not argue that society has six socioeconomic or political classes—but it is most useful in comparing the ranking of groups. If a group is over- or underrepresented in the upper sixth of either scale we know something about its hierarchial position. More important, the division into equal groups opens the possibility of comparing between the two hierarchial scales.

Having divided the entire population into six equal size levels on a socioeconomic scale [Figure 10-1(a)] and into six equal levels on a political participation scale [Figure 10-1(b)], we divide each of these levels in turn into the proportions of blacks and whites who fall in each level. These divisions allow us to estimate the degree to which either of the hierarchies is skewed in such a way so that blacks are overrepresented at the low levels. More important, they allow us to compare the degree of inequality across the two hierarchies. Blacks form about 11 percent of our sample. If they are equally represented at all levels of the socioeconomic hierarchy, one would expect them to form about 11 percent of each level of that hierarchy. But they are 36 percent of the lowest socioeconomic level of the American society, and as we go up the socioeconomic scale the representation of the blacks decreases. Thus only 2 percent of the highest level—that is, the top sixth of the population in terms of receipt of the benefits of society—is black, rather than the 11 percent we would find if there were equality.

If we consider Figure 10-1(b), which presents the distribution of blacks and whites on the various levels of the participation scale, we also see a clear pattern of deprivation. Blacks are more likely to fall in the lowest participation categories than one would expect, given their proportion in the society. If they were equally represented in participation, they would represent 11 percent of each level of the scale. In fact, they are 16 percent of the two bottom categories. However, on the upper levels they are fairly equally represented.

The comparison across the two hierarchies is what is important. The distribution in relation to participation is quite a bit less skewed in favor of whites than is the distribution in relation to socioeconomic benefits. If one compares Figures 10-1(a) and 10-1(b), one sees that blacks are much more underrepresented in the top sixth of the socioeconomic scale than in the top sixth of the participation scale. Equal representation would have 11 percent of them in the top category on each scale; in fact, they form 11 percent of the

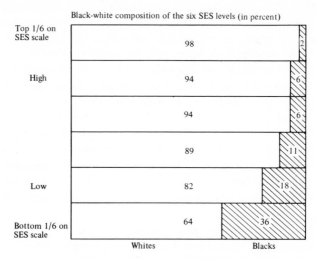

(a) Family socioeconomic status (SES) scale: Proportion of blacks and whites at each level (r between SES and race = .29)

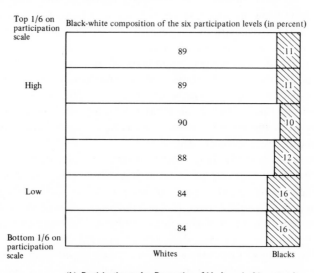

(b) Participation scale: Proportion of blacks and whites at each level (r between participation and race = .05)

Figure 10-1. Representation of Blacks and Whites on Socioeconomic and Political Participation Hierarchies

top category on the participation scale, and only 2 percent of that category on the socioeconomic scale. Switching to the bottom of the scale, we find that the lowest sixth of participation contains 16 percent blacks, whereas the lowest sixth on socioeconomic benefits contains 36 percent blacks (compared with the 11 percent one would come to expect in each case). The greater disparity between the races on the socioeconomic scale is also demonstrated by comparing the measures of association for Figures 10-1(a) and 10-1(b). We see that the correlation between race and the socioeconomic scale is .29, whereas the correlation between race and the participation scale is .05.

One further point should be noted in comparing the two distributions: On the socioeconomic scale, blacks are as underrepresented at the top as they are overrepresented at the bottom. The participation scale presents a less symmetrical pattern. Blacks are more likely to be overrepresented in the most inactive group than they are to be underrepresented in the most active group. On the highest level of activity, blacks produce as many activists as one would expect, given their proportion of the population. This suggests that when blacks break through the barrier that separates the totally inactive from those who engage in at least some activity, they are likely to move to quite high levels of such activity.[3]

On the basis of these data, can one say that the political system is more open for blacks than is the socioeconomic system? Our answer is yes, but one must be cautious in interpreting this. It is legitimate to compare the scales of participation and of socioeconomic benefits. Insofar as we think of the comparison as one between similar positions on different hierarchies, we are not comparing incomparables. When one considers that proportion of the population that receives the most of the social and economic benefits of the society, one finds disproportionately few blacks. When one considers a similar size group that participates most frequently in political life, one finds a number of blacks proportionate to their numbers in society.

On the other hand, the comparison across the socioeconomic and the political status systems is difficult. The socioeconomic variables along which we array blacks and whites represent "payoffs": income, possessions, education, a high-status job. Participation is also a payoff in and of itself, insofar as it is valued as a token of social worth and full membership in the society. But insofar as it represents access to channels of influence that may eventuate in other payoffs, other things must be taken into account. If an individual has an economic benefit, he has it no matter what others do. But if participation is to lead to such benefits, what others do is important. The responsiveness of the government is crucial and the level of participation of one's fellow citizens is important too.

When we consider the types of political activity we shall see that the relative equality in raw amount of political activity does not necessarily imply equality in the benefits received from such activity. Nevertheless, the data do clearly

[3] Matthews and Prothro report a similar finding. See Donald R. Matthews and James W. Prothro, *Negroes and the New Southern Politics* (New York: Harcourt, 1966).

suggest that opportunities for political participation are more equally distributed between the races than are social or economic benefits.[4]

Thus far we have considered the relationships between race and economic stratification on the one hand and race and political stratification on the other. But if we are to understand the relation among all three characteristics—race, socioeconomic position, and participation—we must consider all three simultaneously. Blacks, as Table 10-1 told us, participate less than whites, though the difference is not striking. And as Chapter 8 indicated, citizens of lower socioeconomic status also participate less frequently. The question one can ask is simply: Is it their being black or is it the lower income and education of the black citizens that inhibits their participation? We shall deal with the question in terms of an overall summary measure of participation. The answer we obtain would differ somewhat if we looked at the several modes of participation separately, which we shall do shortly. But for present purposes, the overall measure of participation suffices.

The answer to our question is quite simple. If we compare the general participation scores of the blacks and whites in our sample, we find that whites are more active on the average. Their average participation score is +1 on our standard scale; the average black score is —12. However, consider the data in Table 10-2, which presents the average score on general participation by blacks and whites in the six levels of socioeconomic status. Here we see a very different picture: at five out of the six socioeconomic levels blacks participate more than whites.

We can obtain a summary of the effects of socioeconomic status on black-white participation differences by using our corrected measure of participa-

Table 10-2
Mean Participation Score of Blacks and Whites Within Levels of Socioeconomic Status

	Mean participation score	
	Blacks	Whites
Entire Group	−12	+1
Socioeconomic Status		
1. lowest	−32	−41
2.	−6	−28
3.	+22	−4
4.	+1	+2
5.	+38	+26
6. highest	+98 (8 cases)	+56

[4] There is evidence, furthermore, that the same difference exists in relation to the availability of channels of upward occupational mobility. Upward mobility for blacks through higher status occupations is more open through the governmental sector of the economy than through the private. See Verba, Ahmed, and Bhatt, *Caste, Race, and Politics,* Chapter 8.

tion—a measure that takes out simultaneously from the participation rate the effects of education, income, and occupational level. If we use this corrected measure, we again find that blacks score higher in rate of participation than whites—the corrected mean rate for whites being -1, that for blacks being $+10$. In other words, rather than the average black being an underparticipator, we find that he participates in politics somewhat more than we would expect given his level of education, income, and occupation, and more than the white of similar status. In short, the evidence seems clear that it is not being black per se but the socioeconomic conditions that usually accompany being black that lead to lower participation.[5]

A word of caution must be introduced immediately. These data ought not to be interpreted to mean that race is an unimportant variable in understanding participation. Quite the contrary. It is just the coexistence of lower social status and race that creates some of the most severe social tensions in American society. That we can "control away" the effects of race means that we have used our statistical techniques to help understand how race relates to participation, but we do not thereby eliminate race as a significant social distinction. Furthermore, we have not in fact eliminated the effects of race by taking into account social class. As we shall discuss later, the situation is more complicated if one considers various modes of participation. Last, as our data show, blacks and whites are not equal in participation when one removes the effects of social class. When one removes these effects, blacks are *more* active. Race plays a role, but it is one of increasing the rate of participation of blacks *over* what one would expect given their socioeconomic level. If we return to our base-line socioeconomic model of political participation, we see that race does lead to deviation from that model in the direction of somewhat diminishing the disparity in participation between upper- and lower-status groups. Let us consider why this is the case.

The Role of Group Consciousness

We mentioned that groups might overcome the inhibition to participation that accompanies their deprived status by developing a sense of group consciousness. If such a mechanism were operating for a group we would expect to find that an average member of the group would participate more than one would expect given his socioeconomic conditions. This, we have shown, is the case for blacks.

But of course, the key variable in the group consciousness model is group consciousness itself. If blacks participate more than one would expect of a group with a similar socioeconomic status (SES), the explanation may lie in the fact that they have, over time, developed an awareness of their own status as a deprived group, and this self-consciousness has led them to be more politically active than members of the society who have similar socioeconomic levels but do not share the group identity.

[5] See Thompson, *The Democratic Citizen*, pp. 158-159, for a summary of data consistent with this point.

In order to measure the level of group-consciousness we considered the number of times that black respondents referred to race in answer to a series of open-ended questions about the groups that were in conflict within their community, and on the problems they faced in personal life, in the community, and in the nation. Sixty-four percent of our black respondents mention race spontaneously in response to one of these questions and 24 percent mention race more than once. In Figure 10-2 we compare the rates of participation of blacks at varying levels of group consciousness with the average participation rate of whites. The participation measure is our usual one of overall participation. The upper dotted horizontal line represents the mean activity level of the white population (a bit above zero); the lower, the mean rate for blacks. The slope represents the level of participation of the blacks at various levels of group-consciousness as indicated by frequency of mention of race.

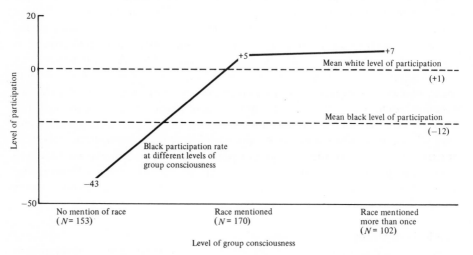

Figure 10-2. Level of Political Activity of Blacks and Three Levels of Group Consciousness

The data in Figure 10-2 are quite clear and striking. Blacks who do not mention race in response to our questions participate substantially less than the average white. But those who mention race—once or more—participate a bit above the average white. Consciousness of race as a problem or a basis of conflict appears to bring those blacks who are conscious up to a level of participation equivalent to that of whites. Or, to put it another way, this awareness overcomes the socioeconomic disadvantages of blacks and makes them as active as whites. Furthermore, it seems that any level of awareness of blackness creates the higher level of participation—whether race is mentioned once or more than once makes little difference. It may, of course, make a difference in terms of attitudes or in terms of more extreme political activities than we have measured in our study. But in terms of ordinary political activity, there appears to be a kind of threshold between those who are aware of the political significance of race and those who are not. The blacks in our sample, thus, manifest the characteristics we suggest we would find among a group brought to political participation by a sense of group-consciousness. They participate less than whites but more than one would expect given their social and economic conditions. And among those blacks who manifest some consciousness of group identification, the rate of participation is as high as that of whites and higher than one would expect given their other social characteristics.[6]

The relationship between socioeconomic status as an inhibitor of black participation, and group consciousness as a means of overcoming that inhibition is seen quite clearly in Figure 10-3. The various bars represent the participation rate both of whites and blacks and the participation rates of blacks controlling for group consciousness, for social status, and for both simultaneously. Consider the data in Figure 10-3. In the first place, blacks participate on the average less than whites (bars *A* and *B*.) The cross-hatched horizontal bar is a measure of the gap between the two races in average participation. The gap, we have indicated, largely derives from the difference in education, income, and occupation level between the two groups.

Second, the average black participation rate illustrated in bar *B* is made up of both those blacks who manifest group consciousness and those who do not. If one considers separately those who do not manifest group consciousness (bar *C*), one finds that blacks participate substantially less than whites. But if one considers those blacks who are conscious of group identity in relation to politics (bar *D*), one finds that they participate somewhat more frequently than whites. Despite the somewhat lower socioeconomic status of this group, their group consciousness bridges the gap between the average black rate and the average white rate.

Third, the situation is clearer if we consider the participation rates of blacks corrected for their lower social status. In bar *E* we see the corrected level for all blacks. This corrected level moves above that of the average white. And if we correct the participation rate of those blacks who are conscious of group identity (bar *F*), we find a participation rate far exceeding that of the average white.

In short, there are two ways black participation rates can be brought up to

---

[6] The causal direction, of course, cannot be ascertained from data such as these. Participation may lead to group consciousness. Indeed, it is likely that group consciousness and participation mutually reinforce each other among blacks—those who have the orientation participate more and in so doing strengthen the orientation. But what is important is that group consciousness and participation rise together. As we shall see in Chapter 14, longitudinal data support the group mobilization interpretation.

Another interesting question about group consciousness is whether it rises along with more general political orientations such as psychological involvement in politics. The evidence is that the two are related, but not identical. Each makes a separate contribution to the participation rate of blacks. For an analysis that separates group consciousness from other attitudes see Verba, Ahmed, and Bhatt, *Caste, Race, and Politics*, Chapter 9.

Last, we were concerned with age differences in the development and effects of group consciousness—our assumption being that the pattern we describe would be most manifest among younger blacks. In fact, we find little systematic age difference.

the level of white rates: If blacks were not disadvantaged in social-status terms they would not be disadvantaged in terms of participation (bar E). Given the fact of disadvantage, however, we find that they overcome this through group consciousness (bar D). If blacks were to close the socioeconomic gap that separates them from whites and still maintain a sense of group consciousness, they would far exceed whites in participation. The situation is of course hypothetical. If the socioeconomic gap were closed perhaps much of the basis for group consciousness would be gone. The most significant fact is that the gap in participation can be so completely closed by the awareness of group identity. Those who argue for the potency of symbols such as Black Power and the need to create cohesion among blacks as a step toward full participation in society would find support for their position in these data.[7]

Race and Modes of Participation

We have consistently argued that one must consider the alternative modes of political participation because they relate the individual to his government in significantly different ways. When we analyzed political participation in Chapter 4 we began with a distinction among four modes: voting, campaign activity, cooperative activity, and citizen-initiated contacts. In that chapter we revised the four modes somewhat because there was evidence that the two types of contacting—on particularistic issues and on social issues—were quite different from each other, and that social contacting was closely related to cooperative activity. The latter combination of cooperative activity and social contacting became our communal activity factor. In general we have used the second set of four modes of activity because of the importance of the scope-of-outcome dimension so clearly distinguished when we separate the two types of contacting. This distinction based on scope of outcome is important for blacks as well. But there is a more important dimension when one compares blacks and whites that leads us to analyze their participation rates in terms of our first set of modes. The distinction that our first set of four modes makes clear but the second obscures has to do with the barriers to contacting government officials that blacks face.

Blacks are separated from white society by a variety of social norms that make communication across the racial barrier difficult. And they are separated, in addition, by the sense of group consciousness to which we have alluded. The barriers separating blacks from the white population suggest that cooperative activity, fostered by a sense of group membership, should be particularly characteristic of black political behavior. Such activity, through informal groups or formal organizations, can be carried on without any need to cross the racial barrier; or at least no need to cross the barrier until the group is internally cohesive. On the other hand, citizen-initiated contacts may,

---

[7] See Aberbach and Walker, "The Meanings of Black Power."

for the same reason, be particularly lacking among blacks because such contact usually requires the crossing of the ascriptive boundary between black and white. From this point of view, the two types of contacting—on a particularistic or a social matter—are similar, and social contact is quite different from cooperative activity. Thus we have fairly clear expectations about racial differences in participation *vis-à-vis* the first set of modes, but less clear ones *vis-à-vis* the second.

When it comes to voting and campaign activity, our expectations are somewhat mixed. Legal restrictions have traditionally impeded black voting in the South and are not fully overcome as yet. On the other hand, blacks are a potent voting body, and their participation in elections may represent a major way to advancement, particularly if the local political setting gives their votes decisive or close to decisive weight. Last, depending on the racial composition of the local voting district, campaign activity may or may not require a crossing of the racial boundary. Black participation in voting and campaign activity is, therefore, likely to lie between the higher participation rates we expect in connection with cooperative activity and the lower ones we expect in connection with contacts—and to depend alot on contingencies of location.

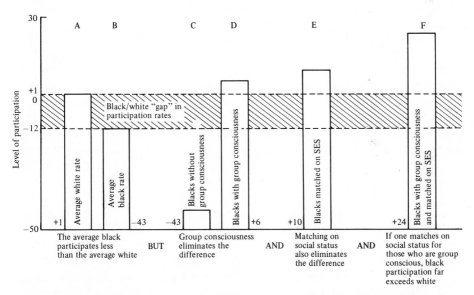

Figure 10-3. Effect of Group Consciousness and Social Status on Black/White Differences in Participation

We can test our expectations with the data in Table 10-3, where we compare blacks and whites in terms of their average scores on our standardized participation scales. The scales are for the four modes of activity we are considering: voting, campaign activity, cooperative activity, and citizen-

Table 10-3

**Mean Participation Scores (Uncorrected and Corrected)
for Blacks and Whites on the Several Modes of Participation**

	Mean level of activity, uncorrected scores			Mean level of activity, corrected for social class		
	Blacks	Whites	Difference	Blacks	Whites	Difference
Voting	−8	+4	−12[a]	−7	+2	−9
Campaign activity	−6	+1	−7	+12	−3	+15
Cooperative activity	−6	0	+6	+29	−1	+30
Citizen-initiated contact	−31	+8	−39	−13	+2	+15

[a]Figure is black activity rate minus white activity rate. If the number is negative, blacks have a lower score than whites; if positive, blacks have a higher score.

initiated contacts. (The scales are built like those described in Appendices B-2 and B-3.) And we report the comparable scores for blacks and whites for the uncorrected and corrected scales, i.e., both without a correction for the difference in social class between the two groups and with such a correction.

If we consider the left side of Table 10-3, we can see the difference between the races in the mean level of participation. The white scores are always close to 0 because the measure is standardized with a zero mean and because whites are the bulk of our sample. The important figures are the differences between the races. The data indicate that blacks are less active in voting, slightly less active in campaign activity, and slightly more active in cooperative activity. They are most different from whites in contacting, which they do less frequently. If we consider the corrected participation figures on the right side of Table 10-3, from which we remove the effects of the difference between the two races in education, income, and occupation level, we find that blacks still vote slightly less frequently than one would expect given their social class. But they engage in campaign and cooperative activity more than one would expect, the "over-participation" being greatest in connection with cooperative activity. And, even controlling for social class, they are less likely to contact a government official than are whites. The disparity between black and white contacting behavior that remains after one has removed the effects of education, income, and occupational level clearly suggests that there is indeed some racial barrier to such activity, as there is to a lesser extent with voting. Being black does not inhibit per se the overall activity rate of blacks—rather, their social-class characteristics do—but it does clearly inhibit contacting government officials.[8]

This interpretation receives further support if we return to our consideration of our measure of group consciousness. The blacks who manifested group consciousness were as likely to participate as whites, and more likely to participate than one would expect given their social characteristics (Figure 10-3). But if we are dealing with an ascriptive barrier that separates the black contactor from the usually white target of the contact, such group consciousness ought to be less useful in overcoming the inhibition to that kind of participation. That this is indeed the case is seen clearly in Figure 10-4, where we compare the activity rates of blacks at the several levels of group consciousness with the rate for the average white American. The measures of participation are the same as on Table 10-3. The average participation score for whites is represented by the horizontal line and is close to zero in each case. For cooperative activity, campaign activity, and voting, those blacks who do not manifest group consciousness—i.e., who do not mention race on the series of open-ended questions we considered—are less likely to be active than are whites. But their level of campaign and cooperative activity moves above that of whites if they are self-conscious of their group position, and voting moves to the white level. For cooperative activity and for campaign activity, the graph shows the same threshold pattern found for overall activity rates: One mention of race in response to an open-ended question is sufficient to bring the participation of blacks above that of whites; additional mentions do not raise the level further. For voting, it is only those who mention race more than once who participate on a par with whites, though those who mention race once vote more frequently than do those who do not mention race. The striking thing is the contrast with citizen-initiated contacts. Group-consciousness seems unrelated to the likelihood that an individual will contact the

---

[8] These considerations about the possible racial differences in type of political activity seem to contradict the data presented in Table 10-1. The reader will remember that we compared blacks and whites in terms of the proportions who fell in the various categories of our typology of political participators. And we found that, though there was a tendency for blacks to be somewhat less active, there did not seem to be much systematic difference in the type of activity in which blacks and whites took part. But our typology of participation—based on the revised four factors—blurs the distinction between contacting and cooperative activity.

The comparable scores for the communal participation scale and the particularized contact scale—which we usually use—are as follows:

	Uncorrected Scores			Corrected Scores		
	Blacks	Whites	Difference	Blacks	Whites	Difference
Communal activity	−10	1	−11	6	−3	9
Particularized contacting	−16	2	−18	−12	0	−12

These data illustrate why using the first four factor scores was more useful. Blacks are somewhat less active in communal activity than whites on the uncorrected scores, and somewhat more active on the corrected scores. But the situation is not as clear as in Table 10-4 because the communal activity scale combines cooperative activity, where the blacks are well ahead of the whites, and contacting, where they are behind. And if we look at the particularized contacting scores, we see that the blacks participate less, as we expect—though the difference is not as great as when we combine particularized contacting with other social contacts.

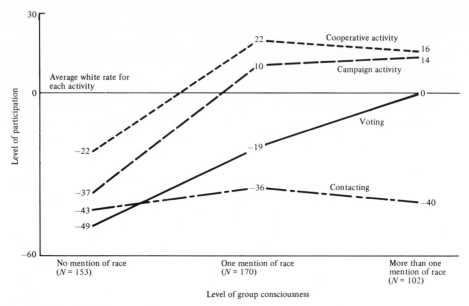

Figure 10-4. Black Level of Activity for Several Activities by Level of Group Consciousness

government. No matter how frequently race is mentioned in response to our questions, blacks are less likely to contact than are whites.[9]

Blacks and Contacting

The disparity between the races in frequency of contacting is perhaps the sharpest racial distinction we have found in our data, and it deserves closer scrutiny to clarify the role of participation as an instrumental act used by blacks to overcome their deprived socioeconomic status. The nature of the boundaries preventing blacks from being able to contact governmental officials is suggested in Tables 10-4, 10-5, and 10-6.

Table 10-4 reports answers to a question on whether the respondent thought that a go-between would be needed if he wanted to approach a

[9] If one were to reproduce the data in Figure 10-4 for the corrected participation rate from which the effects of social class have been removed, the pattern would be, if anything, more striking. When one removes the inhibiting effects of lower education, income, and occupation, the self-conscious black is found to participate substantially more than the average white in all ways but contacting. Even when one creates a group having the "advantage" of group consciousness and with the disadvantage of lower social class removed statistically, one finds that this group participates less frequently than whites in contacting.

In this connection it is also interesting to see the male/female differences in the four acts. When we use "corrected" participation figures, we find, as pointed out in the text, that blacks participate more than whites in campaign and cooperative activity. This difference between the races is greater among women than men, i.e., black women "overparticipate" in campaign and cooperative activity more than black men. But the situation is reversed in connection with contacts. Blacks in general participate less than whites, even when we correct for social class. And it is the black women who this time "underparticipate" much more than the men. This difference is consistent with our argument for the existence of an ascriptive barrier between the races: Black women may have to cross two ascriptive barriers at once—that between the races and that between the sexes.

government official. Blacks are more than twice as likely as whites to think that a go-between would be needed; half of the former and about a fifth of the latter think this. Table 10-5 adds one more bit of information to our understanding of blacks as contactors (or, rather, as noncontactors). Respondents were asked whether they believed they could find a go-between if they needed one. Blacks are less likely to report that they believe they could find such a go-between than are whites.

Table 10-4

Perceived Ability to Contact Governmental and
Political Figures Directly by Race (in percent)

	Total	White	Black
Connections are necessary to contact the official	25	21	52
Depends	3	3	3
Can contact officials directly	72	76	45
Total	100	100	100

Table 10-5

Ease of Availability of Connections for Contacting Elite
for Those Who Need Connections to Approach Elite
(in percent)

	Total	White	Black
Cannot find connections	5	5	7
May find connections	37	35	43
Can easily find connections	58	61	50
Total	100	100	100
Number of cases	(724)	(539)	(185)

The situation is summed up in Table 10-6, where we report the proportion of blacks and whites who (1) have actually contacted the government; (2) have not contacted the government but report that they could contact directly if they wanted to; (3) have not contacted, think one needs a go-between, and believe they could find one; and (4) have not contacted, believe one needs a go-between but believe also that they would have trouble finding one. The difference between blacks and whites is quite striking. A third of the blacks are in the last category in contrast with 13 percent of the whites. At the other end of the table, we find that a full 79 percent of the whites have either contacted or believe they could, if they wanted to, contact officials directly. But only 48 percent of the blacks are in these categories.[10]

Table 10-6

Black/White Differences in Elite Contact (in percent)

	Total	White	Black
Have contacted elite	30	33	14
Have not contacted but: Feel that they can contact elite directly	43	46	34
Feel that contact with elite is possible through connections	10	8	19
Feel they need connections but could not find them	17	13	33
Total	100	100	100

The data add up to a picture of frustration for blacks. The situation is exacerbated by the greater "pressure" for such contacts among blacks—a pressure that derives from the nature of their problems and with their perception of the role of government as the agency able to solve their problems. Blacks have more serious personal and family problems than whites, an assumption consistent with their lower objective social status and with data we have as to their subjectively perceived personal and family

[10] In Table 10-6 we compare blacks and whites in terms of their likelihood of contacting and, if they do not contact, in terms of their perception of the need for and availability of a go-between. One can look at the matter slightly differently by asking how the perception of the channels affects the likelihood that one will in fact contact. This is presented in the following table. The entries in the cells are the proportions who have actually contacted among blacks and whites.

Percentage who have contacted among:	Blacks	Whites
Those who think one can contact directly	16% (162)	39% (1850)
Those who think one needs a go-between and could find one	16% (92)	28% (313)
Those who think one needs a go-between and could not easily find one	15% (92)	16% (208)
The whole group	16% (346)	35% (2371)

The results are interesting, though not completely clear. Very few whites, as we have pointed out, believe that a go-between is needed and that they would have difficulty finding one. But the group of whites who do believe this, contact at the same rate (16 percent) as do blacks, and much less frequently than do the whites who think one can contact directly (39 percent). This is consistent with our argument that the perception of the need for a go-between and its unavailability impedes black contacting. But among blacks, the perception of the restrictiveness of the channels has no effect on the likelihood of contacting. This is less consistent with our argument. One would have expected the blacks who felt they could contact directly would be more likely to contact. Perhaps one has here an effect of the restrictiveness of channels that affects the group as a whole no matter how any individual perceives his own position *vis-à-vis* the need for and availability of a go-between.

problems. For instance, when asked to name the major personal or family problems they face, 19 percent of the blacks mention problems that could be considered subsistence problems—adequate food and clothing—in comparison with 6 percent of the whites. These data are consistent with black and white differences in responses to a question we asked of those who did not contact any official. Fifty-two percent of the whites who had never contacted an official said it was because they had no problem for which such contacts were relevant; only 26 percent of the black noncontactors gave this reason. The most frequent reasons given by blacks were that it would do no good (22 percent), that they would not know whom to contact (9 percent), and that (ambiguously) they had never thought of it (31 percent).

More important for our purposes is the perception of the institution that is relevant for the solution of such problems. As a follow-up to our question on the most salient problem they faced, we asked our respondents an open question on what group or institution they considered most able to solve that problem—or whether they had to solve the problem themselves. There is a sharp difference here between blacks and whites in the frequency with which they mention the government. Of those who mention some problem, thirty-nine percent of the black respondents mention the government as the problem solver in contrast with twenty-three percent of the whites. Blacks are clearly more likely to believe they need the aid of the government to deal with those problems they consider most pressing.

The contrasting situation for blacks and whites is summarized in Figure 10-5. Eighty-nine percent of whites report having a pressing personal or family problem. Of that group, 23 percent think that the government can help solve it. These citizens we call "governmentalized"—i.e., they see the government as the relevant institution for solving their most pressing problems. Of this group, 40 percent have contacted the government on such a problem, compared with 60 percent who have not.

A similar percentage (92 percent) of blacks report a pressing personal or family problem. A higher proportion of this group than among whites considers the government the relevant problem solver—39 percent. But of the group that considers the government relevant, only 23 percent have contacted the government; 77 percent have not. Thus more than three out of four of the blacks who see the government as relevant to their personal problems have not contacted it. The figures in parentheses above the boxes on Figure 10-5 refer to the proportion that the particular group is of all blacks or of all whites. Thus we find that 29 percent of all blacks see the government as relevant but have not acted to contact it, in contrast with 12 percent of the whites.

One further comparison is interesting. Twenty-four percent of the whites contact the government about some problem, though they do not mention the government as the relevant problem solver for their most pressing personal and family problems. The parallel group among blacks, who contact but do not see the government as the agency relevant for their most pressing problems

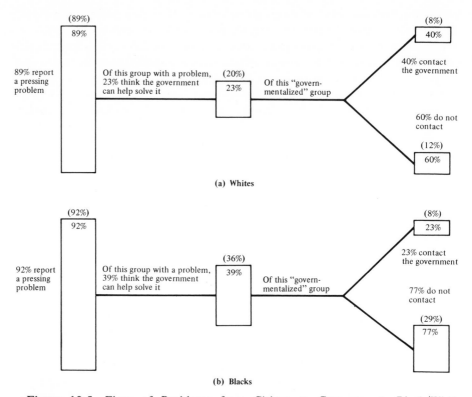

(a) Whites

(b) Blacks

Figure 10-5. Flow of Problems from Citizen to Government: Black/White Differences

is 6 percent of the black population. This suggests that whites often contact the government even when they do not consider it the relevant institution for solving their most pressing problems, obviously enjoying the "luxury" of contacting about less pressing problems. Black contact, when it takes place, is more likely to be on pressing problems. But it is much less likely to take place. In short, when it comes to the precise problems for which contacts are relevant, one finds that for blacks the objective problems exist, they are perceived as problems, and the government is perceived as relevant to the problems. The gap is in the conversion of these perceptions into activity.

One can take the discussion one step further. We have thus far been talking of the conditions under which individuals might contact the government and have found a greater likelihood that whites would contact despite the greater level of need among blacks. But the imbalance might go further, for we have not yet considered the result of the contact. Not only might blacks contact less often, but the results of their contacts might differ as well. We have been interested in the type of problem that respondents bring to governmental offices, in particular in the extent to which individuals raise with governmental officials problems that referred to themselves or their family or problems referring to the larger community or society. This distinction separates our two types of contacting. We dropped this distinction in order to consider the racial differences in contacting more closely but it will be useful now to return to it.

The relevant data are provided in Table 10-7. Thirty-four percent of the white contactors report raising a problem whose referent is limited to themselves and their family in comparison with 48 percent of the black contactors. There are a number of possible sources for this difference. It may simply reflect the greater level of need of the blacks that requires that those who manage to contact an official focus on the most immediate problems with which they are faced. Or the difference may merely reflect a greater ability to articulate problems at a general level among better-educated whites, those with low education being less likely to phrase personal problems as if they were problems of general political relevance.

But our concern here is not with the source of this difference but with some possible consequences. If this difference in the type of problem individuals report bringing to officials is a valid one, it means that officials receive different kinds of messages from the different groups. From blacks they receive messages about problems, the solution of which aids the deprived individual (assuming a favorable response on the part of the official) but has little general impact. From whites, the message is about more general problems, the solution of which (again assuming a favorable response) has a general impact. The black who asks for a particularized benefit does not further the cause of his group. The situation is shown more clearly if we compare the figure in parentheses in Table 10-7. These simply report the

Table 10-7

Contacting on a Particularized Problem or a Social Problem:
Black vs. White Contactors

	Total	White	Black
Percentage who contact on	35^a	34	48
a personal or family matter	$(11)^b$	(12)	(6)
Percentage who contact on			
a communal or social	65	66	52
matter	(20)	(22)	(8)
Total	100	100	100

[a]The figures not in parentheses are the proportions of contactors who contact in a particular manner.

[b]The figures in parentheses are the proportion of the entire group who contact in a particular manner. For instance, the upper left cell indicates that 35 percent of the Americans *who contact officials* contact on a personal matter, while 11 percent of the entire *American sample (contactors and noncontactors)* contact on such a problem.

percentage of *all* blacks or *all* whites who have contacted on the two types of problem, not just the percentage of black and white *contactors.* Whites contact more frequently than blacks on both types of problem, but the difference is most striking in terms of contact on a social problem: 20 percent of the whites as against only 6 percent of the blacks.

Our purpose is not to argue that the problems of American blacks could be solved by contacting government officials. Broader solutions are needed, and these must go through the legislative process. But the data make clear that one important component of the participatory system in America, contacting, is much more open to whites than to blacks, and they indicate how the structure of interracial relations affects access to this important kind of participation.

Race and Region

One last consideration of the differences in political participation between blacks and whites is needed: the impact on these differences of the region within which the individual lives. In Table 10-8 we present some data relevant to this question. We compare the samples living in the South with those living in the rest of the country. We are not interested in the absolute level of participation in different regions but in the way region affects the difference between blacks and whites—i.e., in the question of whether the difference between blacks and whites is greater in the South than in the North.[11] We use our standardized measures of participation and compare scores uncorrected and corrected for the effects of other social characteristics. If a figure is negative it means that blacks participate less than whites; if it is positive, it means they participate more.

Table 10-8

**Black/White Difference in Participation Rates in North and South:
Corrected and Uncorrected[a]**

	Black/White differences (uncorrected participation scales)		Black/White differences (corrected participation scales)	
	North	South	North	South
Overall activity rate	−6	−16	+14	+8
Voting	−6	−37	+13	−20
Campaign activity	−6	−6	+12	+18
Cooperative activity	+1	+9	+20	+45
Citizen-initiated contacts	−38	−38	−15	−17

[a]Plus figures indicate that blacks participate more than whites; minus figures that they participate less.

[11]We use the term "North" for all sections outside of the South.

The data are most interesting if we look across the rows of the table. Consider first the top row of Table 10-8 on the overall participation score. On the left side of the table we see the uncorrected difference in the participation rates between blacks and whites in the North and South. In each region blacks participate less, and there is a somewhat greater disparity in the South. If we look across at the corrected differences, where the effects of education, income, and occupation level have been removed, we find, as expected, that blacks actually participate more. And the regional difference in the racial gap is reduced, indicating that a major reason for the greater racial difference in overall participation rates in the South compared with the North derives from the greater gap in the socioeconomic status of the races in the South.

But we would be greatly misled if we took the previous paragraph to suggest that race plays the same role in North and South, once one has controlled for social class. If one looks at the rest of Table 10-8 (containing the data for the various modes of activity) one finds sharp differences between the regions in the role of race, differences that are by no means eliminated by controlling away the effects of class. Table 10-8 very strikingly illustrates the extent to which a summary measure of participation that assumes no difference among the modes of participation may mask significant differences among the various acts.

Consider voting. Using the uncorrected (actual) levels of participation we see that there is a sharp difference between the regions. Blacks vote almost as regularly as whites in the North, much less regularly in the South. And when one takes out the effects of social class one finds that in the North blacks are more active in voting than their class would predict, whereas in the South they are less active than their class would predict. Clearly this reflects the fact that historical legal discriminations against black voting in the South still make a difference.

For campaign activity the situation is different. In both North and South blacks participate almost as frequently as whites, and when one corrects for social class one finds that blacks participate more in both places. And they over-participate more in the South than in the North. This pattern is even stronger in relation to cooperative activity. Blacks participate a touch more than whites in this way in the South, and when one takes out the inhibiting effect of social class they participate substantially more in both regions, with the over-participation greatest in the South. The data are relevant to our contention that cooperative activity is particularly characteristic of blacks because it requires less crossing of racial boundaries and because it can capitalize on group consciousness. The fact that it is more characteristic of southern blacks—where the boundaries between the races are more restrictive—is consistent with this interpretation.

The data on citizen-initiated contacts is generally consistent with our findings that these are activities for which racial status is particularly inhibiting. In both regions, the black-white disparity is greatest on this measure of participation, and the disparity remains even when one takes out the effects of social class.

On the other hand, the regional data on contacting are not consistent with the argument just made about the reasons why cooperative activity is most distinctively a southern black phenomenon. The greater restrictiveness of racial boundaries that we argued would make for particular emphasis on cooperative activity among southern blacks should form a particularly high barrier to citizen-initiated contacts on the part of the same group. Yet blacks seem equally constrained *vis-à-vis* contacts in both regions. The inconsistency disappears, however, if we distinguish between citizen-initiated contacts directed at local officials and those directed at officials on an extra-local level, in most cases the federal government. If we do this, we find that in relation to contacts with local officials, for which we would expect the hypothesized regional differences to hold, blacks are worse off in the South than in the North, whereas there is little regional difference in relation to extralocal officials. Blacks are less likely to contact such extralocal officials than are whites, but no less so in the South than in the North. In the South, the difference between blacks and whites in the proportions contacting *local* officials is 13 percent (9 percent of the blacks do compared with 22 percent of the whites), whereas in the North the difference is 6 percent (15 and 21 percent, respectively, for blacks and whites). Thus if we consider local government officials, we can support our hypothesis that there is a greater racial barrier to contacting in the South than in the North.

The regional differences, thus, generally support our contentions about the different modes of political activity engaged in by blacks and whites. They support our contention that race per se—or rather the barrier between the two races—particularly inhibits citizen-initiated contacts and may lead to emphasis on cooperative activity. And the data suggest that what seems to be a similarity of role of race in the two regions, when one considers an overall measure of participation, actually masks some sharp differences between the regions that become apparent when one looks at the several different modes of participation. In this way, we hope the comparison of black and white participation has been illuminating in terms of the politics of race in America and has also firmed up the general theoretical argument that we have been making about modes of participation.

SUMMARY

Our analysis of black-white differences in political participation reveals some striking patterns. The analysis also illustrates, we believe, the usefulness of considering the alternative modes of participation. Black-white differences in participation vary depending on the mode involved. In particular, direct contacts with government officials reveal a pattern of disparity, which suggests that insofar as the various components of the participatory system in the United States are useful for different purposes, blacks are blocked from one important channel of influence. And, of course, our data may not reveal the full extent of the disparity between the races. We measure, it must be remembered, political participation, not political power or influence. The same act may in one case lead to success, in another to failure. Whatever disparities we observe in rates of participation may be minor compared with disparities one would observe in terms of successful participation.

The chapter illustrates the usefulness of the standard socioeconomic model as a base line for analysis. For one thing, it becomes clear that socioeconomic differences explain a good deal of the difference in the participation rates of blacks and whites. If there is any impact on participation associated more directly with race, it is one that gives some boost to black citizens—particularly if they have a sense of group consciousness. Black Americans have, in group consciousness, a great resource for political involvement.

Chapter 11
The Organizational Context
of Political Participation

We have thus far dealt with the individual citizen as participant and related his participation to a set of personal characteristics: his social status, his race, his position in the life cycle, and certain of his attitudes. But participation is fully comprehensible only if one takes into account the individual's institutional context. In this and the following chapters we shall take into account various institutions with which the citizen may be involved that may affect the likelihood that he will be a participant. In this chapter we consider the role of organizations and voluntary associations in relation to political participation. We will then turn to the effects of affiliation with a political party and the effects of the type of community within which one lives.

Voluntary associations have figured in many theoretical speculations about the social bases of democracy and, in particular, about some special features of American democracy. A rich associational life has been considered the hallmark of American democracy. Such associations provide an intermediary level of organization between the individual and the government. And this, it is claimed (sometimes supported by data, other times not), prevents the development of mass political movements in this society, mediates conflict, and increases citizen efficacy, participation, and influence. Our interest is in the latter function of organizations and their role in relation to the political participation of American citizens.

Do organizations increase the potency of the citizenry *vis-à-vis* the government? Organizations could play such a role in a number of ways. Voluntary associations and other organizations can themselves, through the activities of their officers or other paid officials, participate in the political process. In this way the organization participates *for* its members. Or the citizen who is a member of an organization may use that affiliation as a channel to gain access to the government: either the organization itself (through its officers or representatives) may transmit the grievance of the individual to the government, or the individual may use connections made within the organization to further his acts of participation. Here the member participates *through* the organization. Last, organizations may have an impact on political life in a society through the influence they have on the participatory activities of their members. Citizens may participate directly *because of* their affiliation with an organization. In studies in a variety of countries, organizational affiliation has been shown to be one of the most powerful predictors of citizen activity, a predictor of political activity that remains strong over and above the social class of the individual. A rich political participant life, these data suggest, may rest on a rich associational life.[1]

This last point is the main concern of the present chapter: how does organizational involvement affect the political activity of citizens? We are, here, separating social from political participation in order to observe their relationship to one another. We are concerned with the replication and elaboration of the relationship that others have found between organizational affiliation and political participation. Thus we shall ask, as others have, about the extent to which such affiliation leads to political activity. The question will be raised within the framework of our base line model of participation as deriving from social status. We will be concerned with the way organizational affiliation affects participation over and above the effects on participation of the other social characteristics of the citizen. Second, we want to explore the process by which organizational affiliation leads to political participation. In addition, we shall elaborate our dependent variable in order to estimate the relative impact of organizational affiliation and its variants on the alternative modes of political participation. And last, we want to see how organizations affect the difference in participation between upper- and lower-status individuals. Does organizational affiliation reduce, increase, or leave unchanged the participation disparity among the several social levels?

To begin with, we will sketch out the facts of organizational participation in the United States, asking what kinds of individuals participate in what ways

---

[1] Nie, Powell, and Prewitt, "Social Structure and Political Participation;" Almond and Verba, *The Civic Culture,* Chapter 12.

in what kinds of organizations. This preliminary sketch will present some descriptive information about participation in organizations and its distribution in the population. In addition, it introduces the various aspects of organizational membership in which we are interested. These characteristics include: (1) the number of organizations to which an individual belongs; (2) the type of organization to which he belongs; (3) the degree to which he is active in them; (4)the degree to which he is exposed to politically relevant stimuli—in particular, to discussions about politics within the organizations; and (5) the degree to which the organizations themselves are actively involved in community and civic affairs.

These characteristics are the raw material of an analysis of the process of political mobilization that takes place within organizations.

Let us turn to our descriptive sketch first.

ORGANIZATIONAL MEMBERSHIP: AN OVERVIEW

The data on the amount and character of organization membership in the United States are reported in Table 11-1. The basic data are quite consistent with a number of other studies of organizational affiliation in the United States. The overall amount of organizational membership found by one study or another will vary somewhat with the question asked and with whether one includes membership in unions (as we do) as part of one's overall indicator of organizational membership. But most studies have found a figure for membership usually close to the figure of 62 percent that we report in Table 11-1.

Table 11-1

Organizational Involvement of American Population

Percentage of sample reporting:	
That they belong to an organization	62
That they belong to more than one organization	39
That they are active in an organization	40
That they belong to an organization in which political discussion takes place	31
That they belong to an organization active in community affairs	44

Is this figure high or low? The question is unanswerable, unless one first asks "compared to what?" Those who have heard the United States described as a nation of joiners may be somewhat disappointed to find that roughly four out of ten Americans belong to no organization. But such characterizations are usually based on broad tendencies and ought never to be taken to imply that an entire nation—something close to 100 percent of all Americans—are involved in organizations. In fact, the figure of 62 percent is roughly equivalent to that found in other industrialized societies.[2]

As the data in Table 11-1 also indicate, four out of ten Americans (or two out of three organizational members) are members of more than one organization. A more important figure, perhaps, is the proportion who are active members in some organization. Most theories that relate organizational affiliation to participation in democratic politics suggest that the private voluntary association offers more opportunities for individual activity than does the larger political system. Our data indicate that 40 percent of our sample, or about half the organizational members, are in some way active within the organizations to which they belong. In this particular respect, the data for the United States do differ from those for other industrial societies. Though the United States appears quite similar to such societies as Britain, Germany, and Japan in terms of the overall membership rate, American organizational members seem to be much more likely to be active within their organizations when they are members.[3]

In our study we included two other characteristics of organizational membership that may help us understand the way in which affiliation operates to increase the participation potential of the average citizen. We asked whether individuals were exposed to political discussion at the meetings of the organizations to which they belonged. These might be formal discussions initiated by the organizational leadership or informal political conversations. In either case, the organization would be acting as a channel of political communication or as a potential means of arousing political interest in the citizen. As the data on Table 11-1 indicate, 31 percent of our sample (about one out of two of all organizational members) belong to organizations within which political discussions take place. Last, we were interested in whether the organizations to which individuals belong were themselves active in the kinds of community-oriented activities about which we asked our individual respondents. Forty-four percent of our sample (a little more than two out of three organizational members) indicate that they belong to organizations that take some active role in dealing with general community problems.

Table 11-2 contains the data on the specific kinds of organizations to which our respondents belong. The range of organizations to which individuals belong is wide. The most frequently reported memberships are in such groups as trade unions, school-service clubs, fraternal groups, and sports clubs. In addition, respondents report membership in a wide range of other kinds of associations, some connected with their work, such as professional associations; some involved in political or communal activities, such as service groups and political clubs; and some purely recreational, such as hobby clubs or art and literary groups.

The data in the next two columns give us a better understanding of the

[2] Almond and Verba, *The Civic Culture*, Chapter 12.
[3] Ibid.

Table 11-2
The Types of Organizations to Which Individuals Belong

Type of organization	Percentage of the *population* who report membership	Percentage of *members* who report the organizations involved in community affairs	Percentage of *members* who report that political discussion take place in the organization
Political groups such as Democratic or Republican clubs, and political action groups such as voter's leagues	8	85	97
School service groups such as PTA or school alumni groups	17	82	54
Service clubs, such as Lions, Rotary, Zonta, Jr. Chamber of Commerce	6	81	64
Youth groups such as Boy Scouts, Girl Scouts	7	77	36
Veterans' groups such as American Legion	7	77	56
Farm organizations such as Farmer's Union, Farm Bureau, Grange	4	74	61
Nationality groups such as Sons of Norway, Hibernian Society	2	73	57
Church-related groups such as Bible Study Group or Holy Name Society	6	73	40
Fraternal groups such as Elks, Eagles, Masons, and their women's auxiliaries	15	69	33
Professional or academic societies such as American Dental Association, Phi Beta Kappa	7	60	57
Trade unions	17	59	44

Table 11-2 (Continued)

Type of organization	Percentage of the *population* who report membership	Percentage of *members* who report the organizations involved in community affairs	Percentage of *members* who report that political discussion take place in the organization
School fraternities and sororities such as Sigma Chi, Delta Gamma	3	53	37
Literary, art, discussion, or study clubs such as book-review clubs, theater groups	4	40	56
Hobby or garden clubs such as stamp or coin clubs, flower clubs, pet clubs	5	40	35
Sports clubs, bowling leagues, etc.	12	28	20

nature of some of these organizations, at least in terms of the two character-istics of involvement in community affairs and political discussions that we have been stressing. The data in the second column indicate the proportion of members of each kind of organization who report that it is involved in community affairs and the data in the third column present the proportion who report that political discussions take place in their organizations. Where 70 percent or more report either community involvement or political discus-sion we have enclosed that figure in a solid line; where between 50 and 70 per-cent report such involvement the figure is enclosed in a dashed line; and where less than 50 percent report such involvement the figure is unshaded. Thus a quick glance at the columns of figures indicates that we have several kinds of organizations. Political clubs are frequently involved in dealing with general community problems, and as one would expect, they are almost universally the site of political discussions. A number of other organizations are highly in-volved in communal affairs, though political discussions are somewhat less frequent than in the political clubs. This is the case with school-service organiza-tions, service clubs, veterans' groups, farm associations, and nationality associa-tions.

In several types of organizations there appears to be a heavy stress on communal activities with a relatively low frequency of reporting of political conversation. This includes youth groups, religious associations, and fraternal groups. The disparity between the amount of communal involvement and infrequency of political discussions suggests—as does the character of these groups more generally—that these may be organizations within which political discussions are generally avoided. Among professional associations, trade unions, and school fraternities or sororities, one finds a moderate amount of involvement in community problems coupled with, in the case of professional associations, a moderate frequency of political discussion and, in the case of unions and fraternities, relatively infrequent political discussions. Because political discussions represent something that may go on informally at organization meetings, the high rate of these discussions in professional associations may simply reflect the higher social-class composition of such groups.

Three kinds of groups seem decidedly less involved in political or community affairs. These are art and literary groups, hobby clubs, and sports clubs. There is a moderate amount of political discussion in the first kind of group, which is a likely reflection of the social-class composition of such groups.

One further point should be made about the organizations listed on Table 11-2. When one looks at the groups near the bottom of the table, one finds quite a bit less involvement in general community problems and quite a bit less political discussion compared with some of the groups near the top. However, when one considers the manifest character of these organizations, such as the three recreational organizations at the bottom of the list, the amount of communal and political discussion activity may seem much larger. Even among sports clubs, which are the least likely to become involved in community problems and the least likely settings for political discussion, 28 percent of the members report that their club has been involved in some general communal activity, and 20 percent report political discussions. Much of the speculation about the role played by voluntary associations in relation to democratic participation has been based on the assumption that these organizations have an impact on the political attitudes and activities of their members even when the explicit purpose of the organization is totally nonpolitical. The data suggest that such may indeed be the case, and we shall look at this question more closely. (For data on activity rates within the various types of organizations, see Table 2-3, p. 42.)

Who Belongs to Organizations?

Our purpose in this chapter is not to explain why individuals join organizations but rather to see the link between organizations on the one hand and political activities on the other. However, we will be better able to understand that link if we have some information on the characteristics of people who join organizations. The rates of organizational membership and of organizational activity for a few select groups in the population are presented in Table 11-3. They can be briefly described. Men are somewhat more likely to be organizational members than women, though the difference is not very great. The higher the level of education one has, the more likely one is to be a member of an organization, and here the difference is somewhat more substantial. About one in two of those who have not graduated from high school belong to some organization while over three out of four of those with some college education are organizational members. Whites are more likely to be organizational members than blacks, and again the difference is fairly great. With age one finds a curved pattern. Organizational affiliation seems greatest among those in the middle group, between 30 and 49. The younger group is the least active in organizations and those over 50 also fall off.

The same patterns apply to active membership in organizations. If one's education is higher, if one is white rather than black, and middle-aged rather than old or young, one is more likely to be an active member in organizations. The one variation on this theme is the difference between men and women. Women are as likely to be active in organizations as are men. When this is coupled with the somewhat lower rate of organizational membership among women, it becomes clear that the average female member is more likely to be an active member of that organization than is the average male member. A good deal of this difference derives from the higher rate of male membership in trade unions, organizations in which the average level of activity tends to be quite low.

Table 11-3

Some Demographic Differences in Organizational Membership and Activity

	Percentage reporting	
	Belonging to at least one organization	Active in at least one organization
Total sample	62	40
Men	65	41
Women	57	39
Not high-school graduate	49	27
High-school graduate	67	43
Some college	78	59
White	66	41
Black	52	30
Age 17-29	52	31
Age 30-49	70	47
Age 50 and above	57	37

THE PROCESS OF POLITICIZATION IN ORGANIZATIONS

The previous data make clear that the universe of organizational membership in the United States is rich and varied. Many are members, many are active, and the range of organizations is vast. Also there is important variation in what goes on within organizations. This provides an opportunity to look more closely than others have at the process that leads organizational members to be active in politics.

Our approach will be to look at the relationship between organizational affiliation and our standard participation scale to see how the scores on that scale differ among those with various forms of organizational experience. However, we must modify that participation scale somewhat to remove from it two items that measure political activity but that are also aspects of organizational activity—membership in a manifestly political organization like a political club and active membership in an organization that takes part in community activities—which we have considered to be measures of political participation. This measure, which removes the danger of auto-correlation, is used throughout this chapter.[4]

To begin with, our data confirm the findings of others that organizational members are more likely to be active in political life than are nonmembers. The average score on our standard participation scale is —46 for those who are not members of any organization, compared with 18 for those who are members of at least one. The average participation rate for those who are members of more than one organization is 50. If one were to take the actual number of political acts engaged in by our respondents, one would find that organizational members engage in, on the average, twice as much political activity as nonmembers, and those who belong to more than one organization engage in almost three times as much activity as nonmembers.

These data are consistent with the findings of others and support the general contention that organizational affiliation is associated with democratic participation. But they leave three questions unanswered:

1. Is the relationship between organizational membership and political participation a real or a spurious one? The data we presented indicate that upper-status individuals are more likely to be members of organizations than lower-status ones, men more than women, whites more than blacks, and middle-aged more than young or old. Our previous chapters indicated these are characteristics also associated with increased political participation. It may be that the association between political participation and organizational affiliation is a spurious result of the association of both of these with the other social characteristics. Thus we shall have to consider, as we have been doing with other characteristics, the residual effect of organizational affiliation "correcting" for these other social characteristics.

2. Assuming that the relationship is not purely spurious (as we shall demonstrate), the next question one can ask has to do with the process by which membership in an organization leads to greater political participation. Does mere membership in an organization lead to increased political partici-

---

[4] The possible overlap between our political measures and our measures of organizational activity illustrates the great difficulty that exists in determining the exact boundary between political participation and participation in the nonpolitical sphere. There is no clear conceptual answer. Our procedure at least eliminates any auto-correlation between the two spheres. The organizational affiliations which form our independent variable in this chapter are all manifestly non-political.

pation or does political participation depend upon a more active organizational involvement? Does the impact of the membership on political life depend upon the extent to which the organization is itself involved in some way in politics—the extent, for instance, to which the organization itself is a political actor or is the setting for political activities? The answers will bring us a long way toward an understanding of the process by which organizational affiliation leads to political participation.

3. Even if we demonstrate that the association between organizational membership and political participation is not the spurious artifact of the association of both with certain other social characteristics, and even if we explicate the process, does the direction of the causality really run from organizational involvement to political participation? If we demonstrate (as we shall) that the organizational members who are exposed to political stimuli within organizations are more likely to be politically active, does this mean that the exposure within the organization led to that activity, or do citizens with certain propensities seek organizations in which they can be exposed to political stimuli and also engage in political activity? Or, if we show (as we shall) that active organizational membership has a strong relation with political activity, does this mean that the respondent's organizational activity makes him politically active, or is it some proneness to activity that makes him an activist both in organizations and in politics? We will not be able to answer these questions definitively, but we will be able to shed some light on them.

Organizational Affiliation, Political Participation, and Other Social Characteristics

To begin with, we can make it clear that the association we noted between organizational membership and participation rate is not merely the spurious result of the relationship of both organizational affiliation and political participation with various other social characteristics such as those listed in Table 11-3, sex, age, race, and education. In Figure 11-1 we plot the relationship between the number of organizations to which individuals belong and their average political participation scores. We plot that relationship twice, once using an uncorrected participation score and once with a corrected score from which we have removed the effects on participation of the respondent's socioeconomic status, age, sex, and race.[5] The uncorrected participation score (the solid line) reflects the strong relationship already noted between organizational affiliation and participation rate: There is a steep rise in participation scores as one moves from the nonmembers in organizations to those who are highly active. For instance, those who are members of six or more organizations have an average political participation score almost two standard deviations above the mean for the population as a whole.

The dotted line represents the participation score corrected for the other social characteristics. Two things are clear from a comparison of the lines for

---

[5] See Appendixes B.3 and G.2.

the corrected and uncorrected measures: First, the relationship between organizational membership and participation is clearly due in part to other social characteristics. The line for the corrected measure has a less steep slope. On the other hand, it is also clear that the relationship that remains after we have corrected for other social characteristics is strong and positive. Indeed, it would be difficult to find another social characteristic that would have as strong an association with political participation after one had corrected for such characteristics as social status, race, sex, and age. Let us consider the sources of that association.

The Impact of Organizational Activity The more organizations to which an individual belongs, the greater is his rate of activity. But what accounts for this? Is it mere membership in an organization or is more active involvement necessary before this has some impact on his rate of political participation? The latter would be consistent with one of the interpretations of the way voluntary associations relate to political participation—i.e., that they increase the propensity of the individual to be a participant because they give him an opportunity for training in participation within the organization that can be transferred to the political realm. The assumption is that voluntary associations allow more opportunities for participation in small units than does the polity. And what counts is not mere membership but the opportunity for activity that the organization affords.

If this is the process at work we should find that passive organizational members are no different in their rate of political activity from those who belong to no organizations, whereas those who are active organizational members are also more politically active.

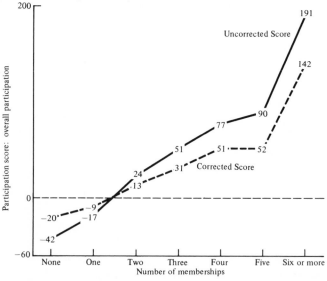

Figure 11-1. Number of Organizational Memberships and Participation Rate: Uncorrected and Corrected Scores

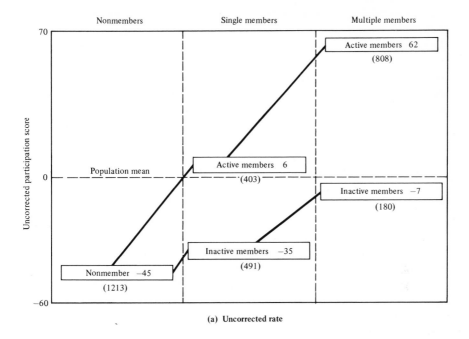

(a) Uncorrected rate

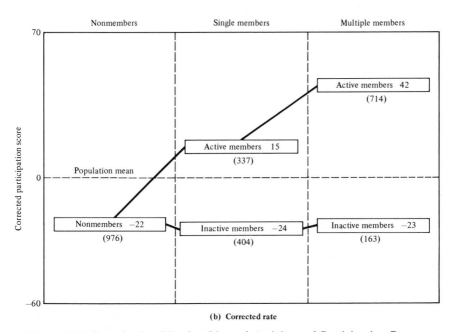

(b) Corrected rate

Figure 11-2. Organization Membership and Activity and Participation Rate[a]
[a]Number of cases appear below the boxes; average group scores are in the boxes.

In Figure 11-2 we attempt to separate the effects on participation of passive and active membership in organizations. In the left column are the participation rates of those who belong to no organizations; in the middle column are the participation rates of those who belong to one organization, divided into those who are active in that organization and those who are not; and in the right column are the participation rates of those who are members of more than one organization, divided again into those who are active within at least one of the organizations and those who are not. In Figure 11-2(a) we present the data for the uncorrected participation score, while 11-2(b) contains the data for the corrected score.

Consider the data for the uncorrected participation scores. Participation increases with both the number of memberships and with organizational activity. Individuals who belong to no organization have an average participation score of —45. If we look at those who belong to one organization but who are inactive in it we find an average participation score somewhat higher at —35; and if we look at those who belong to one organization and are active in it, we find an average score of 6. The pattern continues if we consider those who are multiple members. The participation score increases as one moves from single membership to multiple membership, but it increases more for those who are active in their organizations than for those who are inactive.

The corrected participation scores in Figure 11-2(b) reveal the relative role of membership and activity in organizations. When we remove from the participation score the effect of other social characteristics, which are correlated not only with the likelihood that an individual will be a member of an organization but with the likelihood that he will be an active member, we find that inactive organizational membership is not associated with an increase in political participation, while active membership is. The individual who is a *passive* member in one or more organizations is *no more likely* to be active in politics than the individual who belongs to no such association. In contrast, the active organizational member is much more likely than the nonmember to be politically active, and this political activity rate increases as one moves from single membership to multiple membership. These data strongly suggest that affiliation with associations relates to increased political activity because it affords the individual an opportunity to be active within the organization.

What Goes On in the Organization? We have found activity within organizations to be a potent characteristic affecting the impact of the organization on the participation of the members. We now turn to questions revolving around the nature of the organizations themselves and the kind of activities that take place within them.

There are two possible interpretations of the way organizational affiliation might lead to greater political involvement. One is that organizations expose their members to specifically political stimuli. The member is exposed to conversation about politics or he is exposed to the politically relevant activities of the organization itself. These political exposures, in turn, increase his interest in politics and lead him to greater levels of political activity outside the organizational framework. According to this interpretation, organizations have an impact on the political involvement of their members, either because it is the manifest function of the organization to be involved in political matters or because—whether or not that is the purpose of the organization—it is a location for a large amount of explicitly political stimuli.

An alternative interpretation is that organizational affiliation has an impact on an individual's involvement in politics, whether or not the organization itself has any explicit involvement in political matters. Even if the individual is exposed to little political stimuli through his organization—i.e., there is little political discussion at the organization, the organization is involved in no politically relevant activities—his very association with that organization may increase his level of political activity. For one thing, such affiliation—even, say, with a totally apolitical sports club—offers him a wider view of the world, thereby making it more likely that he will be politically involved. Also, nonpolitical organizations may give an individual greater opportunity for being active, and as we have demonstrated in the previous section, organizational activity, if not mere membership, is a potent predictor of political activity.

In our study we have several ways of distinguishing between organizations within which there are explicitly political activities and those in which the organization focus is more purely nonpolitical. In the first place, we asked respondents whether there were ever political discussions at the meetings of the organizations to which they belonged. A second measure of the degree to which the organizational affiliation entailed explicit exposure to politically relevant stimuli involved asking our respondents whether any of the organizations to which they belonged dealt with the problems of the local community. Because one of our major set of measures of political activity involves the individual as an actor *vis-à-vis* community problems, this measure of the extent to which organizations were themselves involved in such problems can be considered a measure of the extent to which organizational affiliation exposes the individual to organizational activities analogous to the individual political activities we have been studying.

In Figure 11-3 we see the relationship between exposure to political discussions in organizations and political participation. Since we have found that it is organizational activity rather than mere membership that seems to create the greatest impetus toward political participation, we distinguish among members who are inactive, those who are active in one organization, and those who are active in more than one organization. The figures are the corrected participation scores to remove the contaminating effects of other social characteristics. The data in Figure 11-3 make clear that exposure to political discussion in an organization has an impact on one's political participation score. But it has that impact only on those who are *active* in organizations. If one looks at the passive members, one finds that, whether or not they are exposed to discussion, they have participation scores close to those of the nonmembers. As one moves to the active members one finds an increase in political participation for both those exposed to discussion and those who are not (consistent with our findings on the importance of activity) and, more important, a difference between those who are exposed and those who are not. This suggests that organizational activity not only increases the political participation rate of an individual, but it enables him to benefit from the exposure to political discussion within the organization. If he is an inactive member, the exposure to political discussion within the organization makes no difference in his level of political participation.

In Figure 11-4 we repeat the analysis for a different form of organizational exposure. Here we deal with the extent to which individuals belong to organizations that are involved in the solution of community problems. The data form a similar pattern to that in Figure 11-3 on exposure to political discussion. Passive members who report that their organization is engaged in the solution of community problems are only a bit more active in politics than those who are members of no organization (scores of —17 and —22 respectively).

On the other hand, among the organizationally active, those who report their organizations as having some community involvement score substantially higher in political participation than those who do not.

Thus far, the data seem to support a "manifest" rather than a "latent" theory of organizational exposure. When the organization provides explicit

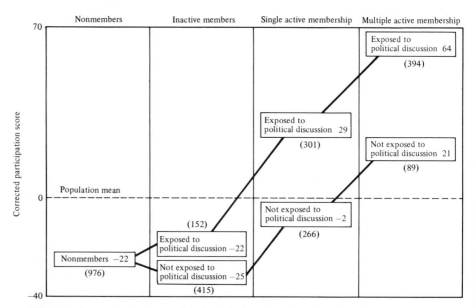

Figure 11-3. Exposure to Political Discussion in Organization and Corrected Participation Scores[a]

[a]Number of cases are below the boxes; average group scores are in the boxes.

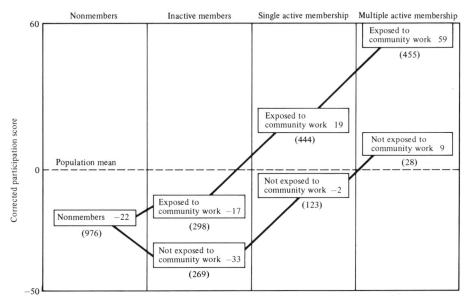

Figure 11-4. Exposure to Community Activities and Political Discussion in Organization and Corrected Participation Scores[a]

[a]Number of cases are below the boxes; average group scores are in the boxes.

political stimuli—as indicated either by exposure to political discussions or to communally oriented activity within the organization—the individual so exposed is more active in politics than the one who is not.

In Figure 11-5 we combine the data from Figures 11-2, 11-3, and 11-4 to show the joint effect on participation rates of activity within organizations, exposure to political discussions, and exposure to community-oriented activity (using, again, our corrected measures). The data are somewhat complex but worth careful attention. Consider first the section to the far right. There we present the data for respondents who are active in more than one organization. Within that group of multiple-activists we show the participation rates of four types of respondent: those who are exposed neither to discussion nor community activity, those exposed to discussion, those exposed to community activity, and those exposed to both. If an individual is a multiple-active member and is exposed to neither organizational stimulus, his participation rate is roughly at the average for the nonmembers (there are few such cases). But when exposure to one or both of the organizational stimuli is added, his political participation rate moves well above that for the sample as a whole. The same pattern, at a somewhat lower participation level, appears for the active members in a single organization (second section from the right of Figure 11-5). When exposure to either or both of the organizational stimuli is added to active membership, political participation rates climb substantially.

The second section from the left of Figure 11-5 contains data for inactive

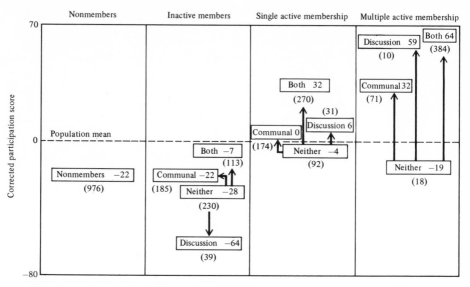

Figure 11-5. The Joint Effect of Number of Memberships, Activity, Exposure to Political Discussion, and Exposure to Communal Activity by One's Organization[a]

[a]Number of cases are in parentheses below the boxes; average group scores are in the boxes.

members of organizations; and these data offer a contrast. Among those who are inactive members, exposure to both organizational stimuli increases the political participation rate but much less than both stimuli increase the political participation rate of the organizationally active. Furthermore, exposure to community activity has little effect on the organizationally inactive, whereas exposure to discussion actually depresses their activity rate.

The data clearly indicate that it is a combination of organizational characteristics that leads to participation. If one is an active member in an organization, additional stimuli increase one's political participation rate, and the more memberships, the more this happens. Activity within the organization appears to make the individual receptive to other stimulation. On the other hand, if one is an inactive member, the additional stimuli have little effect on participation or, in relation to discussion, the additional stimulus is associated with a lower political participation rate.

We saw earlier that it was organizational activity and not mere membership that was associated with increased political participation. It now becomes clear that this activity is important as a necessary condition for the individual to benefit from the exposure to further stimuli within the organization.

We have, thus far, dealt with the first two questions we raised at the beginning of this chapter: We have tried to demonstrate that the relationship between organizational affiliation and political participation is not merely the spurious result of the relationship of those two characteristics with other social characteristics, and we have attempted to explicate the process by which affiliation with an organization leads to greater participation. In relation to the latter question we can see that mere passive affiliation with an organization has little if any positive association with the political activity of the citizen. If organizations operate to increase the political participation of citizens, they do so by giving the citizen an opportunity to be active within organizations and, when he is active, to be exposed to politically relevant stimuli, such as political discussion and community activity.

POLITICAL AND NONPOLITICAL ORGANIZATIONS

Let us return to a question raised earlier about the process of politicization within organizations: Does affiliation, even with manifestly nonpolitical organizations, increase the political participation of the citizen or does organizational affiliation affect participation through more political exposures? The data presented would seem to favor the latter interpretation: Participation increases when the citizen is exposed to political stimuli. But this does not refute the argument of those who say that even nonpolitical organizations lead to civic participation. Quite the contrary. As the data presented on Table 11-2 showed clearly, even in manifestly nonpolitical organizations the citizen is likely to be exposed to politically relevant stimuli; 40 percent of the members of hobby groups, for instance, report that their group takes some part in community affairs, and 35 percent report that there is political discussion in such groups. For nationality groups, to take another example, the figures are 73 percent and 57 percent, respectively, for the proportions reporting community activity and political discussion. In other words, even manifestly nonpolitical organizations are the settings for politically relevant activity.

And these manifestly nonpolitical organizations appear to have an impact on the political participation rate of their members, providing that the internal processes we have specified take place within them—i.e., the combination of activity and exposure to politically relevant stimuli. We can demonstrate this by looking more closely at two quite different types of organization: recreational organizations and trade unions. The two types are similar in that neither has a manifest political purpose. This is more clearly the case with recreational groups—hobby groups, literary groups, sports clubs, and the like—but it is usually true of unions as well.

The two types of groups, on the other hand, differ in the frequency with which political activities—political discussion and community-based activity—go on within them. Thirty-three percent of the members of recreational groups report that these organizations are involved in community-oriented activities and 30 percent report that political discussions take place in such organizations. These are the lowest figures for any category of association. There is more politically relevant activity in unions than in recreational groups. Fifty-nine percent of the members of trade unions report that their union is involved in some way in community activities, and 44 percent report political discussions.

Last, these groups differ in the frequency with which their members are active within them. Members of trade unions are less likely to be active in such associations than are members of recreational associations: 37 percent of union members are active in some way, compared with 52 percent of the members of recreational groups. In short, the two types of organizations are similar in their manifestly nonpolitical nature, but they differ in the extent to which they offer their members the chance to be active and to be exposed to political stimuli.

What we want to know is whether affiliation with either of these manifestly nonpolitical organizations is related to an increase in an individual's political participation rate. An active member of a union or a recreational group does score higher on our general participation scale than does the average citizen, even when we correct the scores for social-status differences. That, however, does not settle the question. The reason is that members of one type of organization are likely to be members of other organizations as well and the positive relationship between, say, activity in a recreational organization and political participation might result from the fact that those who belong to recreational groups are also active in more manifestly political organizations. Thus we attempt to examine the relationship between affiliations with union or recreational groups and participation independent of other affiliations.

We do this in the following manner: First we create dichotomous variables measuring whether the respondent is a member of, active in, exposed to political discussion in, and exposed to community activity in a union, a recreational group, or in all other types of organization together. Thus we have four measures of organizational involvement for each of three types of organizations—unions and recreational groups whose impact on participation we wish to observe, and all other organizations grouped together whose impact on participation we wish to control.

This gives us twelve dummy variables summarizing the individuals' involvement in recreational groups and unions, as well as in all other types of organization. All twelve variables were entered into a multiple-regression equation at the same time, where the overall participation scale was the dependent variable. The corrected participation scale was used to remove the confounding effects of socioeconomic characteristics.

The results are reported in Table 11-4. The figures are unstandardized partial regression weights (B's). These regression weights tell us how many units of participation are gained or lost by having each of the twelve organizational characteristics, while holding constant all the others. Thus the coefficients reflect the independent effects of each of the organizational characteristics. By putting all the characteristics into the equation at the same time we can assure ourselves that a positive relation between union or recreational group affiliation is the independent effect of unions or recreational groups on participation. Because we use our standard participation scale (with mean of zero and standard deviation of 100) one can interpret the magnitude of the regression weights. Let us consider the data in Table 11-4. For each type of organization the pattern is similar. Membership per se has no positive effect on one's participation score, but activity in the organization, exposure to political discussion, and (to a lesser extent) exposure to community activity do. Because the figures are unstandardized regression coefficients based on

Table 11-4

Impact on Participation Score of Affiliation with Union or Recreational Organization, Correcting for Socioeconomic Status and Other Organizational Exposures[a]

	Effects of each organizational characteristic	
Unions		
Effect of union *membership*	−11	
Effect of *activity* in a union	25	
Effect of exposure to political *discussion* in a union	24	
Effect of exposure to *communal activity* in a union	2	
	40	Summary effect of union affiliation
Recreational Groups		
Effect of *membership* in a recreational group	−19	
Effect of *activity* in a recreational group	24	
Effect of exposure to political *discussion* in a recreational group	37	
Effect of exposure to *communal activity* in a recreational group	−7	
	35	Summary effect of recreational group affiliation
"Other" Groups		
Effect of *membership* on "other" groups	−1	
Effect of *activity* on "other" groups	24	
Effect of exposure to political *discussion* on "other" groups	8	
Effect of exposure to *communal activity* on "other" groups	4	
	35	Summary effect of "other" group affiliation

[a]The figures are unstandardized regression coefficients reflecting gains or losses in mean participation score as units above or below the population mean of zero.

dichotomous variables, we can add up the effects for each type of organization. We find that the summary effects of each type are roughly the same—in
each case increasing participation by over a third of a standard deviation.

The data offer strong support for our model of the way organizational
affiliation affects political participation. Unions and recreational groups are
manifestly nonpolitical in their goals. However, these goals differ substantially
between the two types of groups. Furthermore, the types differ in the
opportunities they offer for activity and in the political stimuli they provide.
But despite these differences they appear to operate in the same way in
relation to the individual's participation rate. And all "other" groups operate
in the same way.[6]

To sum up the argument thus far, affiliation with manifestly nonpolitical
organizations does increase an individual's participation rate but only if there
is some political exposure within the organization. And in order to "benefit"
from that exposure the individual must be active in the organization. The
process within quite diverse organizations is similar in this respect. But this
does not mean that associations are all similar in the extent to which they
increase the political activity of their members. Hobby clubs, for instance do
not have as much impact on the political activity of their members as do
political clubs or civic associations. The groups differ in the opportunities they
afford for activity and in the political exposures that take place in them. Thus
political clubs have a greater impact on the participation rates of their
members, because more members of such groups are active and there are more
political stimuli than is the case for recreational groups. On the other hand,
the latter kind of group also has its impact, because it provides similar
opportunities to be active and similar stimuli, even if somewhat less frequently.

"PARTICIPATION PRONENESS"

We raised a third question at the beginning of this chapter: Do the
experiences within organizations really lead to increased political participation, or are those who join organizations, become active members, and are
exposed to political stimuli simply those citizens who are "participation
prone," who for personality or other reasons are more likely to become
politically involved anyway? We cannot deal with that question fully with our
data, but we can make some attempt at an answer. As we pointed out, we are
uncertain as to the causal direction of organizational affiliation and political
participation: Does the individual who is "participation prone" join organizations and also become involved in politics, or do individuals join organizations
and, because of the exposure to stimuli within those organizations, become
involved in politics? The fact that it is not membership per se but active

---

[6] Our technique probably underweighs the magnitude of impact of "other" organizations because they are
reduced to a "dummy" variable, where one is either a member or not (no matter how many), active or not (no
matter how often), etc. However, this does not affect our general finding of the independent residual effect of
recreational groups and unions.

membership combined with exposure to political stimuli that appears to be associated with political participation does not help us answer the question. A general participation proneness might lead to greater activity within organizations and to exposure to political stimuli as well as to political participation.

One way of obtaining at least a partial answer to this question is to see whether organizational exposure has an impact on the individual's political participation rate over and above his general tendencies to be active. We attempt to do this in Tables 11-5 and 11-6. In these tables we reconsider the relationship between exposure to political discussion and to community activities in organizations on the one hand and political activity on the other. Our purpose is to separate the component that reflects exposure to these political stimuli in organizations from the component that reflects the general level of activity of the individual. By this we mean simply that individuals who report that political discussions go on in the organizations of which they are members are also individuals who are quite likely themselves to engage in political discussion. Indeed, there may be political discussion in their organizations simply because they themselves initiate such discussions, or political activists may interpret as political a discussion that less politicized members would consider totally nonpolitical. One would, in that case, not be dealing with an effect of the organizational involvement of the individual, but rather with a characteristic that the individual brings to his membership. The same could be said for exposure to community activities.

Therefore we attempt to assess the impact of organizational exposure while controlling for the impact of the individual's general propensity to engage in political discussion or to engage in community-oriented activity. The data on political discussions are reported in Table 11-5. We know already that there is a fairly large gain in mean participation rate when one compares active organization members exposed to political discussion with other individuals. If the citizen is exposed to political discussion in an organization where he is active, his corrected mean participation rate is about 43 points greater than if he is not exposed. In Table 11-5 we enter into a multiple-regression analysis several dummy variables representing other characteristics of the individual: whether or not he discusses national politics and whether or not he discusses local politics. In addition, because those exposed to political discussion are also more likely to be active in other organizations, we enter a variable summarizing the individual's activities in other organizations. Having removed the effects on his political participation rate of the respondent's propensity to discuss politics as well as his other organizational activities, we can see the residual effect of his exposure to discussion in his organization. The resulting figures are unstandardized regression weights, as in Table 11-4. The interesting finding is that, having partialed out the impact of *his own* discussion of politics, we find that exposure to political discussion in organizations still has a large impact on his participation rate as measured by the unstandardized regression coefficient. Indeed, the impact on his participation rate does not decline very much and is as large as the impact of the combination of his own discussion of local and national politics.

These data clearly support an interpretation that the exposure to political discussion in organizations does lead to an increase in political activity and

Table 11-5

The Impact of Exposure to Political Discussion in Organizations, *Controlling for* the Respondent's Own Political Discussion and All Other Organizational Activities

	Gain in corrected mean participation rate[a]
Independent effect of exposure to political discussion in organizations while controlling for:	34
1. Discussion of national politics	8
2. Discussion of local politics	26
3. Activity in other organizations	2

[a]Figures are unstandardized regression coefficients.

does not reflect merely a general propensity to engage in political conversation and activity. If it were the latter, one would assume that these exposures would have no residual impact on activity once one had controlled for the individual's own frequency of political discussion.

This interpretation is also supported by the data in Table 11-6. Here we are asking a similar kind of question in relationship to exposure within organizations to community-oriented activity. Over and above the information we have about individual membership in organizations that engage in trying to solve community problems, we also have a number of measures of the individual's own activity in similar kinds of cooperative community problem-solving activities, specifically whether he has worked with local groups active on community problems and whether he has helped form such a group. In Table 11-6 we relate the individual's exposure to community activities in organizations to his propensity to engage in political activities, controlling for his own involvement in cooperative community activity (and controlling again for his other organizational activities). In order to do this, we must change our dependent variable, which has been a general measure of political activity and which includes the cooperative activity that we want to use as a control. Thus Table 11-6 reports as the dependent variable three kinds of activity from the general participation scale—campaign activity, citizen-initiated contacts on a social issue, and voting. Each of these is independent of the measure of cooperative political activity. The measure of the dependent variable is the

Table 11-6

The Impact of Exposure to Communal Activity in Organizations, *Controlling for* the Respondent's Communal Activity and His Other Organizational Activity

	Gain in corrected campaign activity score[a]	Gain in corrected social contacting score[a]	Gain in corrected voting score[a]
A. Original effects of active membership in an organization that takes part in community affairs	31	49	21
B. Independent effects of active membership in an organization that takes part in community affairs while controlling for:	20	32	14
1. Working with a local organization	37	58	30
2. Taking the initiative in forming a local organization	35	47	7
3. Activity in other organizations	20	28	19

[a]Unstandardized regression coefficients.

score on the standard scale for each political activity corrected as usual for other social characteristics.

In Part A of Table 11-6 we consider the impact of active membership in an organization that engages in community activity on the three modes of participation. We find that such membership has an impact on all three modes—increasing, for instance, a citizen's campaigning score by 31 points. In Part B of the table we enter the measure of the individual's own activity rate in community-oriented activities (as well as his other organizational activities) and then see whether there still remains a residual impact of exposure to such community activities in organizations. The results appear to be that the impact of exposure to community activities in organizations declines once one has removed the impact of the individual's own propensity to engage in such activities. But there remains a significant residual impact of this exposure to organizational activity. The data are, thus, consistent with the data in Table 11-5. Exposure within organizations to either political discussion or to community-oriented activities is associated with increased rates of political activity, even when one has taken out the individual's own propensity to engage in political discussion or to engage in community activities.

Let us try one more test of our hypothesis that there is an independent effect of organizations over and above the participation proneness of the individual citizen—a test that is about as stringent as we can attempt with our data. Just as we have used a residual measure of political participation from which we have taken out the effect of social position on participation in order to test the effects of organizations over and above such position, we can create a residual measure of political participation from which we take out the effects of social position as well as the effects of those psychological variables that our analysis has told us best predict political activity. Thus we create a "supercorrected" measure of political participation from which we take out the effects of the respondent's social characteristics (socioeconomic status, sex, race, age) plus the effects of his psychological involvement in politics (partisan strength, political attentiveness, sense of contribution to the community, and psychological involvement in politics).[7] If organizational affiliation relates to this supercorrected measure of political participation, it will indicate that organizations have an effect on participation over and above both the individual's social characteristics and his psychological propensities to be politically involved.

The relationship between organizational affiliation and this supercorrected measure is shown in Figure 11-6. The data make clear that organizational affiliation has a positive effect on political participation over and above the social and psychological factors that lead to political participation. The data take the now familiar shape whereby it is active organizational involvement that is decisive. Passive membership makes no difference. Thus, when we control for the psychological participation proneness of the individual, we still find organizations playing an independent role.

Having created our supercorrected score, we can also use it to demonstrate that our model of the process by which organizations increase political participation rates holds, even when one has controlled for these psychological factors. In Figure 11-7 we see the relationship between exposure to political stimuli within organizations—to political discussions and to community

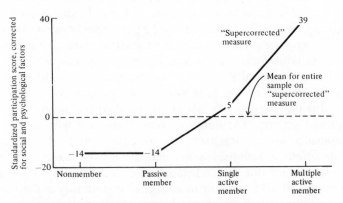

Figure 11-6. Relationship of Organizational Membership and Activity to Political Participation, Controlling for Social and Psychological Characteristics

[7] See Appendix D for these attitude items.

action—and our supercorrected measure of participation, and we plot this relationship separately for inactive members, for members active in a single organization, and for members active in more than one. The figure shows clearly the interactive process at work. Exposure to political stimuli within organizations has an effect on political participation—even when we control for psychological propensity to be involved in politics—but it has that effect largely on those who have high rates of activity within their organizations.

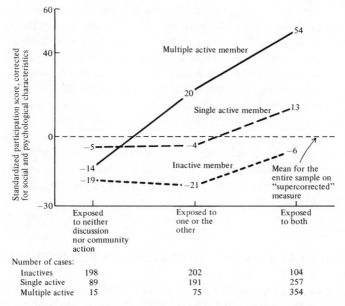

Figure 11-7. Relationship of Exposure to Organizational Stimuli and Political Participation for Active and Inactive Organizational Members, Controlling for Social and Psychological Characteristics

We can summarize this section by returning to the questions we asked at the beginning of our exploration into the link between organizational affiliation and political participation:

1. Is the association between organizational affiliation and political participation the spurious result of the relationship of both to other social characteristics of the individual? The answer is No.

2. What is the process by which organizational affiliation leads to political participation? The answer is that mere passive membership means little for political activity. What counts is a combination of active membership and exposure to political stimuli. And if such activity and exposure are available, affiliation even with manifestly nonpolitical organizations will be associated with a gain in political-participation rates.

3. Is there really an independent effect of organizational affiliation, or is it just that a certain type of citizen is participation prone? Our answer here is more tentative because participation proneness is something we can measure

only indirectly. But the tentative answer is that organizations do have an independent effect over and above any such general propensity toward activity.

ORGANIZATIONS AND THE MODES OF PARTICIPATION

We have thus far been considering the relation between organizational affiliation and political participation in general—the latter measured by our standard participation scale. What of the several modes of participation? The relationship between organizational affiliation, divided into passive and active membership, and the scores for each of the four modes of participation are reported in Figure 11-8. The data can be quickly summarized. Organizational affiliation seems to have the closest relationship with communal activity, followed by campaign activity, and then by voting. It has no relationship with particularized contacting. For the more "intense" political activities—communal and campaign activity—passive membership leads to a somewhat lower score on the respective participation scales, whereas for voting, even passive membership is associated with an increased likelihood of activity. These data are consistent with the distinction we have drawn between voting and other acts. The lower effort and initiative needed to vote perhaps explain why, in contrast to the other acts, passive organizational membership can increase an individual's voting.

One could go further into these differences, but let us turn to another question.

ORGANIZATIONS AND THE DIFFERENCE IN PARTICIPATION
AMONG STATUS GROUPS

How does organizational affiliation interact with socioeconomic status? In particular, to what extent does organizational affiliation lead to deviations from the base-line socioeconomic model we spelled out in Chapter 8? To begin with, it is clear already that organizational affiliation does lead to deviations

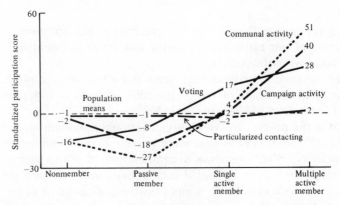

Figure 11-8. Organizational Affiliation and the Four Modes of Participation: Corrected Scores[a]

[a]Autocorrelation that would be due to overlapping questions has been removed.

from the amount of political participation that one would predict on the basis of socioeconomic status alone. Organizational affiliation is an independent force.

But from the point of view of our concern with social stratification and participation, what is important is the way organizational affiliation changes the shape of the relationship between socioeconomic status and participation. We know there is a disparity in political participation between upper- and lower-status groups. Does organizational affiliation increase that disparity or lessen it? Organizational affiliation could have an effect on the disparity in one of two ways. First, affiliation with organizations could have a differential impact on the political participation of individuals at different levels of the status hierarchy. It might "boost" the political activity of members coming from one status group more than it boosted the activity of members from some other status group. Second, even if organizations had no differential impact on individuals at various points in the status hierarchy, organizational affiliation would still change the disparity between upper- and lower-status groups if the proportions of the upper- and lower-status individuals who were exposed to organizational stimuli differed. If a higher proportion of lower-status citizens were affiliated with organizations, the lower stratum *as a group* would gain more in participation from organizations than would the upper—even though only a single lower-status *individual* received no more of a boost upward than any single upper-status *individual.*

Thus organizations can change the participation disparity between upper- and lower-status citizens through differential impact on the *individual* level (increasing one type of citizen's participation more than another) or through differential impact on the *group* level (because more of one group rather than another are exposed to these stimuli). On the individual level, organizational affiliation would *reduce* the participation disparity between upper and lower groups if it gave *lower-status citizens more of a boost* in their participation scores than it gave to upper-status citizens. It would *increase* the disparity if it gave *upper-status citizens more of a participatory boost.* On the group level, organizations would tend to *reduce* the participation disparity between upper- and lower-status citizens *if more lower- than upper-status citizens* were active members of organizations. It would tend to *increase* the disparity if *more upper- than lower-status citizens* were involved in organizations.

The net effect on the participation disparity between socioeconomic levels depends on the joint workings of two factors: the relative amount of boost received by the average individual in each status group and the proportions of these groups that take advantage of the boost. If both effects tended to favor lower social-status citizens, organizational affiliation would reduce the participation disparity. If both effects tended to favor the upper levels, it would increase the disparity. If one effect favored one level and the other the other level, they might cancel each other out, or the disparity might be increased or decreased depending on which effect—the individual or the group—was stronger.

Let us consider the individual impact first. The data on the impact of organizational affiliation on individuals at different points in the status hierarchy are contained in Figure 11-9. There we plot the relationship between organizational membership and activity on the one hand and the standard participation scale on the other, but we do this separately for individuals in the upper, middle, and lower thirds of the socioeconomic hierarchy. The data indicate that organizational affiliation boosts the activity rate of all three status groups. The lines for the three socioeconomic groups all slope sharply upward. But the data also suggest that there is some tendency for organizational

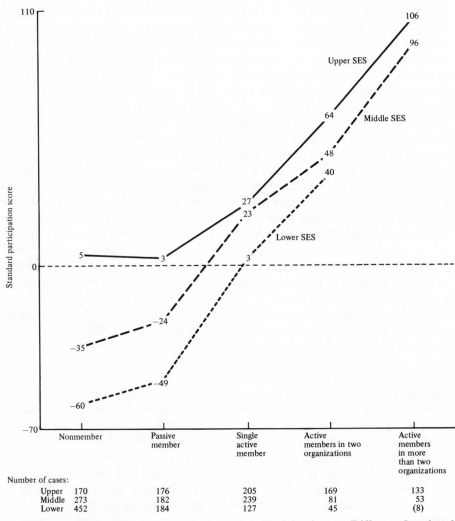

Figure 11-9. Organizational Affiliation and Participation at Different Levels of Socioeconomic Status

involvement to boost the participation rate of lower-status citizens more and thereby to reduce the difference in participation rate between those of lower status and those of higher status. The difference in participation scores between the upper- and lower-status groups is greatest among those who are nonmembers and diminishes as one moves toward those who are more organizationally active. The difference in the participation scores between the upper- and lower-status groups is 65 points among nonmembers, 52 points among passive members, 24 points among those who are active in a single organization, and 24 points among those who are active in two organizations. (There are too few cases of lower-status individuals who are active in more than two organizations to allow comparisons further up the organizational-activity scale.)

In short, on the individual level organizational affiliation has a greater impact on the political participation rate of those lowest in the socioeconomic hierarchy, and thereby works in the direction of lowering the participation gap between upper- and lower-status citizens. If a lower-status citizen becomes an active organization member he is much more like a comparable upper-status citizen in terms of participation than if he is a nonmember. One could speculate on the reasons for this, and two possible interpretations are worth mentioning. One is that additional stimuli to participation—like affiliation with an organization—benefit most those who would not otherwise receive stimuli toward participation. The upper-status individual is exposed to others who are politically active, probably has more resources for effective participation, and has attitudes conducive to participation. He does not "need" the exposure to organizational stimuli as much as does the lower-status individual whose environment and experiences may be more barren in this respect. Another interpretation, not inconsistent with the first, is that the lower-status individuals who are active members represent a group that is deviant from their general social group. Thirty-five percent of the upper-status individuals are active in more than one organization compared with only 6 percent of the lower-status individuals. Thus the upper-status individuals who are organizationally active may represent more individuals whose organizational involvement is a result of conformity to social expectations among those at their social level.

The fact that lower-status individuals are less likely to be among the organizationally active brings us to the next component of our discussion of the way organizational affiliation might affect the disparity in political participation between upper and lower socioeconomic groups: through differences in the proportions exposed to organizational stimuli across the various status groups. Lower-status individuals receive a larger boost in their participation scores by activity in organizations, but a smaller proportion of them receive such a boost because fewer are active in organizations. This fact is seen in Table 11-7, where we compare the three socioeconomic status groups in terms of their amount of organizational involvement. Lower-status individuals are much more likely than upper-status individuals to be nonmembers (56 percent compared to 20 percent) and less likely to be active members (22 percent versus 59 percent fot the lower- and upper-status groups respectively when we combine single and multiple activity).

Table 11-7

Proportions Organizationally Active in Lower, Middle, and Upper Third of SES (in percent)

	Lower SES	Middle SES	Upper SES	Total
Nonmember	56	34	20	38
Passive member	23	22	21	22
Single active member	16	28	24	22
Multiple active member	6	16	35	19
Total	101	100	100	101

Thus the *individual* effects of organizations push in the direction of reducing the participation disparity between upper- and lower-status groups, whereas the *group* effects push in the direction of increasing the disparity. We can measure the net result by combining the two effects. If we weight the amount of "gain" in political participation associated with a particular increase in organizational involvement by the number of people who "take advantage" of that gain, we will have measured the "net" group gain from organizational involvement. For instance, among lower socioeconomic status people there is a difference in average political participation scores of 52 points between those who are passive members and those who are active in a single organization. (As seen in Figure 11-9, among the lower-status citizens, passive members score —49 on participation; members active in a single organization score 3.) This difference we consider to be the "gain" associated with "movement" from passive to single active membership. And as Table 11-7 shows, 16 percent of the lower socioeconomic group "take advantage" of this gain—i.e., 16 percent are active in a single organization. In contrast, upper socioeconomic citizens gain less in political participation from a move from passive membership to single active membership—they gain on the average 24 points. But a larger proportion—24 percent—take advantage of this. To calculate the net gains for the two groups, we multiply the gain in score by the proportion making that gain and divide this, in turn, by the proportion of the population as a whole that is in the single active membership category to obtain figures comparable with those on individual gain. For instance, we multiply the gain of 52 points on the participation scale that a lower-status individual gets from being active in one organization rather than being a passive member by the 16 percent who are active members among that status group, and divide this by 22 percent, which represents the proportion of active members of a single organization in the population as a whole. The result is a net group gain of 24 points on the participation scale for the lower-status group associated with the transition from passive to single active membership.

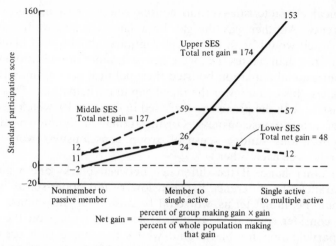

Figure 11-10. Net gains in Participation Rate Through Organizational Affiliation

In Figure 11-10 we plot the net group gains for each step upward in organizational involvement—from nonmember to passive member, passive to active membership in a single group, and single active membership to multiple active membership.[8] The data in this figure offer a sharp contrast to those in Figure 11-9. On the individual level, the disparity between upper and lower status in terms of participation rate was reduced somewhat by organizational affiliation. When we look at the net group effects, we find that the disparity is greatly increased. So many more upper-status individuals are organizationally active, particularly in the multiple active category, that their gain in participation as a group far exceeds that of the lower-status group. One can meaningfully add up the amount of gain that each status group achieves in participation from the three steps upward in organizational involvement. And one finds a net gain for the upper-status group of 174, for the middle group of 127, and for the lower group a net gain of 48. In other words, if we weigh the increase in participation that comes with increased organizational involvement by the numbers who are organizationally involved, we find that the upper-status group has a net increase in participation more than three times greater than that of the lower-status group. In short, organizations increase the disparity in participation between upper- and lower-status groups because upper-status individuals are more likely to take advantage of that gain.

PARTICIPATION OF BLACKS AND WHITES AND THE ROLE OF ORGANIZATIONS

When we considered the difference in rate of participation between black and white Americans in Chapter 10, we stressed the importance of a

[8] The gain in participation for individuals in the various status groups associated with "movement" from single to multiple activity is not directly apparent in Figure 11-7. The reason is that we combine those active in two organizations with those active in more than two to calculate that gain. In Figure 11-7 we had separated these two groups.

psychological characteristic—group consciousness—as a means of reducing that difference. Another way the gap between black and white participation might be closed would be through organizational affiliation. If blacks became more organized than whites (i.e., were active in more organizations) and/or if their organizational affiliation boosted their political activity more than it did among whites, this could lower the racial gap in participation. (This would not be inconsistent with the processes discussed in Chapter 10, which depended on a sense of group consciousness. Organizational affiliation—particularly in black organizations—and a sense of group consciousness would probably mutually reinforce each other.)

On the other hand, if the difference between blacks and whites in this respect parallels the difference between lower- and upper-status individuals, blacks would be, in net terms, worse off because of organizations.

Let us consider some data. Figure 11-11 presents data on the individual gains in participation for blacks and whites that come with organizational affiliation. Such affiliation clearly "benefits" black citizens more: among nonmembers and passive members, whites are quite a bit more politically active than blacks; among active members in a single organization the gap is reduced; among active members in more than one organization the situation is reversed, with blacks somewhat more active than whites.[9]

But what about the net effect, which depends on the rate of organizational membership as well? As Table 11-8 indicates, whites are somewhat more likely to be active organizational members than blacks, though the disparity is not nearly so great as that between upper- and lower-status citizens reported in Table 11-7. In Figure 11-12, we combine the two effects. What we find is a circumstance quite similar to that in relation to the various socioeconomic

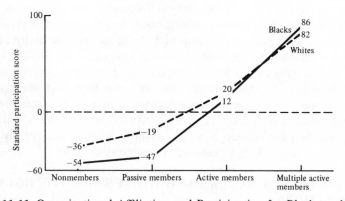

Figure 11-11. Organizational Affiliation and Participation for Blacks and Whites

[9] The data in Figure 11-11 are uncorrected for the effects of social status. If we were to make such a correction, the line for blacks would generally shift upward but it would not change the overall shape of the difference between the two racial groups. Among those inactive in organizations or passive members, blacks would be a bit more active than whites. Among those active in organizations, blacks would be ahead of whites in political participation by a larger amount. In other words, the point we are making here—that the black citizen receives more of a boost from his organizational activity than does the white—would not change.

Table 11-8

**Proportions Organizationally Active
Among Blacks and Whites (in percent)**

	Blacks	Whites
Nonmember	48	34
Passive member	22	22
Single active member	15	24
Multiple active member	15	20
Total	100	100

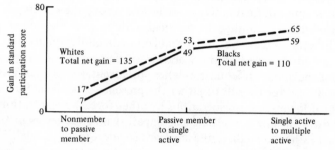

Figure 11-12. Gains in Participation Rate Through Organizational Affiliation for Blacks and Whites

status levels reported in Figure 11-10. At each step upward in organizational involvement, the net gain for whites is somewhat greater than it is for blacks. And the overall net gain for whites is 135 points on the standard participation scale, while that for blacks is 110 points. Therefore, when one considers the overall effect of organizations on blacks and whites—how much of a gain in political participation an individual receives from his affiliation and how many individuals from each racial group are affiliated—one finds that the gap between blacks and whites is increased somewhat.[10]

However, the gap does not expand as greatly as it does between citizens from upper- and lower-status groups, as can be seen clearly if one compares Figure 11-10 with Figure 11-12. This is so for two reasons: On the individual level, blacks receive a particularly large boost from their affiliation with organizations and, indeed, participate politically more than whites if they are

[10] The fact that the lines for blacks and whites are roughly parallel and do not diverge as one moves to the right in Figure 11-12 does not mean that the relative positions of the two groups remain the same. What is plotted on Figure 11-12 is the *net gain* in political participation for each of the groups as one moves up the steps of organizational activity. Thus, Figure 11-12 shows that at each succeeding step in organizational involvement the net gain in participation is greater for both groups (i.e., both lines slope upward) but at each step the gain for whites is greater than that for blacks.

active in more than one organization. And, though they are somewhat less likely to be organizationally active than whites, the difference is not as severe as that between citizens of lower and upper socioeconomic status.

SUMMARY

In sum, what can we say about the role of organizational affiliation in relation to citizen participation and, in particular, in relation to the disparity in participation between more advantaged and less advantaged groups? Do voluntary associations increase political equality, or diminish it? One may have to answer in terms of actuality and potentiality. In fact, organizations increase the political gap, for the simple reason that those who come from advantaged groups are more likely to be organizationally active. Upper-status groups are, to begin with, more politically active. They are also more active in organizations. And, because the latter type of activity has an independent effect in increasing political activity—over and above the effects of socioeconomic status—their advantage in political activity over the lower groups is increased. In short, when we add organizational affiliation to our standard socioeconomic model, we find the workings of that model accelerated.

This is not inevitable. In countries where disadvantaged groups have a better organizational base (as a result of either the presence of socialist movements or the creation of lower-class organizations by other forces), organizational affiliation and activity do not exacerbate participatory inequalities as in the United states, but act rather to mediate the standard socioeconomic model.[11]

Therefore organizations remain an important "potential" source for reducing the participation gap between the socially advantaged and disadvantaged. As our data show, the latter gain more in their political participation through organizations than do the more advantaged groups. If rates of membership among the disadvantaged were to increase, the net effect would be to reduce the political-participation disparity. Currently, this potentiality seems greater for black Americans than for lower-status citizens in general. Though their rate of organizational activity is still lower than that of whites, the gap is not large. Furthermore, blacks appear to receive a particularly large boost upward in political participation from organizational activity. And, as our discussion in Chapter 10 made clear, they have the basis for increased organizational activity, a sense of group consciousness around which organizations can be formed. But this is a potential result. In actual fact, voluntary associations lead to greater inequalities in participation.

[11] See Nie, Powell, and Prewitt, *Social Structure and Political Participation,* Part 2. As we shall see in Chapter 12, some of the same factors are crucial for political parties—their effects on participatory equality may have a great deal to do with the extent that they, like voluntary associations, are organized around lower-status citizens.

Chapter 12
Political Parties
and Political Participation

Most voluntary associations are nonpolitical in purpose. If they bring citizens to political participation, it is often an unintended consequence of the citizen's experiences in such organizations. Political parties, on the other hand, are purposefully political, and one of their major purposes in most cases is the creation of politically active citizens out of politically passive ones. In this chapter, we will examine the role of political parties in relation to citizen participation in politics. And we will be particularly interested in the role of parties in relation to our standard socioeconomic model of political participation. Political parties often attempt to increase the participation of otherwise inactive groups: Labor or socialist parties attempt to mobilize the votes and political activity of workers; agrarian parties attempt the same for farmers; ethnically or religiously based parties often attempt the same for inactive minority groups. Thus political parties may operate, explicitly and purposefully, to modify the workings of the standard socioeconomic model.

However, this may be more likely in circumstances where the parties are themselves based in particular social groups. A labor or a socialist party will be more effective in mobilizing the activity of workers than will a party with a clientele from across the socioeconomic spectrum. Campbell and Rokkan have shown that this is indeed the case when one compares the class-based parties of Norway with the broad-based parties in the United States.[1] The former are more effective in drawing in participants from lower socioeconomic groups. Our argument about the standard socioeconomic model helps explain why this is so: Where a party draws supporters from various socioeconomic levels, the same processes that lead citizens from upper-status groups to higher levels of participation in the society at large operate within the parties as well, leading to the over-participation of the upper-status groups. Thus in the United States, where both political parties are broadly based, it may be that they do not reduce the disparity in participation between upper- and lower-status groups.

We shall pursue this question in a somewhat different manner from the way we pursued the impact on participation of affiliation with voluntary associations. In relation to voluntary groups we asked whether membership or activity in such a group led to greater political participation. We cannot ask the same question about parties—i.e., whether membership or activity in a party leads to greater political participation—because we define party membership and activity as political. We shall, therefore, consider in this chapter the relationship between subjective identification with a political party and political activity. Is the party identifier more active than the nonidentifier? How does this relate to the participation disparity among the socioeconomic groups? In some sense, we shall be exploring the role of a psychological orientation (party identification) rather than the working of a particular institution (the political party). But because that psychological orientation derives from association with an institution, we believe we are nevertheless dealing with the role of party organizations. If, by identifying with one or another of the American political parties, lower-status citizens are brought to participate more, and if that participation reduces the participation disparity between upper- and lower-status groups, then the parties will be playing an important democratizing and equalizing role.

Party identification would act to modify the workings of the standard socioeconomic model under the following conditions:

1. Those who identify with a political party are more active politically than the nonidentifiers.

2. This greater level of activity is not merely the reflection of a higher social status among party identifiers.

These first two conditions merely mean that party identification has an independent effect on participation, over and above any effect associated with differences in the social composition of the identifiers and the nonidentifiers. For this identification to be associated with a reduction in the participation disparity between social groups, the following would also have to hold:

[1] Rokkan and Campbell, "Norway and the United States of America," *Int. Social Science Journal,* op. cit.

3. There is some combination of the following "individual" and "group" effects such that the joint effect is to create a net increase in the participation coming from lower socioeconomic groups in comparison with upper groups.

(a). The average *individual* from lower socioeconomic groups receives a greater "boost" in his participation rate from his partisan identification than does the average upper-status citizen.

(b). More citizens from the lower status *group* have partisan identifications and, therefore, "take advantage" of whatever boost in participation comes from such identification.

If the boost received by lower-status citizens is substantially larger than that received by upper-status citizens, condition 3(b) does not have to hold. Conversely, if the proportion of lower-status citizens who are party identifiers is substantially larger than the proportion among upper-status citizens, the participation disparity will be reduced even if lower-status citizens do not receive as large an individual boost in their participation rate. What counts is the joint effect of the gain in participation associated with party identification and the number of citizens who make this gain.

We must elaborate these hypotheses in one way: In relation to conditions 3(a) and 3(b) we expect differences between the two parties. The Democratic Party is much more likely than the Republican to play a role in diminishing the gap between lower- and upper-social-status citizens for several reasons. First, the Democrats draw their support more heavily from lower socioeconomic groups. If there is a gain in participation associated with party affiliation, more lower-status individuals will gain from Democratic affiliation than from Republican. This would be consistent with the traditional role of the Democratic Party, which, particularly in urban areas, has attempted to mobilize working-class political activity as a way of countering the political power of the more established social groups. Second, one would expect a greater boost upward in participation on the individual level for the lower-status citizen who identifies with the Democratic Party than for the one who identifies with the Republicans. This is to be expected because the policies of the Democratic Party are more likely to be congruent with the interests of such citizens. Republican identifiers from lower socioeconomic strata will be in more of a dissonant situation, and we might expect this to lower their rate of participation. In short, we can modify conditions 3, 3(a), and 3(b) by saying that we expect the differential effects on lower-status groups to work more through Democratic Party affiliation than through Republican.

Let us now consider some data. In Figure 12-1 we present the participation scores for five kinds of citizens: strong Democrats, weak Democrats, independents, weak Republicans, and strong Republicans.[2] We present their participation scores on our overall scale of participation, as well as scales representing their activity rates on each of the four modes of participation. We have put the strong supporters of the two parties at opposite ends of the horizontal axis of the graph, and the independents in the middle. Thus the U-

---

[2] For the items used to define party supporters, see pp. 377-378.

shape of the curve for overall participation, for voting, and for campaign activity indicates that the strong party identifiers are, on the average, more active than those whose identification is weaker, and that both groups of identifiers—the strong and the weak—are more active than the independents. For overall participation, for voting, and for campaign activity, strong party identifiers (with either party) participate more than the average for the population as a whole. Weak identifiers and independents are, on the other hand, less active than average.

There is, however, an asymmetry between the parties. Republican identifiers are, on the average, more active than Democratic identifiers, and this disparity is greatest among those with strong identifications. Thus the average strong Democrat scores 10 on the standard participation scale, whereas the average strong Republican scores 52.

When it comes to communal activity, we see a pattern somewhat different from that for overall participation, for voting, and for campaign activity. For one thing, the relationship between partisan identification and activity is weaker than that with voting and campaign activity—a fact to be expected, given our previous discussion of the nonpartisan nature of communal activity. On the other hand, we also find that the strong Republicans are substantially more active in this way than any other group. In particular, they are strikingly more active in communal activity than are the strong Democrats. The strong Democrat is, in fact, a bit less active than the average citizen in this mode of participation.

However, the asymmetry may be the result of the higher average socioeconomic level of the strong Republicans. Communal activity, as we showed, is relatively weakly related to partisan identification but is strongly associated with social class. And because strong Republicans have higher average social status than strong Democrats, their greater activity rates may simply reflect this.[3]

We can, thus, turn to some corrected measures of participation, where we use our usual procedures to remove the effects on participation of the social background of the individual. There are two points for which this corrected measure is important. We wish to see, for one thing, whether the correction flattens the U-shaped curve; that is, whether the higher participation rates among strong identifiers is merely a reflection of a higher average social status. Second, we wish to see if the asymmetry whereby Republican identifiers are more active than Democratic identifiers is removed when we control for social status.

The relevant data are in Figure 12-2; the groups are the same but the measures ot participation are corrected for social status. (The dotted line repeats the uncorrected measures for comparison.) The U-shaped pattern remains in relation to overall activity, to voting, and to campaign activity. It

---

[3] There is no relationship between particularized contacting and party identification, a fact consistent with the nonpolitical nature of such activity.

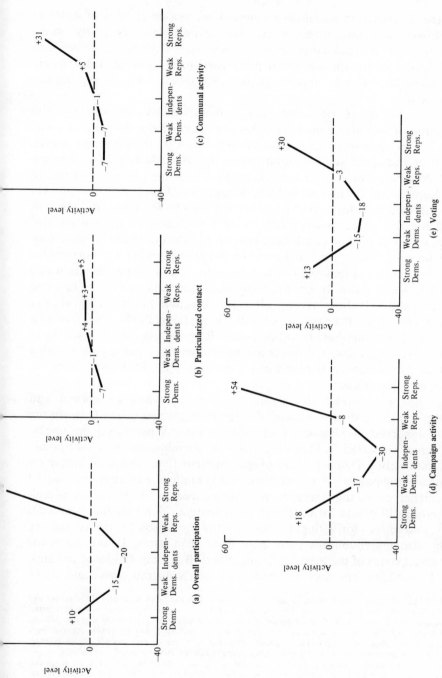

Figure 12-1. Party Identification and Participation: Uncorrected Scores[a]

[a]In all sections of this figure, the number of cases in the sample were strong Democrats, 697; weak Democrats, 1,057; independents, 207; weak Republicans, 603; and strong Republicans, 347.

(a) Overall participation

(b) Particularized contact

(c) Communal activity

(d) Campaign activity

(e) Voting

is not the difference in social-class composition among citizens at different levels of partisan identification that explains the higher level of activity among those with closer psychological ties to political parties. Those who have such strong identification with a political party participate more than one would expect, given their social composition; those with weaker ties or with no ties participate less.

The fact that the participation rates of those who identify strongly with either party are well above the population average when one corrects for social class indicates an independent relationship between partisanship and participation over and above socioeconomic status. But one additional fact is worth noting. When one corrects for socioeconomic status, the participation rate of strong Republicans declines somewhat, whereas for Democrats it goes up. On the uncorrected scale for overall participation, the rate for strong Republicans was 52, but the corrected score falls to 40. For Democrats the uncorrected score was 10, but the corrected score rises to 22. The difference is interesting. The decline in participation rate for strong Republicans when one corrects for social status indicates that one of the reasons for their high participation rate is their high social status. It is not the only reason, as indicated by the fact that their rate is still well above average after the correction, but it is a reason. For Democrats this is not the case. Social status, if anything, holds down their rate of participation somewhat. In other words, Republicans clearly come from high social-status groups, and this is one reason why they participate as much as they do. Democrats do not, and this is one reason the Democratic activists participate so much less.[4]

This change—whereby Democratic rates go up when we correct and Republican rates go down—reduces the asymmetry noted earlier between the participation rates of Democrats and Republicans. Whereas on the uncorrected scores (reported in Figure 12-1) strong Republicans scored 42 points higher than strong Democrats on overall participation, 36 points higher on campaign participation, 38 points higher on communal participation, and 17 points higher on voting, these figures are reduced to 18 points for overall participation, 19 points for campaign participation, 17 points for communal activity, and to zero for voting. In short, part of the reason for the asymmetry whereby strong Republicans participate more than strong Democrats is the higher social status of the Republican identifiers. But some difference remains. Strong Republicans are more active than strong Democrats—over and above

[4] The situation *vis-à-vis* strong Democrats and strong Republicans may be made clearer if the reader will remember two parallel sets of relationships. The situation in relation to strong Republicans is like that found *vis-à-vis* organizational membership. Organizational members were found to be much more active in politics. When we corrected for socioeconomic status their activity rate fell, indicating that one reason for their high level of activity was their higher than average social status. But their activity rate was still above average, indicating also that there was a relationship with organizational affiliation independent of social status.

The situation in relation to strong Democrats is similar to, but not exactly like, that in relation to blacks. In each case, a correction for socioeconomic status raises the participation rate. The meaning of this is that blacks and strong Democrats are somewhat lower than average in socioeconomic status and that fact "depresses" their participation rates. Remove that effect and we find that blacks participate about as much as the average white, and, similarly, the strong Democrats' above average participation is even greater.

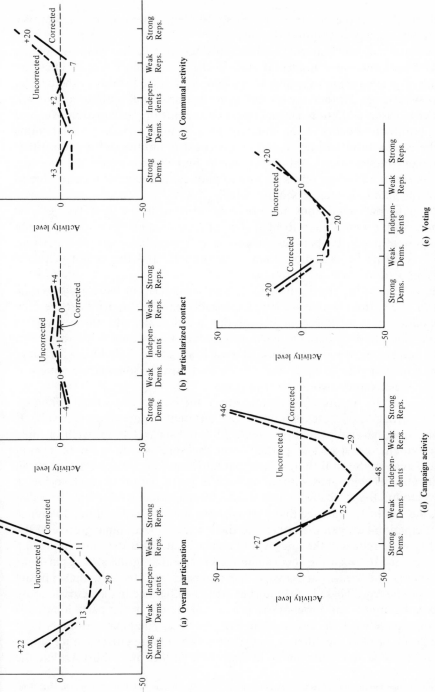

(a) Overall participation

(b) Particularized contact

(c) Communal activity

(d) Campaign activity

(e) Voting

Figure 12-2. Party Identification and Participation: Corrected Scores[a]

[a]The number of cases in Figure 12-1 apply to this figure.

the difference that the disparity in their social composition would predict. We shall return shortly to inquire why this is so.

The data indicate that party affiliation does modify the workings of the standard socioeconomic model, at least to the extent that it has an effect on the rate of participation over and above that of the social status of the citizen. If one were to go further, as we did with organizational affiliation, and ask whether partisan affiliation has an impact on the rate of participation over and above both components of the standard socioeconomic model—social status and the civic attitudes (interest and involvement in politics, information) that accompany higher social status—we would find this is indeed the case. In short, partisan affiliation offers a route to political participation alternative to that of the standard socioeconomic model.

The data presented thus far are consistent with the first two of our conditions that would have to hold if partisan affiliation were to reduce the participation disparity between upper- and lower-status groups; partisan identifiers do participate more than nonidentifiers, and this is not merely a reflection of their social background.[5]

Let us turn to the third point: Does partisan affiliation have a *differential* effect on the various socioeconomic levels such that the disparity between the participation rate of those higher in the social scale and those lower is reduced? For that to happen, partisan identification would have to have a greater impact on the participation rate of lower-status individuals, or more lower-status individuals would have to be partisans, or some combination of the two circumstances would have to occur.

In Figure 12-3 we present data relevant to the impact of partisan affiliation on the participation rate of citizens at different socioeconomic levels. It contains data parallel to that on Figure 12-1, but separately for each of three socioeconomic groups. The participation measure is our scale of overall political activity. Several things are apparent from Figure 12-3. First, partisan identification is associated with an increase in participation for each socioeconomic group; the U-shaped curve exists for all three levels. On the other hand, there is little evidence that partisan identification reduces the difference in participation between the upper and the lower socioeconomic groups. If the disparity were reduced, the lines would converge at either extreme, indicating less difference between the socioeconomic groups among the strong partisans than among the weak partisans or the independents. In fact, the opposite appears to be true. There is a somewhat greater difference in participation rate between the upper- and lower-status groups among the strong party identifiers than among the weak partisans or the independents. The figures at the bottom of the graph present the difference in score between those citizens in the upper third of the socioeconomic hierarchy and those in the lower third. Unlike the

---

[5] The fact that the process seems to work more strongly for Republican than Democratic identifiers is not inconsistent with these two points. It was only in relation to point 3—that there be differential impact on the social classes—that we expected a stronger relationship with Democratic than with Republican affiliation.

situation with voluntary associations—the boost in participation that comes from party identification is greater for upper-status groups than for lower. Thus condition 3(a), whereby lower-status citizens get a bigger participating boost, does not hold.

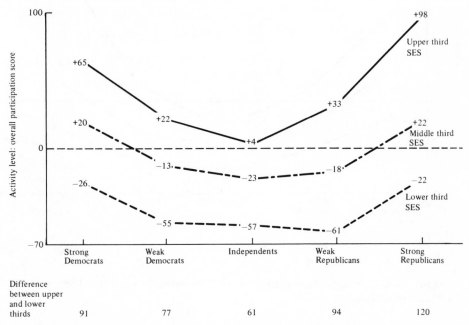

Figure 12-3. Overall Participation Score (Uncorrected) and Party Identification for Three Socioeconomic Levels

In one sense the data are consistent with our expectations. Though the disparity between the social levels grows with increased identification with either political party, the disparity increases more with Republican identification. The biggest gap in participation rate between those in the upper and those in the lower socioeconomic groups is found among strong Republicans. Thus, the expected difference between the political parties does appear, though in a somewhat different form. We had expected Democratic identification to reduce the gap between the social levels more than did Republican identification. Both identifications increase the gap, but Republican affiliation increases it more.

Figure 12-3 reports data for overall participation. Is a similar pattern apparent for the various participatory modes? Figure 12-4 and 12-5 present relevant data for the two electoral modes of activity—voting and campaign activity—for which partisanship is most important. The pattern is quite different for the two modes. In Figure 12-4 we see that the relationship between partisan identification and campaign activity for the three socioeco-

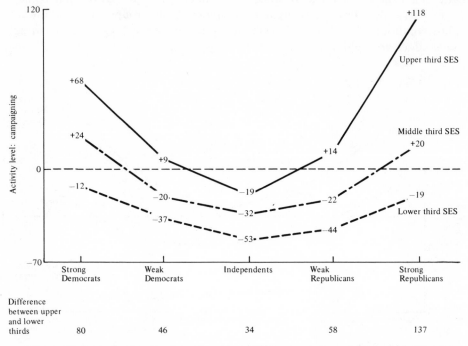

Figure 12-4. Campaign Participation Score (Uncorrected) and Party Identification for Three Socioeconomic Levels

nomic levels closely resembles the pattern for overall participation: The gap in participation between the upper and lower socioeconomic groups is greatest among those with strong party identification and especially great among strong Republican identifiers.

When it comes to voting, the pattern is quite different. Indeed, in relation to voting we find that partisan identification greatly reduces the participation-rate gap among the social levels. Among those with strong partisan identification, there is almost no difference in voting rates between the upper and the middle social levels. And the difference between the lower and the upper two levels in voting rate is much smaller among the strong identifiers of either party than among weak identifiers or independents.

Thus the data for voting fit condition 3(a): Lower-status citizens receive more of a participatory boost from partisan identification than do upper-status citizens. But the data for campaign activity form the opposite pattern, with a bigger boost being received by upper-status citizens. (And, though we do not present the data, the latter is true as well for communal participation.) The finding is important, and suggests a possible revision in our view of the way partisan identification affects the difference in participation among social levels.

When it comes to voting, partisan identification is a most useful orientation,

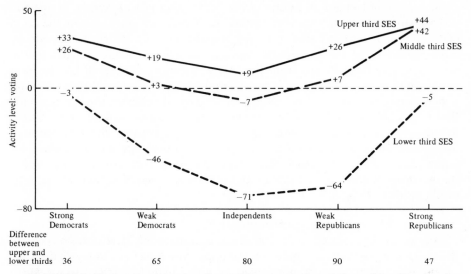

Figure 12-5. Voting Participation Score (Uncorrected) and Party Identification for Three Socioeconomic Levels

for it both guides the direction of the vote and helps bring the citizen to the polls. It is, however, not as important as a key to voting for upper-status citizens as it is for lower-status citizens.[6] Among upper-status citizens, general interest in politics, norms about voting, peer pressures, and the like are well developed. They lead the citizen to vote even if he has weak partisan identification. Hence, among upper-status citizens voting rates differ little across the various levels of partisan identification. But among lower-status groups, in which such civic attitudes and norms are not as fully entrenched, partisan identification becomes an all-important orientation. When a lower-status citizen has a weak or nonexistent partisan identification, there is little to bring him to the polls, so his voting rate is low indeed. A strong party identification changes this substantially. In this sense, it can be said that partisan identification mobilizes to political activity lower-status citizens who might otherwise be inactive, and it does this more than it mobilizes upper-status citizens.

But partisan identification can do this only in relation to the vote—an act that, as we have seen, requires relatively little initiative and can be performed in the absence of general political interest and involvement. When it comes to those activities that depend on a deeper political involvement—on psychological involvement in politics or on information—partisanship gives a bigger boost in participation to those upper-status citizens who are likely to have these other requisites as well.

[6] One reason why party identification might have so little effect on the voting rate of upper-status citizens might be that they vote so regularly already there is little room to move upward. But this is not the case. Our measure of voting includes local voting and even for upper-status citizens, they could vote at a higher rate.

One last point ought to be noted about the data just presented. If one considers Figures 12-3 to 12-5, an interesting point becomes clear *vis-à-vis* the asymmetry in participation between strong Republicans and strong Democrats. As those figures show, the asymmetry depends entirely on the higher participation rates of strong Republicans from the upper socioeconomic level. On the other two socioeconomic levels there is no difference between strong Republicans and strong Democrats. As we have shown previously, this higher level of participation is not solely due to the higher average socioeconomic level of the strong Republicans in contrast to the strong Democrats, because the difference remains even when we correct for social status. Thus we are left with the interesting phenomenon of a particularly high rate of activity coming from upper-status strong Republicans, a rate that exceeds what even their high social status would predict. We shall return to them later.

The "Net" Effects of Partisan Identification.

As we have pointed out, the overall impact of partisanship on the differences in participation between the upper and lower social levels depends on the boost in participation received by individuals from the various social levels as well as the proportions of those levels that "take advantage" of the stimulus of partisanship. We have seen that citizens from all status levels receive a boost in participation if they are partisans, but that upper-status individuals receive more of a boost when it comes to difficult modes of participation—campaigning and communal activity—while lower-status individuals receive more of a boost in voting participation. The overall net effect of partisan identification may depend, therefore, on the proportions at the various socioeconomic levels who are partisan. Table 12-1 presents data on this. It is clear from this table that lower-status citizens are more likely to be strong Democrats, and upper-status citizens to be strong Republicans. But the number of strong partisans is so much greater on the Democratic side, that lower-status citizens are more likely to have a strong party identification: 43

Table 12-1

Party Identification at Various Socioeconomic Levels (in percent)

	Lower socioeconomic level	Middle socioeconomic level	Upper socioeconomic level
Strong Democrat	34	23	15
Weak Democrat	38	39	31
Independent	6	7	8
Weak Republican	13	20	30
Strong Republican	9	11	16
Total	100	100	100

percent do in the lowest socioeconomic group, 34 percent in the middle socioeconomic group, and 31 percent in the upper group. Thus condition 3(b) holds: Lower-status citizens are more likely to be strong party identifiers, and therefore more likely to "take advantage" of whatever boost in participation is associated with such identification.

What then is the combined effect of the differential in the individual boost in participation received at the several social levels and the differential in proportions who are strong identifiers? We can answer this by using the same approach as in Chapter 11 to see the effects of organizational involvement on participation at each social level: We multiply the gain in participation associated with increased partisan identification by the proportion of that social level taking advantage of that gain,[7] i.e., by the proportion who have a partisan identification.

Thus, if the difference in participation rate between weak and strong Democrats is 10 points for a particular socioeconomic group, we consider that to be the gain in participation associated with movement from weak to strong Democratic identification. We then multiply this by the proportion of the group that takes advantage of this gain—i.e., that has a strong Democratic identification. The result is the net gain for that group. (We divide these figures by the proportion of the population as a whole that makes that gain, but this merely puts the figures on a comparable scale without changing the results.)

As our previous results have told us, it would be misleading to consider this question from the point of view of our measure of overall participation; the difference between voting and the other modes of participation is great. Thus, we will consider the data separately for the two electoral modes of participation—campaign activity and voting.

Figure 12-6 contains the data on campaign activity. Across the horizontal axis of the graph we place the four steps upward in partisan identification that are possible—from independent to weak identifier and from weak to strong identifier for each of the two parties. We then plot, for each socioeconomic level separately, the net gain associated with that step upward—i.e., the size of the average gain multiplied by the proportion making it. The results are quite striking. For one thing, there is a sharp difference in the net group gains at the Democratic end of the scale and at the Republican. The net gain from strong Democratic affiliation is about the same for all three socioeconomic levels. In particular, there is hardly any difference between the top and the bottom socioeconomic groups—the former have a net gain of 37, the latter a gain of 35. Though the net gains are similar, however, the figures are differently composed for the two groups. The individual members of the top socioeconomic group gain on the average twice as much from being strong rather than weak Democrats, but about twice as large a proportion of the bottom socioeconomic group are strong Democrats. The two effects cancel each other out, and the two socioeconomic levels gain about the same amount from their identification with the Democratic Party.

---

[7] For a description of the technique, see Chapter 11, pp. 200-204.

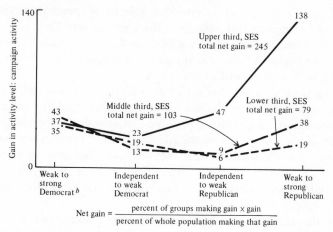

Figure 12-6. Net Gains in Campaign Participation Rate Through Party Identification for Three Socioeconomic Levels[a]

[a] This refers to the gain in participation associated with a movement from weak to strong Democratic affiliation.

On the Republican side of the graph, the individual and the group effects work in the same direction, leaving the upper socioeconomic group with a great net advantage in campaign participation from Republican identification. And as the figures for the total net gain in campaign participation associated with partisan identification indicate, the upper socioeconomic group gains more from association with the two parties combined than does the lower.

The figures for the net gain in voting (Figure 12-7) form a sharp contrast with those for campaign participation. Here is a case where both forces—the individual level gains in participation and the proportions taking advantage of such gains—work in the same direction to benefit the bottom socioeconomic group. More of that group have strong party identification and gain on the average more from such affiliation than do upper-status citizens. Thus at both the Democratic and Republican ends of the continuum, the lower group gains more in voting rate from partisanship than does the upper. In fact, the net gain for the bottom socioeconomic group is larger than that for the other two socioeconomic levels for three out of four of the possible "steps upward" in party identification. Only for the "step" from independent to weak Republican identification do the other levels gain more. Furthermore, consistent with our expectation, the gain is greater on the Democratic side. And, reversing the situation in relation to campaign activity, the total net gain in voting associated with partisanship is greatest for the bottom socioeconomic group, and least for the topmost group.

Where does this leave us *vis-à-vis* our earlier question as to the extent to which partisan identification increases or decreases the disparity in participation across the various socioeconomic levels? The results are somewhat more

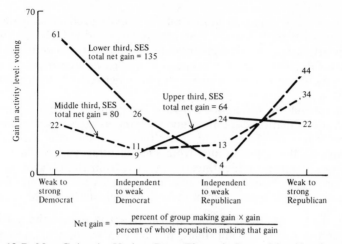

Figure 12-7. Net Gains in Voting Rate Through Party Identification for Three Socioeconomic Levels

complicated than expected but quite interesting. We cited several conditions that had to hold if the disparity were to be reduced:

1. Partisanship had to be associated with greater activity.

2. This had to be more than a mere reflection of the social-class composition of the various partisan identifiers.

3. The multiplicative effects of the following two conditions had to have the net effect of helping the lower group.

(a) Individuals from the lower socioeconomic levels had to receive more of a participatory boost from party identification than did those from higher levels.

(b) A higher proportion of lower-status citizens had to be partisan identifiers.

We added the subsidiary hypothesis that, if identification worked to help lower-status citizens, it would do so to a greater extent on the Democratic than on the Republican side of the scale.

The results of our analysis are as follows:

1. The first two conditions clearly hold: partisan identifiers are more active, and this does not merely reflect their socioeconomic status.

2. When it comes to the gain in participation for the individual citizen, the results differ depending upon the mode of participation. The upper groups gain more from partisan identification in campaign activity; the lower groups gain more than the upper in voting.

3. Lower-status citizens are more likely to be strong party identifiers.

4. The result is that when it comes to voting, the individual and the group effects both aid the lower socioeconomic group, and the net effect of partisanship is to greatly diminish the difference between the various socioeconomic levels in voting rate.

5. But when it comes to more difficult activity such as campaigning, the greater gain in participation that upper-status individuals get from their partisan affiliation overwhelms the advantage that lower-status citizens get from the fact that a greater proportion are party identifiers. In this case, partisan identification increases the disparity between the upper- and lower-status groups.

6. In general, the difference between the political parties is as expected. Democratic affiliation does more good for the lower socioeconomic groups because more are Democratic identifiers and because the differential advantage to the upper groups from identification with a party is not as great from Democratic identification as it is from Republican. In fact, we found on the Republican side that upper-status strong Republicans are particularly active, more so than even their high status would predict.

In sum, party identification does appear to act to reduce the participation disparity across socioeconomic lines, but only in relation to the vote. As a mobilizer of lower socioeconomic groups to the polls it is effective. But when it comes to more difficult political activity, partisan identity seems to accelerate the workings of the standard socioeconomic model: It leads upper-status citizens to participate more. As with voluntary associations, partisanship has equalizing·potentialities, but these are not realized.[8] It can mobilize citizens to the easy act of voting, but for more difficult acts, more is needed, such as psychological involvement in politics. Upper-status citizens tend to have such involvement, and party identification helps them more. For lower-status citizens, party identification is not enough to lead to more difficult political acts.[9]

Policy Preferences and the Hyperactive Republicans

We have not yet solved one puzzle: the very high activity rates of the strong Republicans. They participate more than do strong Democrats even when one takes into account the differences in the socioeconomic status of the two groups. One possibility is that they are motivated to political activity not simply by attachment to their party, which is probably what partisan identification measures, but by their preference for policies that they expect to be furthered by the Republican Party. For this to explain the asymmetry between the two parties, the motivating force of policy preferences would have to apply more strongly to Republicans than to Democrats. The higher activity

---

[8] The parallel between the net effects of voluntary association and party identification is interesting. But note that the acceleration of the workings of the standard socioeconomic model come about in different ways. For voluntary associations, lower-status individuals gain more from exposure, but fewer are "exposed." For party identification, lower-status citizens gain less, but more are "exposed." The difference may derive from the fact that we are dealing in the former case with a measure of actual activity in organizations, and in the latter with a psychological measure of identification. The former is harder to achieve but more potent once achieved; the latter is easier to achieve but has less impact on behavior. As with organizational affiliation, we find that partisanship has an independent impact on participation over and above that of socioeconomic status.

[9] We wished to attempt a similar analysis for black and white citizens. But almost all the blacks in our sample are Democratic identifiers. That causes no substantive problem and, indeed, suggests some interesting results. But it causes a methodological problem: We are left with only a dozen or so black independents. Because all our measures of "boost" in participation require a comparison of independents with identifiers, this made the intended analysis impossible.

rates among strong Republicans than among strong Democrats would then be explained by commitment of the former to a particular set of political beliefs—to a political "ideology," if one wants to use that word.

That participation is more closely related to policy position among Republicans than among Democrats is something that various studies of party activists would lead us to expect. These studies find that Republican leaders differ more from rank-and-file Republicans in policy preference than is the case among Democrats.[10] And our data support this position. Table 12-2 reports the correlation between political-activity rates and various measures of political preferences arrayed in a left-right direction. The correlations are higher in each case for Republicans than for Democrats. In other words, one's preference on issues relates more strongly to politica! activity among Republicans than among Democrats. And, as one would guess, the political beliefs of Republicans that are having this effect on participation rates are conservative in direction. The political preferences that we are correlating with participation have to do with the extent to which the government has responsibility for welfare in various fields, the extent to which further efforts are needed to reduce income disparities between rich and poor in the United States, and the extent to which civil rights for blacks ought to be pursued vigorously by the government.[11] On all these issues, strong Republicans have more conservative views than other citizens. And, as Table 12-2 makes clear, these views are related to their rate of political activity.[12]

The consequence of the difference between strong Democrats and strong Republicans in the relationship of political beliefs to participation is shown in Figure 12-8. There we compare the participation rate of strong Democrats with that of strong Republicans first in terms of actual participation rate, then

[10] See McClosky et al., "Issue Conflict and Consensus among Party Leaders," pp. 422–423. See also David Nexon, "Asymmetry in the Political System: Occasional Activists in the Republican and Democratic Parties, 1954–1964," *American Political Science Review*, vol. 65 (Sept. 1971), pp. 716–730.

[11] The figures in the table are multiple correlation coefficients (r's) between the set of political attitudes and the levels of voting and campaign participation for the two sections of the sample. Five sets of attitudes were used, including three measures of the respondent's attitudes toward the government's role in social welfare: (1) whether he thought the difference between the rich and the poor in American society was too great, about right or too small; (2) whether he thought that in general the government or the poor themselves had the major responsibility for the care of the poor; and (3) the number of specific welfare areas for which he thought the government (as opposed to private groups or individuals) had the main responsibility. (This last measure was a scale based on eight separate questions.) Two measures of the respondent's attitude toward race were also used: (1) whether he thought that the speed of change for blacks was being pushed too quickly, about right, or not quickly enough; and (2) whether the government ought to see to it that fair housing and integrated schools be obtained or whether the government ought to stay out of such matters. The latter was a scale composed of two items. The questions used and the scale construction techniques for the multiple item scales are presented in Appendix D.2.

Strongly held and more extreme attitudes tend to increase rates of participation for both Democrats and Republicans, but much more so for Republicans. The increase for Republicans comes from the conservative direction on race, and much more strongly, welfare attitudes. The Democratic relationships are more mixed, but also lean slightly in a conservative direction. We shall discuss this seeming anomaly as far as Democrats are concerned and consider the relationship between each of these attitudes, party identification, and rates of participation in greater detail in Chapter 16.

[12] We were concerned with the effect on this conclusion of regional differences among Democrats. Perhaps the lack of relationship of political beliefs to activity level among Democrats is the result of the averaging of two different relationships: conservative views leading to participation in the South, liberal ones leading to participation in the North. But the correlations between political belief and participation, run separately for southern and northern Democrats, do not support this counterproposal. The data are as follows:

Table 12-2

Multiple Correlations Between Political-Policy Preferences
and Participation: Republicans and Democrats

Correlation of political-policy preferences and → for ↓	Over all participation rate	Voting rate	Campaign activity rate	Communal- activity rate
Democrats	.07	.08	.06	.10
Republicans	.28	.21	.24	.27

corrected for the impact of socioeconomic status, and finally corrected for socioeconomic status and their attitudes toward welfare and race. (We use our overall measure of participation because the same pattern exists for all modes.)

The contrast between the strong adherents of the two parties is sharp. On the actual participation rate, as we have already seen, there is a great disparity between the strong adherents of the two parties in their activity levels. Strong Democrats score 10 on the overall participation scale; strong Republicans score 52. When we correct for socioeconomic status, the disparity is reduced. Democratic rates go up, and Republican rates go down, a situation we interpreted as indicating that high socioeconomic status is one source of Republican participation, while their lower socioeconomic status dampens down the participation rate of Democrats. But the disparity between the two groups remains when we correct for socioeconomic status. This is what creates our "puzzle" of the hyperactive Republicans.

The data on participation rates corrected both for socioeconomic status and for political beliefs offer a solution to the puzzle. When we add a correction for political belief there is no change for Democrats; when we add such a correction to the Republican rate there is a sharp decline in participation. The difference in activity rates between the two groups of strong party adherents

Correlation of political policy → preferences and for ↓	Overall participation rate	Voting rate	Campaign activity rate	Communal activity rate
Southern Democrats	.14	.12	.13	.15
Northern Democrats	.06	.09	.02	.09

For both kinds of Democrats, the relationships are much weaker than for Republicans. However, there is a tendency for the southern Democrats to resemble the Republicans more than the northern Democrats do. For southern Democrats, there is a slight relationship between activity and belief, none for northern Democrats. And, as with the Republicans, the political beliefs that affect activity come from a conservative direction, as an analysis of the various policy issues that went into our scale makes clear.

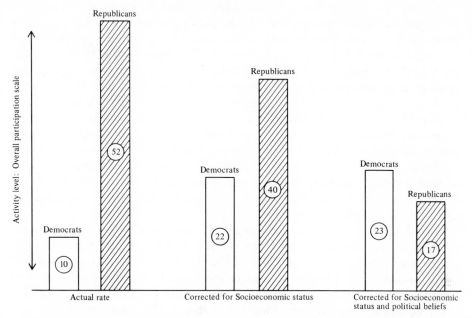

Figure 12-8. Overall Participation Rate of Strong Democrats and Strong Republicans, Correcting for Socioeconomic Status and Political Beliefs

largely disappears.[13] In fact, the Democrats participate at a slightly higher rate. In other words, one of the reasons for the high rate of participation among strong Republicans is their political beliefs. Political beliefs appear to play no such role among strong Democrats.

The difference between the strong partisans of the two major parties is striking. Strong Democrats participate more than the average citizen. But this higher rate depends neither on their socioeconomic status nor on their political beliefs. Correcting for the former raises their activity rate; correcting for the latter does not change it. Strong Republicans also participate more than the average citizen, but in this case their higher socioeconomic status and their conservative political beliefs contribute to their activity rate. And these two characteristics—higher social status and conservative beliefs—explain their higher participation rate compared with strong Democrats.

[13] The effects of socioeconomic status were taken across the population, for Democrats and Republicans alike. The effects of the set of political attitudes on rates of participation were of course taken out separately for Democrats and Republicans as a second order residual after the usual correction for class was made. The technique used to control for social class is the same one we have used in many previous chapters. The correction for political beliefs was also done through regression where each of the five attitudes discussed in the previous footnote were independent variables in the regression equation—participation, of course, being the dependent variable. We separated the Democrats and Republicans into separate populations for this regression because the relationship here is clearly a contingent one, operating differently for Democrats and Republicans. See Appendix I for a further discussion of the methodological implications of this type of analysis of residual effects.

Among our strong Republicans, thus, we find a group whose political participation appears to be motivated by policy preferences. They tend to be more conservative in their political attitudes and those attitudes appear to lead to greater levels of political activity. Some of this activity is channeled through the Republican party; political beliefs contribute to the high campaign activity rates of Republicans. But these beliefs also contribute to their high activity rates in the relatively nonpartisan realm of communal activity. As indicated in Figure 12-2, strong Republicans participated much more than the average citizen in communal activity, even after one corrects for their higher socioeconomic status. Correcting for their political beliefs greatly reduces their level of communal activity, indicating that these beliefs lead to that kind of activity as well. In short, we have here a group motivated to high levels of political activity—both in the electoral and the nonelectoral spheres—by a general set of conservative political beliefs.

The data suggest a most intriguing conclusion about the role of political preferences on ideology in American politics. Such beliefs, we argued, can be a means of modifying the workings of the standard socioeconomic model of participation. Certain beliefs can reduce the disparity in participation between upper- and lower-status groups by motivating citizens to participate more than they "ordinarily" would given their social status. This, as we have seen, is a role played by group consciousness among blacks.

But, in general, political beliefs or political ideology seems to have the opposite effect *vis-à-vis* participation in American political life. Political beliefs that we have found to have an impact on the political activity of the mass public tend to be conservative ones, and they affect the participation rates of strong Republicans, particularly, as Figures 12-3 and 12-4 showed, those from the upper-status level. Thus, political ideology—in the sense of preferences for governmental policies—modifies the workings of the standard socioeconomic model. But the modification is to accelerate the workings of that model.[14]

These data appear to fly in the face of much of recent American political activity—the civil rights movement, activity on Vietnam, on ecology, and on women's liberation. All these activities appear to be motivated by a more liberal or radical set of attitudes. But these highly viable (and highly important) tendencies may involve smaller numbers than those brought to politics by conservative beliefs whose activity is not as noticeable. It is impossible to tell which is more potent—a dramatic push to the left from a small group or a steady pressure from a large group on the right. We will return to this issue when we discuss the consequences of participation.

---

[14] As the data in footnote 11 make clear, the weaker impact of political beliefs on activity rate among Democrats pushes in the same conservative direction. There is a slight push in that direction among southern Democrats, and no push in either direction among northern Democrats.

Chapter 13
The Community Context
of Participation:
A Test of Two Models

We have thus far considered a variety of forces that push citizens in the direction of political participation. Many of these characteristics were those of the individual participant—his socieconomic status, his race, or his attitudes toward politics. We also considered certain characteristics of the citizen's environment—the impact of the organizations to which he belongs. But one aspect of the citizen's environment is crucial and, unlike his organizational involvement, not voluntary. This is the nature of the polity within which he lives. The citizen may have all those characteristics that impel one toward political activity, but be inactive if the political environment is uncongenial. This could happen in many ways. His fellow citizens may undervalue participation. Thus, he would violate the norms of those around him if he tried to participate. Or the political structures toward which he would aim his participation might be hostile and unresponsive to such participation. Another possibility is that the channels of participation might not be clearly visible. And so forth. In short, there are many ways in which the individual's environment affects the likelihood that he will participate and the way in which he participates.

A full analysis of the impact on an individual's participation of his environment requires data from a variety of nations. Such analyses lie in the future, when we hope to consider the questions raised in this volume in a comparative perspective.[1] We shall, in this chapter, consider the citizen's community as the relevant political environment. This does not allow consideration of all those characteristics of the political environment that affect the political activity of the individual. All our communities, of course, are parts of the American political system and have much in common. But it does let us consider a few central characteristics of the individual's environment. In particular, it allows us to consider the impact on the citizen's participation of the extent to which he lives in a central urban environment rather than a peripheral and more rural one.

The subject is one for which there are conflicting interpretations and conflicting data. On the one hand, various studies indicate that citizens in urban settings are likely to be more politically active. Milbrath provides an apt summary of these studies:

> Persons close to the center occupy an environmental position which naturally links them into the communications network involved in policy decisions for the society. They receive from and send more communications to other persons near the center. They have a higher rate of social interaction, and they are more active in groups than persons on the periphery. This central position increases the likelihood that they will develop personality traits, beliefs and attitudes which facilitate participation in politics. There are many more political stimuli in their environment, and this increases the number of opportunities for them to participate . . . .
>
> One of the most thoroughly substantiated propositions in all of social science is that *persons near the center of the society are more likely to participate in politics than persons near the periphery*. . . . Persons near the center receive more stimuli enticing them to participate, and they receive more support from their peers when they do participate.[2]

And Milbrath cites twenty-eight studies to support this point.

On the other hand, a variety of studies have found little direct association between urbanization and political participation. This is particularly true when other social characteristics are taken into account—communications structure, social class, or organizational structure. The conclusion of Nie, Powell, and Prewitt is typical of these studies: "It appears that living in an urban environment has no significant effect on rates of national participation."[3]

Furthermore, the somewhat contradictory data are bolstered by somewhat contradictory models of what happens to citizens as one moves from rural peripheral places to urban centers. One model, which can be called the

---

[1] See the preface for a discussion of the larger research undertaking of which this is a part.

[2] Milbrath, *Political Participation,* pp. 113-114 (italics in original). See also pp. 128-130.

[3] Nie, Powell, and Prewitt, "Social Structure and Political Participation," Part 1, p. 368. See also Deane Neubauer, "Some Conditions of Democracy," *American Political Science Review,* vol. 61 (December 1967), pp. 1002-1009, and Donald J. McCrone and Charles F. Cnadde, "Toward a Communications Theory of Democratic Political Development: A Causal Model," *American Political Science Review,* vol. 61 (March 1967), pp. 72-79.

mobilization model, predicts an increase in participation. Another, which we label the *decline-of-community model,* predicts a decrease.

The Mobilization Model

This model predicts increased participation as one of the concomitants of urbanization. The quotation from Milbrath not only summarizes the findings of empirical studies, it summarizes the reasons offered for the increase in participation in the urban setting. The key variable appears to be the stimulation that comes from such an environment: exposure to more communications, interaction with others involved in politics, support from peers for such activity, and the development of personality traits compatible with political activity.[4]

The Decline-of-Community Model

This alternative model predicts the decline of participation as one moves from the smallness and intimacy of town or village to the massive impersonality of the city. In the small town, the community is a manageable size. Citizens can know the ropes of politics, know whom to contact, know each other so that they can form political groups. In the larger units, politics is more complicated, impersonal, and distant. In addition, "modernization" shatters political units. What were once relatively independent communities—providing the individual with the social, economic, political, and cultural services that he needs—become small towns in a mass society. Such communities no longer have clear economic borders as citizens begin to commute to work. They have more permeable social boundaries as recreational and educational facilities move out of the community, and they cease to be well-bounded political units as local services become more dependent on outside governmental authorities.

All these changes, according to the decline-of-community model, should reduce the level of participation within the community. For one thing, the government of the local community loses its importance. Local participation becomes less and less meaningful. Furthermore, the attention of individuals becomes more diffuse. They no longer concentrate upon their local community. Rather, they are exposed to a wider political realm where meaningful participation is much more difficult because of its larger size and greater complexity.[5]

That two alternative models can exist side-by-side is not unexpected, given

---

[4] The mobilization model is largely associated with the work of scholars interested in modernization and political development, particularly Karl Deutsch. See his now classic article, "Social Mobilization and Political Development," *American Political Science Review,* vol. 55 (September 1961), pp. 493-514. A major statement of the theme is in Daniel Lerner, *The Passing of Traditional Society* (New York: Free Press, 1958).

[5] The argument is found in various places, particularly in many contemporary works that call for greater decentralization. One of the strongest advocates of this position vas G. D. H. Cole. See his *The Future of Local Government* (London: 1921) and *Guild Socialism Restated* (London: 1920). For an excellent statement in the relationship of size to participation, see Robert A. Dahl, "The City in the Future of Democracy," *American Political Science Review,* vol. 61 (December 1967), pp. 958-970.

the fact that the study of this subject is in its early stages. But the conflicting testimony of the data is harder to comprehend. We think there are three reasons why contradictory findings appear. First, there is failure to distinguish adequately among community types. Many studies focus on the size of the community as the measure of urbanization. But the size of a community does not tell about the degree to which the community provides a stimulating urban environment, nor the extent to which it is an independent relatively self-governing entity. The small suburb is quite different from the isolated town of similar size. We shall develop a measure sensitive to both size and isolation.

The second reason is suggested by our discussion thus far of the baseline socioeconomic model of politicization. Small towns, suburbs, and big cities are different sociopolitical environments. But they also contain different kinds of people: They differ in the socioeconomic level of their inhabitants and in racial and age composition. If one finds higher activity rates in suburbs, is that the result of the suburban environment or of the fact that suburban dwellers are likelier to be of high socioeconomic status? Unless one separates the effects on participation of individual characteristics from the effects of the environment, one will not understand the impact, if any, of the community. We shall try to separate these two effects.

The third reason is implicit in our discussion of the several modes of participation. Different modes of activity should be more or less sensitive to the nature of the community environment. We will suggest some of these differences and test them against the data.

SIZE AND PARTICIPATION: THE BASIC RELATIONSHIP

Figure 13-1 presents the mean participation rates of citizens in communities of various sizes. The mean participation scores for the community are simply the averages of the respondents' scores. For purposes of comparability these scales have been restandardized to have a mean of zero and a standard deviation of 100. We present the data for overall participation and for voting. The data are not terribly illuminating. In relation to overall participation, there is fluctuation in participation rates as one moves from one size of community to another. Participation is lower than average in places with a population under 10,000 and peaks in places with a population of 10,000-25,000. In other places—those between 3,000 and 10,000 and those over 300,000 participation is about average. The data lend themselves to no clear interpretation, and support neither model of relationship between the nature of the community and participation. The data for voting are equally difficult to interpret—there is much fluctuation but no clear pattern.

COMMUNITY TYPE AND PARTICIPATION: SIZE, AND ISOLATION

As we pointed out, the size of a community is misleading from the perspective of both the mobilization model and the decline-of-community model of participation. From the point of view of the mobilization model, the

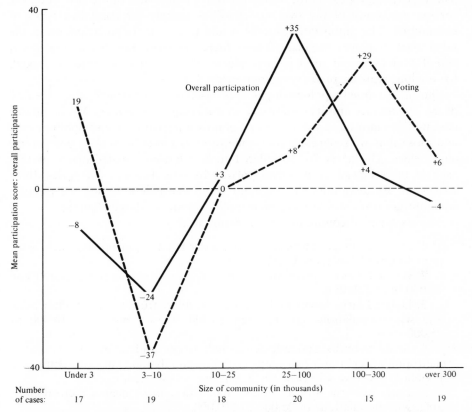

Figure 13-1. Participation Rate and Community Size: Overall Participation and Voting

size of the community in which a citizen lives is important because it gives some indication of the extent to which he is exposed to the stimulation of the urban environment. From the point of view of the decline-of-community model, size is important as an indicator of complexity or loss of intimacy. But another characteristic is important: the extent to which the community is a well-defined social unit. The more the community is a well-defined, autonomous unit (i.e., has a functioning local government and is a meaningful economic unit where citizens live, work, shop, and have recreational, religious, and educational facilities) the more the decline-in-community model would predict high rates of participation.

This suggests a more refined measure of community type based on two characteristics—the community's size and its degree of "isolation." The latter characteristic enables us to separate out the small or moderately sized town that stands as an independent entity far from other communities from the communities of similar size that are embedded in a large urban concentration.

This is particularly useful for it may provide a crucial test of the two models—for the prediction of the two models differ sharply for these two types of community. The mobilization model would predict more participation in the latter type of places because citizens there are more exposed to the urban stimuli than citizens in more isolated places. The decline-of-community model, for obvious reasons, predicts the opposite.

Our more refined typology of places is based on two characteristics: the size of the community and its distance from a metropolitan center. We divide our communities into those within, or in a county adjacent to, a metropolitan area and those that are separated from a metropolitan area by at least one county on all sides. The latter are considered to be relatively isolated places. Within each of these categories we divide places by size. The size categories differ somewhat. By definition, there are no very large places among the isolated communities (they would form metropolitan centers if large enough).

The six types of communities that result are:

1. Isolated villages and rural areas: away from a metropolitan area with populations of less than 3,000.
2. Isolated towns: away from a metropolitan area: between 3,000 and 10,000 in population.
3. Isolated large towns and small cities: away from a metropolitan area and with populations greater than 10,000. Most range from 10,000 to 25,000.
4. Small suburbs and adjacent small towns and cities: in or near a metropolitan area and less than 25,000 in population. They are similar in population to towns in category 3, but are not isolated.
5. Large suburbs and adjacent small cities: in or near a metropolitan area, with populations of 25,000 to 150,000.
6. Core cities: places over 150,000 in population.

The typology needs a few comments. For one thing, it does not eliminate all the heterogeneity of the distinction based on size alone; each category contains a quite diverse set of places. But it does separate some extremely different places that were lumped together by the size criterion. Second, one ought to read carefully our definition of *isolation* so as not to reify the concept. Isolated towns in the U.S. context may still be quite close to major areas and are, with almost no exceptions, linked to the national communications networks of radio and television. They are not the isolated communities of less developed societies where one may have to travel days to see the first paved road. Last, though the six types of community are ranked on what we think of as an "urbanness" continuum, one ought to be aware that there are two distinct sets of communities, the first three being "isolated," the last three not. When we graph the relation between community type and participation the reader should be aware that there are two sets of communities on the graph.

Figure 13-2 presents data relating participation rate to our new typology of communities. The data suggest no clear conclusion; they conform neither to what one would expect given the mobilization model nor the decline-in-community model. The former would predict most participation in large cities. We find participation there to be roughly on the mean for all communities. It is high in large suburbs (exposed to urban influences) but particularly low in small suburbs (also so exposed). The decline-in-community model would predict higher participation in smaller, more isolated places. Participation is high in isolated cities, but low in smaller places that are isolated. In short, the results are inconclusive.

COMMUNITY TYPE AND PARTICIPATION: SEPARATING INDIVIDUAL AND COMMUNITY EFFECTS

As we pointed out, we are interested in the effects of community environment on citizen participation. Figure 13-2 does not clearly reflect this because it combines two kinds of effects. The isolated village dweller in category 1 differs from the suburbanite in category 5 in the nature of his environment, but he is also likely to differ in his level of education, income, or race. If the latter appears to participate more than the former, it could be due to the greater stimulation of suburban living as compared with village life, or simply to the disparity in social status. To sort out these two effects, we can use our usual correction techniques. We ask: For each type of community, how active are citizens over and above what one would have predicted on the basis of their social and economic characteristics? The individual characteristics we

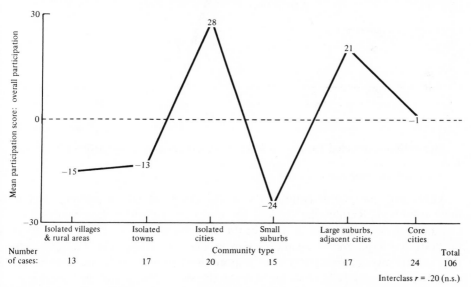

Figure 13-2. Participation Rate and Community Type: Overall Participation

correct for are socioeconomic status, race, and age. These are related to participation and also vary among the community types.[6]

The corrected data are presented in Figure 13-3, where we also present the uncorrected data for comparison. The correction for social characteristics changes the pattern quite a bit. In some places the correction for social characteristics raises the participation rate. This is particularly the case in the rural areas and isolated villages and towns—the two most "peripheral" categories. In others, particularly in the large suburbs, it drastically lowers the rate. The result is that, whereas on the uncorrected data the citizens in rural and small isolated places were participating less than the average for the nation as a whole, when one corrects for their individual social characteristics, one finds them participating more. In the large suburbs, though citizens participate more than average on the uncorrected data, they participate much less than average when one corrects for their socioeconomic characteristics.

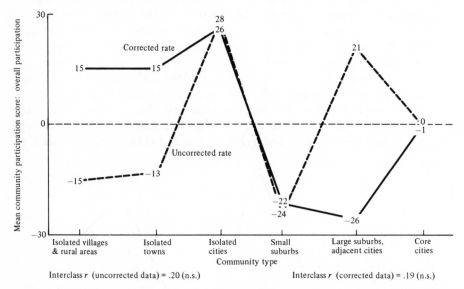

Figure 13-3. Corrected Participation Rate and Community Type: Overall Participation

ᵃNumber of cases same as in Figure 13-2.

The small, peripheral community is not the place where participation is most inhibited. Rather, the citizens there participate more than their social characteristics would predict. It is in the suburbs where one finds citizens to be underparticipators—even more than in the core cities. This fact suggests that of the two characteristics of communities upon which the decline-in-community model is based—the size of the community and the degree to which it is a well-defined and bounded community—the latter is more important. It is in the suburbs, the communities that are least well-bounded

[6] For a discussion of the "correction" technique, see Appendix B.3.

and that merge into urban complexes, that one finds the least activity. This stress on the importance of the boundedness of the community rather than its size is supported by the data on the isolated places. There one finds activity high in general, but particularly high in the larger of such places. The data in Figure 13-3 suggest that failure to take into account the individual effects on participation of the socioeconomic characteristics of citizens in different types of community greatly blurs the impact of the community on such participation. Most striking are the large suburbs. Citizens are in fact quite active there, as the uncorrected data indicate. But this reflects the higher social status of the citizens who live in such places. If we separate out the impact of the nature of the community, we find that in such suburban places citizens participate less— indeed they have the lowest mean score. In fact, the corrected data in Figure 13-3 lend quite a bit of support to the decline-in-community model and seem to refute the mobilization model.

COMMUNITY TYPE AND THE MODES OF PARTICIPATION

We can refine our comparison of the two models of community impact by considering the various types of political activity. As we have shown so often, an overall measure of participation often masks some sharp differences among the political acts. Because the two alternative models usually do not distinguish one mode of participation from another, they do not provide clear predictions about the different modes. One expectation is clear, however: If the decline-in-community model holds, it should hold most strongly for communal activity. This mode of participation, unlike activity in the electoral process, requires informal cooperation among citizens (or, at least, that is one important way citizens engage in communal activity) something that should be easier in the smaller and more well-defined communities further from urban areas. Particularized contacting also might be expected to thrive more in smaller and more "intimate" places because citizens could more easily know and have access to governmental officials. However, there is also a tendency for certain kinds of officials to be unavailable in the most isolated places, thereby lowering the likelihood of contacting.

Figure 13-4 presents data on the electoral modes of participation. We will comment only on the corrected scores. Voting is particularly high in rural areas but also high in large suburbs and core cities—a finding that fits neither model.[7] Campaign activity also has a rather irregular relationship with community type, but one that is quite different from that in relation to voting. Campaign activity is low in rural areas, whereas voting is high. It then goes

[7] Although these data on voting rates are inconclusive in relation to either the decline-in-community model or the mobilization model, one other fact lends support to the decline-in-community model. If we consider the number of voting specialists rather than the rate of voting—i.e., the numbers who limit their activity to the vote—we find that they exist in large suburbs and in the core cities to a much greater degree than one would expect given the social compositions of those places. This is not the case in the rural areas and isolated villages. Voting rates are high, but there is no similar overrepresentation of citizens who do nothing but vote. In fact, voting specialists are found rather infrequently in isolated places. In other words, it may be true that voting rates are relatively high in large suburbs and core cities, a fact that might be taken to support the mobilization model. But the fact that we also find many citizens who do nothing but vote suggests that the high voting rates ought not to be interpreted to indicate high levels of citizen activism.

up in isolated places as size increases, whereas voting rates decrease. One could invent many explanations for that particular pattern, but the most reasonable conclusion may be that no clear conclusion is possible.

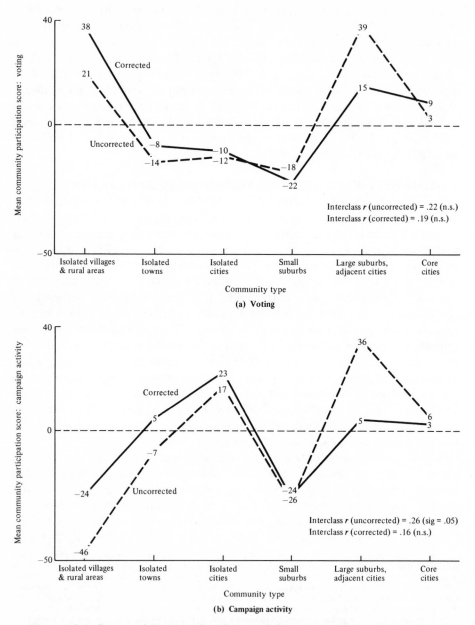

Figure 13-4. Corrected Participation Rate and Community Type: Electoral Activities[a]

[a]Number of cases same as in Figure 13-2.

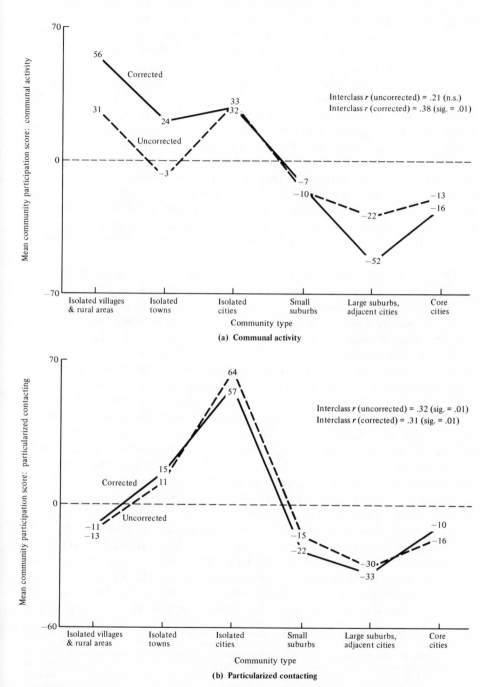

Figure 13-5. Corrected Participation Score and Community Type: Nonelectoral Activities[a]

[a]Number of cases same as in Figure 13-2.

The situation is much clearer in relation to communal activity (Figure 13-5). Here one finds that such activity is much more prevalent in isolated places than in nonisolated ones. Activity rates are above average in all three types of isolated communities, below average in all three nonisolated types. And, in particular, such communal activity is low in large suburbs. Even in the uncorrected data such activity is less frequent in such places than the average for all communities despite the high average socioeconomic status of the citizens there. When one corrects for that status differential as well as for other social characteristics, one finds such activity most infrequent in such places. These data fit nicely into the decline-in-community model: Such large suburbs have both characteristics that, according to this model, would depress the rate of activity—they are large and they do not have well-defined boundaries. Particularized contacting also appears to be more widespread in more isolated places, at least in those large enough to have available officials to contact. In rural isolated places, the distance to government officials may make such contacts difficult. Again, it is in the suburbs where one finds the least such activity.

Figure 13-6 provides further data relative to the community impact on participation. In this figure we compare a measure of local and extralocal participation.[8] The decline-in-community model is largely about the former. As a community loses its clear borders and identity, it should become more difficult or less meaningful for the individual to participate in it. The predicted impact of such changes on participation outside the community—in national or state politics, for instance—is ambiguous from the point of view of the decline-of-community model. One might imagine a "spill-over" effect, whereby the difficulty of participating locally depresses all kinds of participation, but the expectation is not clear. As for the mobilization model, there is usually little specification as to the nature of participation that might be affected by socioeconomic change, though the focus is usually on participation on a wider level than the local community. Thus, one possible reconciliation of the two models might be in terms of the alternative modes of participation to which they apply—perhaps local participation goes up in smaller, more isolated places and extralocal participation goes up in more central places.

The data do indicate a difference between participation focused on the local community and that with a broader referent. The latter shows relatively little variation across communities, at least when one compares it to local activity. It is not more prevalent in smaller isolated places. The situation is quite different in relation to participation within the local community. When one corrects for socioeconomic status, one finds citizens in more isolated places

---

[8] The scales of local and national participation are based on comparable items. The local participation index is constructed from three items: the frequency of voting in local elections, initiating contacts with local officials, and frequency of political discussions about politics and public affairs in the local community. The index of national participation is composed of three parallel items—voting in presidential elections, contacting extralocal officials, and frequency of political discussions about national politics. Both indices were created by standardizing each of the three component items and adding them together. These simple additive indices were then restandardized to have means of zero and standard deviations of 100. Appendix B.1 describes the voting and contacting questions and Appendix D describes the frequency of political discussion times.

generally more active in this way. And the activity increases as one moves to the smaller of the isolated places. Isolation and small size seem to work together to increase participation.

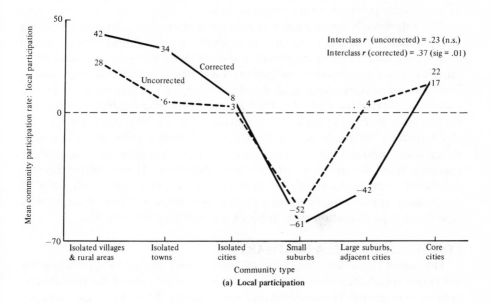

(a) Local participation

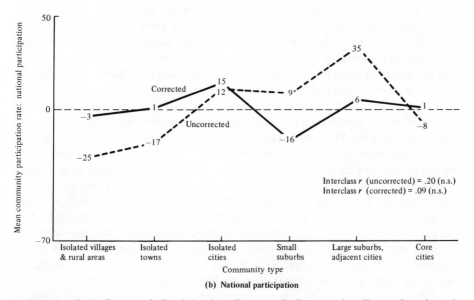

(b) National participation

Figure 13-6. Corrected Participation Rate and Community Type: Local and National Participation[a]

[a] Number of cases same as in Figure 13-2.

In nonisolated places the situation is curiously reversed. As one moves to more populous places, local participation goes up. It is higher in large suburbs than in small ones, and higher yet in core cities. Why this should be the case is unclear, unless it is simply that smaller suburbs, because of their subordination socially and economically (and sometimes even politically), are not seen as worthwhile places in which to participate.

The difference between local and national participation illustrates the value of using our correction technique to separate individual and environmental effects. One would expect the nature of the community to have a greater effect on local than on national participation. But if one compares the interclass r's between community type and the two types of participation using the uncorrected data, one finds that they are similar in magnitude. That for local participation is .23, that for national participation .20, indicating that the type of community relates as well to both types of participation. But the uncorrected data confound the impact of the community type with the impact of the characteristics of individual citizens who live there. If we correct for the individual characteristics of the citizens, we see that the relationship of community type to national participation goes down to .09; that of community type to local participation rises to become a highly significant .37.

COMMUNITY TYPE: A SUMMARY

The use of our refined typology of communities and of the correction for individual social characteristics does provide a clearer view of the relationship between community environment and participation. There are some ambiguities, yet the overall pattern lends support to the decline-in-community model. Participation does indeed decline as communities grow, and, more clearly, as they begin to lose the clear boundaries that separate them from other communities. Participation in general and communal participation in particular are more widespread in more peripheral and isolated places. As one moves to the "center" of society, such activity is inhibited.

We can summarize our findings and, perhaps provide the clearest test of the two models by comparing two kinds of communities: the isolated cities and the small suburbs. These two types of community are fairly similar in size, but sharply different from the point of view of their closeness to the urban environment and the degree to which they are well bounded and autonomous. The isolated city is, of course, much further from the "stimulation" of the urban centers than is the small suburb. For that reason the mobilization model would predict less participation in the former than in the latter. On the other hand, the isolated city is a much better defined community, whereas the small suburb may be merely a bedroom community or in other ways be in the shadow of its larger neighbors. For this reason the decline-in-community model predicts more participation in the former than in the latter.

Table 13-1 presents the mean participation rates for these two types of community on all the measures of participation discussed in this chapter. For

Table 13-1

Isolated Cities and Small Suburbs Compared[a]

Mean participation rates (corrected)	Isolated cities	Small suburbs
Overall activity	26	−22
Voting	−10	−22
Campaign activity	23	−24
Communal activity	32	−7
Particularized contact	57	−21
Local activity	8	−61
National activity	15	−16

[a]Student's t indicates all comparisons on this table are significantly different.

each measure of participation, one finds more participation in the isolated city than in the small suburb. This holds even for participation in national politics, suggesting a possible spill-over effect from activity on the local level. In short, the data support an interpretation that the nature of the community does make a difference in participation over and above the effects of the characteristics of the individual citizens who live there. The difference it makes is related to the degree to which the community is isolated enough so that the citizen has a well-defined political unit within which to participate.

COMMUNITY BOUNDEDNESS: A CLOSER LOOK

The decline-in-community model focuses, as we have pointed out, on two characteristics of the community—its size and the extent to which it is a well-defined community. The latter characteristic we have called the "boundedness" of the community; it refers to the extent to which the community is an autonomous political, social, and economic unit. Of course, none of the communities in our study approaches being a completely autonomous community; all are embedded in American society and are not economically, politically, or socially independent. Nevertheless, there are clear differences among communities in the extent to which they have some autonomous life. Some towns or cities form the center of the lives of their inhabitants—they live and work there, engage in social life there, and their children go to school there. Other places are less central to the lives of their inhabitants. Many who live there may not work there (or vice versa), and other communities may be the focus of social life or the centers of economic activity.

The decline-in-community model clearly predicts that participation would be lower in places that are not well bounded for the simple reason that the attention of the potential participant is diffused across a large number of places. He lives in one place, works in another, and may take part in social life elsewhere. The politics of each place may be relevant to him, as there is no single "center" on which to focus his participation.

We can test these expectations more directly than we have thus far. In a number of the communities that fell into our sample, we gathered data on a wide range of community characteristics; data that were gathered from census records as well as from interviews with local leaders (See Appendix A). We have several measures of the degree of boundedness of the community. One such indicator is the degree to which governmental services—offices of various types of governmental agencies—are located in the community. A second is a measure of the density of voluntary associations within the community, i.e., the number of such associations adjusted for the size of the community. A third is a measure of the extent to which citizens both live and work in the community, a distinction based on the proportion of residents who live in the community but commute to work and of those who work in the community but live outside it. Last, we have two measures of communication: one of the richness of the internal communication channels (are there newspapers or other media specific to the community?) and one of the richness of external media (how available are external newspapers or radio and TV stations?). The more internal communication, the greater the community boundedness. The more external communication, the less the community boundedness.

Each one of this rather heterogeneous set of indicators relates to the degree to which the community can be considered to have a life of its own. In Table 13-2 we relate these characteristics to the degree of local participation within the community by using the local participation scale we introduced, and by presenting data corrected for the socioeconomic characteristics of the citizenry. It is clear from the table that in all cases, communities that are well bounded have more local participation than those that are not. In some cases, the difference is quite striking. In relation to the availability of organizations in the community, about one standard deviation on the participation scale separates the most from the least well-bounded communities. The data on our measure of commuting are even more striking. The measure of the amount of commuting into and out of the community has a quite skewed distribution, separating off at either end a few sharply different communities—one set where very few citizens both live and work in the community and another where there are few commuters either in or out. In places where the population has a high proportion of commuters, the rate of local participation is over one standard deviation below the average for places where there are few commuters. And though the availability of internal communication does not raise local participation much (though it does a bit), the existence of external media significantly depresses local activity, just as the decline-in-community model would predict. When one remembers that we are dealing with rates of participation corrected for the other social characteristics of citizens, these data offer strong support for that model.

Table 13-2

"Boundedness" of the Community and Local Activity: Corrected Scores

	Less well bounded ←————→ More well-bounded			
(A) Availability of services in the community	Few services −19[a] (35)[b]			Many services 24 (29) r = .23[c]
(B) Number of available voluntary organizations per capita	Few −38 (16)	Some −19 (16)	Many −4 (6)	Very many 61 (16) r = .34[d]
(C) Proportion of workforce that commutes in or out to work	Many Commuters −62 (5)		Some Commuters 2 (48)	Few Commuters 60 (7) r = .28[c]
(D) Density of internal communications channels	Low −5 (33)			High 6 (28) r = .09
(E) Density of external communication channels	High −26 (32)			Low 3 (28) r = .29[d]

[a]Figures are mean corrected participation scores on a local participation index.
[b]Figures in parentheses are the number of communities in that category.
[c]Significant at the .05 level.
[d]Significant at the .01 level.

We can take the argument one step further by seeing how the boundedness of the community relates to the different modes of participation. In particular, we can contrast campaign and communal activity—the latter being much more susceptible than the former to the impact of the nature of the community. In Figure 13-7 we relate two of our measures of boundedness—the number of organizations in the community and the proportion of commuters—to the rate of campaign and communal activity. As one can clearly see, communal activity is much more sensitive to the boundedness of the community than campaign activity is. The degree to which the community forms a clear focus of attention for citizens appears to affect, in particular, the extent to which citizens can come together to work on community problems. Where the community declines, this kind of activity declines, but this cooperative activity thrives where the community is well bounded.

This interpretation is supported by one last bit of data. In Figure 13-8 we relate campaign and communal activity to the availability of external communication media in the community. Campaign activity *increases* somewhat and communal activity *decreases* quite a bit the more the citizen is exposed to communications from outside the community. Clearly, communal activity is susceptible to those forces associated with the decline of the community

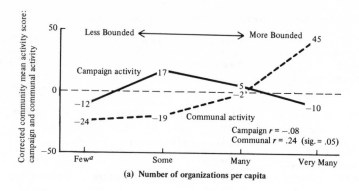

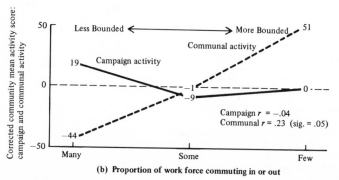

Figure 13-7. Community Boundedness and Campaign vs. Communal Activity[a]
[a]Number of communities in each cell same as in Table 13-2.

(where the community loses its boundedness). When communications flow in or commuters flow out, or when one must go elsewhere for governmental services or voluntary associations, communal activity declines precipitously.[9]

The data in Figure 13-8 on the relationship between external communications and participation provide perhaps the most crucial test of the two models. The availability in the community of such external media (newspapers from other cities, network radio, and television) clearly represents the kind of stimulation that the mobilization model predicts would increase participation; and it clearly represents the kind of loss of community boundedness that the decline-in-community model predicts would depress participation. For campaign activity, there is some weak support for the mobilization model. External communications are associated with an increase in such activity. But the stronger finding is for communal activity. The stimulation of external communications *lowers* that activity—as the decline-in-community model would predict.

---

[9] What has been said about communal participation in relation to community boundedness also applies to particularized contacting, though not to as dramatic an extent. The pattern associated with voting is, on the other hand, rather mixed, showing little regular relationship with boundedness.

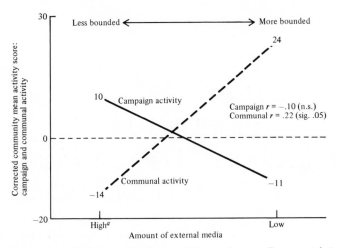

Figure 13-8. External Communication and Campaign vs. Communal Activity[a]

[a] Number of communities same as in Table 13-2.

CONCLUSION

The data presented in this chapter give, we believe, an interesting picture of the relationship between the nature of the community and participation. In general, the decline-in-community model seems to hold. As communities grow in size and, more important, as they lose those characteristics of boundedness that distinguish the independent city from the suburb, participation declines.[10] And it does so most strikingly for communal participation, a kind of participation particularly well attuned to deal with the variety of specific problems faced by groups of citizens. One last obvious point must be made here, for it has important implications. The communities that appear to foster participation—the small and relatively independent communities—are becoming rarer and rarer.

---

[10] At first glance our conclusions differ from those of Robert Alford who found that when he controlled for a series of individual characteristics, no residual effect was found of the community within which the citizen lived. See Robert R. Alford, *Bureaucracy and Participation: Political Cultures in Four Wisconsin Cities* (Chicago: Rand-McNally, 1969), pp. 159-160. He was, however, dealing with only four cities all of which would fall in the same category of our typology.

Chapter 14
Participation: The Record of the Past Two Decades

Survey techniques have many limitations. One of the most serious is that they usually are time-bound: They give a snapshot of a population at a particular moment in time. The survey on which this study is based is no exception. Our questionnaires were administered in April, 1967 and the data we report are largely bound within that time frame.

Such a limitation is particularly unfortunate for a study such as ours, dealing with an important political problem in a time of rapid political change. For one thing, our description of the participation input—how much, what kind, from what citizens—may reflect a situation at that point in time. The problem is not that serious looking backward from 1967, since we ask our questions about patterns of behavior extending backward into time. But it is not impossible that matters have changed since the time of our field work. More important is the possibility that the relationships we find may be time-bound. Perhaps the close connection we find between social class and participation is something that existed for idiosyncratic reasons in 1967, but not before or after. And most important, is that fact that we attempt to deal with processes—such as the process of politicization—using relationships among variables measured at one point in time.

Such limitations are serious but not fatal to research of this sort. We believe that data on the kinds of behavior we are studying do not vary so idiosyncratically over time so that a particular moment chosen for field work would provide a very distorted picture; and we believe that a pattern of relationships among characteristics—such as the relationship between class and participation—is even less likely to be time-bound. Furthermore, one can deal with process in survey data if one is willing to make assumptions about the causal ordering of variables, for instance, that an individual's social status precedes and determines his political behavior rather than vice versa. To be honest, we would have carried out our analysis without the use of data over time. But, in fact, a rich body of systematic data exists on participation in American politics over the past two decades. We refer to the unique historical record of American electoral behavior contained in the various studies by the Survey Research Center at the University of Michigan. These data have been used to trace changes in the division of the vote over time; but they also contain information relevant to our concern with rates of political participation—data we believe have not yet been exploited from this point of view. Thus we turn to these data to see whether and how participation has been changing over time and, more important, to see whether these data are consistent with our conclusions on the processes of politicization in America. There is one final reason why we turn to these data. As with much survey analysis, many of the hypotheses tested in previous chapters derive in part from our experience with our own survey data. As such, our attempt to test them on our data does not provide independent confirmation. By turning to a new set of data based on other samples we can obtain important independent confirmation of patterns found within our sample.

In seven of the periodic election surveys conducted since 1952, we have been able to locate questions about the same six campaign activities.[1] These questions were asked in each of the five Presidential surveys between 1952 and 1968, as well as in the 1966 and 1970 Congressional election surveys. The questions are similar, but not identical, to questions that we have combined into our measure of campaign activity. The difference in the questions from our own is not significant, since what we are interested in is the change over time, and what counts is that we have the same measures over a period of about two decades. More serious from our point of view is that the data are limited to one of our modes of participation. We would have preferred information on the whole panoply of participatory modes.[2] But secondary

---

[1] For the questions that went to make up the scale of campaign participation see Appendix B.4.

[2] One could, of course, deal with the change in the voting rate over time, and in this case use a much wider historical sweep. This was done, for instance, by Walter Dean Burnham, "The Changing Shape of the American Political Universe," *American Political Science Review*, vol. 59 (March 1965), pp. 7-28. But though a deeper historical account of changing voting turnout was possible, it would not let us consider the specific set of questions we want to consider and that are possible to consider via the S.R.C. election data. Furthermore, we

analysts can't be choosers, and campaign activity may be, of the various modes of activity, the one that is most useful to trace. Of the various modes, it is most closely related to the others and to the overall dimension of participation.

We can begin by presenting the data on campaign participation since 1952. These data are reported in Figure 14-1. For each election we report the mean number of acts, of the six recorded, performed by the American public. The pattern is confused a bit by the fact that both Presidential and Congressional elections are graphed on the same figure; and participation rates in Congressional elections are generally lower. In order to correct for this—since we are interested in tracing changes over time rather than in the difference between these two types of election—we have increased the mean scores for the two Congressional elections by their average deviation from the three Presidential elections between 1960 and 1968. These corrected figures are circled in Figure 14-1. When these corrections are entered, the pattern becomes more regular and quite interesting. The 1950s appear as a decade of steadily increasing rates of campaign activity, peaking in the Presidential election of 1960. The rates then fall a bit below the 1960 peak, but remain fairly steady throughout the 1960s, returning in the 1970 Congressional election to the peak amount of 1960. Clearly there is election specific variation. 1960 was a particularly active year as was, perhaps, 1970 for a Congressional election. But what is most important is that the change in campaign activity rate in the 1950s seems to have produced a plateau of participation in the 1960s on a level higher than in the earlier decade. In all the elections since 1960, the rate has been higher than in any of the elections before 1960.

These data are consistent with the view that the 1950s started as a decade of political disengagement and that political involvement grew steadily as the decade progressed. On the other hand, our socioeconomic model of politicization warns us that an alternative interpretation is possible—that the growth in activity rate is just the "natural" concomitant of change in the social composition of the population, a population that over time has become more educated and affluent. Indeed, if one compares the samples of the American population taken over the eighteen-year period from 1952 to 1970 one finds a steady increase in the proportions with higher levels of education, as can be seen in Table 14-1.[3] Does this increase in educational level account for the growth in rate of campaign activity? The likely answer is that it accounts for some increase, but not all of the change, since one would expect a steadier pattern of growth if it were solely due to the change in the educational level of the sample.

---

believe that voting is probably the worst indicator of political activity, because the meaning of the vote as a political act may differ substantially over time and at different levels of socioeconomic development. Thus, comparative data indicate that voting has a different meaning (in terms of the reasons why citizens vote) in India and the United States, whereas campaign activity has a similar meaning in both places. See Verba, Nie, and Kim, *The Modes of Democratic Participation,* pp. 59-61; and Verba, Ahmed, and Bhatt, *Caste, Race, and Politics,* Chapter 6.

[3] The slight decline in educational level between 1968 and 1970 is, we believe, simply an artifact of sampling error.

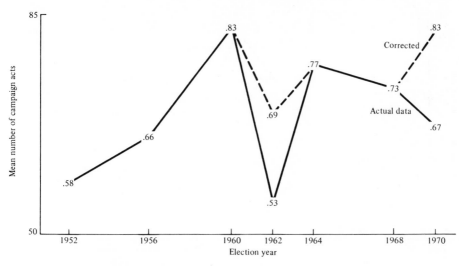

Figure 14-1. Mean Number of Campaign Acts by Year

Table 14-1

Proportion with High School Diploma or Higher Education

1952	1956	1960	1962	1964	1968	1970
24%	29%	31%	32%	34%	39%	38%

Fortunately we can test this more directly, using a technique analogous to the correction techniques we have used to remove the effects of social status on participation. Taking the participation rate and the relationship of participation to education in the first election year as our base line, we can project the rate of campaign activity in each succeeding election based on the educational composition of the population at that later time. (For a discussion, see Appendix B.4.) In other words, we can project the increase in participation we would have found based simply on the changing social composition of the population. In Figure 14-2 we present that projection, and compare it with the actual data we have on campaign activity. (We use the corrected scores for Congressional elections.) As Figure 14-2 indicates, we would have predicted steady growth in participation based on the increased educational level of the population. The actual increase during the 1950s was quite a bit higher, and the resulting rate of participation that has remained during the 1960s is above what the socioeconomic forces alone would have predicted.

The data suggest an increase in political activity over and above the "natural" growth associated with the changing social composition of the population. However, the exact reason for this increase is unclear. One possibility is that politics in the 1950s and early 1960s involved an increase in

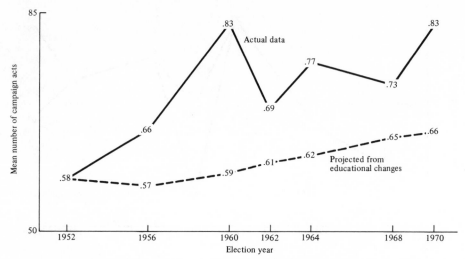

Figure 14-2. Mean Number of Campaign Acts: Actual and Projected

political concern and interest over and above what a changing social composition would predict. Alternatively, it may be that our base year is an
unusually inactive one and what seems like a secular growth in the 1950s is
actually the return to an earlier high level. There is one other possibility we
have neglected to consider: the fact that citizens with higher levels of
education also are likely to be more active in voluntary associations and that
this, because it has an impact on participation over and above social status,
might cause an increase above that shown in Figure 14-2.

We cannot disentangle these processes here for the population as a whole.
But we can use the data to look at some subgroup patterns and thereby to test
some hypotheses derived from our more static analysis.

SOCIAL STATUS, RACE, AND POLITICIZATION

The over-time data on campaign participation allow us a crucial test of the
workings of our standard socioeconomic model and of the forces that lead to
deviations from it. The data allow this test in relation to our consideration of
the differences in participation between black and white Americans.

As our analysis in Part II of this book made clear, the standard socioeconomic model is a powerful predictor of political activity. The result of the
workings of that model is that upper-status citizens participate more than
lower-status ones. Furthermore, a variety of other social and psychological
forces accelerate the workings of that model and result in an even greater
disparity between the upper- and lower-status groups. Thus we found that
affiliation with voluntary associations, party affiliation, and political beliefs (in
particular, conservative beliefs among Republicans) all lead upper-status
individuals to participate more than their socioeconomic status would predict.

The one counterforce that we found was the sense of group-consciousness among blacks. This tended to increase black political participation above the level their socioeconomic status would predict and thereby tended to reduce the participatory gap between them and white Americans.

The data over the past two decades allow us to test our interpretation of the role of group-consciousness as a mobilizer of black participation. The reason is that the period from 1952 through 1970 has been, we may assume, a period of rapid growth of group-consciousness. Thus the situation that we found in 1967—in which the black-white disparity in participation was relatively slight and much less than one would have expected given the disparity in socioeconomic level—should not have been the case in earlier years. In short, the change in black group-consciousness that we assume took place during the 1950s and 1960s should be reflected in accelerated participation rates for blacks that go well beyond what would have been projected based on their increasing socioeconomic level; and such an acceleration in participation rates should be reflected in a steady narrowing of the participation gap between the two races.

Furthermore, though group-consciousness among blacks changed rapidly in the last two decades, the more general working of the standard socioeconomic model among whites should show little change. The relationship between social status and participation is a relationship that we expect to be rather steady and long term. A reduction in that relationship might come with the development of a set of political beliefs among lower-status white Americans that performed an equivalent function to group-consciousness among blacks, i.e., a class consciousness that led to political activity. But we found little evidence for this. We found the contrary—the only political beliefs among whites that were related to participation rates were conservative beliefs among upper-status Republicans. Thus the reduced participation gap between blacks and whites that we expect to find ought not to be matched by a reduced gap between upper- and lower-status whites. If anything, the role of conservative beliefs as an impetus toward participation might increase the participation gap among whites.

We can begin by considering the extent to which the relationship between socioeconomic status and political activity—which we consider basic to our model of participation in America—is steady over time rather than being a relationship found uniquely in our study in 1967. Table 14-2 reports the correlations between social class (measured by level of education) and campaign activity in seven election studies from 1952 through 1970. The

Table 14-2
Correlation of Class and Participation by Year

1952	1956	1960	1962	1964	1968	1970
.24	.22	.20	.19	.31	.23	.32

correlations are somewhat lower than those based on our data on the relationship between class and campaign activity, but this may be an artifact of our somewhat different and more precise measure of social status compared with the educational measure used here. What is most relevant from the point of view of our current concern is that the relationship has been remarkably stable over time. The relationship increased in the 1964 election (for reasons we shall discuss later) but otherwise it remains relatively unchanged until 1970 when it rose again. The socioeconomic forces that push to participation seem to be steady, changing little over time.

Let us consider the difference between the races as they evolved in the last two decades. In Figure 14-3 we plot the actual and the projected participation

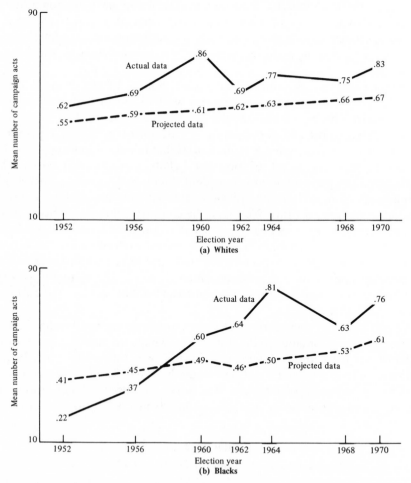

Figure 14-3. Actual and Projected Mean Number of Campaign Acts: Whites and Blacks

rates for whites and blacks from 1952 to 1970. The data for whites, in Figure 14-3(a), are, as one would expect, quite like those already reported for the population as a whole. Their changing educational composition projects a steady and gradual rise in participation; their actual increase in participation goes somewhat beyond this. The contrast with Figure 14-3(b) is quite sharp. The projected line for black participation is similar to that for whites; a gradual and steady growth accompanying a steady increase in educational level. The actual evolution of black participation is quite different. In 1952 black participation was well below what one would have predicted given their level of education. At that time they were underparticipating *vis-à-vis* their expected level. From 1952 through 1964 one finds a sharp growth in campaign activity rates well above what would have been projected on the basis of their increasing educational level. There is a dip in the 1968 election, but a rise again in 1970. From 1960 on, blacks have been participating above what one would have projected based on their socioeconomic level. Thus, in this period we expect a growth in group consciousness to be accompanied by a rapid increase in black activity rates over and above what the socioeconomic model would predict. And we find such an increase.

The result of the rapid growth in black campaign activity is seen in Figure 14-4, where we plot the actual rate of campaign activity over the two decades for blacks and whites. What is most apparent is the rapid narrowing of the participation gap between the two races between 1952 and 1964. In 1964, blacks were slightly more active than whites in the campaign, and though their rate declines somewhat from the peak of 1964, the gap between the races remains narrow.

The data over time are quite consistent with those that our analysis of static

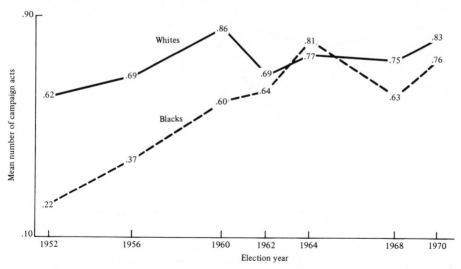

Figure 14-4. Campaign Activity Rate: Whites and Blacks

data in Chapter 10 would have predicted. Using our data gathered in 1967, we found a relatively narrow participation gap between blacks and whites, a gap narrower than that expected on the basis of the difference between the races in socioeconomic status. We interpreted the narrow gap as reflecting the results of a process of political mobilization through the development of group-consciousness. And when we consider a series of studies over time—based on data quite independent of our own—we find a relatively narrow gap between blacks and whites in 1964 and 1968 (the years bracketing our own study). In addition, we find, as our static analysis led us to expect, that this narrow gap is of recent origin, in all likelihood reflecting the workings of an evolving group consciousness.

The data in Figure 14-4 are in clear contrast to those in Figure 14-5, where we plot the rate of campaign activity over time for three different white educational groups—those who have not completed high school, high school graduates, and those with some college. Unlike the situation *vis-à-vis* the black-white differences, we see no such tendency for a diminution of the participation gap between the social levels among whites. Rather, as would have been predicted from the steadiness of the correlation between social status and participation, the gap remains roughly the same throughout the two decades

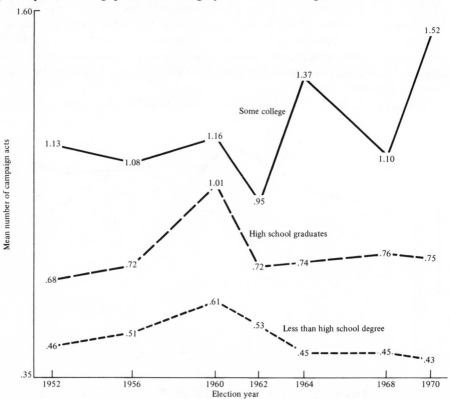

Figure 14-5. Mean Number of Campaign Activities for Three Educational Levels: Whites Only

or, if anything, it increases. Most noticeable is the increase in the gap in 1964, when the upper-educated group came out in large numbers. (For reasons not clear to us, the gap expands again in 1970.) Were these upper-status Republicans mobilized to work for Goldwater? Were they liberal intellectuals mobilized to oppose him? Our discussion in Chapter 12 suggests that they are the former. But we'll consider them more closely in a moment.

Figure 14-6 summarizes the situation with respect to black-white participation differences and participation differences among upper-educated and lower-educated whites. The figures plotted are simply the difference in mean number of campaign activities between the two races and between whites with some college education and those with less than a high-school degree. For the black-white difference one finds a decline from the situation in 1952. Among whites there is, if anything, an increase, with the difference between whites with high and low education reaching a high in 1964 and 1970.

These data are so interesting—in terms of their relationship to our earlier developed model of participation and, more important, because of what they tell us about some major changes in American politics in the past two decades—that it is worthwhile to consider one more set of data on the subject. The "group-consciousness" model of politicization was presented as an alternative to the standard socioeconomic model. It predicts that a sense of group-consciousness leads citizens to participate well beyond what their socioeconomic status would predict. But the group-consciousness model is somewhat unclear as to what to expect *vis-à-vis* social differences *within* the group that develops that consciousness. On the one hand, the fact that the

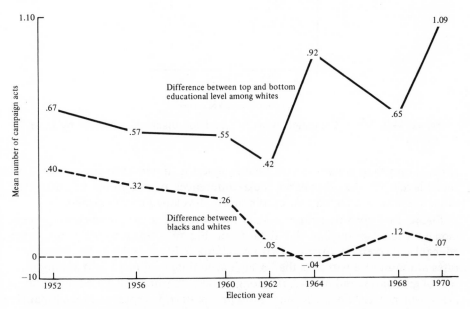

Figure 14-6. Differences in Campaign Activity Rates Between Upper- and Lower-Educated Whites and Between Whites and Blacks

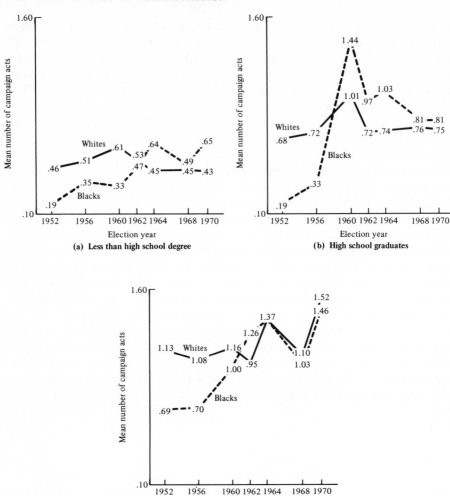

Figure 14-7. Mean Campaign Activity Level for Blacks and Whites by Level of Education

stress is on group-consciousness would suggest it should have effects across all social levels. On the other hand, social differences among group members may influence who is affected first by the newly developed consciousness.

Figure 14-7 gives us a closer look at the workings of the group-consciousness model. There we repeat the data from Figure 14-5 separately for three educational levels. In Figure 14-7(a) we compare black and white participation rates among those with less than a high school degree, in 14-7(b) among high school graduates, and in 14-7(c) among those with some college. Several points are worth noting. For one thing, the same pattern is repeated in each panel: Black participation starts, in 1952, well below white participation at each educational level. As the two decades progress, black participation rates grow until they surpass the rate among whites in most elections and on most educational levels. Apparently the process of politicization through group-consciousness works across the board.

The fact that the data by educational level show a generally higher black rate at the end of the time period (whereas the data for the two races as a whole showed a slight advantage to whites) is, of course, consistent with our finding in Chapter 10 that blacks participate more than average when one corrects for their socioeconomic level.

Furthermore, there is an interesting difference in the timing of the increase in black campaign activity across the several educational levels. For those in the higher educational levels—high school graduates or those with some college training—the crucial increase seems to come between the 1956 and 1960 elections. For those with the lower educational levels, the increase comes a bit later. The latter show no increase in activity from 1952 through 1960, but a sharp increase after 1960. One must be cautious in interpreting such data because sample sizes among blacks are small and there may be some random perturbations. But the data would be consistent with a time lag, whereby better educated citizens "get the message" first, and it is then picked up by the less educated group.[4]

The over-time data, thus, neatly illustrate the workings of the socioeco-nomic model of participation and confirm our expectations as to the deviations from it. Where there has been a growth of a belief system (e.g., group-con-sciousness among blacks) that countervails the general tendency for upper-status citizens to participate more, we see a clear diminution of the participation gap between upper- and lower-status citizens. Where no such belief system has developed, as appears to be the case among lower-status whites, the gap persists.

One last point is worth noting about the data. Much attention has been focused on black militancy in recent years. New political tactics, often direct and sometimes violent, have been adopted by various black groups. The data we report indicate that such activity has been accompanied by a remarkable growth of participation "within the system." Black consciousness does not lead merely to activities outside ordinary channels; it leads as well to greater use of the existing channels.

THE HYPERACTIVE REPUBLICANS: FURTHER CONSIDERATIONS

One of our most striking findings, reported in Chapter 12, was that the most potent belief system affecting participation rates among whites was the conservative political beliefs of strong Republicans. These beliefs, held as they are by an upper-status group, accelerate the workings of the socioeconomic model by increasing the participation gap between the upper- and lower-status groups. The over-time data allow us to test whether this is a long-term tendency or an artifact of the particular moment of our study.

---

[4] We also compared age groups over time, expecting younger blacks to have larger increases in participation. In fact we found, as we did in Chapter 10, that there were few age differences. The rise in activity cuts across all age groups.

Unlike the situation in relation to blacks, we do not expect a particularly great change in the conservative ideology among strong Republicans during the two decades for which we have data. They should be quite steady over-participators, if the data and argument in Chapter 12 are valid. On the other hand, the basis of their activity in strong conservative views on matters of welfare would predict a particularly strong mobilization in the Goldwater campaign of 1964—where the Republicans offered a truly conservative "choice" rather than a more moderate "echo." (We have already seen the high rate of participation among the college-educated in that election.)

Figure 14-8 compares the rate of campaign activity for citizens who identify themselves as strong Democrats with those who identify as strong Republicans across the seven elections. We also repeat for comparison the data on the average campaign activity for the population as a whole. Consistent with what we found in our static data, both sets of strong partisans participate more than the average citizen does. More striking is the large and consistent difference between the participation rates of the strong partisans of the two parties, with strong Republicans participating much more in each election.[5] Equally striking is the particularly high rate of campaign activity they manifested in 1964. Though we cannot test directly the assumption that conservative political beliefs are the driving force among these strong Republicans, the great increase in the 1964 election is consistent with such an interpretation. If the Republican leadership "guessed wrong" about voter preference for a true conservative in 1964, they guessed quite correctly about the preferences of those Republicans committed enough to engage in campaign activity.

The data are quite consistent with our argument that political beliefs that lead to greater participation among the mass public tend to be conservative rather than liberal. In the 1964 election the ideological split between the candidates was unusually large—a split reflected in Goldwater's campaign posture and a split apparently recognized by a large proportion of the public, many of whom were Republicans who defected to support Johnson.[6] Such an

[5] The data for all five types of partisan identifiers are remarkably stable over time and quite consistent with the asymmetrical U-shaped pattern reported in Chapter 12—i.e., a pattern where strong identifiers are the most active and independents the least active, with the particularly high score for strong Republicans creating the asymmetry. The data for all five groups across time follows:

Mean Campaign Activity Rate for Strong and Weak Partisans and Independents
(Figures are mean number of campaign acts)

Year	Strong Democrats	Weak Democrats	Independents	Weak Republicans	Strong Republicans
1952	.67	.41	.39	.58	.99
1956	.81	.52	.42	.69	.98
1960	.99	.55	.59	.87	1.42
1962	.82	.32	.28	.41	1.03
1064	.79	.52	.41	.78	1.75
1968	.83	.59	.53	.74	1.31
1970	.94	.50	.43	.60	1.26

[6] See the account of the 1964 election in Nelson W. Polsby and Aaron B. Wildavsky, *Presidential Elections: Strategies of American Electoral Politics* (New York: Scribner, 1968), Chapter 4. They present evidence from a variety of studies on the particularly strong conservatism of the Republican activists. See also Converse et al., "Electoral Myth and Reality . . . " and Field and Anderson, "Ideology and the Public's Conception of the 1964 Election."

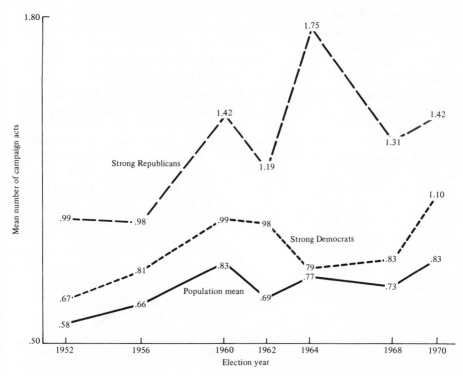

Figure 14-8. Mean Campaign Activity Rate for Strong Democrats and Strong Republicans

ideological split can be expected to motivate those with conservative beliefs to higher levels of participation, but one might expect it also to mobilize those with opposite beliefs to increased effort. Yet as Figure 14-8 makes clear, there is no evidence for an increase in campaign activity among strong Democrats in 1964 (nor any evidence for a special increase in activity among weak Democrats or independents). Nor did we see in Figure 14-5 any increase in participation among whites on the lower educational levels—another possible source of participation motivated by beliefs counter to those of Goldwater. In fact, aside from the strong Republicans and college-educated whites, the only other place where we see a particularly large peak of activity in 1964 is among blacks, who were more active in that campaign than in any before or after. And, of course, it is among blacks that we have found political beliefs that effectively lead to participation.[7]

Furthermore, although we cannot test directly for the role of conservative beliefs, we can eliminate the possibility that the higher participation rate of strong Republicans is merely a reflection of their higher social status. Figure

---

[7] This is not to argue that one never finds liberal or radical political beliefs in America and that these are never motivations for political activity. The 1950s and 1960s saw a large amount of this centered around Vietnam and civil rights. But our data suggest that this is more characteristic of smaller populations or special populations; and that it is less likely to be channeled into ordinary partisan activity.

14-9 presents relevant data. There we give the participation rate of the two partisan groups, corrected for the rate that one would have predicted based on the educational level of that group for the year when the measurement is presented. The strong Republicans still out-participate the strong Democrats by quite a bit, and their peak activity in 1964 still remains.

The participation rate for strong Republicans goes down a bit when we correct for social status, that for Democrats up a bit. Again, this happens consistently from election to election.[8] These data are also consistent with those found in our static data and reflect, we believe, the fact that strong Republicans participate as much as they do in part (but only in part) because of their higher status; for Democrats, their lower social status acts as somewhat of a depressant on their activity level. Correct for that and Democratic activity goes up. For instance, the quite low campaign activity rate one finds for strong Democrats in 1964—where they hardly participate more than the average citizen—moves up when one corrects for social level.

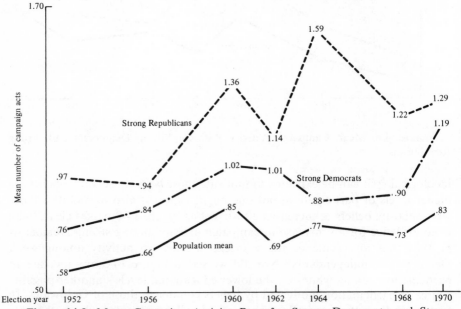

Figure 14-9. Mean Campaign Activity Rate for Strong Democrats and Strong Republicans: Corrected for Socioeconomic Status

[8] See the following table. In each of the years we find that the correction for social status leads to a slight increase in the participation rate of strong Democrats, a decrease in the rate of strong Republicans. The changes are not great, but we are dealing with residual effects. And the consistency over time does lend support to our contention as to the different role of social status among the two groups.

Change in Mean Campaign Participation Rate after Correction for Socioeconomic Status: Strong Democrats and Strong Republicans

	1952	1956	1960	1962	1964	1968	1970
Strong Democrats	+.11	+.05	+.03	+.03	+.09	+.09	+.10
Strong Republicans	0	−.04	−.05	−.04	−.16	−.07	−.13

CONCLUSION

In general, the data are consistent with the arguments based on our static data. For neither blacks nor strong Republicans do we have measures of the relevant political beliefs in the over-time data. But the data on their behavior patterns are remarkably consistent with what our analysis of the role of political beliefs would lead us to expect. They illustrate how political beliefs affect the participation input in America: group consciousness among blacks increasing the participation of a deprived group, conservative beliefs among strong Republicans increasing that of an already advantaged group.

The data suggest that the patterns found in our study in 1967 represent long-term patterns in American politics. But one ought not to confuse long-term trends with inevitable ones. Just as we have seen the rise of group consciousness among American blacks bring new participants into the political process, so might other political views mobilize groups of citizens to greater political activity—"poverty consciousness" among poor Americans of all ethnic backgrounds, liberal or radical beliefs among broad segments of the population. This might reduce the participation disparity between upper- and lower-status citizens—a disparity particularly apparent in the high activity rates of conservative upper-status Republicans. Students of American politics in the 1950s and 1960s have learned to be cautious in projecting past trend lines into the future.

THE PROCESS OF POLITICIZATION: A SUMMARY OF PART II

In Part I of this book we demonstrated that the participators in American politics come disproportionately from those more advantaged in education and income. This section has attempted to explicate the reasons for this. Our findings can be briefly summarized:

1. We presented first a standard socioeconomic model of politicization whereby citizens of upper socioeconomic status come to participate more through the development of a general set of "civic" attitudes. This explains a good deal of the over-participation of such citizens.

2. We then considered a variety of other forces that modify that socioeconomic model. Most tend to accelerate its effects.

   (a) Affiliation with voluntary associations increases the participation gap between lower- and upper-status citizens.
   (b) So does affiliation with a political party—at least for more difficult political acts such as campaign or communal activity.
   (c) And, perhaps most striking of all, is that those political beliefs among the mass public that we discovered to be associated with increased political activity increase the participation disparity as well. They tended to be conservative policy preferences among upper-status Republicans.

3. The one strong countervailing force we found was the impact of group-consciousness among blacks, which greatly reduces the participation disparity with whites.

4. Our data over time illustrated clearly the effects of the standard socioeconomic model when there are such countervailing forces and when there are none. Blacks, with group-consciousness, have narrowed the participation gap between themselves and whites over the past decade. Lower-status whites, without any apparent parallel of class consciousness, are faced with an undiminished gap. Such participation gaps have consequences—as we shall see in Part III.

5. There are also some interesting differences among the political acts. Communal activity and campaign activity are those acts for which the socioeconomic model works best and for which the additional forces do most to increase the participation gap between lower- and upper-status citizens. Voting is less skewed in the direction of the upper-status citizens, and party affiliation (particularly with the Democratic Party) acts as a countervailing force reducing the participation gap for voting.

Particularized contacting also stands out. It is least affected by the standard socioeconomic model reflecting, we believe, the fact that it communicates contingent problems that can arise in any social group. However, we did find a clear black-white disparity in the degree to which such activity is used.

6. We should refer to what we have learned about the impact on participation of the nature of the community within which the citizen lives. As Chapter 13 showed, participation appears to decline as one moves from the smaller, more isolated community to the larger, less clearly bounded one. This fact deserves emphasis, for it may help us understand some of the tensions associated with participation in recent years. There are two countertendencies in our data. On the individual level we see an increase in participation over the last two decades. Furthermore, not only are more citizens active, but more have the characteristics that lead to activity—advanced levels of education, higher-status jobs, and so forth. Thus, the potential and actual participant populations have grown.

Yet, when we look, not at the individual characteristics of citizens, but at the social settings within which they participate, we find that participation is more extensive in smaller, more isolated communities, especially participation of a communal sort. And, of course, these are circumstances that are gradually fading in America—the small, isolated community is the community of the past. Furthermore, this situation reflects a more general situation. More and more, the setting of participation and the subject of participation make effective citizen control more difficult. The setting becomes the large city, not the small town; the subject becomes national, not local policy. The kind of participation that produces the most direct and tangible benefits becomes more and more difficult.

Part III
THE CONSEQUENCES
OF PARTICIPATION

In this section we ask whether citizen participation makes any difference, and if so, how. We attempt to answer this question first by considering the kinds of messages communicated to political leaders through the mechanisms of participation. Second, we deal with the responses that citizens receive from leaders. In dealing with the responsiveness of leaders, we are concerned with the way participation affects how responsive leaders are and how equally they respond to all citizens. This section deals with consequences of the processes of politicization described earlier, particularly the consequences of the fact that socioeconomic status predicts participation so well, and that social and psychological forces tend to increase the participatory gap between upper- and lower-status citizens.

Chapter 15
Participation
and Policy Preferences

In this section of our book we are interested in the consequences of participation: in particular the extent to which political participation raises the likelihood that those who make governmental decisions will be responsive to the preferences of the citizens. But we are immediately faced with a problem. The participators are, as we have seen, not coterminous with the citizens. Rather, they are a subset of those citizens. More important, the subset of citizens who participate in politics is by no means a random sample of the citizenry. This group is heavily drawn from certain parts of the society—particularly from wealthy, white, and middle-aged citizens. Thus when we investigate the extent to which participation leads to greater responsiveness on the part of governmental officials, we must keep in mind the question: "responsive to whom?" To all citizens whether or not they participate? Only to those who participate? And, if the latter, to all who engage in any participation, or only to those whose participation level is fairly high?

The answer to the question, "responsive to whom?" will tell us quite a bit about the social consequences of democratic participation. In Chapters 17 through 20 we shall try to provide an answer. Our purpose here and in Chapter 16 is to indicate why it makes a difference whether officials respond to all citizens or just to those who participate. And we will do this by comparing the preferences that would be communicated to leaders by the citizenry as a whole with those communicated by the participators. If there were no differences between the preferences of the activists and those of the rest of the population, it would not matter that the activists were but a small part of that larger population. Their preferences would represent the preferences of all. But if the preferences of political activists differ from those of the inactive citizenry, it would make a big difference in policy outcome if leaders attended to all the citizens or just to those who were active.

The issue we are dealing with in this chapter can be made clearer if we imagine the situation from the point of view of the governmental leader who attempts to discover the preferences of his constituents. Consider two polar strategies a leader can use: He can go out and ask the citizenry about their preferences, being careful to speak to all citizens or a representative sampling of them; or he can wait until citizens come to him to present their points of view. These two strategies correspond fairly closely to the distinction between the public-opinion poll on the one hand and political participation on the other as means of eliciting public attitudes. We can call them the *polling* and the *participation strategies*. In the former case, the attitudes of the citizenry are sought out. Assuming a well-run public-opinion poll, the procedure has the following consequences: All members of the society have equal opportunity to express their views; the views elicited are "representative" in the statistical sense; the opinions of individuals who do not come forward voluntarily to give them are recorded; and the opinion of each individual receives equal weight in estimating the preference distribution in the society.

"Participation strategy" involves waiting for citizens to come forward voluntarily with their views. The consequence of this strategy is that the political leader sees the opinions of the participators. The rest of the population is invisible to him. This participant population is likely to be more intense in its beliefs and to differ somewhat from the rest of the population in the shape of its opinions. In addition, the leader is likely to see a distribution of opinion somewhat closer to his own views than the distribution of opinions in the population as a whole, due to the propensity of individuals to write to "friendly" government officials.[1] Thus the "participation" means of eliciting opinion, unlike the public-opinion survey based on a random sample, does not weigh all citizens equally. Interest, intensity of opinion, resources, skill and all the other characteristics that determine successful participation give greater voice to some citizens than to others.

The contrast between the two techniques is striking. The polling strategy covers the entire population and seeks out the inarticulate. But at the same

---

[1] See Lewis A. Dexter, "What Do Congressmen Hear: The Mail," *Public Opinion Quarterly*, vol. 20 (Spring 1956), pp. 16-27; and Converse, *et al.*, "Electoral Myth and Reality: The 1964 Election."

time it records both the opinions of the thoughtful and the opinions of those who have given the problem little thought; it equates the intensely concerned with the citizen for whom the problem may not have existed until the pollster showed up at his door. The participation method records only the views of those who have views; it takes into account intensity of opinions, and it eliminates the "noise" from a mass population that has little to say on the subject. In so doing, this method leaves a large proportion (indeed often an overwhelming proportion) of the population unheard from. It gives differential access to social groups, and it turns particular problems over to particular groups—often the special interests rather than the general but less intense interests. Which technique reflects reality and which distorts it? The question is important but unanswerable. Each technique elicits a reality of sorts.

If the political leader wants to respond to the preferences of the population, how different will his response be if he views the populace through the eyes of the public-opinion poll rather than through the participatory mechanism? We can answer this by comparing what the political leader would see if he viewed the policy preferences of the entire society—as he would if he read accurate poll results—with what he would see if the only visible preferences were those of the political activists.[2]

Our technique is simple: We compare the distribution of policy preferences of the population as a whole as reflected in our entire sample (which gives a good estimate) with the activist population. However, this requires some decisions. What exactly *is* the activist population? How much activity makes an individual a member of this population? Is the population made visible by the participation strategy made up of those who have engaged in any political act, or only those who constantly engage in all sorts of acts? A firm answer to this question would depend upon an intensive study of the strategies used by political leaders. And, indeed, this would probably reveal that different leaders use strategies that tap into different populations. In any case, we have not conducted such a study.[3] Even if we had, it might be a mistake to choose one definition of the activist population, for the interesting question may be how differently defined activist populations differ from the overall population. Thus we have created a series of activist populations to compare with the population as a whole. Using our measure of overall participation, we create

---

[2] The term *accurate* to qualify poll results is important. Candidates for office, Congressmen, and other political leaders often read inaccurate poll results—the returns, for instance, of a mass mailing to constituents with response rates of less than one-quarter.

[3] There are several studies that attempt this. John W. Kingdon in *Candidates for Office: Beliefs and Strategies* (New York: Random House, 1966) inquired into the information sources of candidates for office in Wisconsin. He was interested in how they got information on the campaign chances, not on the policy preferences of the citizenry. However, the results are instructive. Only about one-fourth used polls. And only half of these relied upon them without reservations (for good reason, since most of the polls were highly amateur). More reliance was placed on party workers, and the most reliance was placed on the "warmth of reception" to them at meetings and rallies. But few were aware of the special characteristics of the public one meets at such rallies (pp. 91-101).

David A. Leuthold, *Electioneering in a Democracy: Campaign for Congress* (New York: Wiley, 1968) found that candidates rely on three sources of information: mail, personal contacts, and polls. The latter are usually done badly, are inaccurate, and are subjected to little analysis.

several alternative activist populations based on more and more stringent criteria in terms of amount of activity—for instance, the top third of the population in terms of participation, the top 15 percent, the top 5 percent. We can then compare the image of societal preferences that a political leader would get if he were attuned to those who were only somewhat active, with the image he would get from the most active segment. In addition, we can consider the consequences of observing the preferences only of those active on a particular issue and, in Chapter 16, of those who are active from one party or the other.

At the outset, it might be useful to make one additional comment on how we are interpreting the data in this chapter. We are trying to look at the data from a political-systems perspective rather than a perspective of individual political attitudes and behavior. Any difference in policy preferences between the activist population and the population as a whole depends upon a relationship between policy preference and participation—i.e., it depends upon the finding that those with particular policy preferences are more likely to participate. If such a relationship exists, it may well be that it is spurious—that neither causes the other, but that both the particular policy preferences and participation are the result of some third factor, such as social status. Whether there is a causal relationship between preferences and participation is not of interest to us here. We are interested in the fact that, if citizens with different policy orientations participate at differing rates, the "messages" that are carried into the political process by such participation are affected accordingly. The dependent variable in this chapter is not the participation of the individual, but the distribution of preferences in the visible and participant population in comparison with the population as a whole. However, in Chapter 16 we shall deal with some reasons for the difference in preferences between the activist and nonactivist populations.

Before beginning, there is one more question with which we must deal: What is the issue or set of issues on which we shall compare the activists and nonactivists? This, too, is a complex problem and one for which it is hard to avoid at least semiarbitrary solutions. By what criteria does one select the major political issues? As survey researchers have come to learn, the presentation to an individual of questions about some preselected issues may produce responses with little content or structure. Thus to compare our respondents on a series of issue scales runs the risk of artificiality in two ways: It might compare them on issues that are not salient from their own point of view, and it might introduce great arbitrariness in choosing the major issues of the day.

We shall try to get around the problem of the arbitrary choice of issues by comparing the various activist and nonactivist populations in terms of what problems and issues *they* think are important. The comparison of the various populations in terms of the issues they consider salient should be relevant to the important question of what kinds of issues are put on the political agenda. If it turns out that the nonparticipants are interested in a different set of problems from the participants, we shall have some evidence that the selection of issues through the political process is indeed skewed, omitting the concerns of certain citizens. In addition, the comparison of the salience of issues helps avoid the problem of arbitrariness because the respondent chooses the issue.

We shall also compare these populations in terms of preference in relation to several policies. These do not capture all major political issues of the day, though we do believe they tap some of the major controversial matters before the government. The issue areas are:

1. Attitudes toward the responsibility for the welfare of citizens. Is the government responsible for the welfare of citizens or is the individual largely responsible for taking care of himself?
2. Attitudes on race relations. Is the attempt to improve the lot of American blacks proceeding at too rapid or too slow a pace, and how much ought the government to push actively for further improvement?
3. Vietnam. Should the United States increase its military effort in Vietnam or seek a reduction in its involvement?

If we had chosen other issues—civil liberties perhaps, or women's rights— we might have found differences in specific patterns, but little change in our overall argument. Furthermore, our stress on issues of welfare and race relations is consistent with our concern with the role of participation in relation to social equality, for these are two issue dimensions closely related to status, and no one could deny they represent crucial issues.

THE SALIENCE OF POLITICAL ISSUES

The first political question may not be "where does one stand on the issues?" but "what *are* the issues?" Political access and participation may be most relevant as ways of bringing issues to the fore. It may not be that the *preferences* of the inactive on the issues of the day are replaced by the *preferences* of those who are active if political leaders pay attention to the activist population. It may be, rather, that the issues of the day are *selected* in a way that ignores whatever matters most to the inarticulate members of the population. It is in this most crucial sense that the inactive and inarticulate are likely to be politically invisible.

This problem is at the heart of the controversy over issues and "nonissues."[4] Studies of decision-making in local communities, it is argued, are inadequate to determine whether community decisions are sharply skewed so as to benefit a limited elite group. The crucial problem is, which issues come into the decision-making arena and which are left out? But how can one tell what issues are blocked from entry into the political arena? Certain arguments about the reasons for such blockage are hard to deal with empirically. For

---

[4] This problem underlies much of the debate on "issues and nonissues." On this subject, see, among others, Peter Bachrach and Morton S. Baratz, "Decisions and Nondecisions: An Analytical Framework," *American Political Science Review*, vol. 57 (September 1963), pp. 632-642; and Raymond E. Wolfinger, "'Nondecisions' and the Study of Local Politics," *American Political Science Review*, vol. 65 (Dec. 1971), pp. 1063-1080; and the following "Comment" by Frederick W. Frey, pp. 1081-1101.

instance, does the population not know its own needs and interests because of "false consciousness" or because of systematic biases in the socialization process? We can obtain some insight into the nature of the problem by looking at blockages that might derive from differential rates of participation among those faced with different problems. If those with a particular type of problem are less likely to participate and if leaders learn about the salient problems in the society through the participation strategy, we will have some empirical evidence that "nonissues" (in this limited sense of the word) exist.

We can explore this question by comparing various activist populations with the population as a whole and with various inactive populations in terms of the problems that the several groups consider most salient. We can begin with the data in Figure 15-1. These data are on the personal problems reported by various active and inactive populations. Because we shall be using the graphic presentation of Figure 15-1 throughout this chapter, it may be worthwhile to describe it fully. Each one of the bar graphs on Figure 15-1 reports the attitudes of several populations on a particular issue (in the first case, the proportions reporting that they were faced with particular personal problems). We report the attitudes for the least active 5 percent of our sample, for the least active 15 percent, and for the least active 33 percent, as well as for the most active 33, 15, and 5 percents of the population. (The groups partially overlap because the less stringently defined groups contain the more stringently defined ones.) The less active groups are found to the left of each bar graph, the more active to the right.

We have tried to make our substantive point more visually apparent in two ways. The width of each bar reflects the size of each group, and the darkness of the coloration within the bar reflects its degree of "visibility," that we assume is directly proportional to how active it is. Thus the bar on the far right of each of the bar graphs represents the most active 5 percent of the population. It is thin (because it represents the views of only 5 percent), but dark (because their high level of activity makes this group particularly visible to the leader using a participation strategy of information gathering). Above each bar graph we present the figure for the proportion of the population as a whole holding that particular view.

We can relate these graphs to our substantive concern. The political leader using a strict polling technique would be aware of the position of the whole population on a particular matter. The leader using the participation strategy would be more aware of the position of the activist groups (on the right of the graph) and would be less aware of the position of the inactivist groups (on the left). If he paid attention only to those most active, he might be unaware of any preferences but those of the most active 5 percent of the population. Thus the more the bars on the right side of the graph (representing the activists) differ in height from the left side, the more would a participation strategy of information gathering create a "distortion" of the preferences of the population and leave some parts of that population with preferences that are invisible.

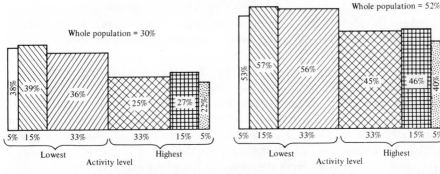

(a) Proportion reporting a serious personal problem in obtaining adequate housing, employment, or in paying for medical care (closed question)

(b) Proportion volunteering basic income or material need as the most important personal problem (open question)

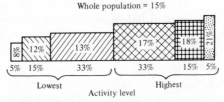

(c) Proportion volunteering educational problems as the most important personal problem (open question)

Figure 15-1. Salience of Personal Problems

Consider now the data in Figure 15-1. In each of the three sections of that figure we report the proportions who said, in response to our questions, that they were faced with particular types of serious problems in their personal and family lives. In two cases (b and c) the answers were volunteered to open-ended questions on the major problems the respondent faced; in the other case (a) respondents were asked specifically whether they had faced a particular problem in the past year within their family. In Figure 15-1(a) we report the proportion indicating that in the past year they had had a serious "welfare" problem—finding adequate housing or employment or paying for medical care. As we can see, the political leader using a polling strategy would find that about one-third (30 percent) of the population had such a problem. But if he used a participation strategy and considered only the activist groups on the right of the graph, he would find such problems to be much less frequent. (Only 22 percent of the most active group reports such a problem in contrast to 38 percent among the least active group.)

A similar pattern appears in Figure 15-1(b), where we report the proportions responding to an open-ended question that income problems were the most serious in their personal lives. In both cases, the participation strategy would produce an underestimation of the extent to which citizens were faced with such serious welfare problems. It would particularly underestimate the extent of such problems in the least active segments of the population. On the other hand, a leader attending to the participants would find much more concern about educational problems among the activists than among the inactives. In 15-1(c), 21 percent of the most active mention educational problems in answer to an open-ended question, in contrast with 8 percent among the least active.

Figure 15-2 presents similar data on the salience of various community problems. Bar graphs 15-2(a) and (b) present the proportions answering closed questions on whether air pollution or crime were important problems in their community. The two graphs illustrate one issue (air pollution) in which the more active are much more aware of a problem than are the inactives and another issue (crime) in which there is little difference in the degree to which a problem is perceived across the various active and inactive groups.

Graphs 15-2(c) and (d) present the proportions giving alternative answers to an open-ended question about community problems. Graph (c) shows the proportions saying that the community was faced with serious problems of subsistence (problems of families below the poverty line, for instance). Graph (d) shows those saying that the major community problem was high taxes. The proportion giving either answer is low, because so many other answers were possible, but the contrasting pattern in relation to subsistence and taxes is striking. As graph (c) shows, whatever perception there is that subsistence problems exist within the community is found among the inactive citizens. No one in the topmost activist group mentions such problems. And the opposite is the case in relation to taxes, as graph (d) shows. Taxes are mentioned as a problem by the upper participators, but almost never by the lower ones.

Last, graph (e) illustrates the great attention paid to matters of education among the activist segments of the population in comparison to the inactivist.

What do these data suggest about participatory mechanisms as a means of reporting to political leaders the problems that exist within the society? In terms of problems that citizens consider important in their personal lives or that they perceive as priority needs for the community, political leaders attuned to the groups who participate more would be less likely to be aware of certain basic income and subsistence needs of the whole community and somewhat more likely to be aware of educational needs. It is clear that participation, or the lack of it by those who report economic problems as their most pressing problem, may add to the invisibility of the poor. Furthermore, the leader attuned to the activists would find a greater concern about high taxes than exists in the population as a whole. In sum, it would seem that the leader who used the participation strategy would be less sensitive to the existence of severe personal economic problems in the society than would a leader who used the polling strategy. And the more narrowly he limited the population he observed—if he were attuned only to the most active 5 percent of the population, for instance—the more such personal economic problems would be obscured. Participation makes some problems more visible and others less so.

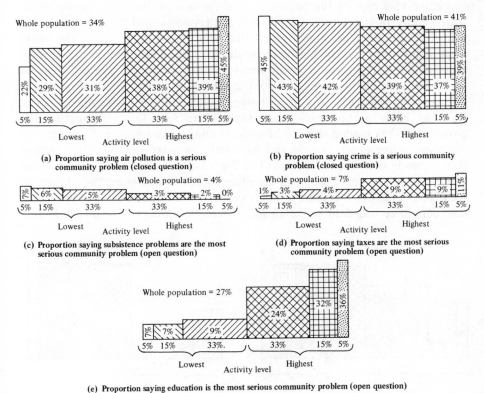

(a) **Proportion saying air pollution is a serious community problem (closed question)**

(b) **Proportion saying crime is a serious community problem (closed question)**

(c) **Proportion saying subsistence problems are the most serious community problem (open question)**

(d) **Proportion saying taxes are the most serious community problem (open question)**

(e) **Proportion saying education is the most serious community problem (open question)**

Figure 15-2. Salience of Community Problems

Participation and Policy Preferences

We have demonstrated that the problems an observer of the activist population would see differ somewhat from the problems seen by an observer of the entire population. What about the solutions to these problems? Would the participatory strategy in contrast with the polling strategy produce different views as to the policy preferences of the populace on some of the major issues of the day? As indicated earlier, we can deal with this question in terms of some of the issue controversies facing the American people in the spring of 1967. Data on the preferences of various populations (the population as a whole and various activist and nonactivist populations) are reported in Figures 15-3 and 15-4. Again, one can imagine the political leader observing various policy-preference distributions depending on the information strategy he uses. If he uses the polling strategy, he observes the distribution of the entire population as reported above each figure. If he is attuned only to participant groups, he sees a populace with a preference distribution found on the right side of the bar graphs, and he is unaware of the preferences expressed by the inactive groups on the left.

Figure 15-3 reports the responses to three sets of questions having to do with welfare policy. Graph (a) presents the proportion of the various groups who believe that the poor rather than the government have the main responsibility for improving their conditions. Graph (b) reports the proportions rejecting the idea of governmental responsibility in various areas of social welfare. The patterns of response are quite similar for the two sets of questions. In each case the most active segment of the population is about twice as likely as the least active segment to take the position that the government has limited responsibility for welfare. For instance, 51 percent of the most active group believe the poor have primary responsibility to help themselves in contrast to 26 percent of the least active group. Graph (c) adds another example, consistent with the other two parts of Figure 15-3. There we see that the inactive members of the population are more likely than the active members to consider the income gap between rich and poor to be too large.

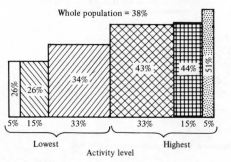

(a) **Proportion responding that the poor have an obligation to help themselves and that the government does not**

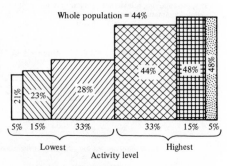

(b) **Proportion rejecting government responsibility in more than two of the following areas: housing, employment, care of aged, and medical care**

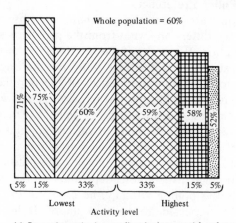

(c) **Proportion saying income disparity between rich and poor is too great**

Figure 15-3. Welfare-Policy Preferences

The data on the welfare issue are fairly clear. The activist population is more in favor of individualistic solutions and somewhat less in favor of government intervention in welfare matters than is the population as a whole. If one adds to this our earlier finding that problems of personal economic welfare are likely to be less apparent to political leaders using a participation strategy, one can see that this strategy may substantially obscure popular concern with welfare matters and popular preferences for governmental intervention in such matters.

Figure 15-4 provides one more illustration of differences in preferences across populations divided in terms of their degree of political activity. Here we present some attitudes on matters of race relations: in graph (a) the proportion saying that change in relations between the races is being pushed too fast, and in graph (b) the proportion saying that the government should enforce both fair-housing laws and school integration. In both parts of Figure 15-4 we find an increase in antiintegrationist attitudes as one moves from the inactive to the active members of the population: in graph (a) an increase in the proportion saying that things are changing too quickly, and in graph (b) a decrease in the proportion saying that the government ought to enforce integration in housing and schools. But in each case, the most active segment of the population (the top 5 percent of the activists) are somewhat more prointegration than the moderate activists. In this case it would make a difference which of the activist groups the political official observed. But the difference among these groups is not great, and, as with most of the other issues reported, the activists differ from the inactives more than they differ among themselves. On racial matters, as on welfare matters, the participation and polling strategies for gathering information would produce different results.

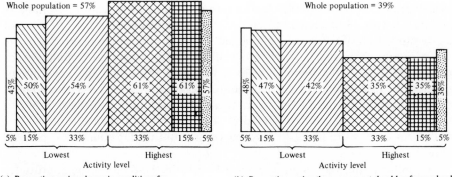

(a) **Proportion saying change in conditions for blacks is too fast**

(b) **Proportion saying the government should enforce school and housing integration**

Figure 15-4. Policy Preferences on Racial Matters

ISSUE-SPECIFIC PARTICIPATION

There is a major weakness in our argument that leaders attuned to the participators would see preferences different from those that characterize the population as a whole. The participators do have different preferences on welfare, for instance. But our data do not show that they communicate those preferences when they participate. The main reason is that we are comparing those who are more or less active *in general* in terms of their preferences on *specific issues*. The activist groups that we find somewhat more conservative on social-welfare issues are not necessarily participating with specific reference to that issue. They may be participating in election campaigns where the issues are unclear, in community activities on some subject other than governmental responsibility for welfare, or contacting officials on other issues.

Fortunately, we can look at this question from the point of view of individuals who have participated with relation to several specific issues: problems of income and economic welfare, problems involving race, and the issue of the Vietnam war. To do this, we turned to data on citizen-initiated contacts because in relation to contacting we know the specific subject matter, and we also asked a series of questions about participation *vis-à-vis* Vietnam. We can then ask how those who have participated on a specific issue differ from the population as a whole and from the rest of the contactors in their attitudes on that issue.

The data on the welfare and race issues are shown in Figure 15-5. On the welfare issue, we compare three groups in terms of their preferences for individual vs. governmental responsibility for welfare: the entire population, all citizens who have contacted, those who have contacted officials in relation to a personal or family economic problem (jobs, income, standard of living, etc.), and those who have contacted officials in relation to such basic needs as food, clothing, or shelter.[5] The latter two groups represent 6 percent and 1.5 percent of the population respectively. As Figure 15-5(a) shows, contactors differ from the population as a whole in that they are somewhat less in favor of governmental responsibility for welfare problems (29 percent of contactors compared with 33 percent in the population as a whole). On the other hand, as we move to those who have contacted in relation to economic problems we see a sharp change. They are more likely than either the population of contactors and/or the population as a whole to think that the government ought to be responsible for citizen welfare. Forty percent of those who contact on an economic matter favor governmental responsibility. When we move to that small group that has contacted in relation to a subsistence problem, we find them even more likely to favor governmental responsibility—54 percent take that position.

A similar pattern is found in Figure 15-5(b) in the data on racial attitudes

---

[5] The group that has contacted on economic problems also contains the subsistence contactors; i.e., the latter group represents a further breaking apart of the former.

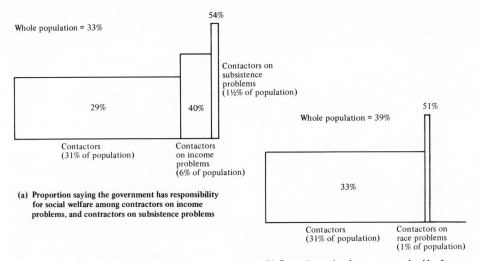

Figure 15-5. Issue-specific Participation

when we compare contactors with the population as a whole and with those who contacted on racial matters. Whereas the population of contactors is somewhat less likely than the population as a whole to take a prointegrationist position (33 percent of contactors as against 39 percent in the population as a whole), the group that has contacted officials on a specifically racial matter is more likely than either the contactors or the population as a whole to take this position. Fifty-one percent want the government to take action to enforce fair housing and school integration.

These data are quite striking, especially in light of the fact that the citizen contactors, as a whole, differ from the population as a whole on the welfare and racial issues in the *opposite* direction from the way citizens who contact on those specific issues differ from the population as a whole. In other words, the contactors are more conservative than the population as a whole on welfare and racial matters, but those who have contacted on those specific issues are more liberal than the population as a whole. The key is the nature of contacting as a political act and the ability of the individual to set the agenda. Those who contact on economic problems or on the race issue are those for whom this is a most important issue; it is directly salient to their own lives. And these are more likely to be people who feel themselves deprived along these lines. Though the general population of activists may present the policy preferences of those of higher social status, the policy preferences of those who are active on specific issues may be sharply different from the preferences of the more generally activist group.

It is worth pursuing this matter a bit further, because it tells us something about contacting as a mode of citizen activity. The data reaffirm the importance of citizen-initiated contacts in the relations between citizen and government, and they particularly reaffirm the importance of such contacts in situations where the general preferences of the activist population would skew opinions in a direction opposite to that of particularly needy groups. But the data also suggest that contacts tend to fill a gap for needy groups, not by presenting to officials alternative policy preferences on welfare matters, but by presenting the particularized needs and problems of needy citizens. This is because those who contact in relation to basic economic needs are more likely to refer to problems that affect themselves or their families than to refer to problems that are generalized to the entire community. Consider Table 15-1. It compares the proportions of the contactors of local officials who refer to particularized problems (mention themselves or their families as the referent of the problem) rather than community problems among all the contactors, among those who contact officials in relation to educational matters, and among those who contact in relation to job or other basic economic problems.

Table 15-1

Proportions of Contactors Who Refer to Particularized Problems and Community-Level Problems Among All Contactors, Contactors on Educational Issues, and Contactors on Basic Economic Needs

	All contactors	Contactors on educational matters	Contactors on basic economic pattern
Refer to self or family	32%	13%	55%
Refer to community	61%	76%	34%
Refer to subgroups and miscellaneous	7%	11%	11%
Total	100%	100%	100%
Number of cases	616	55	59

The numbers are small but the difference is clear. In contrast to the contactors in general, and even more in contrast to those who contact on an issue like education, those who bring basic economic problems to officials do not appear to carry messages about general social policies for dealing with welfare matters, but rather to carry messages dealing with their own particularized problems. More than half refer to particularized needs and only a third refer to community problems in contrast with the situation in relation to education, where three out of four refer to community problems.

These data illustrate the strength and weakness of the citizen-contact channels as ways of getting messages into the political system—and the importance of distinguishing between contacts on a social issue and on a particularized issue. On the one hand, particularized messages about economic needs may be terribly important and have meaningful consequences for those with severe economic needs who contact officials with such messages. But, because the contacts are so particularized, these benefits are not generalized to others. The results are gains for a few, but little impact on social policy.[6]

Let us now turn to participation and preferences in relation to Vietnam. This is a good example of a generally relevant political issue that was, at the time, highly salient. And in this case we have several different measures of activity with specific reference to the war. We asked respondents if they discussed Vietnam with others, if they tried to convince others to change their positions on it, if they ever wrote a letter to a newspaper or government official about the war, or if they ever took part in a demonstration or march about it.[7] This allows us to look even more closely at the relation between issue-specific participation and policy preferences because we can compare the policy-preference distribution that would be communicated by alternative activist populations.

Figure 15-6 compares the policy positions on the Vietnam war of five groups: the entire population, those who report that they have discussed the war with others, those who report that they have tried to convince others to change their minds about it, those who have written to a newspaper or a government official about it, and those who have taken part in some march or demonstration. Each succeeding type of activity would seem to reflect a more and more intense involvement, and this is supported by the fact that the proportion who engage in that activity falls as one moves across the page, from 68 percent who have discussed the war, to 13 percent who have tried to convince others to change their minds, to about 2.5 percent who have written

---

[6] The reader ought to remember that the difference between contacting on a social and on a particularized matter depends on how the citizen phrases his contact. We are not arguing that a citizen who complains about a specific economic need of his family is not dealing with an issue that is of more general social importance. Indeed, some of the difference between social and particularized contacting may involve habits of language. Perhaps those who contact on educational matters (who have on the average a higher level of education) tend to use more general language—to say "there are disciplinary problems in the school" rather than to say "some kid keeps beating up my Johnny at school." Conversely, those who contact on economic matters may talk about the job needs of their families rather than about unemployment in general.

The upper-status and more sophisticated groups in America have often managed to clothe their particular interests in the language of general reform, and to sound "public-regarding" when they may be as "private-regarding" as their less sophisticated compatriots. But for our purposes, what counts is that the particularized contactor articulates only a specific problem for his family. There is no request for a general response. They do not ask for a general response and they do not get it. Government leaders may respond by dealing with the specific problem, but this has little effect on their views of social problems in general.

[7] See Chapter 7 for further discussion on this issue. For further analyses of the Vietnam data, see Sidney Verba and Richard Brody, "Participation, Policy Preferences, and the War in Vietnam," *Public Opinion Quarterly,* vol. 34 (Fall 1970), pp. 325-332; Brody and Page, "Policy Voting and the Electoral Process"; and Brody, Page, Verba, and Laulicht, "Vietnam, the Urban Crisis and the 1968 Election."

letters on the subject, down to less than 1 percent (8 cases out of 1,495) who have taken part in a demonstration or march.[8]

Figure 15-6 indicates why one might receive a different impression, depending upon the population one viewed. At the time of our survey, the population divided on a "hawk-dove" scale according to the distribution seen at the top of the figure.[9] Eighteen percent could be considered "hawks," 12 percent "doves," and the rest fell in between. The specific distribution of opinions on the war at that time is not what is relevant here; the distribution depends heavily on the specific items that went to make up the scale. What is relevant is the difference between the population as a whole and the more activist population.

As one moves from the population as a whole to the group that has discussed Vietnam with others, one finds a slight shift of the attitude distribution in a hawkish direction. But the difference is very small. By the time one moves to the more intensive level of activity of attempting to change someone's attitude, we notice a tendency for the views of that activist public to be somewhat more polarized. About 6 percent more respondents are found in the most hawkish position and about 6 percent more in the most dovish position. Among the even smaller group (2.5 percent of the population) that has written to an official or a newspaper on the war, there is an increase in the proportion in the most hawkish position but no rise in the proportion who are doves. Thus if an official were to "read" the state of public attitudes on the basis of letters written, he would find a little more than one and a half times as many hawks as in the population as a whole and a little less than one and a half times as many doves.

Yet the story seems only partially told by these comparisons, for the time of our survey, spring, 1967, was a time of great agitation and activity about the war, and the activity seemed to be largely against it. This is hardly reflected in the distribution of public opinion, and even less so in the distribution of opinions of those who had written letters about the war. The puzzle is in part solved if we look at the last population distribution on the far right of the figure. Here we have the very small number of our sample—8 out of 1,495— who report having taken part in a march or demonstration about the war. The numbers are too small for any reliable estimates, but the figures are suggestive. The distribution of opinion among this group is strikingly different from that of any of the other groups in Figure 15-6. Six out of 8 of this group (75 percent) are in the most dovish category, in contrast with 12 percent in the population as a whole. Clearly, this particular mode of participation carries a distribution of Vietnam opinion quite different from other modes of activity and from the population as a whole.

---

[8] The Vietnam questions on our survey were asked of only a part of our sample.
[9] See Verba and Brody, "Participation, Policy Preferences, and the War in Vietnam," for a discussion of this scale.

Figure 15-6 is an excellent illustration of the proposition that the image of public preferences may depend heavily on the particular population that is observed. In addition it vividly illustrates one of the problems of the sample survey in dealing with public attitudes, which, in turn, reflects a general problem in democratic theory. The eight demonstrators in our sample are, indeed, quite small in number. They are about 0.5 percent of the sample and represent the kind of tiny group that often winds up in the "miscellaneous response" category on a table of survey responses. But small percentages can mean large numbers. One half of 1 percent of the adult population of the United States in 1967 was over half a million, and if the half-million are engaged in marches or demonstrations (and are located in strategic places such as university campuses and large metropolitan areas where they are highly visible) they are a large number indeed.[10] Furthermore, these figures illustrate the fundamental ambiguity in any answer to the question posed earlier in this

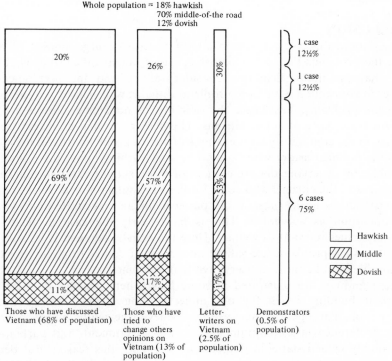

Figure 15-6. Hawkish and Dovish Preferences Among Various Activist Groups *Vis-à-Vis* Vietnam

[10] We are fully aware that our eight respondents do not let us extrapolate to the actual number of demonstration in the society. The data illustrate the point we are making; we do not offer hard evidence on the basis of so few cases.

chapter: Which is reality and which is distortion? Is reality the mass opinion reported on Figure 15-6 for the entire population, or is reality the opinion in the thin line on the far right? Or is it somewhere in between, among the letter-writers or the opinion-leaders? The answer is, of course, that the entire figure represents reality; the passive and slightly mass hawkish public, the articulate and more polarized (but leaning in a hawkish direction) public that has written to officials and newspapers; and the small proportion (but substantial numbers) of intensely involved antiwar demonstrators.

These data are relevant to a question left dangling in Chapter 12. There we showed the strong impact on participation of generally conservative attitudes held by upper-status Republicans. How, we asked, could this be reconciled with the obvious growth of more liberal and radical tendencies associated with race, ecology, Vietnam, and the like? The answer may simply be that the latter represents a smaller, more noticeably active group. The former represents a larger, if less apparent (but perhaps more constant), pressure. We will return to this issue.

CONCLUSION

The data in this chapter demonstate that, across a large number of policy areas, the problems that participators consider salient differ somewhat from those that the nonparticipators consider salient, and the preferences for policies in connection with these problems differ as well. This is not inevitable. There are problem areas where the opinions of nonactive citizens are little different from those of active citizens. The perception that crime is a serious problem in the community is an example of such a problem. But on most other issues the political leader who thought he was learning about the attitudes of the public by observing the preferences of those activists around him, or the preferences of the citizens who come forward to contact him, or of the citizens who write letters to the press would be receiving an inaccurate impression of the population as a whole.[11] This is particularly the case in relation to economic issues relevant to welfare. Here the activist segment is less likely to think that such problems are salient and, when it comes to policy positions, they are likely to be more conservative than the inactives.

These findings are illustrated at some length here because they form an important building block for our understanding of the consequences of participation. Participatory acts are, we believe, the major means by which citizen preferences are communicated to the government, and participation has a highly valued status in democratic theory for this reason. But because all citizens are not participants and because the mechanisms that bring citizens to participate do not "select" those citizens at random, the preferences of citizens that are communicated via political participation will not reflect the preferences of all. It is not our purpose in this chapter to blame participation

[11] Converse et al., in "Electoral Myth and Reality: The 1964 Election," offer a classic illustration of how this can affect party leaders looking for a winning candidate.

and praise the public-opinion poll. Each strategy of information gathering—participation and polling—communicates a different aspect of reality. What is important is that one is aware of the difference and of the ambiguities in the meaning of democratic responsiveness that this creates.

The findings presented in this chapter are hardly surprising. Others have observed the same phenomena.[12] And they are what one would expect, given our earlier demonstration that various demographic characteristics—in particular socioeconomic status, race, and age—are closely associated with participation. What this chapter shows is that the close link between various sociological characteristics and participation is paralleled by a link between political preferences and participation. In Chapter 16 we will consider this triangular relationship—sociological characteristics, preferences, and participation—more closely, and then we will turn to some striking differences between the two major political parties in the way these three characteristics relate to each other.

[12] Converse et al., "Electoral Myth and Reality: The 1964 Election"; and V. O. Key, Jr., *Public Opinion and American Democracy* (New York: Knopf, 1961). In a recent study (available to us only after the completion of this manuscript) Austin Ranney reports differences in preferences between the public at large and the voters in primary elections. For this reason, he points out, preferential primaries are not necessarily ways of introducing greater representativeness into the presidential nomination procedures. Our data indicate that the phenomenon is more general and affects not only preferential primaries but all mechanisms that highlight the views of activists. See Austin Ranney, "Turnout and Representation in Presidential Primaries," *American Political Science Review*, vol. 66 (March, 1972), pp. 21-37.

Chapter 16
Participation
and Preferences:
The Role of Social Position
and Party

Preferences and participation are associated with each other. This has important consequences for what is communicated by participation. But preferences probably do not lead to participation (or vice versa). Rather the association between preference and participation is likely to be due to the association of these two phenomena with social position. Certain types of individuals—such as those with high socioeconomic status—participate more than others (for reasons spelled out in Part II). These individuals are also likely to face different problems and to favor different solutions. The combination of high participation rate and particular preferences within particular groups quite likely leads to the differences in attitudes between the active and inactive parts of the population. We shall explore this problem in this chapter.

Let us start with a specific example involving the relationship between high socioeconomic status and political participation. Upper-status citizens are more likely to be participants. They are also less likely to report salient problems within the welfare area and more likely to be "individualistic" in their preferences for the solution of welfare problems. They carry these attitudes into the participant population. Thus that population is heavily weighted by upper-status individuals expressing the particular economic views associated with their position. For example, in Figure 15-3(a)(p. 276) we show that those in the top 5 percent activist group are more likely than the average citizen to believe that the individual, rather than the government, is responsible for dealing with problems of poverty (51 percent of the top 5 percent activists so believe, in comparison with 38 percent for the population as a whole). A major reason for this is the overrepresentation of upper-social-status citizens with individualistic views in that activist group. For instance, upper-status citizens (i.e., from the upper third of our socioeconomic scale) who take the position that the individual is responsible for his own welfare form 16 percent of the population as a whole. When we look at the top 5 percent activist group, we find that they form 38 percent of that group. In contrast, lower-status individuals (from the bottom third of our socioeconomic scale) who hold the government responsible for welfare form 14 percent of the population as a whole. But when we look for them among the actives, we find that they are but 5 percent of that group.

The pattern of under- or overrepresentation of particular sociological groupings with particular attitudes is most evident in relation to social class, which, as we know, is a good predictor both of participation and of political beliefs, but it is found whenever a particular set of policy preferences is held by a group that participates above or below the average for the population as a whole. Sex differences in attitudes on Vietnam and in participation rates explain, to a large extent, the pattern of attitudes on that issue reported in Figure 15-6 (p. 283). Men were almost twice as likely as women to be hawkish on the war in Vietnam, and they were about twice as likely to be active *vis-à-vis* the war. Thus much of the dovish sentiment on the war was carried by citizens who were less likely to express it publicly. The result is an active population of letter-writers and opinion-leaders more hawkish in inclination (at least at the moment of our study in 1967) than the population as a whole.[1]

We can consider this matter more closely by seeing what happens when we "correct" the political attitudes of active and inactive citizens by eliminating the impact of the difference between them in sociological characteristics. We use the same technique we have developed for removing the effects of socioeconomic status from our measure of participation. But in this case we remove from our attitude measures the effects of various sociological characteristics associated both with attitudes and participation. These characteristics are socioeconomic status, sex, race, and age.[2] Thus when we use our corrected attitude measure to see the proportions holding individualistic views on

---

[1] See Verba and Brody, "Participation, Policy Preferences, and the War in Vietnam."

[2] The method we use to control for the impact of the demographic variables on the attitudes is the same type that we have frequently employed to "control" or "correct" for the effects of various demographic variables on rates of participation. Linear regressions utilizing SES, sex, race, and age as independent variables were computed for each attitude measure—the dependent variables. On the basis of the B's from the regression equations, residual attitude measures were constructed with all of the variance related to the demographic

matters of welfare policy in various activist groups, we will see differences only if they exist over and above what one would expect given the sociological composition of these groups. If such differences remain, we may have evidence that preferences have an independent effect on participation. If they disappear, the relation between preference and participation has been explained away by the relation of sociological characteristics to both.

An illustration may make what we are doing somewhat clearer and also present our first substantive finding. Consider the data in Figure 16-1. In that figure we repeat data from Figure 15-1(a)(p. 273) showing the proportions of various active and inactive groups who report that they were faced with a serious personal welfare problem. These data are plotted on the solid line. As we saw in Chapter 15, the proportions with such severe welfare problems decline as one moves from the inactive to the active population. But if we correct the attitude measure for the expected frequency of such problems among various sociological groups, we find that the result (the dotted line) presents almost no difference among the groups on various levels of activity. In other words, the underrepresentation in the activist population of citizens with severe welfare problems can largely be explained away by the underrepresentation among the activists of those with higher social status.

If any more direct relationship between the salience of welfare problems and participation remains, it is in the opposite direction of the uncorrected data—those with such problems are slightly more likely to be active. We found in Chapter 15 that people whom one would expect to need governmental assistance the most—those with severe personal welfare problems—were also those who were least likely to be active. The data in Figure 16-1 do not change that substantive finding. But they do indicate that if one compares citizens

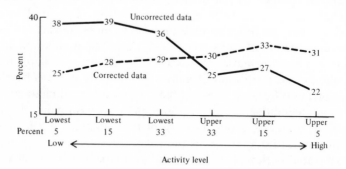

Figure 16-1. Proportion Reporting a Serious Personal Welfare Problem Among Activists and Inactives: Uncorrected and Corrected Data

---

factors removed. These residual attitude variables can then be said to be a reflection of an individual's political attitudes, independent of his socioeconomic characteristics. On any attitude a given individual may be more, less, or about as liberal or conservative, as one would predict, given his particular demographic characteristics. In this way we can determine the degree to which other variables outside of the demographic set are related to his political beliefs. Appendix D contains a discussion of the various implications of using this type of residual control.

with similar sociological characteristics (by correcting for the relationship between their attitudes and their sociological characteristics), one finds that those with more severe problems are somewhat more active. Apparently, serious welfare problems do lead citizens, at least to a small degree, to be more active politically—a fact consistent with our view of participation as an instrumental act. But this tendency is very weak and is overwhelmed by the opposite tendency for citizens with certain sociological characteristics (of which the most important is upper socioeconomic status) to be more active.

Let us turn now from the salience of particular problems to policy preferences. These are reported in Figure 16-2, where we repeat two measures of welfare attitudes from Figure 15-3. In Figure 16-2(a), the solid line represents the proportion saying that the poor have the main responsibility for helping themselves. Data corrected for social characteristics are reported on the dotted line. When we remove the effects of sociological characteristics on this "individualistic" political position, we find that the differences among the various activist and inactive groups is reduced. Again it appears that the more conservative or individualistic views on welfare found among the activists are the result of their sociological characteristics. But in this case the original relationship whereby the more active were more conservative remains even after we have corrected for sociological characteristics. Thus there remains a tendency for those with more conservative views on public policy to be more politically active over and above what their sociological characteristics would lead us to expect. This is somewhat harder to explain than the tendency for those with serious welfare problems to be more active (after one corrects for their social status). In the latter case, the problems themselves could be the motivating force. But why should those who have individualistic views on matters of public policy be more active—beyond the fact that they come from ordinarily active sociological groups? We shall return to this puzzle when we consider some differences between the two political parties.

In Figure 16-2(b) we see data on the question of whether the difference in income between the rich and the poor is too great. Again, correcting the data for social characteristics, we find that there is less difference among the various active and inactive groups than with the uncorrected data. But a slight tendency remains for the more active—particularly those in the most active group—to reject the notion that income disparities ought to be less.

Last, we consider attitudes on racial issues in Figure 16-3. In Figure 16-3(a) we report the proportions saying that the government should enforce integration in housing and in education, while in Figure 16-3(b) we report the proportions saying that conditions for blacks are changing too fast. When we correct the data for the social characteristics of the respondents, we find that the particular curve for both issues—whereby the actives are somewhat less prointegration, except for the most active group—also largely disappears. When the difference in the social composition of the various activist groups is removed, attitudes on race differ hardly at all across the activity levels.

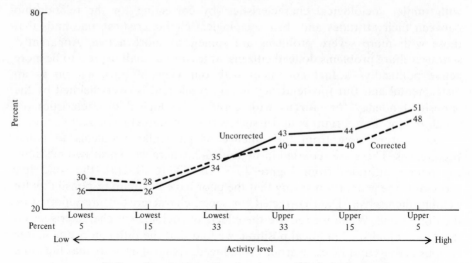

(a) **Proportion saying the poor have the main responsibility for helping themselves**

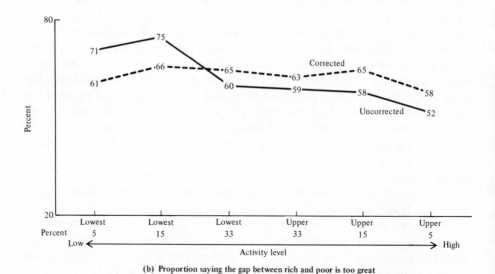

(b) **Proportion saying the gap between rich and poor is too great**

Figure 16-2. Welfare Attitude of Activists and Inactives: Corrected for Demographic Characteristics

The data in Figures 16-1, 16-2, and 16-3 make fairly clear that sociological characteristics account for most of the differences among the activity levels in both the salience of issues and in policy preferences. However, there is some tendency for those with serious personal welfare problems to be more active than one would expect, given their sociological characteristics, as there is for those with preferences for individualistic social policies to be more active than otherwise expected. It should be clear, however, that, when we say that we can account for the more conservative bent of the activists or the lesser degree to which they are faced with serious welfare problems by the nature of the social groups to which they belong, we are in no way changing the conclusion of Chapter 15 as to the extent to which participatory mechanisms provide an image of public preferences different from that which would obtain from a

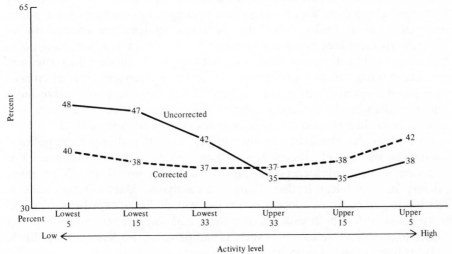

(a) Proportion saying the government should enforce school integration and fair housing

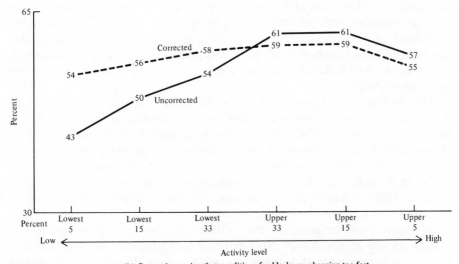

(b) Proportion saying that conditions for blacks are changing too fast

Figure 16-3. Race Attitudes of Activists and Inactives: Corrected for Demographic Characteristics

random sample. We are presenting some reasons why this takes place; we are not changing the fact that participation brings forth the preferences of an unrepresentative sampling of the population.

THE ROLE OF THE PARTY

We have thus far considered differences among groups at various levels of political activity for the population as a whole. But we have ignored some important aspects of the way preferences are channeled into politics. We compared the polling and participation strategies for learning about public preferences as if leaders who use the latter strategy are attuned to all participants or, if they pay more attention to some than to others, they do so to the most active. However, leaders do not necessarily allocate their attention to citizens solely on the basis of how active they are; certain types of citizens may receive more attention than others: White activists may receive more attention than blacks (or under certain circumstances, vice versa), men may receive more than women (again sometimes vice versa), and so forth.

One particular characteristic that might focus the attention of political leaders on one set of citizens rather than another is party affiliation. For Democratic political leaders, Democratic activists are likely to be more salient; for Republican leaders, Republican activists.[3] Unlike the situation in relation to voting, where a leader in one party might find it expedient to appeal to voters identified both with his own party and with the opposition, when it comes to more intense activities such as campaigning, leaders are more likely to be attuned to the activists in their own party.

It is, therefore, quite useful to consider how the active citizens differ from the inactive within each of the parties. If a leader of the Democratic Party were to choose a participation strategy over a polling strategy for learning the preference of Democrats, would it make a difference? And how does this compare with the situation in relation to Republicans? Do the parties differ in the extent to which the activists are similar in attitude to the more inactive party supporters?

The findings of others, particularly McClosky, suggest that there are differences between the parties in this respect. Republican delegates to the national convention differed more from a sample of all Republicans than Democratic delegates differed from a sample of Democrats.[4] By using our more general activity measures we found a similar difference between the parties in the extent to which policy preferences related to activity. These data were reported in Chapter 12. We can now see the consequences of this in terms of preferences of activists and inactivists.

In Figure 16-4 we compare the welfare attitudes of citizens within the various activity groups, but do this separately for Democrats and Republicans. There is a strong contrast between the party groups. There is much greater

---

[3] See Kingdon, *Candidates for Office*, pp. 91-101. He shows that candidates pay particular attention to the views of their own supporting partisan coalition.

[4] McClosky et al., "Issue Conflict and Consensus Among Party Leaders and Followers."

difference between Republican activists and Republican inactives than there is between the active and inactive Democrats. As one moves toward greater levels of activity among Republicans, one finds many more saying the poor should help themselves and many fewer saying the income gap between rich and poor is too great. Among Democrats, there is also a tendency for the

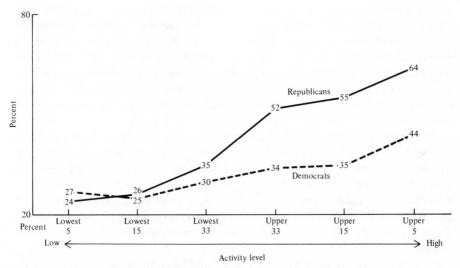

(a) Proportion saying the poor have the main responsibility for helping themselves

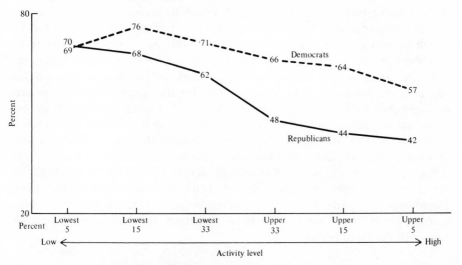

(b) Proportion saying the gap between rich and poor is too great

Figure 16-4. Welfare Attitudes of Democrats and Republicans at Various Activity Levels

more active to take more conservative positions on the welfare items listed on Figure 16-4, but the tendency is not nearly so marked. Indeed we find, as did McClosky, that the inactive Republicans have attitudes on welfare matters closer to those of the active Democrats than to those of the activists in their own party, largely because the attitudes of the activists in the Republican Party are so conservative.

Last, the data indicate (as did McClosky's) that there is greater similarity in attitude between the inactives of the two parties than between Democratic and Republican activists. As we move toward the activist groups on the right-hand side of Figures 16-4(a) and 16-4(b), we see the distances between the supporters of the two parties increase. But the divergence does not appear to be due to the increased polarization between the two parties. The Democratic activists are not more liberal and the Republicans more conservative. Rather, the Democrats are somewhat more conservative as one moves toward the activist groups, but the Republicans move much further in a conservative direction.

Naturally this situation will differ from place to place, and we do not contend that in all cases and all constituencies the activists are likely to be more different from the inactives among Republicans than among Democrats. Nor will activists in both parties always tend to be somewhat more conservative than inactives.[5] But in general, these data clearly indicate a difference in the parties in the extent to which the activists diverge from the less active. The Republican political leader who chooses a participation strategy to gather information on the preferences of those in his party runs a greater risk of attending to a set of preferences quite skewed from those of Republicans as a whole than does the Democratic leader with a similar strategy.[6] We can take the argument one step further by attempting to account for this difference between the parties. The main explanation that we have found for the disparity between the views of the active and the inactive citizens is the difference in their social characteristics. Such a difference might account not only for the somewhat more conservative bent within each of the parties as one goes up the levels of activity, but also for the greater disparity between activists and inactives among the Republicans. For while the activists in each party are in general of higher status than the inactives, the difference is somewhat greater among the Republicans. Figure 16-5 gives the proportions at various activity levels of Democrats and Republicans who have a high-school education or better. Republican activists do differ more from the inactives within their party in terms of social status than is the case among Democrats. The pattern resembles that for political attitudes, with Republican activists much more different from the inactives in their party than is the case with the Democrats.

---

[5] Regional differences among Democrats may play a role, but as we showed in Chapter 12, the difference is not great. See Chapter 12, footnote 12, p. 225.

[6] This is one explanation of the Republicans' nomination of Barry Goldwater in 1964 and the ensuing electoral vote. See Converse et al., "Electoral Myth and Reality."

We can see if the difference between the patterns found within the two parties is explicable in these terms by using our corrected measures of political preferences. Suppose we correct for the fact that Republicans differ from Democrats in social characteristics and, more important for our purposes, that there are differences in social characteristics among partisans at different activity levels. Does the pattern apparent in Figure 16-4 disappear?

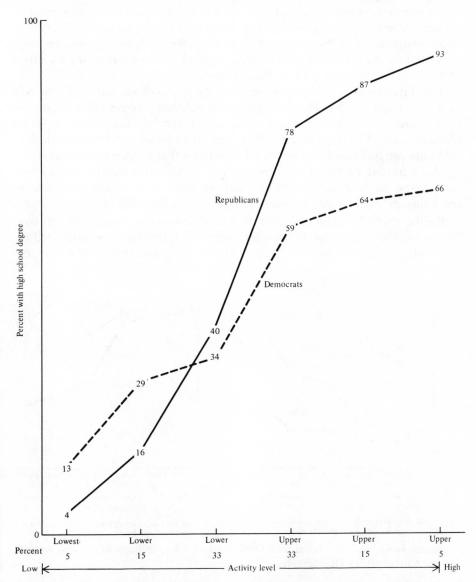

Figure 16-5. Proportion of Republicans and Democrats at Various Activity Levels with High School Education or Better

The answer is anticipated by our analysis in Chapter 12, where we found that policy position had an independent effect on the activity rate of Republicans over and above their higher social status, but not on the activity rate of Democrats. Consider Figure 16-6. When we control for the impact of the social characteristics of citizens on their attitudes, we find that the tendency for Democratic activists to be somewhat more conservative than Democratic inactives largely disappears.[7] If those Democrats who are most active in politics were found in Figure 16-4 to be somewhat more conservative on welfare matters, the reason appears to be that they differ on the average in social characteristics. Not so for Republicans. Republican activists are more conservative than Republican inactives, even when one corrects for the effect of their social characteristics on their attitudes.

The data reflect the difference between the two political parties in the role of political beliefs. That Democrats who are politically active differ in attitude from those who are not can be accounted for by differences in social characteristics. For Republicans, there appears to be an independent relationship between political belief and level of activity that cannot be accounted for by demographic composition. Ideology (or conservative beliefs *vis-à-vis* welfare, to be more specific) seem to play an important independent role in recruiting individuals into political activity among Republicans.

Furthermore, the data in Figure 16-6 shed some light on a puzzle left over from an earlier section of this chapter: Why was it that when we corrected for social characteristics, we still found activists to be somewhat more conserva-

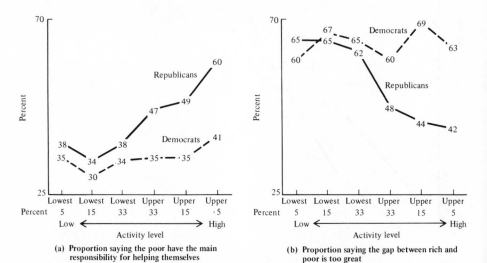

Figure 16-6. Welfare Attitudes of Democrats and Republicans at Various Activity Levels; Corrected for Demographic Characteristics

[7] This is exactly the same measure described in footnote 2.

tive on matters of social welfare? Figure 16-6 makes clear that this depends on the tendency among Republican activists to be more conservative. Thus, if there is a conservative "bias" in the preferences on welfare held by political activists, there seem to be two sources for this: the tendency for activists from both parties to come from upper socioeconomic groups, and the tendency among Republicans for those with conservative views to become more active than one would expect, given their social characteristics.

Figure 16-7 provides some supporting data for this difference between the political parties. The data are from the area of race relations. In Figure 16-7(a) we report the proportions of Democrats and Republicans at various activity levels who say that conditions among blacks are changing too fast; and in Figure 16-7(b) we repeat these data, but correct them for social characteristics. A pattern appears that is similar to that in relation to welfare attitudes. As Figure 16-7(a) shows, Republican activists differ from the Republican inactives much more than Democratic activists differ from Democratic inactives. And, in general, as one moves in the more active direction, Republicans become more conservative on racial matters, with higher proportions saying that change is coming too fast. (Among the most active group of Republicans there is a slight decrease in the numbers taking this position, but the most active Republicans are still quite a bit more conservative on racial matters than any of the inactive Republican groups.)

The corrected data in Figure 16-7(b) show a marked similarity to the data for social-welfare policy. As one goes up the ladder of activity among the

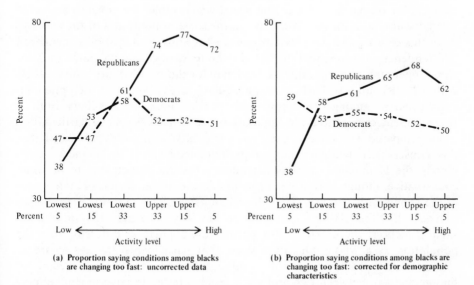

(a) Proportion saying conditions among blacks are changing too fast: uncorrected data

(b) Proportion saying conditions among blacks are changing too fast: corrected for demographic characteristics

Figure 16-7. Racial Attitudes of Democrats and Republicans at Various Activity Levels

Republicans, the proportions taking the conservative position increase, over and above the differences to be expected due to differences in social composition. But among the Democrats, correction for social characteristics results in the activists being a bit more liberal.

CONCLUSION

Our consideration of the role of party affiliation and of social characteristics has sharpened our understanding of the way participation could affect the preferences that a political leader would observe if he attended to political activists. If there is a skewing of the preferences of activists away from those found in the population as a whole—and, in particular, a skewing in the direction of greater conservatism on welfare matters and lesser salience of serious welfare problems—the main source of this is the social composition of the activist groups. But beyond this, there is a difference between the two political parties. The Republican activist differs much more than does the Democratic activist from inactives in their respective parties, and he differs in a conservative direction. This increased disparity within the Republican ranks has its source, as we said in Chapter 12, in the association of conservative political beliefs with activity within the Republican Party that goes beyond what one would expect on the basis of the social composition of the Republican activists. Among Republicans, political beliefs play a much more important independent role in recruiting citizens to activity than is the case among Democrats. It is this conservative bent among Republican activists that explains why the activists in the population at large are somewhat more conservative on matters of race and social welfare than the nonactivists—even when one discounts for the differences in the social composition of the activists.

In this chapter and the previous one we have observed the consequences of two tendencies documented in Part II—the tendency of participants to come from upper-status groups, and the tendency for those with conservative beliefs within the Republican Party to be particularly active, while no such phenomenon occurred among Democrats or those with more liberal beliefs. Both of these tendencies contribute to the more conservative cast of the participation input compared with the population as a whole. Within the Republican Party, this conservative tendency among participants is most pronounced. Even among the Democrats, there is a tendency for the participants to be more conservative, though here it has its source in the higher socioeconomic status of the Democratic activists. Thus the relationship of social status to participation as well as the relationship of political ideology to participation push in the same direction: the creation of a participant population different from the population as a whole. Our data show that participants are less aware of serious welfare problems than the population as a whole, less concerned about the income gap between rich and poor, less interested in government support for welfare programs, and less concerned with equal opportunities for black Americans.

Chapter 17
Participation and
Leader Responsiveness:
I. A Measure
and Some Data

We have stressed the role of participation as an instrumental activity, an activity by which citizens attempt to influence the government. Thus far we have considered a number of questions on how citizens can act to influence the government, which citizens are in fact active, and why activity rates differ among citizens. In the previous two chapters we began to consider the most crucial question in relation to participation: What difference does it make? But in those two chapters we dealt with the question somewhat indirectly and hypothetically—by considering what leaders *would* respond to if they responded to the preferences of the activist population rather than to the preferences of the citizenry as a whole. In this chapter and the next two we wish to tackle the question of the consequences of participation more directly.

Our focus thus far has been on the citizen-participant, rather than on the results of participation as reflected in the responses of leaders. To use the language of systems theory, we have concentrated on the "inputs" but have not directly studied the "outputs." This is within the tradition of most research on citizen behavior. Good survey data can be obtained on what citizens believe and on what they do, but it is more difficult to measure *the results* of what they believe or do.[1] Analyses usually focus on the individual citizen, either ignoring the question of the effects of citizen activities and beliefs or dealing with the question by speculation.[2] We wish to go further and attempt to measure the impact of participation on the responsiveness of political leaders to the citizenry. Responsiveness is what democracy is supposed to be about and, more specifically, is what participation is supposed to increase. But responsiveness, as far as we can tell, rarely has been defined precisely, almost never has been measured, and never has been related to participation.[3]

There are a number of reasons for this, not the least of which is the difficulty of defining and measuring responsiveness. The term refers to a relationship between citizen and government, one in which the citizen articulates certain preferences and/or applies pressure on the government and the government in turn—if it is responsive—attempts to satisfy these preferences. To measure responsiveness, therefore, one needs measures of citizen preferences and activities as well as information on the attitudes and activities of leaders. If the former can be shown to influence the latter, one will have demonstrated that indeed political participation does make a difference.

In order to deal with this question, we shall use data from interviews with local community leaders in the same sixty-four communities in which our interviews with a sample of citizens took place.[4] The availability of data from both sides of the citizen-government interaction makes it feasible to consider

[1] The exception is, of course, voting. One can tell the impact of voting on the macropolitical system because it affects the election. There are two reasons why students of voting have been able to make the connection upward between the individual voting decision and the system consequences. For one thing, there are clear "composition" rules provided by the electoral laws, on how one adds up the individual acts into a general social outcome. Second, there are a series of replicated macroevents—the periodic elections—that provide the units of analysis for making this linkage. The present chapter may be thought of as attempting to perform a somewhat analogous task for participation in general, in particular to suggest some nonelectoral composition laws.

[2] In some cases the consequences of participation for the individual citizen are considered, particularly in terms of his satisfaction with, or his loyalty to, the political system. See for instance, Almond and Verba, *The Civic Culture,* Chapter 10. Such consequences are important, but they refer to events within the individual citizen and only inferentially to actual interactions between him and the government. We are interested in attempting to link the citizen more directly to the government.

[3] Miller and Stokes, in their analysis of the relationship between constituency attitudes and Congressmen, do deal with responsiveness in ways similar to ours. However, they do so in relation to a fixed set of policy alternatives which, we believe, artificially limits the range of responsiveness. And they do not, as we shall attempt, relate the rate of participation to the responsiveness of leaders. See Miller and Stokes, "Constituency Influences in Congress," in Campbell et al., *Elections and the Political Order,* pp. 351-372. Some of the work relating aggregate characteristics of states to the performance of the government is also relevant here. See Brian R. Fry and Richard F. Winters, "The Politics of Redistribution," *American Political Science Review,* vol. 64 (June 1970), pp. 508-522. Gerald Pomper studies responsiveness indirectly by considering the relationship between campaign pledges and performance. See his *Elections in America* (New York: Dodd, Mead, 1968) Chapter 8. For an important attempt to determine how a variety of electoral, organizational, and participatory characteristics of communities effect electoral accountability as well as community policy profiles, see Heinz Eulau and Kenneth Prewitt, *Labyrinths of Democracy* (Indianapolis: Bobbs-Merrill, 1973. In press.)

Norman Luttbeg relates citizen and leader preferences on local issues, a concern similar to that of ours. But he is more interested in the similarity of difference in structures than in the question of responsiveness. See Luttbeg, "The Structure of Beliefs Among Leaders and the Public."

[4] Seven to nine leaders were interviewed in each of the sixty-four target communities. These leaders were selected by formal position and included the highest elected governmental official in the community, the heads of the local Republican and Democratic parties, the highest official of the local school system, president of the local chamber of commerce, the editor of the local newspaper, and the highest elected official of the county in

how and whether the government is responsive to citizen activities. The fact that the data we introduce now come from a body of interviews separate from those we have been analyzing thus far means that we can provide truly independent tests of some hypotheses derived from our earlier analyses.

Before one can turn to the data, we must specify more clearly the notion of responsiveness. The people ask for or demand something and the government does or does not do it; in this sense responsiveness is a fairly clear intuitive notion. But two matters have to be cleared up if we want a more precise measure of responsiveness: On what subjects does the government respond and how does it respond?

On What Subjects Are Leaders Responsive?

We raised a similar question in Chapter 15 when we compared the preferences of the active and inactive citizens. The problem there was: on what subject should we compare the preferences of various groups of citizens? For the researcher to choose a set of issues and ask about responsiveness in relation to those issues may introduce a bias. The issues may not be the ones most salient to the citizenry or to the leaders. The problem is compounded by the fact that we shall be considering responsiveness within the context of the local community—do local leaders respond to the activities of citizens in their communities?—and we shall be doing this across a wide range of communities. The relevant issues may differ from community to community. We shall get around this problem, as we did in Chapter 15, by measuring responsiveness in terms of the "setting of the agenda" for community problems; that is, we will measure the extent to which community leaders agree with the citizenry as to the most important problems facing the community and the extent to which the leaders act on these problems. This approach is reasonable because it allows great flexibility across communities where the objective situations may differ considerably, and because one of the first and most important political tasks may indeed be the setting of the agenda for governmental activity. In fact, this approach may represent the only way to deal precisely with a measure such as responsiveness—a measure that has to be relative to its context.

Responsive in What Way?

Community leaders can be responsive to citizens in many ways. They may be responsive in terms of knowing what the citizens want, in terms of agreeing

---

which the community was located. Additions and replacements and deletions from this basic set were made according to guidelines described in Appendix H. Appendix H also contains more detailed information on the community leadership sample. See Appendix A for the community sample description.

Though not all of these leaders are explicitly governmental figures, they do represent the leadership who by position are most likely to serve as links between the citizens and the government. A rather extensive analysis parallel to that in this chapter but comparing patterns of concurrence for leaders who do and do not hold positions of governmental leadership indicates few if any significant differences among the patterns of concurrence for the different types of elites. See Susan Hansen, *Concurrence in American Communities: The Response of Local Leaders to the Community Political Agenda*, unpublished Ph.D. dissertation, Stanford University.

with those priorities, in terms of making an effort to deal with those priorities, or in successfully dealing with those priorities. Each meaning of responsiveness is important. The last is probably the most meaningful, but it is the least accessible to us without detailed community case studies over an extended period and without some complicated assumptions about what success entails. We will focus on the first three meanings: Leaders are responsive if they accurately *perceive* citizen priorities, if they *agree* with the citizenry on the nature of the community problems, and if they are *active* in trying to solve those community problems seen by the citizenry. At several points we shall distinguish among these three ways leaders can be responsive, but the ways are closely related to each other, and the primary measure used in the following chapters will combine them all.

A Measure of Concurrence   The key to our analysis of the effects of participation is a measure of the *concurrence* of leaders with the citizens in their community. In our interviews with citizens we asked a very broad question about the most important problem facing their communities. The respondent could choose freely what problem to mention. Several answers were recorded and coded. In our leadership interviews we asked three similarly broad questions. One was on the perception of community leaders as to the problems citizens thought important; another was on the problems the leader himself thought most important; and the third was about the problems to which the community leader devoted most time and effort. Again several answers were recorded and coded. Thus for the citizenry we have a measure of the problems to which they give priority in the community. For the leaders we have their schedule of priorities, in terms of their perception of what citizens desire, their own perception of problems, and the actual allocation of their work time.[5]

Our measure of concurrence depends on how well the priorities of the citizens and the leaders match. Several types of concurrence are possible across the questions asked of citizens and leaders. We constructed separate concurrence measures for the perceptions of leaders, their attitudes, and their behavior. However, we found a close enough connection among these three measures that we have combined them into one summary index of concurrence for our analyses.[6] Thus our measure of the concurrence between citizens and community leaders measures the extent to which citizens and leaders in the community choose the same "agenda" of community priorities.

Specifically, the measures were developed by pooling all leaders' answers about community problems, recording the number of times the problem each citizen mentioned was also mentioned by the leaders in his community, and converting this into a ratio based on the number of "matches" that would have been possible—i.e., on the number of leaders in the community. Citizens and

---

[5] The exact questions asked of both leaders and the citizens are reported in Appendix I.

[6] See Hansen, *Concurrence in American Communities,* for a fuller discussion of some differences among these measures.

leaders could mention any set of problems. If the most important community problems listed by a citizen are mentioned by *all* leaders in the community, the concurrence score would be 100, indicating that 100 percent of the leaders in the community agree with the citizen's community priority schedule. If none of the problems listed by the citizen is mentioned by a leader in his community, his concurrence score is zero.[7]

The measure of concurrence has several advantages. For one thing, the technique allows us to compare concurrence scores of various subsets of the citizenry—active and inactive, upper- and lower-status, and so forth. This allows us to get at the all-important question of whom leaders are responsive to.

Furthermore, we can compute aggregate concurrence scores for each of the sixty-four target communities simply by taking the average concurrence for the citizens in each community. Thus we can distinguish among communities in terms of the degree to which leaders agree with their citizenry on the agenda of community problems. This is important if we want to examine participation and its consequences on the level, not of the individual, but of the political system. When we do this, we shall consider the community as the unit of analysis. Leaders will not be affected by the participation of any particular citizen, but by the *rate of participation* within the community. And the appropriate measure of the extent to which they concur with or are responsive to the citizenry is not the match between their preferences and those of any particular citizen, but the match with the set of citizens in their community. In Chapter 18, where we test some hypotheses on the collective impact of participation on leader concurrence, we shall move to this aggregate community level. In this chapter we shall first present some data on concurrence looked at from the point of view of the individual.

Several other advantages of the measure of concurrence ought to be noted. For one thing, it is a powerful measure in that it represents a relationship across two independent data sets—the interviews with the citizens in a community and with the local leaders. This should eliminate many measurement artifacts that can exist when one relates responses to various questions derived from the same interview. In addition, the fact that the concurrence score depends upon a match in the answers to open-ended questions makes the amount of agreement even less likely an artifact of the research instrument.

The last advantage of the measure of concurrence has to do with the logic of hypothesis testing. In Chapters 18 and 19 we wish to test some hypotheses about the consequences of participation. These hypotheses derive in large part from the analysis of participation we have reported thus far. To use the same body of data we have been analyzing would, of course, not provide independent tests of these hypotheses. But by turning to measures based on relation-

---

[7] The calculation of the measures of concurrence is discussed in Appendix I. The measure as calculated has a mean of 24 and a standard deviation of 14.

ships with another, as yet unanalyzed body of data, we can more confidently consider the tests of our hypotheses to be independent.

Before turning to those data, we ought to mention two problems with the measure of concurrence—problems that we shall try to deal with more directly later but that need mention now. One is that we match citizens and community leaders on the priority they assign to problems. This has the advantage of allowing them to choose the issues. But it has the disadvantage that selection of the same issue by leaders and citizens does not actually imply agreement. Leaders and citizens may both select school integration as the major problem facing the community, but one group may favor it and the other oppose it. To deal with this we shall use a parallel measure based on specific policy attitudes to see whether patterns persist when we take into account the specific content of the policies that the two groups prefer.

Another problem has to do with the direction of causality. Our data are stronger than most survey data in that we have material on both citizens and governmental leaders. But these data share the problem with other survey data of the lack of time perspective: Both leaders and citizens were interviewed at about the same time. If we find that an increase in participation is accompanied by an increase in leader concurrence with citizens, how do we know which is causing which? Is it that participation induces leaders to agree with the citizenry (a result consistent with an independent role for participation)? Or is it that participation has the opposite effect and helps leaders induce citizens to agree with them (a result consistent with the notion that participation makes citizens more open to persuasion by political leaders)? Or perhaps both concurrence and participation are caused by some third variable. In short, the problem is whether we have the warrant to consider our measure of *concurrence* to be a measure of *responsiveness*. Just because leaders agree with citizens and that agreement increases as citizens become more active, can we be sure that it is citizen activity that is causing leaders to *respond* by adopting the priorities of the citizens?

As the reader can see, this is a complicated issue that goes to the heart of the question of the effectiveness of participation. We mention it here so that the reader will be aware of the problem. We shall then temporarily ignore the problem and assume that our measure of concurrence actually does measure responsiveness, and we will use the terms interchangeably. We shall test the hypothesis that participation induces leaders to concur with (respond to) citizens. After that we shall entertain the rival hypothesis that if participation increases concurrence it does so because leaders influence citizens rather than vice versa. And we shall entertain some other rival hypotheses: that participation and concurrence are the result of some third variables.

Participation and Concurrence: The Individual Level   We can begin our analysis of the relationship between citizen participation and leader concurrence by asking a simple question: Are citizens who participate more likely to be the ones with whom leaders concur? If participation in some way induces leaders to concur with citizens, we should expect active citizens to have the highest concurrence scores. Such a finding, as we shall see, is but a first step in determining the effects of participation. But it is a crucial step. If we find that the community leaders are no more likely to agree on community priorities with the active than with the inactive citizens it would certainly suggest that participation makes little difference, or, perhaps, that our measure of concurrence was not sensitive enough to pick up the difference.

As Figure 17-1 makes clear, however, our measure of concurrence does pick up differences among citizens in the extent to which leaders concur with them. And these differences are consistent with the assumption that participation does indeed make a difference. In that figure we divide our citizens into five groups based on their degree of political activity, and for each level report the average concurrence score. As one can see, the average percentage of concurrence doubles as one moves from the least active to the most active citizens: The least active citizens receive, on the average, 16 percent concurrence while the most active citizens receive an average of 32 percent.

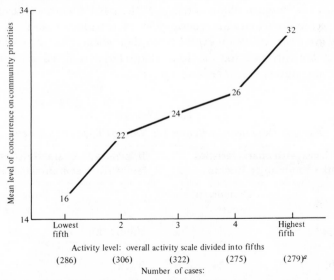

Figure 17-1. Individual Participation Scores and Concurrence Scores[a]

[a]The total number of cases for the tables in this chapter is about 1,500, less than that in other parts of this book. The reason is that elite interviews were not conducted in all communities, and only part of the cross-section sample could be used. (For further details, see Appendix A.)

Our analysis of participation thus far should make it clear that Figure 17-1 is but a weak test of the hypothesis that participation *induces* community leaders to concur with citizens. The participants are, as we have shown, a quite unrepresentative group—they are more likely to be of upper social status, to be male, white, and middle-aged. And these are exactly the characteristics that differentiate the local leaders we interviewed from the rest of the population.[8]

[8] See Hansen, *Concurrence in American Communities.*

Perhaps the pattern found in the figure depends on the simple fact that community leaders are more like the participants in social characteristics than they are like the inactives; and this is the reason they agree with the former on priorities.

Such an interpretation of Figure 17-1 is consistent with the data in Table 17-1. There we compare the average concurrence scores of citizens with social characteristics similar to those of our sample of community leaders—citizens who are in the upper third of our status hierarchy, who are white, male, and middle-aged—with those whose social characteristics differ from the local leaders. In each case, those citizens sociologically similar to the leaders have higher concurrence scores: upper-status citizens, whites, males, and middle-aged citizens score higher on concurrence than those whose characteristics differ from those of leaders.

Which leads to greater concurrence, political activity or the social similarity of leaders and citizen-activists? We can test the two alternatives. Suppose we take the data in Figure 17-1 and reconsider them, correcting the concurrence score for the sociological characteristics of the participants, i.e., use our usual technique to see if participants receive more concurrence than nonparticipants *over and above what one would expect* given their social characteristics. And we can correct concurrence for the four characteristics listed in Table 17-1— socioeconomic status, sex, race, and age.

Table 17-1

Average Concurrence Scores for Various Types of Citizens

Citizens with characteristics like community leaders		Citizens with characteristics different from community leaders	
	Concurrence score		Concurrence score
Upper third of SES scale	28	Middle third SES	24
		Lower third SES	22
White	24	Black	18
Male	26	Female	22
Middle years (30–60)	26	Older (61+)	23
		Younger (under 30)	21

The results are in Figure 17-2. There is relatively little diminution of the relationship between participation and concurrence, indicating that the source of the increase in concurrence that comes with participation is not the sociological characteristics of the citizens who participate. Even when we eliminate the effects of the particular social characteristics of the participants

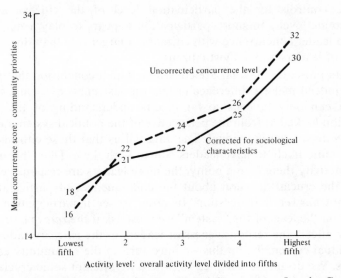

Figure 17-2. Individual Participation Scores and Concurrence Levels: Corrected for Sociological Characteristics

on their concurrence scores, we find a sharp difference between the activists and the inactives.

We can reverse the analysis to demonstrate further that participation and not similarity in social status is more important for concurrence. In Figure 17-3 we show the relationship between socioeconomic status and concurrence, correcting for rate of political participation. In contrast with Figure 17-2, we see the relationship between socioeconomic status and concurrence disappear

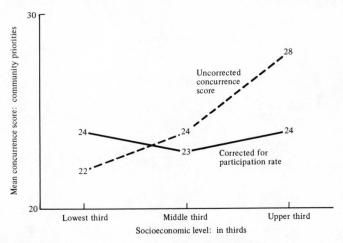

Figure 17-3. Socioeconomic Level and Concurrence Score: Corrected for Rate of Participation

when one controls for the participation level of the citizens at various socioeconomic levels. In short, participation appears to play a major role in relation to leader concurrence with citizens—a larger role than does the social similarity of leaders and activist citizens.

The data presented thus far are consistent with a conclusion that participation does indeed make a difference in the responsiveness of local leaders. But such data can only take us so far in our understanding of the effects of participation looked at from the perspective of the political system rather than the perspective of the individual. The data tell us that those citizens who are active are more likely to have leaders concur with them. Does this mean that the more activity there is in a polity, the more leaders are responsive? That of course is the crucial question about the consequences of participation. The data do not answer that question. In order to see if participation makes a difference on the level of the "system" we must ask if the *rate of citizen activity* in a polity affects the responsiveness of leaders to the *citizenry* rather than to any individual citizen. To do this we must turn to the community as the unit of analysis. We do this in Chapter 18, where we attempt some crucial tests of hypotheses as to the systemic consequences of participation.

Chapter 18
Participation and
Leader Responsiveness:
II. The Basic Hypotheses

Our measure of concurrence, as we pointed out, can easily be aggregated to the community level by averaging the concurrence scores of the citizens in each of the sixty-four communities we studied. In a similar manner we can move to the community level of analysis with our measures of participation by computing the average rate of participation within each community. This allows us to relate the mean rate of participation in a community to the degree to which the leaders of the community are responsive to the citizenry.

We consider our sixty-four communities to be "polities" in this analysis—i.e., political units in which citizens participate and in which leaders respond or do not respond. We are aware that as polities they differ from independent societies, and we cannot be sure that we could generalize from one level to another. Yet such analysis does allow us to move to a "systemic" level (although the systems are small and not independent) and it allows us to ask some crucial questions about democracy in general.

Our assumption is that the relationship between participation and concurrence looks like this:

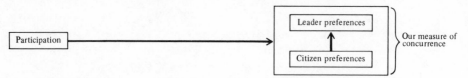

Participation leads to responsiveness of leaders to citizens

We assume that as participation goes up in a community so does our measure of concurrence (i.e., citizen priorities come to resemble leaders' priorities) and that concurrence goes up because participation induces leaders to agree with citizens (i.e., the more participation, the more effectively citizen preferences are communicated upward to leaders).

The notion of leader concurrence or responsiveness is complicated by one other factor: To whom are leaders responsive? Citizens differ in their priorities, and leaders may be differentially responsive to different groups. One can ask how responsive leaders are to the community as a whole, i.e., to the modal views of citizens. And one can ask how responsive they are to various groups within the community, particularly, to the activist citizens in comparison with the inactive ones.

Thus we shall be focusing on two broad issues:

1. How does participation affect the *overall level of responsiveness* of leaders—i.e., the extent to which they come to agree with the most widespread views in the community as a whole?

2. How does participation affect the *differential responsiveness* of leaders to active and inactive citizens? We saw in Chapter 17 that they respond more to active citizens. But that does not tell us how the *rate* of activity in the community affects the difference in leader responsiveness to active and inactive citizens. One can imagine several alternative situations: As participation rates in the community increase, leader responsiveness goes up *vis-à-vis* all citizens whether or not they participate; or as participation rates increase, leaders become more responsive to the participant citizens, but no more so to the nonparticipants; or as participation rates go up, leaders become more responsive to the participant citizens, and *less* responsive to those who are not active. In other words, participation can help everyone, it can help only the participants, or it can help the participants and hurt the nonparticipants.

The first question deals with participation and the *level* of responsiveness of community leaders to citizens; the second with participation and the *equality* of responsiveness of community leaders to citizens. Both are important for understanding the consequences of the pattern of participation that has been presented in this book. And both are important for understanding the relationship of participation to democracy.

EXPECTATIONS AS TO THE RELATIONSHIP BETWEEN PARTICIPATION AND RESPONSIVENESS

We will start with the question of the relationship of participation to the overall level of responsiveness of community leaders to the citizenry. Our general hypothesis is that citizen activities increase responsiveness because they both inform community leaders of the preferences of the citizens and put those leaders under pressure to conform to those preferences. If this is the case, one might expect a relationship of the sort depicted in Figure 18-1 between participation in the community and the overall level of concurrence between leaders and citizens. As participation increases, concurrence of community leaders with the modal preferences of the citizenry would increase.

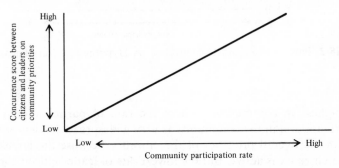

Figure 18-1. Participation and Concurrence: A Hypothetical Linear Relationship

The data analysis in Chapter 17 suggest such a linear relationship between participation and leader concurrence. The shape of the relationship between participation and concurrence was monotonically linear (as reported in Figure 17-1, p. 305). The more the citizen participated, the more it was likely that leaders would concur with him. But those were data on *the individual level.* They indicate that citizens who participate are more likely to have leaders concur with them. But that does not tell us what the relationship between the rate of activity in the community and leader responsiveness to the entire citizenry is likely to be.

Indeed, most of our analysis thus far suggests that a monotonically linear relationship is unlikely for data on *the community level.* As we have demonstrated, the participators are only a small and unrepresentative part of the citizenry. The participation input is heavily skewed in the direction of upper-status individuals. And, as we showed in Chapter 15, because of this difference in status, the participants differ from the citizenry as a whole in their preferences, including their priorities for community action. Thus, if participation does have an impact on the attitudes and behavior of leaders, it may not be an impact that results in their greater concurrence with the modal priorities of the citizens, simply because the participants do not necessarily represent that modal pattern. Rather, as participation increases in a community, the views and actions of community leaders may diverge from the preferences of the bulk of the population toward the preferences of the activists. This suggests a differently shaped relationship between participation and leader concurrence, as diagrammed in Figure 18-2.

The hypothetical relationship depicted in this figure is curvilinear. Concur-

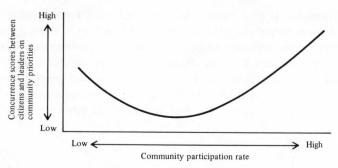

Figure 18-2. Participation and Concurrence: A Hypothetical Curvilinear Relationship

rence is highest in communities where the rate of participation is highest. Where participation in the community is very widespread, leaders are likely to concur with the overall priorities of the citizenry because the largest proportion of that citizenry is active. But the lowest rate of leader-citizen concurrence is not in communities where the rate of participation is lowest. Where there is very little participation, leaders are neither under pressure to respond to citizens nor are they informed of their preferences. In these cases, they may or may not follow the dominant priorities within the community—it depends on factors other than those associated with participation: their social backgrounds, the views they bring into office, the exigencies of their positions, and so on.

The rate of concurrence would be lowest in communities with moderate amounts of participation. As one moved from very low participation communities, where leaders are relatively free to act on whatever priorities they choose to communities of moderate participation, where leaders are under pressure and receive information about citizen preferences from participants—but from a small minority—the attitudes and actions of leaders would tend to diverge from those of the citizens as a whole. Thus our previous data analysis leads us to expect that the relationship between participation and concurrence, if indeed such a relationship exists, is curvilinear.

With this expectation in mind, we can consider some data. The basic relationship between the amount of participation in the community and the degree to which leaders concur with citizens on community priorities is plotted in Figure 18-3. We have divided our sixty-four communities into four levels of political activity.[1] (We use the measures of participation corrected for the

---

[1] Much of the data analysis in this chapter depends on comparisons among the four types of community that are created by dividing our sixty-four communities into quartiles based on their mean scores on our corrected standard participation scale. The reader might, therefore, be interested in a more concrete description of the extent to which these communities actually differ in the frequency of participation. The division provides us with communities that are substantially different in terms of the amount of political activity that goes on in them.

If we compare those communities in the "very low" quartile on participation with those in the "very high"

average socioeconomic status of the citizens because we want to make sure we are measuring the effects of participation rates, not the effects of the socioeconomic level of the community.)[2] The dependent variable on the vertical axis is the average level of concurrence between the leaders of the community and the citizenry.

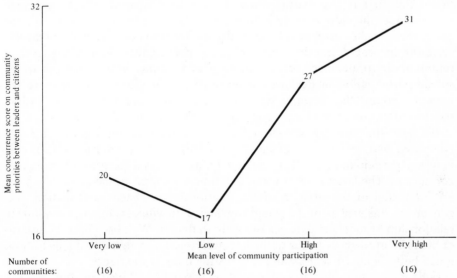

Figure 18-3. Corrected Community Participation Rates and Concurrence on Community Priorities Between Citizens and Community Leaders[a]

[a] Linear r = .32 (sig. = .01)
Interclass r = .36 (sig. = .01)
Nonlinear/linear ratio = 1.2

quartile we find, for instance, that 14 percent of the citizenry in the least active communities have contacted a local official on a problem, whereas 27 percent in the most active communities have. Twenty-five percent of the citizens in the least active communities have worked with a local group on some community problem, and 9 percent have led in the formation of such a group. In the most active communities, the figures are 37 percent and 22 percent, respectively. In the least active communities, only 5 percent of the citizenry regularly work for political parties during campaigns, whereas in the most active communities 18 percent do. The other two types of communities lie between the most and least active. The same situation exists for voting turnout. In communities of the lowest quartile in voting, over one-third (37 percent) report that they never or only rarely vote in local elections, whereas in the higheest quartile only 10 percent so report.

We thus feel confident that we have a real distinction between types of communities in terms of the activeness of the citizenry. In communities we label "very high" we find about twice as many citizens active as in the communities labeled "very low." This activeness appears to go beyond specifically political activity. In the least active communities, only about a third of the citizenry (34 percent) report active membership in a voluntary organization. In the most active communities over half (52 percent) report such active membership.

[2] We have divided these communities on their participation rates corrected for the socioeconomic characteristics of the citizens living in the community. This gives us differences in participation that are more than a reflection of differences in level of affluence. Though the patterns of concurrence reported in this chapter are quite similar whether one uses the uncorrected or the corrected community participation scores, the corrected scores make the patterns somewhat clearer. We have used the corrected measures throughout this chapter because we feel they are better indicators of the relative amounts of pressure placed upon, and information communicated to, the community leadership. The uncorrected score gives heavy weight to the class,

The data indicate that concurrence does go up with participation, but in the curvilinear manner suggested. Concurrence is substantially higher in the two categories of community where participation is high, but the lowest rate of concurrence is not in the quartile of communities with the lowest rate of participation, but in the next quartile, where participation exists but is relatively limited in amount. Thus the data conform to two of our expectations. The first is that participation does indeed have an effect on leader concurrence; the more participation there is, the more leaders concur with the preferences of the citizenry. The data also conform to our expectation that the relationship would not be linear because participants do not necessarily represent the preferences of the citizenry as a whole. Where there is widespread participation, leaders are indeed responsive to citizens; where there are limited amounts they seem to respond to those who are participating and to pay less attention to the large proportion of the citizenry that is quiescent.

To test the strength of the relationships reported in Figure 18-3 we computed two measures of association: a measure of the linear relationship between participation and concurrence (r) as well as a measure of interclass correlation. The latter is sensitive to curvilinear patterns in the data.[3] Since we are interested in the strength of the relationship between participation and concurrence as well as in the extent to which a curvilinear rather than a linear relationship best fits the data, we report both figures. We also report the square of the ratio of the curvilinear to the linear correlation, a figure that tells us how much better a curvilinear assumption fits the data. If the figure is above 1.0, a curvilinear relationship fits better; if it is below 1.0, a linear relationship fits better.

The correlation coefficients are consistent with our argument. Both the linear r and the interclass r (for curvilinearity) are positive and statistically significant (each at the .01 level), and the fact that this relationship is found

age, and race distributions in the community, which are part of the national trends of participation. The corrected mean, on the other hand, controls for the kinds of people who live in the community and thus permits us to classify communities as more or less participant, holding constant the demographic make-up of the community. We believe that this corrected rate of community participation is more meaningful, given our desire to isolate participation without the confounding influences of variables such as status, race, age, and sex. In employing the corrected measure we know that its relationships to concurrence are not simply the reflections of differences in concurrence that may be associated with the wealth, race, or age composition of the community.

[3] The interclass r is computed by creating a series of dummy variables, one corresponding to each of the classes or levels of community participation rates (actually to avoid multicolinearity it is the number of participation levels minus 1—in this case 3). These dummy variables then become predictors in a standard multiple regression equation where the dependent variable is the level of community concurrence. The multiple r from the regression equation reflects the amount of variance in concurrence that can be explained by levels of participation. When the relationship is linear, this multiple r is either identical or very similar to the simple linear correlation. (The small differences in this case are simply due to the fact that we are dealing with grouped data rather than the relationship of the continuous participation variables). When both the linear r and the interclass r are small, it indicates that the participation has little or no effect, linear or nonlinear, on concurrence. Finally (and perhaps most important) are those cases where the simple r is zero or small, while the interclass r is much bigger. This indicates that although there is an absence of a linear monotonic relationship, there exists a strong curvilinear one. That is, participation explains a significant amount of the variance in concurrence, but the prediction is neither linear nor likely to be even monotonic. As we proceed through this chapter and the next we will see that in some instances our greatest ability to predict variance in concurrence is in nonlinear situations.

across two independent data files makes it quite convincing.[4] The fact that the linear relationship is significant indicates that, on average across all communities, the generalization "the more participation, the more responsiveness" holds. However, the somewhat greater magnitude of the interclass r indicates that a curvilinear relationship fits the data a bit better. This is reflected in the ratio of 1.2 between the linear and the nonlinear correlations.

Thus, the data conform with our general hypothesis that the relationship of participation to concurrence would be a curvilinear one. But they are certainly not substantial enough to reinforce our entire argument as to the consequences of participation. The downturn in concurrence between the "very low" activity communities and the "low" is slight and might not reflect the process we assume to be operating by which participation relates to leader concurrence. But we can test more directly to see if that process is operating.

PARTICIPATION AND DIFFERENTIAL RESPONSIVENESS

Our argument on the effects of participation rests heavily on the *differential responsiveness* of leaders to citizens, i.e., on the extent to which leaders respond to participation by accepting the views of the participants and ignoring citizens who do not participate. Thus far we have considered this question from the point of view of the extent to which leaders concur with the average position of a cross section of the community. We have shown that their average level of concurrence goes down and then up again as participation increases and have assumed that this is due to the differential attention they pay to participators.

We can perform a crucial test of our analysis of how participation relates to governmental responsiveness by comparing what happens to community leaders' degree of concurrence with those who are active and with those who are inactive as the participation rate goes up in the community. If our analysis is correct, an increase in participation should lead to greater concurrence of community leaders with the activist citizens, and the increase in concurrence should be linear. On the other hand, as participation increases, particularly as one moves from very little participation to a moderate amount, concurrence with those citizens who are inactive should decline. We interpreted the curvilinear pattern in Figure 18-3 as reflecting the fact that leaders were turning away from the citizenry as a whole to concentrate on the activists.

---

[4] We believe that such relations across separate data files are very powerful methodologically. In this light, it is most encouraging to note that one finds a similar positive relationship between participation in the community and leader-citizen concurrence when one uses as the measure of participation the actual percentage voting in the community (as reported in official statistics) rather than the data from our sample survey. The relationship is not as strong as that found using our sample data. The correlation between concurrence and our sample data on voting rate was .41; the correlation between concurrence and the official statistics on voting was .22. But in both cases the figures are positive and statistically significant.

The correlation between official voting statistics and citizen-leader concurrence is a relationship across *three independent data files:* our interviews with a cross-section sample of citizens, our interviews with local leaders (the combination of these two data files going to make up the index of concurrence) and official statistics on voting. Such relations across data files eliminate many of the problems of response set or biased reporting that can artificially raise relationships among variables taken from a single data file.

Thus, for the activists, concurrence should rise in a linear manner; for the inactive citizens it should display the curvilinear pattern.

The data in Figure 18-4 test this hypothesis. This figure is similar to Figure 18-3 in that we plot the relationship between the overall participation rate in the community and the concurrence of leaders with citizens. But we plot separately the concurrence of leaders with citizens at various levels of political activity. The data fit our expectations quite closely. For the top third activists, concurrence goes up in a linear manner: The more participation, the more leaders respond. The linear correlation is statistically significant, and nothing is gained by using a curvilinear assumption. But for the less active, increased participation has a curvilinear relationship to concurrence. (For both of the less active groups the interclass correlation coefficient fits the data better.) For less active citizens, increased participation, at least as one moves from communities with very little participation to those with a somewhat greater amount, leads to a decline in the responsiveness of leaders. As one then moves to communities with higher levels of activity, the low-participators begin to reap the benefits of the overall high participation rates. Thus in communities where participation is the highest, leader responsiveness is the highest for all three types of citizens. Very active, moderately active, and inactive citizens in high-participation communities are all better off in terms of the concurrence of leaders with their preferences than citizens in any other type of community.[5] But in the very high participation communities, there is still a great gap between the concurrence rates of leaders with active and inactive citizens.

Figure 18-4 deserves close attention, because it presents the best answer to the two questions raised at the beginning of this chapter: What is the relationship between participation and the *level* of leader responsiveness to citizens, and what is the relationship between participation and the *equality* of responsiveness of leaders to citizens? Indeed, it offers the best general answer to the question of the difference participation makes.

Consider the situation in the various types of community:

1. In communities with *very low* rates of political activity, responsiveness of leaders is relatively low. But leaders concur to a fairly equal degree with all three types of citizens. Where very few people are active, leaders are fairly free to do as they want and they respond equally to all citizens, though they are not very responsive to any level.

2. In communities where participation is *moderately low* (where a small segment of the population is participating) the gap between leader respon-

---

[5] In relation to this point, it is important to note that we have divided citizens into upper, middle, and lower thirds on participation by using the distribution across the whole population, not that found in each community. This is important for establishing that the higher concurrence received by the lower-third participants in active communities results from the "spill-over" effect of that activism on the inactives. If we had divided citizens into participation levels on a community-by-community basis the absolute level of activity of the lower-third citizens would go up as we moved to more active places. Because we used the same absolute standard in each type of community, lower-third activists in highly active communities are no more active than lower-third activists in less active communities (with the possible exception of small grouping effects). If they get more concurrence, it must come from the effects of the general level of activity in the community. It does not come from their own activity.

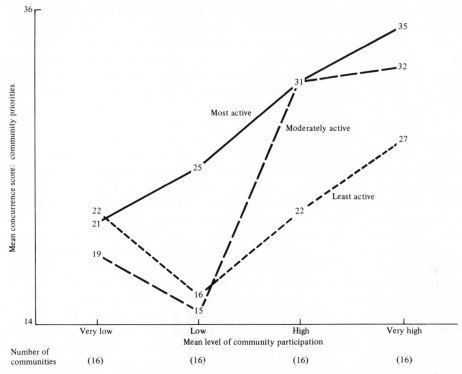

Figure 18-4. Corrected Community Participation Rates and Concurrence on Community Priorities Between Community Leaders and Citizens at Three Levels of Activity[a]

[a]Most active:
Linear r = .32 (sig. = .01)
Interclass r = .30 (sig. = .05)
Nonlinear/linear ratio = .89

Moderately active:
Linear r = .38 (sig. = .01)
Interclass r = .41 (sig. = .01)
Nonlinear/linear ratio = 1.1

Least active:
Linear r = .12 (not sig.)
Interclass r = .23 (not sig.)
Nonlinear/linear ratio = 3.6

siveness to the most active citizens and to the others is most severe. Leaders in such communities are more attentive to the activists and less attentive to the inactives than are the leaders in the communities with very little participation. In moderately active communities, the inactives are least well off than in any other type.

3. In the communities where there is a *moderately high* rate of participation, leaders are quite responsive to those who are active, and there is a wide gap between the active and inactive citizen. In such communities the least active are just about as well off in terms of leader responsiveness as they are in the communities where there is little activity.

4. In communities where there is *most citizen activity,* concurrence between leaders and citizens on all three activity levels is highest. But a relatively wide gap remains between the level of concurrence of leaders with the activist and the inactivist citizens.

In short, all citizens—active and inactive—are absolutely better off in terms of leader responsiveness in communities where there is high activity. On the other hand, equality among citizens in terms of leader concurrence is greatest where participation is the least. If one preferred *equal* treatment of all citizens, even if this implied *equally bad* treatment, one might choose a community with very little participation. If one preferred a *higher level* of treatment for all citizens, even if this meant *unequal* treatment, one might choose a community with high levels of activity.

In sum, the data in this chapter make clear that when we consider participation from the perspective of the polity (i.e., by using our sixty-four communities as political units) we find that it makes a difference in the behavior of leaders. In general, the more participation there is, the more leaders concur with citizens on community priorities. But this increased concurrence is a benefit coming most unambiguously to the participants. Nonparticipants may or may not benefit from this. It depends on the overall amount of activity in the community.

The data confirm the importance of the socioeconomic model of participation. The fact that the participation input comes from a small and unrepresentative sample makes a difference in how leaders respond. Participation is a powerful mechanism for citizen control, but how that mechanism works depends on who participates. This is our most basic conclusion. But we can take the argument several steps further by considering how the relationship of participation to governmental responsiveness is affected by several conditions, one set having to do with the nature of the community and another with the mode of participation. These further considerations, to which we shall turn in Chapter 19, will enable us to elaborate the basic pattern we have found, and also to confirm further the existence of the process we have suggested by which citizen activity affects leaders. We shall also consider some rival explanations to those offered here.

Chapter 19
Participation and Leader Responsiveness: III. Elaboration and Some Counterhypotheses

In Chapter 18 we found that the relationship between participation and concurrence, while strong, was not monotonically linear; and this was especially the case when one considered the concurrence of leaders with less active citizens. We can test our model further in two ways. There are certain circumstances in which one would expect participation to be related to concurrence in a more or less linear way: one has to do with characteristics of the community and the other with the mode of participation.

COMMUNITY CONSENSUS AND THE RELATIONSHIP OF PARTICIPATION AND CONCURRENCE

The major reason we expected a somewhat curvilinear relationship between participation and concurrence was that the participant population does not *represent* the population as a whole—they differ, as we have seen, in social characteristics and in preferences. Thus they do not speak for the whole community. If leaders pay attention to this small but active segment of the population, they will be paying less attention to the community as a whole.

But there is a circumstance under which the participants would represent and speak for the community as a whole. This would be the case if the community were a highly consensual one, where all or almost all of the citizenry agreed on the priorities for the community. In such a case, participation by even a small group of citizens would induce leaders to concur with the preferences of the citizenry as a whole for the simple reason that there would be little difference in preference between the activists and the inactives.

We can use our measure of concurrence to differentiate among communities in terms of the amount of agreement on community priorities between the activist portion of the citizenry and the rest of the citizens. We do this by computing for each community a measure of concurrence between the top activists in the community and the rest of the citizens. The measure is exactly analogous to the concurrence measures between citizens and community leaders.[1] The higher the concurrence measure, the more consensus there is on community priorities between the activist and inactivist population. Using this measure we can deal with the joint effects of the amount of citizen consensus and the amount of participation on the responsiveness of leaders. We do this by dividing the communities into those above and below the median on agreement between activist and inactive citizens. We can then see how participation relates to leader concurrence in communities that are more or less consensual.

In Figure 19-1 we compare the effects of participation on concurrence in communities where there is a low level of agreement between activists and inactive citizens with the relationship where there is a high level of agreement. The contrast between the two types of community is striking. In low-agreement communities, participation has almost no impact on the concurrence of community leaders with the citizenry as a whole; in high-agreement communities it has a major impact. In the former communities there is no linear correlation between participation and leader concurrence, whereas in the latter the linear relationship is quite strong (linear $r = .48$, significant at .01).

Thus the data conform nicely to our expectations about community conditions under which participation can play a representative role. Where there is a high level of agreement among citizens, the segment of the population that participates can speak for the entire community, and concurrence goes up monotonically. Where the active segment of the community

---

[1] The measure of agreement between high and low participators is actually the mean concurrence on community priority schedules between the upper-third activists (i.e., all citizens scoring 60 or above on our standard participation index—about 33% of our sample) and all other citizens in the community. The calculation of the agreement or consensus score is directly parallel to the calculation of our measure of community concurrence. In this case the activists were treated in a manner identical to the leaders in the original concurrence measure. The community priority schedules of these citizens treated as a group were then compared to the priority schedule of each of the less active citizens. By such means each of the less active citizens was given an agreement score reflecting the degree to which the activists in the community did or did not share his priority schedule of community problems. Average agreement scores for the communities were obtained by simply averaging these individual agreement scores. For more details on our measure of concurrence, see Appendix I.

does not speak for the whole community—where there is little agreement between the activists and the rest of the citizenry—participation does not lead to greater leader concurrence with the citizenry.[2]

Thus, community consensus, at least between the activist and the nonactiv-

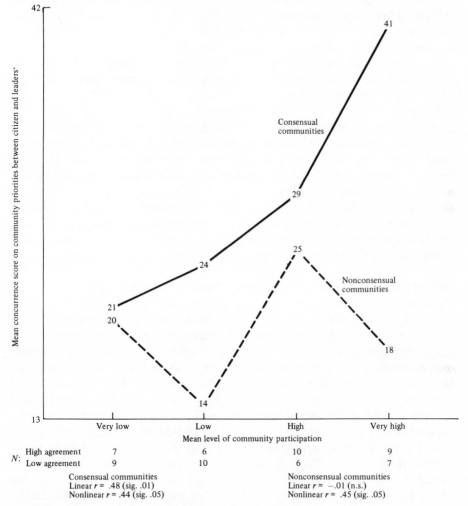

Figure 19-1. Corrected Community Participation Rate and Concurrence on Community Priorities in More or Less Consensual Communities

[2] The difference between consensual and nonconsensual communities predicts that the differential responsiveness reported in Figure 18-4 should hold most strongly for nonconsensual communities. The data for that figure were rerun for the two types of community. In general they are consistent with our expectations. In consensual communities all kinds of citizens—participant and nonparticipant—benefit more than in nonconsensual ones. In the nonconsensual communities, however, there were too few cases in various cells for reliable estimates.

ist, becomes a crucial factor in understanding the role of participation in relation to leader responsiveness. This brings us back to our concern for the importance of social status. One of the main reasons communities vary in the amount of agreement between activists and inactives is that in some places social status is more strongly related to participation than in others. Where it is more strongly related, there is less agreement on community priorities between activists and inactives. The correlation between social status and overall participation is .34 in the high-consensus communities, but .45 in the low-consensus ones. To put it another way, social status explains twice as much of the variance in participation in low-consensus communities ($r^2 = .20$) than in high-consensus ones ($r^2 = .11$).[3] (A similar pattern holds for all the modes of participation.)

The point is that where the socioeconomic model works most strongly, the largest differences in preferences between the participants and the rest of the population appear simply because the former come more heavily from upper-status groups. We have made that point often. What the present data show are the consequences of that fact. Where socioeconomic status plays a bigger role in determining who participates, leader responsiveness to the citizenry as a whole is not increased by citizen activity. Only where the model works less well—where the status-participation relationship is weaker—does a participant population emerge that can speak for all. And only then does participation increase responsiveness to the citizenry as a whole.

THE MODES OF PARTICIPATION AND CONCURRENCE

If our explanation of the way participation affects concurrence is correct, one would expect differences among the modes of political activity. To see why this is so we can return to a distinction among the various modes of activity first mentioned in Part I—the *type of influence* that the different modes exert over policy. Participation affects the behavior of leaders for two reasons: It conveys to them information on the preferences of the citizenry and it applies pressure on them to conform to those preferences. But as we pointed out, the modes differ in the extent to which they are influential via the communication of preferences or via the exertion of pressure. Voting can provide a lot of pressure on leaders (especially if they wish reelection) but it conveys little information per se on the preferences of the participants. Campaign activity is high in pressure as well (for the same election-related reason that voting is potent) but it can convey more information because the campaign activists are a visible population with whom leaders are likely to be in contact.[4] Communal activity communicates much more information because of the specificity of the issues to which it can be related. How much pressure it exerts is uncertain, depending on how many citizens are active and

---

[3] These correlations are based on individual data. That is, the correlations between status and participation are computed from the 718 interviews in the consensual communities and the 656 in the nonconsensual ones.
[4] See Chapter 15, footnote 3 for relevant literature on attention paid to campaigners.

how active they are. Furthermore, particularized contacting is high in informational content, but exerts somewhat less pressure on leaders to conform because they are faced with the activity of single citizens.

In sum, the four modes rank in the following way:

	Type of Influence
Voting:	Low information/high pressure
Campaign activity:	Moderate to high information/high pressure
Communal activity:	High information/low, moderate or high pressure
Particularized contacting:	High information/low pressure

The distinction is important in terms of our expectations about the shape of the relationship between citizen activity and leader responsiveness. If citizen activity influences leaders by exerting general pressure without communicating precise information on the nature of their preferences, one would expect a more linear relationship between activity and concurrence because leaders could not divert their attention to satisfy the preferences of the participant few, since they do not receive information on the nature of these preferences. Rather, they would be under diffuse pressure to conform to the citizenry's preferences, which should lead to concurrence with the citizenry as a whole.

On the other hand, if the mode of participation was rich in its information content, leaders responsive to that participation might indeed divert their attention to the participants and away from the inactive population. This suggests the likelihood of finding a linear relationship between the rate of voting participation in the community and the concurrence of leaders. With other modes, especially communal activity and particularized contacting, one should find a more curvilinear relationship.

However, our previous data suggest that one must compare the impact of the various modes of activity in consensual and nonconsensual communities. The relationship between participation and concurrence took quite a different shape in these two different types of community. And this should be related to the informational and pressure components of participation. If a community is consensual, the distinction between information and pressure should be unimportant, for even if leaders receive information as to the preferences of the participants, these preferences will not differ from those of the nonparticipants. On the other hand, where there is a disparity in the priorities of the active and inactive portions of the citizenry, the difference between influencing leaders through pressure rather than through information should be important. In such communities, modes of participation that convey a lot of information should *lower* responsiveness to the citizenry as a whole, unless a very large proportion of the population takes part in that mode.

In Figure 19-2 we differentiate between the communities where there is a high degree of consensus between participants and nonparticipants and those where there is less consensus, and relate this to the rate within the community of the four modes of participation. The data fit quite closely to our expectations. Consider first the high-consensus communities (plotted by a solid line on all subsections of the figure). In relation to all modes of participation the situation is fairly similar. Each mode of participation has a linear relationship to concurrence in such communities. The relationship with the electoral modes is statistically significant; that with the nonelectoral modes is significant in one instance and close to it in another. The result is consistent with our expectation that the mode of participation—particularly whether the mode of activity is effective through pressure or information—would make little difference under such circumstances.

On the other hand, differences appear among the modes when one considers the nonconsensual communities (plotted by a dotted line on the graphs). For communal activity and particularized contact—those modes of activity high in informational content—increased rates of participation are coupled with a *decline* in the overall level of concurrence. That is, where the activist citizens do not agree on priorities with the inactives (i.e., in our low-consensus communities), increased nonelectoral activity leads to a lower level of agreement between the leaders of the community and the modal priorities of the citizenry. This result is consistent with our notion that under such conditions leaders pay attention to the special views of the activists, views that do not represent those of the rest of the citizens.

The pattern is clearest in relation to communal activity, where the relationship in nonconsensual communities is *linear but negative.* A similar pattern is observable in relation to particularized contacting, where—at least in communities highest in this type of activity—a general decline in responsiveness is found. (Crucial to this argument is the fact that, even in the high-activity communities, neither communal activists nor particularized contactors approach being a majority of the population. They just become a more noticeable minority.)[5]

Perhaps the most striking characteristic of Figure 19-2 is the distinction between the electoral and the nonelectoral modes of activity. All the modes of activity relate similarly to concurrence in consensual communities. But where there is less consensus, the nonelectoral modes—by communicating the specific problems of the participants—result in a decrease in responsiveness of leaders to the community as a whole. The data seem to be consistent with arguments in favor of control over governmental officials through the blunt but powerful techniques of the electoral process. By putting relatively diffuse pressure on leaders to respond to citizens but *without specifying how they should respond* (because of the low informational content of the electoral situation) electoral participation does not result in the decline of overall responsiveness

---

[5] Even in the communities where communal activity is highest, the communal activists remain a minority, though a substantial one. In such places, for instance, 37 percent reported having worked with a local group.

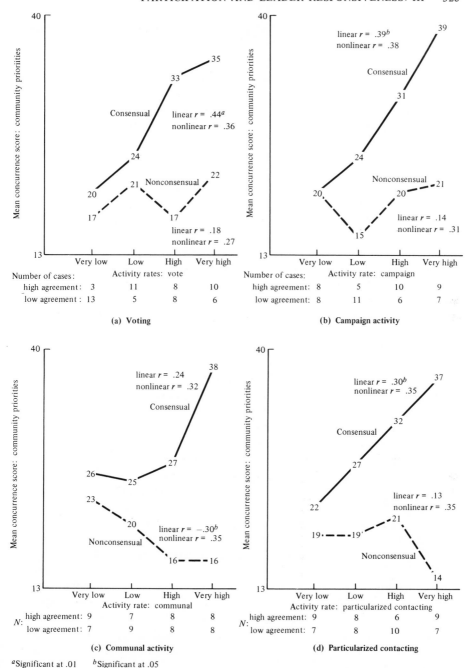

Figure 19-2. Corrected Community Participation Rate and Concurrence in More or Less Consensual Communities: Four Modes of Activity

that one finds with nonelectoral participation in communities where there is little consensus among citizens.

The data in Figure 19-1 and 19-2 tell us a lot about the role of participation in relation to leader responsiveness. Above all they indicate that the relationship is a rather mixed one, depending upon the nature of the polity where the participation takes place and on the mode of participation. Where the active portion of the citizenry can speak for all the citizens, participation leads to a higher overall level of leader concurrence. But where citizens are divided on preferences, such a clear relationship is not found. In such cases it depends on the mode of activity.

One of the strong points of communal activity and particularized contacting is their ability to convey to leaders fairly precise information on citizen preferences. But that means that leaders receive distorted views, for the activists may not represent the views of all citizens. Where the activists and the inactives do not agree, high rates of activities that are rich in information lead to a decline in the overall level of leader responsiveness.

The data in Figure 19-2 also make clear the importance of both pressure and information as means by which participation influences government leaders. Both voting (an act high on pressure and low on information) and particularized contacting (high on information and low on pressure) result in higher leader concurrence—at least in consensual communities. The impact of voting is especially interesting, for at various times in this book we have appeared to denigrate the vote compared with other political activities because it requires so much less initiative than the other acts and because it is such a blunt instrument of citizen control. But, as we have also pointed out, the vote in its aggregate effects is perhaps the most important means of citizen control because it can keep pressure on leaders.

In Figure 19-3 we present data that offer strong support for the importance of voting, particularly in combination with other modes of activity. We divide our communities into those where voting turnout is high and those where it is low (by dividing communities on the median on voting turnout). Within these two types of community we consider the relationship between the other three modes of activity and concurrence.

The contrast is clear. In communities where voting rates are high, the other three modes of activity are quite powerful in increasing concurrence. Where voting turnout is low, the other modes of activity make little difference. In short, the vote per se may not carry much information about citizen preferences, and elections themselves may not be capable of dealing with the vast array of specific problems faced by citizens and groups, but the general pressure of the vote appears to enforce the effectiveness of the other, more specific modes of participation.[6]

---

[6]The importance of the pressure component of voting is underscored by the fact that voting rates have their biggest impact on concurrence in communities with competitive elections, and, in such communities, on elected leaders. See Hansen, *Concurrence in American Communities,* for a fuller discussion of the data on competition.

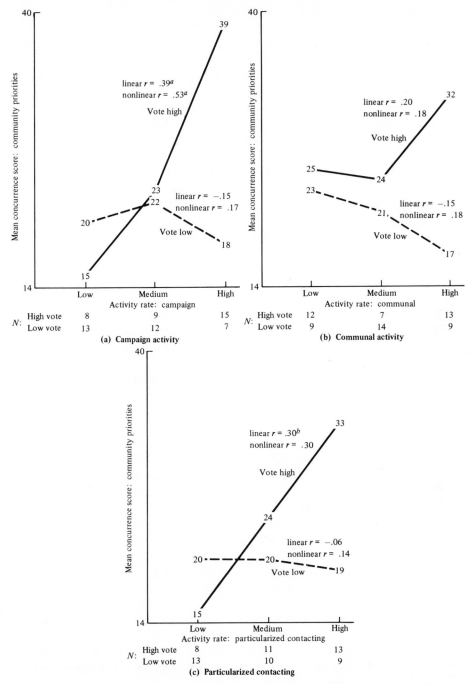

Figure 19-3. Corrected Community Participation Rate and Concurrence in Communities with High and Low Voting Rates: Three Kinds of Activity[a]

[a]We have divided the communities into three levels of activity rather than the usual four in order to have enough cases for analysis.

SOME COUNTERARGUMENTS

Since our measures in this chapter are unusual, as are our modes of analyses, they leave some ambiguities in our argument. It may be useful to end this chapter by considering some counterarguments to the ones we have made. First we will consider the argument that our measure of concurrence does not measure concurrence at all. Second we will consider some "plausible rival hypotheses" that involve alternative causal patterns within the data.[7]

Does Our Concurrence Score Measure Concurrence?

Our measure of concurrence focuses on the selection of problem priorities by leaders and citizens and not on their desired policies *vis-à-vis* those problems. This has the advantage, we argue, of allowing respondents to choose freely among issues for the community, but it has the disadvantage of possibly masking disagreements. Citizens and leaders might both choose the same problem as salient in the community, but have diametrically opposed views on what to do about it. We think that this reservation about our measure is reasonable, but we believe that it is not likely to happen. The problems mentioned were most often those for which agreement on the selection of a problem would imply agreement on the direction, if not the details, of a solution. Citizens and leaders complain about shortages of community facilities, job shortages, traffic, crime, pollution.[8]

Furthermore, we do have a measure of the attitudes of citizens and leaders on one specific set of issues where one might expect to find groups with opposing policy preferences agreeing that the problem was indeed a problem. This is the issue of race relations. We asked both the citizens and leaders in our sample a series of questions on race relations: whether the government should enforce school integration, whether it should enforce fair housing, and whether the blacks in America were pushing too fast for change. Then we created a scale of attitudes on race relations, and developed a measure of concurrence between citizens and leaders on this issue. The measure is of concurrence on a policy *direction*, not on the salience of an issue. The data offer some, but not perfect, support for our position. The correlation between the corrected rate of participation in the community (the measure we have been using) and concurrence on this specific issue is .12—positive but not significant. However, the correlation between the uncorrected measure of the rate of participation in the community and concurrence on the racial issue is .25 (statistically significant at the .05 level). This is a rare case where sizeable differences appear when one uses the corrected rather than the uncorrected rate, and possibly the uncorrected rate is better in this instance. To remove the effect of race from the rate of participation is to remove too much when race

---

[7] The term *plausible rival hypotheses* is used by Donald T. Campbell. He suggests, following Popper, that confirmed scientific knowledge is what survives the challenge of alternative hypotheses. In this section we submit our findings to such a challenge.

[8] Furthermore, where answers focussed on the same issue but clearly implied opposite positions on the issue, our coding scheme separated them—at least in the most frequent circumstances where that occurred. Citizens who said that the *high cost* of schools or other facilities were a problem were put in a different category from those who thought the *inadequacy* of such facilities a problem.

itself is the issue. In general, then, the data seem to be consistent with a view that concurrence on the priority of problems does not mask disagreement on the nature of solutions. On the issue of policy preferences on racial matters we find a pattern similar to that on choice of priorities for the community.

Some Alternative Causal Patterns

Our argument thus far has been that particiaption increases responsiveness of leaders to the citizenry. The causal argument is that the amount of participation in the community increases the degree of concurrence between leaders and citizens by making leaders more responsive to citizens. The assumed relationship looks like this:

Participation leads to responsiveness of leaders to citizens

The data presented thus far would be consistent with a variety of other hypotheses. One alternative is that the relationship between participation and concurrence is the result of some third factor and is, therefore, spurious. Another alternative is that participation increases concurrence not by making leaders responsive to the citizenry, but by making the citizenry responsive to the leadership. Let us consider each.

Participation and Concurrence as the Result of Some Third Factor   If some third factor were causing the relationship between participation and concurrence, the situation vould look something like the following:

A third factor leads both to participation and to concurrence

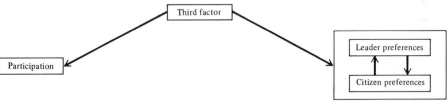

On the face of it, such an alternative pattern would be hard to square with the particular pattern of relationships we found between participation and concurrence. But two alternative third factors come to mind: the social similarity between community leaders and participators, and the smallness and isolation of the community.

Leaders and citizens might concur on problem priorities for the community because they come from similar social backgrounds. This might explain the patterns we have found. Community leaders tend to have higher socioeconomic status than the average citizen, and so do participators. Hence in communities with higher median income or education there would be more participation (because of the well-established relationship between socioeconomic status and participation) as well as more concurrence (because leaders would be similar in social background to more of the citizens). Such a situation would be consistent with the pattern we reported in Chapter 18 whereby leaders manifest more concurrence with the participating citizens as participation goes up because it is the participants who are similar in social background to the community leaders.

However, the data presented in Chapter 17, where we considered the concurrence scores for individual citizens, are inconsistent with this rival hypothesis. As indicated in that chapter, it is true that citizens who have social characteristics similar to those of the community leaders do have higher concurrence scores (see Table 17-1, p. 306). This is consistent with the rival hypothesis that concurrence is based on social similarity. But, as was also shown in Chapter 17 (see Figure 17-3), the relationship between social characteristics and concurrence disappears when one controls for the citizen's rate of political activity. Participation is what counts, not social similarity.

We can also test for this rival hypothesis on the community level. If similarity of social status and not participation is important for concurrence, this would imply that the third factor we have ignored is the wealth of the community, for in wealthier communities participation would be higher and so would concurrence because leaders would be more like the average citizen in social background. To test this rival hypothesis we use a measure of the socioeconomic level of each of the communities we studied—based on a combination of the average income of citizens, the average value of property and houses, the median school years, and the percentage in tertiary occupations (all derived from census data). The rival hypothesis—that similarity in social background is what counts—predicts that a control for community socioeconomic level would reduce or eliminate the relationship between participation and concurrence. But this does not appear to be the case. The linear correlation between the rate of overall participation in the community and our concurrence measure is .32; when we control for our measure of community wealth it is .30. Apparently the third factor is not community wealth.

One other plausible rival hypothesis can also be dismissed. Perhaps the third factor we have not considered is the size and isolation of the community. In smaller, more isolated communities citizens might participate more (as our data indicated) and leaders would be more attuned to their preferences. This could explain the pattern we have found. But, just as we controlled for community socioeconomic level, we can control for a measure of the size and isolation of the community. When we do so, we find no change in the relationship between our participation measures and concurrence. Our findings survive that challenge as well.

There are, of course, many other possible "third factors" we have not dealt with. In fact, the number of such additional explanatory variables is unlimited. And our readers may think up more. But at least we have shown that our argument survives two of the most plausible additonal factors—the similarity in social background between leaders and citizens, and the size and isolation of the community.

Concurrence Because Citizens Respond to Leaders   This may be the most crucial alternative hypothesis. The reader will remember that we have used the terms *concurrence* and *responsiveness* interchangeably in this chapter. But the terms are different. Though we clearly measure concurrence between leaders and citizens, does this imply that leaders are *responding* to citizens? If leaders and citizens agree, might not the causal relationship run in the other direction? Agreement might come, not because leaders respond to the initiatives of citizens, but because citizens respond to the initiatives of leaders. This would be compatible with data indicating that concurrence goes up as participation goes up, and particularly with data indicating that concurrence between leaders and participants goes up as participation goes up.

Rather than indicating that citizens were applying pressure on leaders, participation might simply indicate that more citizens are open to influence from leaders. The participant citizens are also those who receive more communications. Therefore, the more participation, the more leaders may be able to convince citizens to accept their views of community problems. And the participant citizens—because they were more available for influence by leaders—would be those for whom the citizen-leader concurrence measures would be the highest. In short, what looks to us like citizen control of leaders through participation might indeed be just the opposite. The causal relationship, in this alternative situation, would look like this:

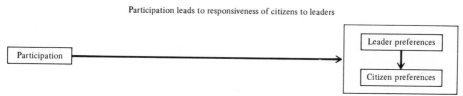

Participation leads to responsiveness of citizens to leaders

We are faced here with a plausible rival hypothesis, one we cannot easily eliminate without data gathered over time. Even then it would be hard to design a study to disentangle these processes. However, we can try one indirect test of the alternate hypotheses. Just as we have measures of citizens' activity rates, we have measures of leaders' activity rates—how active they are in communicating with citizens and in working with community groups. If the process were the reverse of the one we have just described (whereby the extent of leader influence over citizens affects the level of concurrence) one would expect that the measures of leader activity would have a stronger relationship to concurrence than would the measures of citizen activity.

Data on this are reported in Table 19-1. We present the correlations between three measures of citizen participation and concurrence and between four measures of leader activity and concurrence. The measures of the leaders' degree of activism within the community are the frequency with which they report they have formed local groups to work on community problems, the frequency with which they report that they talk to people in the community as

Table 19-1

Correlation between Citizen and Leader Activity Measures and
Concurrence on Community Priorities

Correlation between citizen activeness and concurrence		Correlation between leader activeness and concurrence	
Concurrence and overall participation	$.32^a$	Concurrence and leader activity in forming groups	.14
Concurrence and voting	$.41^a$	Concurrence and leader activity in talking to citizen	.11
Concurrence and campaign activity	$.27^b$	Concurrence and leader membership in organization	.12
		Concurrence and leader activity in problem-solving organization	.11

^{a}Significant at .01 level.
^{b}Significant at .05 level.

a source of information, the number of memberships they report in community organizations, and the number of memberships they report in organizations active in solving community problems. In all cases, the correlations between citizen activity and concurrence are much stronger than those between leader activity and concurrence. The data support our original hypothesis, not the rival one. Our measure of concurrence seems to be a valid measure of responsiveness of leaders to citizens rather than a measure of citizen responsiveness to leaders. Indeed, to add one more bit of evidence, the leadership characteristic that relates most strongly to concurrence is a measure of how positively leaders evaluate *citizen* interest and concern with community affairs—a result consistent with our emphasis on the positive impact of participation.[9]

THE CONSEQUENCES OF PARTICIPATION: A SUMMARY

In Part III we have presented some complicated data and tested a variety of hypotheses. It is useful to summarize some highlights.

1. The first point to repeat is the main conclusion of Chapter 15: Participants differ from nonparticipants in the problems they consider most important and in the solutions they favor for social problems.

2. In Chapter 17 we showed that community leaders are more likely to concur with the problem priorities of participants than with those of nonparticipants. This is not the result of the social characteristics of participants, but appears to be an independent effect of participation.

These two facts about participants as individuals largely determine the effects of participation considered from the point of view of the political system.

[9] For a further elaboration of these data on leader characteristics, see Susan B. Hansen, *Concurrence in American Communities.*

3. The first major finding of our analysis on the level of the polity (community) is that participation does indeed make a difference. If we think of the community as a whole, there is a tendency for leaders to be more responsive to the citizenry in communities with high participation rates.

4. However, as our analysis of the participation input led us to expect, the relationship between participation rate and the responsiveness of community leaders is not linear. Participants are not a representative group of the population. Where there is a moderate amount of participation, leaders pay attention to the unrepresentative participant groups and are less responsive to the community as a whole.

5. We distinguished between the *level* and the *equality* of leader responsiveness. Where participation is lowest, the level of leader responsiveness to the public as a whole is low; but active citizens receive no more responsiveness than inactive ones. As participation rates rise in a community, the level of leader responsiveness goes up but the equality of responsiveness declines. In more active communities, there is a wide gap between the responsiveness received by active and inactive citizens.

6. In the most active communities, however, though inactive citizens receive less responsiveness than active ones, the former receive more responsiveness than do similarly inactive citizens in less active communities. In this sense, the inactives appear to reap the benefit of the activity of their fellow citizens.

7. Participation does not increase inequality if the participants are representative of the population as a whole. This can happen in highly consensual communities where the participants have the same preferences as the nonparticipants. In such cases, all modes of participation are associated with an increase in responsiveness.

8. Where community agreement is low—where active and inactive citizens have different preferences—increased participation rates can result in a diminished level of responsiveness. This happens when the mode of participation conveys a lot of information to leaders about citizen preferences.

9. The data make clear some differences between electoral and nonelectoral modes of participation. Elections, as we stressed at the beginning of this book, are relatively blunt instruments of citizen control because they convey little information about citizen preferences. This means that electoral modes of participation do not result in a diminution of the overall level of responsiveness as participation increases since they influence the behavior of leaders via more diffuse pressure.

10. The importance of voting as a force toward leader responsiveness is also clear: It appears to work in interaction with other modes of activity—it supplies pressure and they convey more information.

Chapter 20
Participation and Equality: Who Gets What and How?

The theme of this book has been political participation in America: What is it? Who does it? What difference does it make? We have tried to answer these questions in the framework of some general considerations about processes associated with participation. This in turn leads to a consideration of some fundamental issues and dilemmas of democracy.

The extent of democracy in a nation is often measured by the availability of political rights: the right to vote, to hold office, to speak up and challenge incumbent leadership, to associate freely with one's fellow citizens in political activity. The history of democratic government can be traced in terms of the extension of these rights so that they are equally available to all citizens.

Such rights can and have been justified as ends in themselves—one of the components of the good polity and society is the equality of access to political rights. But political rights are also justified in terms of their consequences: A society in which there is equal political access may be a better society because of the results of that access. Political rights give the citizenry control over the government and lead to better public policy, policy more closely attuned to the needs and desires of the citizenry. Though most theorists of democracy have conceded many weaknesses in public control over governmental policy—the public is ill-informed, short-sighted, changeable, disorganized—most agree that public policy arising from free participation of citizens and contention among them is, in the long run, to be preferred to more despotic policy.

Thus opportunities to participate are valued because they are expected to lead to more responsive and accountable government. In addition, they are expected to have a close relationship to another democratic value—equality. To give the masses of a society political rights is to give them an important resource—power over governmental activities. And if that resource is equally available to all citizens, it can be used to further social equality. Lower-status citizens are numerous. This, coupled with equal political access, should allow those deprived socially and economically to induce the government to carry out policies that will reduce that deprivation. But does it work that way?

One of the simplest but most important findings in our book is that participation does indeed make some difference. If we accept as a measure of responsiveness the extent to which community leaders adopt the same agenda for community action as that of the citizenry, our data support the conclusion that where citizens are participant, leaders are responsive. That participation makes a difference is hardly surprising—most theorists of democracy have assumed it. Yet it has not often been demonstrated that there is indeed a relationship between citizen activities and leader responsiveness.

But the relationship between participation and leadership responsivenes is not that simple. The source of the complexity of this relationship lies, we believe, in the nature of participation and in what it means to make participation equally available to all. Equal rights to participate are just that: *rights,* not obligations. Some may take advantage of these rights, others may not. The result is that participation is unequally distributed throughout the society because the qualities that lead some to choose to participate—motivation, skills, resources—are not equally distributed.

Given unequal distribution of participation, it could still be that those who have the greatest need for governmental services would participate the most. Their greater need would be motivation enough for higher activity levels. Under some circumstances this happens—though more than just objective levels of need are required.[1] As our data in Chapter 16 indicated, there is a slight tendency—when all else is held constant (such as social status and race)—for those with serious personal welfare problems to participate more. The point is that all else is not constant in the actual political world. The slight tendency for those with severe personal needs to participate more is overwhelmed by the fact that such individuals come from lower social and economic groups. In fact, they participate far less than those citizens who do not have such severe problems.

---

[1] Studies of reasons why men revolt have shown that objective deprivation is but one component of a set of forces that lead deprived groups to political violence. See Harry Eckstein, "On the Etiology of Internal Wars," *History and Theory,* vol. 4 (1964), pp. 133-163.

STATUS AND PARTICIPATION

A major force leading to participation, as our study shows, is associated with social status and the civic attitudes that accompany it. This skews the participant population in the direction of the more affluent, the better educated, those with higher-status occupations. Furthermore, most of the other forces that modify the workings of the standard socioeconomic model tend—in the United States—to accelerate its effects. Affiliation with voluntary associations increases the disparity in participation between the social levels. So does affiliation with a political party (except in relation to voting). Furthermore, with the exception of group consicousness among blacks, the political beliefs among the mass public that we have found to be related to participation all tend to increase the participation disparity between the social levels. The conservative political beliefs among upper-status Republicans seem to be the most potent political ideology in America, in the sense that they seem to have an independent effect as motivations to participate. In sum, the standard socioeconomic model of the process of politicization works in America, resulting in an overrepresentation of upper-status groups in the participant population. The additional forces we study increases that overrepresentation.

The fact that the processes of politicization work as they do in the United States has consequences in terms of how governmental leaders respond to citizens. Participation is a potent force; leaders respond to it. But they respond more to the participants than to those who do not participate. Thus, if participants come disproportionately from the upper strata, they are the ones to whom leaders will respond. The "linking" role of participation is crucial here. As shown in Chapter 17, community leaders and activists have similar social backgrounds: leaders, like activists, tend to come from upper-status groups. But it is not simply this similarity in social background that leads to greater concurrence. What counts is that upper-status citizens participate more. In short, the process of politicization and its consequences in the United States looks something like the following:

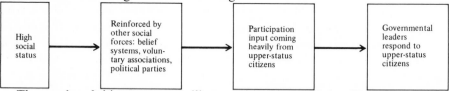

The results of this process are illustrated in Figure 20-1, which summarizes the participation "payoff" received by the different status groups at various levels of participation. In that figure we divide our sample into five groups based on their overall participation rates. Each of these groups is in turn divided into three socioeconomic levels. Last, we indicate the concurrence scores received by each of the fifteen groups. The height of the various bars indicates the concurrence score for each group (the score is circled in the bars). The width of the bars indicates the proportion of each group in the population as a whole (a figure given as a percentage at the top of each bar).

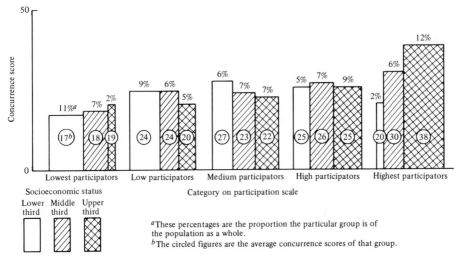

Figure 20-1. Participation and Concurrence for Three Socioeconomic Groups: Individual-Level Data

[a] These percentages are the proportion the particular group is of the population as a whole.
[b]The circled figures are the average concurrence scores of that group.

We can consider our concurrence measure to be an indicator of how much an individual or group gets from the government. The fact that concurrence measures how frequently leaders agree with a citizen on priorities makes this interpretation of the measure quite reasonable. Figure 20-1 can then be interpreted in an interesting way. The higher a bar, the more the average member of that particular group receives from the government; the wider the bar, the larger that particular group is as a proportion of the population. And, indeed, the area of the bar can be thought of analogously to the "net" effects we discussed earlier—how much benefit an average member of a group receives multiplied by the number of members of the group.

Consider the concurrence scores (the height of the bars) received by members of the three socioeconomic groups at various points on the participation scale. Among the lowest participants, there is little if any difference across the three socioeconomic levels in the concurrence received from leaders. Only two points on the concurrence scale separate the upper- and lower-status citizens among the lowest participants. But consider the contrast among the highest participants at the other end of the graph. At the high participation level, a big difference exists in the concurrence scores of the citizens from the several socioeconomic levels; indeed, among high participators, upper-status citizens receive almost twice as much concurrence as lower-status ones (38 v. 20 points on the concurrence scale). In fact, we find that lower-status citizens in the highest participation category receive *less* concurrence than do less active lower-status citizens.

A consideration of the proportions of the population who fall into the various groups (the width of the bars) rounds out the picture. It also helps explain why highly active lower-status citizens, despite their activity, do so poorly when it comes to leader concurrence. Consider the category of highest participators. The upper-status citizens are more likely to be in that category than in any other; indeed, they form more than half of the highest participator category. Citizens from the lower socioeconomic group are less likely to be in that category than in any other; they form only about 10 percent of the set of highest participators. Thus, not only do upper-status citizens receive much higher concurrence when they participate, but there are many more of them who actively participate and receive that high score. The overall effect, roughly indicated by the height and width of the bars, reflects this larger "output" that they receive.

Furthermore, the small number of citizens of lower social status who are found among the highest participators explains why they receive relatively little responsiveness despite their high activity rate. In Chapter 15 we showed that those who are active are likely to differ from the citizenry as a whole. They are less likely to be faced with severe personal welfare problems, less likely to perceive such problems as the major issue in the community, and less likely to think that the government should intervene to deal with such problems. This deviation from the population as a whole is, as we showed in Chapter 16, due to the generally higher social status of these activists.

But those lower-status citizens found in the highest participation category differ sharply from the rest of the activists. Our data indicate that they are much more likely to face severe welfare problems than are the other activists. In fact, of all fifteen groups contained in Figure 20-1—three status groups on each of five participation levels—the lower-status activists report such problems most frequently.[2] The problem is that there simply are not enough of them among the activists. If we look at the category of highest participants we see that upper-status citizens outnumber lower-status ones by six to one. The result is that as individuals, the upper- and lower-status citizens in that highest participant category may be equally active. But the larger number of upper-status citizens—more likely to be opposed to welfare, less likely to be in need of it—drown out the voices of the lower-status ones.

Thus, Figure 20-1 illustrates, as graphically as any data presented in this book, that participation helps those who are already better off. In general, lower-status citizens participate less than do upper-status ones. And even when some of them become active, their preferences are not communicated to leaders as adequately as are those of the upper-status activists, because they are such a small minority of the activist population.

These data are relevant to a puzzle to which we have alluded at various points in our book: How can our data on the conservative bent of the American participant population square with the obvious signs of radicaliza-

---

[2] On a series of closed questions about problems facing the respondent as well as a similar open question, the small group of lower-status activists constantly expressed a higher level of need.

tion in the United States? Our data on the attitudes toward the Vietnam war found among different activist groups—in particular the differences between the demonstrators and the group of letter writers—suggested that we were dealing with two different phenomena: a small group of highly noticeable activists and a larger group active in less dramatic ways. The former were more dovish, the latter more hawkish.

Figure 20-1 is, we believe, a strong illustration of this phenomenon. We find a group of very active lower-status citizens, and a group that differs strikingly from all other groups in the salience to themselves of welfare problems. They are likely to be a highly assertive group. But though quite visible, they remain a small group—only 2 percent of the population, and they are counterpoised against the almost glacial pressure of a much larger number of conservative activists. The latter group may not speak as dramatically, but as our data on the relative concurrence received by the upper- and lower-status activists make clear, they speak very effectively.[3]

The close relationship among social status, participation, and responsiveness is our major conclusion about American politics. This stress on the importance of social status conflicts with some common notions. Observers have often commented on the lack of a class basis for American politics. On the institutional level, political parties in the United States are not organized on a class basis; America is famous for the absence of an effective socialist party. There is less class-based voting in the United States than in most of the other English-speaking democracies,[4] and American political parties are less likely than parties elsewhere to recruit activists from particular class groups.[5] Furthermore, the absence of class-based parties is paralleled by the situation vis-à-vis public belief systems. Citizens in the United States are not known for the strength of their political ideologies. Especially noteworthy is the absence of class-based ideology as a guide to political behavior.[6]

Yet class relates strongly to participation rates. Indeed—and we think these data are quite surprising—social status has a closer relationship to political

[3] One caution should be mentioned. The data in Figure 20-1 come from our sample of sixty-four communities, since it is only in such places that we have the data to measure concurrence between leaders and citizens. They do not, therefore, include data from the urban cores. Perhaps the poor are more active and effective there. Without our concurrence measures in large cities we cannot compare the effectiveness of the poorer strata in the urban core with their effectiveness elsewhere. But we can compare their participation. And there is some tendency for the socioeconomic model to work more strongly outside of the urban core, but only a slight tendency. In the sixty-four communities on which our analysis in Figure 20-1 is based, socioeconomic status correlates at .39 with participation. In the larger cities, it correlates at .33. These data suggest that what we say about our sixty-four communities could be said about larger places, though the disparity between the upper- and lower-status groups on the amount and effectiveness of participation might be somewhat less severe in the latter places.

Another caution is in order. Our data refer to leader-citizen concurrence within the framework of the local community. Would the same general pattern hold if we considered the match between citizens and national policy makers? Our data provide no answer, though we suspect the pattern would not be *that* different. However, the pattern would obviously depend on what kind of administration were in power. The concurrence scores for the lower status activists would be much higher under an administration interested in more radical economic policies.

[4] See Robert Alford, *Party and Society* (Chicago: Rand McNally, 1963).

[5] See Rokkan and Campbell, "Norway and the United States."

[6] See, for example, Louis Hartz, *The Liberal Tradition in America* (New York: Harcourt, 1955), Chap. I.

participation in the United States than in all but one of nine other countries for which it was possible to obtain data based on measurements similar enough to allow comparison. The data are in Table 20-1. The relationship is roughly as strong in India as in the United States; but in the other eight nations the status-participation relationship is weaker than in the United States.[7] As all our analysis has shown, this strong relationship between social status and participation has a significant impact on governmental performance.

Table 20-1

Correlation of Social Status and Participation in Eight Countries[a]

Civic culture data		Cross-national program data	
U.S.	.43	India	.38
U.K.	.30	U.S.	.37
Italy	.28	Nigeria	.31
Mexico	.24	Netherlands	.18
Germany	.18	Austria	.10
		Japan	.07

[a]We present two separate sets of correlation because the data come from two different studies. In each column the measures are comparable, but not across the columns, because different measures are used. This explains the two different figures for the U.S.

Why should class, in its relationship to American politics, appear at once so weak and so strong? The answer may be that it is just the absence of an explicit class basis of politics in an institutional or an ideational sense that explains the close relationship in the behavioral sense. If there were more class-based ideologies, more class-based organizations, more explicit class-based appeal by political parties, the participation disparity between upper- and lower-status citizens would very likely be less. Group consciousness among blacks illustrates how a group-based belief system can reduce the participation disparity. But that, of course, works only for blacks. More generally, the absence of institutions and ideas associated with social status makes, paradoxically, such status a more potent force in American politics.

In this sense, our data may reflect the contemporary results of the historical development of American politics: the absence of a socialist movement, the development of an economically rather than politically oriented trade union

[7] The data in the left column of Table 20-1 are discussed in Nie, Powell, and Prewitt, "Social Structure and Political Participation"; those in the right column in Verba, Nie, and Kim, *The Modes of Democratic Participation: A Cross-National Comparison.* Data such as those in Table 20-1 cry out for further analysis along the lines suggested in this book. Such remain on the agenda for the future.

movement, the development of a dominant ideology in which class had no place. Such an interpretation, of course, goes beyond our data. But it does suggest some intriguing questions that can be asked about the patterns of participation in other nations whose historical developments differ from those in America—a task of comparative analysis to which we intend to turn.[8]

THE MODES OF PARTICIPATION

Along with stressing social status, we have emphasized the multiplicity of ways citizens can participate. The different modes of activity are engaged in by different sets of citizens, citizens who differ in their orientations to politics. More important, the different modes influence leaders in different ways: The electoral modes of activity (particularly voting) influence leaders by the application of diffuse pressure rather than the communication of specific information about the preferences of the activists. The nonelectoral modes of activity influence through communication of information. The differences among the alternative modes of participation closely relate to a long-standing debate on how citizens can best influence the government. For some analysts, the most important control by citizens over leaders is via elections, in which citizens periodically choose leaders. Effective social policy is maximized if citizens limit their participation to that mode, for citizens cannot effectively rule on more detailed matters. Other scholars have stressed the importance of citizen participation in the between-election period, participation more directly focused on the specific needs and interests of the citizens. Governmental policy that most effectively satisfies citizen needs would come in response to the activities of citizens and groups participating *vis-à-vis* their more narrow interests. Out of the clash of such interests effective social policy emerges.

Our data indicate that both means of citizen control—the pressure of the electoral process and the information of nonelectoral activity—are important ways of achieving governmental responsiveness. Indeed, the combination of the two, where the diffuse pressure of high voting rates combines with high rates of more information-rich activity, leads to greatest leader responsiveness. But the electoral modes differ from the nonelectoral, at least in communities where there is less consensus among citizens as to what the government ought to do. In that kind of community, the more communication of preferences through nonelectoral activity, the lower the overall level of responsiveness of community leaders. And, though we must use caution in extrapolating from

---

[8] In this connection it is interesting to consider some data from Yugoslavia—the latest nation to join our cross-national studies of participation. (These data became available only after the completion of this manuscript.) Our argument that the strong relationship between social status and participation in the United States depends, at least in part, on the fact that social status differences receive little explicit recognition in terms of political ideology or political institutions leads to an interesting and somewhat counter-intuitive hypothesis about Yugoslavia. In Yugoslavia, for a quite different set of reasons, social status differences receive little explicit recognition in political institutions or ideology. If our argument is correct, one should find a close relationship between status and participation in Yugoslavia as well. And we do find a correlation of .35 between socioeconomic status (based on a measure of income plus education) and political participation. Thus, Yugoslavia has about the same correlation as the United States and India, the two nations where we had previously found the relationship to be strongest.

The data on Yugoslavia are quite preliminary and require closer analysis. But the point is intriguing.

our analysis of communities to national politics, one can assume that national politics is more likely to resemble that in the less consensual communities— diversity being much greater across the nation than in any particular community. This suggests that in general, nonelectoral politics in the United States (the activity by which specific groups and individuals try to influence governmental policy) is more likely to skew governmental policy in favor of the particular participant groups and away from a more general "public interest"—if we can interpret that term to refer to the modal preferences of the public.[9]

Such a conclusion is not intended to denigrate the nonelectoral modes of politics. They do have the important ability to communicate fairly precise preferences, but for that reason they benefit only those who use them.

* * *

Participation, looked at generally, does not necessarily help one social group rather than another. The general model of the sources and consequences of participation that we have presented could work in a number of ways. It could work so that lower-status citizens were more effective politically and used that political effectiveness to improve their social and economic circumstances. Or it could work, as it appears to do in the United States, to benefit upper-status citizens more. It depends on what organizations, parties, and belief systems exist, and how these all affect participation rates. Participation remains a powerful social force for increasing or decreasing inequality. It depends on who takes advantage of it.

The 1960s, at the end of which our study was conducted, was (it has become a cliché to point out) a time of turmoil and political frustration. A good deal of the frustration focused on the inadequacy of participatory mechanisms in America. Some of our data may explain this. For one thing, the inequality of use of participatory means may be a reason for the search for alternative techniques by citizens who do not find the government as responsive as they would like. Second, the fact that much protest activity comes from an intense but small proportion of the population—a small proportion that is, in turn, counterbalanced by a larger body of steady activists from the other end of the political and social scales—may help explain why so much protest activity flares up, catches the public's attention, and then dies down, leaving behind little substantive change in policy.

Last, consider some changes over time traced by our data. The number of citizens with those characteristics that would lead them to participate in politics—for instance, the number with higher levels of education—has been steadily expanding. Further, the number of citizens actually participating in politics seems to have grown at a rate even faster than that which the expansion

---

[9] This conclusion is, we believe, quite consistent with the powerful argument made by Lowi about interest group politics in America. See Theodore Lowi, *The End of Liberalism.*

in education would predict. But at the same time, political activity takes place more and more in circumstances that are not congenial to effective participation. More and more the setting for participation has become the large city or the suburb, not the well-defined smaller community that fosters political activity. More and more the subject matter of participation has become national or metropolitan issues rather than local issues which citizens can more effectively control.

Thus the actual and potential participant population has grown just when effective participation becomes more difficult. Citizens may be participating more, but enjoying it less.

Appendix A
The Sample Design

The data reported in this book are based on a national population survey, consisting of 2,549 interviews conducted by the National Opinion Research Center in some 200 separate locales in March 1967. The universe sampled was the total, noninstitutionalized population of the United States, twenty-one years or older. The sample was a standard, multistaged area probability sample to the block or segment level. At the block level, however, quota sampling was utilized (to reduce costs to a tolerable level) based on sex, age, race, and employment status statistics of the census tract or division within which the block fell.

SELECTION OF THE PRIMARY SAMPLING UNIT (PSU)
The primary sampling units employed were originally derived from NORC's 1953 Master Sample. The primary sampling units in the Master Sample were selected with probabilities proportionate to their estimated 1953

Prepared with the assistance of John Petrocik.

345

populations and drawn from a list of all PSU's in the nation.[1] The original Master Sample was updated several times to account for population shifts and at the same time to minimize the number of PSU's that needed to be added or dropped from the Master Sample.

A procedure suggested by Nathan Keyfitz was employed.[2] It involved the comparison of the desired 1960 probabilities of selection for PSU's to their original 1950 probabilities. If the originally selected PSU had a lower original probability than was warranted by its 1960 population, it was retained in the new sample and assigned the desired probability. If the originally selected PSU had a higher probability than was now warranted, it was subjected to the possibility of being dropped. The probability of retention for such a PSU was the ratio of its desired probability to its original probability. Replacements for dropped PSU's were made from among those PSU's that had not fallen into the 1953 sample and for which the 1953 probability was lower than that desired in 1960, the probability of the 1960 selection being a function of the amount of growth the unit had undergone.

Basically, this method preserves the stratification based on the 1950 classifications of geographic regions, size of largest town, median family income, economic characteristics, and in the South, of race. Counties that the Census Bureau classified as nonmetropolitan in 1950 but as metropolitan in 1960 were, however, shifted to metropolitan strata. This restratification complicated the computation of selection probabilities but, in all likelihood, served to increase somewhat the efficiency of the sample.

The current set of PSU's is to be used until the 1970 census is available. For this reason, the 1960 census figures were extrapolated to 1967, the midpoint between the availability of the 1960 and 1970 census reports. For each PSU, the extrapolation was based on its population change between 1950 and 1960.

SELECTION OF THE LOCALITIES WITHIN PRIMARY SAMPLING UNIT (PSU)

Within each selected PSU, localities were ordered according to cities with block statistics, other urban places, urbanized Minor Civil Divisions, the nonurbanized MCD's, with the places ordered by 1960 population within each of these categories. Localities were selected from this list using a random start and applying a designated skip interval to the cumulative 1960 population. This provided stratification according to size and urban type of locality and at the same time selection with probability proportionate to size.

Where available, 1960 census block statistics were used. Blocks were selected with probabilities proportionate to the population in the block. In places without block statistics, census enumeration districts were selected with

---

[1] A primary sampling is either a Standard Metropolitan Statistical Area or a county (when the county lies outside a Standard Metropolitan Area).

[2] Nathan Keyfitz, "Sampling Probabilities Proportional to Size," *Journal of the American Statistical Association,* vol. 46 (March 1951), pp. 105-109.

probabilities proportional to the number of households. The selected districts were then divided into segments and estimates of the number of households within each segment were obtained by field count. The selection of segments was then made with probability proportionate to the number of households. The average cluster size in Amalgam Surveys is 7.5 respondents per cluster. This seems to provide a suitable balance of precision and economy. Although sampling errors cannot be computed directly (because this is a quota sample), one can make estimates of variability using procedures such as those outlined by Stephan and McCarthy.[3] Past experience suggests that for most purposes a sample of 1,500 could be considered as having about the same efficiency as a simple random sample of 1,000. Thus, in the simple binomial case, the observed percentages would have the following sampling errors:

Observed Percentage	Estimated One Standard Error
50%	1.6%
40 or 60	1.5
30 or 70	1.4
20 or 80	1.3
10 or 90	0.9
5 or 95	0.7

ENLARGING THE STANDARD CROSS-SECTION SAMPLE AND THE CREATION OF THE SIXTY-FOUR SMALL COMMUNITY SAMPLES

The estimated standard errors in the foregoing table are based on the standard NORC national amalgam sample of approximately 1,500 interviews, a sample we enlarged by almost 1,100 interviews. The sample was increased for two reasons. First, we simply wished to have a larger number of respondents, so that we could statistically examine smaller groups and make finer distinctions in our analysis. Second, the sample was enlarged because we wanted to develop a series of mini-samples in some sixty-four small communities, so that we could relate patterns of participation in these communities to the characteristics of their elites, whom we also interviewed, as well as to the communities' social, economic, and political structure (also factors on which data was collected from a variety of sources).

The sample was enlarged in the following way: A complete list of the localities (secondary sampling units) that fell into our sample, and whose population was less than or equal to 50,000, was constructed. Exactly half of this list was randomly selected to be our sixty-four target localities, and the additional 1,000 to 1,100 interviews were divided equally among these localities, adding to each community approximately sixteen interviews. Since each of these localities had already been selected into the original sampling

---

[3] Frederick Stephan and Philip McCarthy, *Sampling Opinions* (New York: Wiley, 1958), Chapter 10.

frame, the additional interviews tripled the number of respondents in the sixty-four secondary sampling units. This procedure yielded twenty-five to thirty interviews in the communities. The additional interviews were obtained by eliminating the map segment that yielded the initial interviews and selecting the supplementary interviews from two additional map segments in order to maximize the geographical distribution of interviews in the community. When population lists were available, which they often are in communities of this size, all selection was done from the lists. Not all interviews were conducted in incorporated communities. The reality of the spatial distribution of American society is that people live in unincorporated areas and minor civil divisions and individuals living in such places fell into this sample.

In Chapters 18 and 19 the unit of analysis is the sixty-four communities which were overinterviewed as described above. For Chapter 13, the sixty-four communities plus all additional communities in which there were at least twenty interviews are the unit of analysis. Because of the oversampling in the small communities, interviews in localities above 50,000 population are weighted by a factor of 2.0 whenever population parameters are estimated. This produces a weighted sample of 3,095 interviews.

PROCEDURES FOR SELECTING RESPONDENTS WITHIN BLOCKS

At the block or segment level, the interviewer begins her travel pattern at a random dwelling unit that has been previously designated and proceeds in a specified direction until her quotas have been filled. In the South, segments have been selected by race of respondents. This has been done because accuracy of response is increased when blacks are interviewed by black interviewers in the South. Elsewhere, the interviewer is given no race quotas.

The quotas call for approximately equal numbers of men and women with the exact proportion in each location determined by the 1960 census. For women, the additional requirement is imposed that there be the proper proportion of employed and unemployed women in the location. Again these quotas are based on the 1960 census. For men, the added requirement is that there be the proper proportion of men over and under thirty in the location. These particular quotas have been established because past experience has shown that employed women and younger men under thirty are the most difficult to find at home for interviewing. Although the interviewer can interview at any time, the quotas require that a large number of interviews be made on weekends and in the evening. In the following table, we compare our weighted sample with 1967 estimates published by the U.S. Government, on a series of standard demographic characteristics.

Table A-1

Comparison of Sample with Census Estimates on Six Demographic Characteristics[a]

Demographic characteristics	Census estimates	Sample
Sex		
Male	49.2%	48.3%
Female	50.8	51.7
Race		
Black	11.1	13.1
White	88.9	86.9
Urban	64.0	64.5
Rural	36.0	35.5
Occupation		
White collar	46.9	43.9
All others	53.1	56.1
Age		
20-34	33.6	29.2
35-54	36.6	37.3
55-64	14.3	15.5
65+	15.7	17.9
Education		
0-8 years	28.7	27.8
9-12 years	50.7	50.9
More than 12 years	20.5	22.0

[a]All census estimates obtained from the *Statistical Abstract of the United States*, U.S. Department of Commerce, Bureau of the Census. All figures represent estimates for 1967 except those for age and education, which are estimates for 1969.

Appendix B
Description of
the Participation Variables

This appendix describes and discusses the various measures of participation used in this book. Part B.1 presents the questions, coding, and frequency distributions of the individual participation questions; B.2 defines and describes the standard participation scales; B.3 describes the measures of participation corrected for the effects of socioeconomic characteristics; and B.4 contains information on the participation variables in the Survey Research Center's Election Studies that were employed in Chapter 14 in our longitudinal analysis of trends in participation.

B.1. QUESTIONS AND MARGINAL DISTRIBUTIONS FOR THE INDIVIDUAL PARTICIPATION MEASURES
Presented here are the exact wording of the questions, coding categories, relative frequency distributions, and weighted and unweighted number of respondents for each of the individual participation variables used in Chapters 2 and 4. The variables are listed according to mode.

Prepared by John Petrocik.

Question	Raw N	Weighted N	Frequency Distribution	
(a) The Voting Measures				
Can you tell me how you voted in the 1964 presiden-tial election—did you vote for Johnson or Goldwater or perhaps you did not vote. (Codes containing direction of vote not presented.)	1,793 557 199	2,172 671 252	Voted Didn't vote Missing data	70.2% 21.7 8.1
And how about in 1960—can you tell me how you voted in the presidential election —did you vote for Kennedy or Nixon or perhaps you did not vote. (Codes containing direction of vote not pre-sented.)	1,893 467 189	2,280 575 240	Voted Didn't vote Missing data	73.7% 18.6 7.8
What about local elections— do you always vote in those, do you sometimes miss one, or do you rarely vote, or do you never vote?	403 206 730 1,198 12	505 244 885 1,447 14	Never Rarely Mostly Always Missing data	16.3% 7.9 28.6 46.8 .5
(b) The Measures of Campaign Participation				
During elections do you ever try to show people why they should vote for one of the parties or candidates? (If yes), Do you often, sometimes, rarely, or never?	1,516 321 444 264 4	1,849 378 523 340 5	Never Rarely Sometimes Often Don't know or no answer Less than .1	59.7% 12.2 16.9 11.0
In the past three or four years have you attended any po-litical meetings or rallies?	2,063 471 15	2,498 580 17	No Yes No answer	80.7% 19.2 .1
In the past three or four years have you contributed money to a political party or candidate or to any other political cause?	2,201 339 9	2,678 405 12	No Yes Missing data	86.5% 13.1 .4
Have you ever done (other) work for one of the parties or candidates in most elec-tions, some elections, only a few, or have you never done such work?	1,903 301 229 114 2	2,318 354 280 141 2	Never A few elections Some elections Most elections Missing data	74.9% 11.4 9.0 4.6 .1

Question	Raw N	Weighted N	Frequency Distribution	
Now we would like to know something about the groups and organizations to which individuals belong—here is a list of various kinds of organizations: What about *political groups* such as Democratic or Republican clubs, or polical action groups? Are you a member of any of these types of groups? (If yes), Are you an active member, that is, do you regularly attend meetings and play an active role in the organization?	983 538 1,028	1,213 671 1,211	Nonmember Passive member Active member	39.2% 21.7 39.1

(c) Measures of Communal Activity

Question	Raw N	Weighted N	Frequency Distribution	
Have you ever worked with others in this community to try to solve some community problem?	1,758 789 2	2,158 935 2	No Yes Missing data	69.7% 30.2 .1
Have you ever taken part in forming a new group or a new organization to try to solve some community problem?	2,177 366 6	2,655 433 7	No Yes Missing data	85.8% 14.0 .1
We were talking earlier about problems that you and the people of this community have—have you ever personally gone to see, or spoken to, or written to— some member of the local community about some need or problem? (Only contacts with a group or social referent are reported here. Frequencies for contacts with particularized referents are presented under d.)	2,172 349 28	2,653 410 32	No Yes Missing data	85.7% 13.2 1.0

Questions	Raw N	Weighted N	Frequency Distribution	
What about some representa-tive or governmental offi-cial outside of the local community—on the (county, if local unit below county level) state or national level—have you ever con-tacted or written to such a person on some need or problem? (Only contacts with a group or social ref-erent are reported here. Frequencies for contacts with particularized refer-ents are presented under d.)	2,256 284 9	2,755 330 10	No Yes Missing data	89.0% 19.2 .3

The last measure of communal participation is a composite index. It was computed by summing the number of times the respondent reported active membership in an organization that is actively involved in attempting solutions to community problems. Activity in fifteen types of organizations was utilized in building this measure. Thus, organizational activity was counted as an act of communal participation only when the respondent reported active memberships, and when the organization was actively engaged in attempting to solve community problems.

Now we would like to know something about the groups and organizations to which individuals belong—here is a list of various kinds of organizations: Could you tell me whether or not you are a member of each type? The results are shown in Table B-1.

	Raw N	Weighted N	Frequency Distribution	
The measure is based on column C	1,720	2,118	No memberships	68.4%
	506	597	One	19.3
	188	222	Two	7.2
	89	107	Three	3.5
	28	31	Four	1.0
	10	12	Five	.4
	5	5	Six	.2
	3	3	Seven	.1

Mean = .516
Standard deviation = .942

Table B-1
Organization Membership

Organization	A Percentage re- porting active membership	B Percentage of A that were en- gaged in solving community problems	C Percentage of the sample
Fraternal groups	14.7	69.1	9.9
Service clubs	5.9	80.6	4.7
Veterans' groups	7.3	77.1	5.4
Political clubs	8.2	85.0	6.8
Labor unions	17.0	58.8	9.7
Sports groups	12.2	27.6	3.3
Youth groups	7.2	77.2	5.5
School service groups	17.0	81.9	13.7
Hobby or garden clubs	5.4	40.0	2.1
School fraternities or sororities	3.3	52.5	1.7
Nationality groups	2.0	73.0	1.5
Farm organizations	4.0	79.0	3.0
Literary, art, discussion, or study groups	3.9	40.4	1.4
Professional or academic societies	6.6	60.0	3.9
Church-affiliated groups	6.2	72.8	4.3
Any other groups	7.1	68.3	4.9

Weighted N = 3,095   Raw N = 2,549

(d) *Measures of Particularized Contact*

We were talking earlier about	2,362	2,872	No	92.8%
problems that you and the	159	191	Yes	6.2
people of this community	28	32	Missing data	1.0
have—have you ever per-				
sonally gone to see or				
spoken to, or written to—				
some member of the local				
community, or some other				
person of influence in the				
community about some				
need or problem? (Only				
contacts with particularized				

referents are presented here.
Frequencies for contacts
with a group or social referent are reported under c.)

What about some representa-	2,387	2,909	No	94.0%
tive or governmental official	153	176	Yes	5.7
outside of the local com-	9	10	Missing data	.3

munity—on the (county, if
local unit below county
level) state or national
level—have you ever con-
tacted or written to such
a person on some need or
problem? (Only contacts
with particularized referents are presented here.
Frequencies for contacts
with a group or social referent are reported under c.)

B.2. THE STANDARD INDICES OF PARTICIPATION

On the basis of the factor analysis in Chapter 4, standardized measures of
participation were constructed—one corresponding to each of the modes of
activity and one overall or summary measure of political activism. Some basic
descriptive information on these measures was presented in Chapter 8.
Presented here are more detailed descriptions as well as information on the
scale construction techniques utilized. Part A describes the four modes and
Part B the summary index.

A. The Measures of the Four Modes of Participation

The scales for the four modes of participation were computed from the
factor score coefficient matrix, which is a product of the binormamin rotation.
When each of these coefficients is multiplied by the respondents' standardized
scores on the corresponding participation items, and when these products are
in turn summed across all the individual participation variables, the relationship among the resultant scales reflects the exact angles of the binormamin
solution. We, however, altered this exact solution slightly using in each scale
only those coefficients and variables that were central to each of the factors.
The coefficients and the respondents' scores for all variables residual to the
factor were disregarded. The variables used in the construction of each of the
scales are listed under (a)—(d) in part 1 of this appendix.

Each scale was computed by the following formula:

$$FS_i = (ZX_i \cdot L_i) + (ZX_j \cdot L_j) \cdots + (ZX_n \cdot L_n)$$

where

FS_i = the ith factor scale (i.e., of the four)

ZX_i = a respondent's standardized score for the ith item included in the factor
scale score.

L_i = the factor loading of the ith item on the ith factor

As is the case with almost all the features of factor analysis, there is less than complete agreement on the appropriate way of constructing factor scales. Some consider it adequate simply to add variables with substantial loadings on a given factor without regard to the different magnitudes of the loadings.[1] Some prefer, as we have done, to combine variables with differential weights, excluding those with low loadings on the factor. Still others prefer the complete estimation method, which includes every variable in the equation to estimate each factor in proportion to the size of the loading.[2]

For factor solutions as clean as the one presented in Table 4-5, p. 72 (by clean we mean that each variable loads on only one factor and has loadings near zero on the others), it should not make much difference whether one uses only the subset of variables with high loadings or the complete set in estimating the factors because the factor weights on nonrelevant variables will be near zero. We use the partial estimation method rather than the complete one simply to insure that the indices have intuitive validity and the best possible referent to the concrete acts of which they are composed. The following matrix is a product of the complete estimation method and a comparison of the correlations here with those presented in Table 4-7 show how trivial the differences actually are.

The Correlations among the Four Modes of Participation

	Campaign activity	Communal activity	Voting	Personalized contacting
Campaign activity		.53	.33	.05
Communal activity			.26	.07
Voting				.04

Simple additive indices à la Tryon and Baley produce correlations with somewhat larger differences because the rotational solution is ignored.

Even in this case, however, the differences are quite small in our case and would not have changed any of our descriptions of the patterns.

The resultant factor scales were then rescaled so that each would have a mean of zero and a standard deviation of 100. These measures of the four modes of activity are used throughout the volume wherever we refer to *uncorrected* participation scores.

Footnote 5 of Chapter 8 (p. 129) presents more information on the distributional characteristics of these measures, including minimum, maximum, and median.

B. The Summary Participation Index.

The overall participation index was constructed from a higher-order factor analysis of the four factor scales. Higher-order factoring is the same as

---

[1] R. C. Tryon and D. E. Baley, *Cluster Analysis* (New York: McGraw-Hill, 1970), p. 176.
[2] For a fuller discussion of this issue see Harry H. Harmon, *Modern Factor Analysis.*

ordinary factoring except that the variables entered in this case are the four factor scales rather than the individual participation measures. The overall participation index is thus based on a single common-factor model. The assumption of this model is that the main thing that the participation scales hold in common is their reflection of degree of activeness. Thus the model assumes that if we control for the "higher order" there will be no remaining relationship among the lower-order factors. Table B-2 displays the relationship of each of the four modes of participation to the higher-order factor. The higher-order factor is simply the loadings of the four original factor scales on the first principal component when they are refactored, i.e., the numbers are the loadings between each lower-order factor and the higher one. Table B-3 indicates that the assumption of this model is a good one insofar as there is virtually no remaining correlation among the modes once the higher-order factor has been removed.

The scale was constructed using the following formula:

$$SPS = (ZV \times L_v) + (ZCP \times L_{cp}) + (ZCM \times L_{cm}) + (ZPC \times L_{pc})$$

where:

SPS = a respondent's score on the standardized participation scale

ZV = a respondent's standardized score on the voting scale

ZCP = a respondent's standardized score on the campaign participation scale

ZCM = a respondent's standardized score on the communal participation scale

ZPC = a respondent's standardized score on the particularized contacting scale

L_v through L_{pc} = the factor loadings on the first principal component of the higher-order factors given above.

The summary measure was then standardized to have a mean of zero and standard deviation of 100.

Chapter 8 presents information on the distributional characteristics of the summary participation index.

B.3. THE MEASURES OF PARTICIPATION CORRECTED FOR DEMOGRAPHIC CHARACTERISTICS

In many parts of our analysis we attempt to examine one or another social or institutional characteristic while controlling or correcting for the confounding influences of certain basic socioeconomic variables. These corrections are obtained by the computation of residual participation measures where the impact of socioeconomic characteristics is removed by means of regression equations. Appendix G.2 contains a discussion of the implications and validity of this technique. Here we will simply describe how this technique was used

Table B-2

Higher-Order Factor Solution

Campaign	Voting	Communal activity	Personalized acts	Percentage of total variance
.805	.409	.655	.085	44

Table B-3

Residual Correlation Matrices for Higher-Order Factors

	Campaign X_1	Voting X_2	Communal activity X_3	Personalized contacts X_4
X_1	—			
X_2	.000	—		
X_3	.001	−.005	—	
X_4	−.014	.005	.014	—

in conjunction with the standardized participation variables in order to produce these corrected measures. A large number of corrected participation variables are used; some are employed exclusively in one chapter or even in one or two tables of a given chapter. These we will not attempt to describe, though the technique is identical and only the correcting variables differ. Two of the corrected measures, however, appear frequently throughout the volume and thus warrant separate documentation. These are the five participation scales—one for each mode and an overall participation scale—correcting for socioeconomic status, and those five correcting for socioeconomic status plus race, age, and sex. The former measures are used wherever we attempt to determine the independent impact of some social characteristic such as age or race while correcting for differences among these groups in their levels of socioeconomic status. We use the second set of measures when we wish to investigate the independent effect of some institutional, structural, or community factor while holding constant the confounding influences of all of the aforementioned demographic characteristics.

Each of the corrected measures was computed in the following way: (1) A regression equation was constructed where one or more demographic variables were used as predictors of the five standard participation scales. These regressions produced regression weights (b's), which are the best linear estimates of their independent impact on each of the participation scales. (2) Residual participation measures were then constructed by the following formula—the resultant scales were then corrected for or made orthogonal to the socioeconomic variables employed:

$$CPM_L = PM_L - (b_i \times ZX_i) - (b_j \times ZX_j) - \cdots (b_n \times ZX_n) - K$$

where

CPM_L = the resultant score on the corrected participation measure for any given respondent

PM_L = his original score on the Lth standard participation measure

$b_{i,j,\ldots n}$ = the regression weights for the corresponding demographic variables for which the CPM measure is being corrected.

$ZX_{i,j,\ldots,n}$ = the respondent's standardized score on the ith, jth, . . . nth demographic characteristic.

K = the regression constant.

The CPM scales were then readjusted so that they would have a mean of zero, but the variance was left unaltered so that variability was reduced by removing the demographic effects present. The means were set to zero simply so that they could be plotted in relation to the uncorrected measures. Table B-3 contains the standardized regression weights for the complete demographic residual including socioeconomic status, race, sex, and age. The index of socioeconomic status is a continuous variable based on income, education, and occupation and is described in Appendix C. On the race variable whites were coded 1 and blacks 2. Because age had a slightly curvilinear relationship with the modes of participation, it was entered into the regression as age group 30-65 and age group over 65. The age group below 30 was therefore the base line from which the other two age categories operated. Sex was coded as male 1, female 2.

Table B-3
The Socioeconomic Correction Equation (standardized regression weights)

	Voting	Campaign	Communal	Particularized contacting	Overall participation
Socioeconomic status[a]	.282	.309	.351	.049	.389
Race	.008	−.070	−.069	.042	−.071
Age 2	.153	.058	.150	.033	.171
Age 3	.168	.106	.112	.001	.122
Sex	−.006	−.012	.009	−.016	−.062
R =	.31	.31	.36	.08	.40

[a]Described in Appendix C.

"Corrected" Scores on the Community Level

At various places in the book we move to the community level in our analysis of the data. For that purpose we compute the mean participation scores for citizens in each of our sample communities. In addition we compute corrected scores for the communities based on the mean corrected participation scores for the citizens there. (The corrected scores are then simply the average of the corrected scores at the individual level.)

For purposes of comparability in displaying the data, these community means (corrected and uncorrected) were rescaled so that they, like the individual participation scores, would have means of zero and standard deviations of 100. These corrected scores on the community level gives us a purer measure of the participatory characteristics of each community. They are useful in two ways. In Chapter 13 we are interested in community participation rates as a dependent variable—to see how those rates are affected by certain community characteristics such as size or degree of urbanization. We want to eliminate from this analysis the contaminating effects of the socioeconomic characteristics of the citizens living in such communities. The corrected scores allow us to do this.

In Chapters 18 and 19 we use the participation scores in the community as independent variables to see their impact on the responsiveness of leaders. Again we use the corrected participation scores because we want to separate the impact of the socioeconomic characteristics of the citizenry in the community. The use of the corrected measure makes as big a difference in Chapter 13, where we consider participation the dependent variable—as we discuss in the text. In Chapters 18 and 19 the differences in the results using the corrected measures we report and using uncorrected measures is minimal.

B.4. THE SRC PARTICIPATION VARIABLES OF CHAPTER 14

In Chapter 14 we use data from the University of Michigan's Research Center National Election Studies. The over-time campaign participation scale was built from six participation variables that appeared in each of the seven election studies we utilized. These questions are listed here along with their variable number designations from the University of Michigan ICPR Codebooks. Interested readers can locate exact questions and frequencies of these variables in the aforementioned ICPR documents.

1. Did you talk to any people and try to show them why they should vote for one of the parties or candidates?
2. Did you give any money or buy any tickets or anything to help the campaign for one of the parties or candidates?
3. Did you go to any political meetings, rallies, dinners, or things like that?
4. Did you do any other work for one of the parties or candidates?
5. Did you belong to any political club or organization?
6. Did you wear a campaign button or put a sticker on your car?

The following table indicates the variable number of the participation item as it appears in the codebooks distributed by the Inter-University Consortium for Political Research. The variable number of any question for any year can be located at the intersection of the row of the question number and the column for the year of the election study in question.

	1952	1956	1960	1962	1964	1968	1970
Q. 1	203	215	215	49	313	318	155
Q. 2	204	216	216	50	335	423	*
Q. 3	205	217	217	51	314	397	157
Q. 4	206	218	218	52	315	398	159
Q. 5	207	219	219	53	316	400	160
Q. 6	*	220	220	54	317	399	161

The 1958 and 1966 election studies did not ask the full set of campaign participation questions and, for this reason, were deleted from the analysis reported in Chapter 14.

The asterisks in the table above indicate that the question was not asked in that year. The values for the missing variable were estimated with a multiple regression of the missing variable on the existing variable in an election study nearest the one missing the data. To develop a value for the campaign contribution variable in 1970 (Q.2), for example, questions 1, 3, 4, 5, and 6 were regressed with question 2 for *1968* and the coefficients obtained were used in computing the expected value for 1970.

The index of campaign activism was computed in the following way: Answers to the questions were dichotomized with respondents reporting the activity at least once scored as participators on the item. For the estimated variables—question 6 in 1952 and question 2 in 1970—the dichotomization was done in a way that maximized the correspondence with the proportion engaging in the activity in the election which supplied the coefficients (see above on this). In both cases this proportion was less than the proportion in the estimating sample. Respondents whose value on the estimated variable equalled the constant in the regression equation (i.e., did none of the other possible campaign acts) were coded as nonparticipators for the estimated item. The intermediate scores were left as they were estimated. The index of campaign participation is the sum of the six variables.

An individual was not assigned missing data on the index unless he was missing data for each of the component questions. Respondents that were not ascertained or who responded with "don't know" or "can't remember" were regarded as nonparticipators unless they were coded similarly on *all* the remaining questions. If codeable data were obtained for even one of the questions in the set, DK's and NA's were coded as nonparticipation. As a consequence of this rule virtually all the missing data were contributed by respondents not reinterviewed in the postelection half of the Presidential election studies. With this group excluded, less than 1 percent of the cases were missing data on the index.

In order to achieve greater comparability for all the data points, the means presented for Congressional elections were adjusted by adding to them the average difference in campaign activity scores in Congressional vs. Presidential elections in the decade of the sixties. This average distance amounted to sixteen points on our scale and this quantity was added to all reported means pertaining to the 1962 and 1970 Congressional elections.

Chapter 14 also utilizes a projected campaign participation score—projected that is, on the basis of the standard socioeconomic model. Mean levels of participation among each of the educational groups in 1952 were obtained for the 1952 Presidential election. These means were then assigned to each respondent (according to his level of education) in all subsequent election years. New population means were then computed for each election—1965-1970. These means reflect the expected level of participation, given changes in the average educational attainment within the population. In short, these means are an estimate of what the trends in participation should have looked like if only the base-line socioeconomic model was affecting rates of activity during this period. This same procedure was used in constructing the projected means for blacks and whites. (The means are, then, expected campaign activity scores given the changing educational distribution for blacks and whites.)

In order to insure that the projections were not an artifact of some particular characteristic of the 1952 election, similar projections were made using the combined 1952-1956 data files and the data file from the 1956 election by itself. Each of these yielded very similar projections. Furthermore, the correlations between education and participation for each of the election years indicate that similar projections would have resulted using any of the election years as a starting point save 1964 and 1970, when the education-participation relationships were somewhat stronger. See Table 14-2, p. 253.

Appendix C
Descriptions and Frequency Distributions for the Demographic Questions

Listed here are questions, coding categories, relative frequency distributions and weighted and unweighted number of respondents for each of the demographic variables used in this book. In addition the method of scale construction and the distribution of the summary socioeconomic status index are reported in this appendix.

Question	Raw N	Weighted N	Frequency Distribution	
How long have you lived here in this community of (name of place)?	209	243	Less than one year	7.9%
	329	390	From one to three years	12.6
	450	540	From four to ten years	17.4
	1,092	1,332	More than ten years but not all R's life	43.0
	469	590	All my life	19.1

Question	Raw N	Weighted N	Frequency Distribution	
What is your religion?	1,834	2,174	Protestant	70.2%
	560	698	Catholic	22.6
	44	72	Jewish	2.3
	22	30	Other	1.0
	89	117	None	3.8
	3	4	Missing data	.1
How old were you on your	323	404	Up to 25	13.1%
last birthday? (Exact age	250	311	Age 26–30	10.0
was recorded but the fol-	461	552	Age 31–40	17.8
lowing six-fold age class-	485	600	Age 41–50	19.4
ification was used in most	593	718	Age 51–65	23.2
sections of the book.)	433	506	Age over 65	16.3
Mean = 46.2 years	4	4	Missing data	.1
Median = 45.1 years				
Standard deviation = 16.9				
years				
Sex of the respondent	1,232	1,496	Male	48.3%
	1,317	1,599	Female	51.7
Race of the respondent	2,260	2,653	White	55.7%
	261	406	Negro	13.1
	6	7	Oriental	.2
	7	7	American Indian	.2
	13	18	Latin American	.6
	2	4	Other	.1
Type of Community. The	646	646	Rural	20.9%
following variable con-	662	670	Small town	21.6
structed from the size	413	467	Suburb	15.1
and spatial isolation of	782	1,266	City	40.9
the respondents commun-	46	46	Unclassifiable	1.5
ity of residence, was used				
in Chapter 6. In Chapter				
13 where the community				
is the unit of analysis, a				
similar measure was				
utilized and is described				
in some detail within the				
chapter itself.				

Question	Raw N	Weighted N	Frequency Distribution	

Measures of Socioeconomic status

Question	Raw N	Weighted N	Frequency Distribution	
What is the last grade or year in school which you completed?	24	28	No schooling	.9%
	670	804	Grammar or elementary (1 to 8)	26.0
	522	642	Some high school (9 to 11)	20.7
	776	936	Completed high school (12)	30.2
	320	388	Incomplete college	12.5
	158	199	College graduage	6.4
	78	96	Postgraduate college	3.1
	1	2	Don't know	.1
Will you please look at this card and tell me which figure comes closest to your family income for the past year—before taxes that is? Just tell me the letter next to the figure that fits best.	117	139	Less than $1,000	4.5%
	171	202	$1,000-$1,999	6.5
	200	247	$2,000-$2,999	8.0
	208	251	$3,000-$3,999	8.1
	196	240	$4,000-$4,999	7.8
	243	301	$5,000-$5,999	9.7
	215	261	$6,000-$6,999	8.4
	201	244	$7,000-$7,999	7.9
	156	185	$8,000-$8,999	6.0
	158	185	$9,000-$9,999	6.0
	354	439	$10,000-$14,999	14.2
	118	143	$15,000-$19,999	4.6
	24	27	$20,000-$24,999	.9
	28	35	$25,000 or more	1.1
	67	88	Refused	2.8
	93	108	Don't know	3.5
Occupation of head of household: What kind of work did/do you (he/she) normally do?	235	295	Unskilled	9.5%
	598	746	Semiskilled	24.1
	364	395	Independently employed	12.8
	439	534	Skilled	17.3
	409	511	Clerical & sales	16.5
	368	451	Professional & managerial	14.6
	136	163	Other (Includes unemployed women who are head of household)	5.3

Question	Raw N	Weighted N	Frequency Distribution	
The index of family social	413	518	Lowest	16.7%
and economic status was	367	434	2	14.0
based upon the respon-	418	512	3	16.5
dents' education, family	398	471	4	15.2
income and occupation	376	446	5	14.4
of head of household.	417	518	Highest	16.7
Each of the variables were	160	196	Missing	6.3
standardized and then				
summed, creating a simple				
additive index with equal				
weight given to education,				
income and occupation.				
If occupation was unob-				
tainable, it was estimated				
on the basis of income				
and education.				

Appendix D
Descriptions of Attitude
and Orientation Measures

This appendix contains information on the individual measures and composite indices of political orientations and issue opinions used at various points in this book. D.1 describes the political orientations employed in Chapter 5; D.2 describes the policy attitudes used in Chapters 12, 15, and 16.

D.1. THE POLITICAL ORIENTATIONS

1. *The Index of Psychological Involvement in Politics.* Each of the following five items was entered into a principal component factor analysis. Each displayed loadings of .5 or greater on the first principal component—i.e., each passed this test of unidimensionality. These factor loadings were then multiplied by the respondents' standardized scores on each of the items, and these six produces summed into an overall psychological involvement index. This summary index was once again standardized to have a mean of zero and a standard deviation of 1. The items in the scale were:

Question	Raw N	Weighted N	Frequency Distribution	
How interested are you in	628	754	No interest	24.4%
politics and national	896	1,078	Some interest	34.8
affairs? Are you very	793	981	Interested	31.7
interested, somewhat	232	283	Missing data	9.1
interested, only slightly				
interested, or not at all				
interested?				
In general, how often do	374	454	Never	14.7%
you usually discuss pol-			Less than once a	
itics and national affairs	901	1,087	week	35.1
with others—every day,			At least once a	
maybe once or twice a	882	1,063	week	34.3
week, less than once a	384	481	Every week	15.5
week, or never?	8	10	Missing data	.3
How often do you usually	385	461	Never	14.9%
discuss local community	1,140	1,356	Less than weekly	43.8
problems with others in	756	925	At least weekly	29.9
this community—every	260	343	Every day	11.1
day, at least once a week,	8	10	Missing data	.3
less than once a week,				
or never?				
Are there any magazines	2,115	2,539	Read none	82.0%
that you read regularly?	321	407	Read one	13.2
(If yes), Which ones	99	126	Read two	4.1
are they? (One point	13	21	Read three	0.7
was given for each *news*	1	2	Read four or more	0.1
magazine regularly read.				
News magazines were de-				
fined as those predom-				
inantly composed of				
politics and public				
affairs, such as *News-*				
week, Time, U.S. News				
& World Report, The				
New Republic.)				
How often do you watch	133	164	Never	5.3%
the news broadcasts			Less than once a	
on TV—once a day,	68	84	week	2.7
a few times a week,	75	89	Once a week	2.9
about once a week,	441	534	Few times	17.3
or never?	1,820	2,210	Every day	71.4
	12	14	Missing data	.4

Question	Raw N	Weighted N	Frequency Distribution	
And how often do you	118	143	Never	4.6%
read the newspaper—			Less than once a	
every day, a few times	104	120	week	3.9
a week, about once a	161	184	Once a week	5.9
week, less than once a	306	377	Several times	12.2
week, or never?	1,859	2,270	Every day	73.2
	1	2	Missing data	.1

2. *The Information Index.* The index of political information is based on the simple sum of the correct responses to the following five questions. The mean and median number of correct answers for the whole population were 3.3 and 3.2 respectively. When used in the analysis of Chapter 5, however, this measure as all the others was standardized to have a mean of zero and a standard deviation of 1.0

Questions	Raw N	Weighted N	Frequency Distribution	
We are interested in how	1,672	2,117	Correct answer	68.4%
well known the com-			Incorrect answer	
munity leaders are in	877	978	or don't know	31.6
different places.				
What is the name of				
the (Head of the local				
governmental unit) of				
this community?				
What is the name of the	1,146	1,332	Correct answer	57.0%
head of the local			Incorrect answer	
school system?	1,403	1,763	or don't know	43.0
We want to know how	2,254	2,724	Correct answer	88.0%
well-known the dif-			Incorrect answer	
ferent governmental	295	371	or don't know	12.0
leaders are known				
around here. Could				
you tell me the name				
of the governor of				
this state?				
And what are the names			One Senator named	
of the Senators from	674	841	correctly	27.2%
this state?			Two Senators named	
	803	958	correctly	31.0
			No Senators named	
			correctly or don't	
	1,072	1,296	know	41.9
What about the congress-	1,037	1,238	Correct answer	40.0%
man from this district?			Incorrect answer	
Do you happen to know	1,512	1,857	or don't know	60.0
his name?				

3. *The Index of Political Efficacy.* Four items were used to build our index of political efficacy. However, two questions on the difficulty of initiating contacts with public officials were precombined before being used to construct the index. The two individual items and the third precombined measure were then standardized, summed and restandardized, once again producing a measure with a mean of zero and a standard deviation of 1.0. The items employed were:

Question	Raw N	Weighted N	Frequency Distribution	
How much influence do	438	535	A lot	17.3%
you think people like	891	1,092	Moderate well	35.2
you can have over local	718	847	Not so well	27.4
government community	456	559	Not at all	18.1
—a lot, a moderate	46	62	Don't know	2.0
amount, or none at all?				
If you had some complaint	716	852	A lot of attention	27.5%
about a local government	1,099	1,319	Some	42.6
activity and took that	460	575	Very little	18.6
complaint to a member	196	256	None at all	8.3
of the local government	78	93	Don't know	3.0
council, would you expect				
him to pay a lot of at-				
tention to what you say,				
some attention, very				
little attention, or none				
at all?				
Do you think it would be			Could contact an	
necessary for you to find	1,837	2,109	official directly	68.1%
an intermediary or con-			Would need a	
nection in order to con-			"connection" to	
tact a government offi-			get to an official	
cial or do you think you			and a "connection"	
could go directly to him?			could be found:	
(If connection necessary),	300	410	easily	13.2
How easy would it be to	170	251	not so easily	8.1
find such a contact?			A "connection"	
Would you say that such			was necessary but	
a connection could be	66	93	could not be found	3.0
easily found, would be	176	232	Missing data	7.5
difficult but could be				
found, or you couldn't				
find one at all?				

4. *Strength of Partisanship.* Each respondent was asked the standard Survey Research Center partisan identity questions listed below. On the basis of their answers to these questions respondents were classified into three categories:

strong party identifiers, weak party identifiers, and independents. For comparability with the other orientation measures, this measure was also standardized to have a mean of zero and a standard deviation of 1.0. (Note that direction of party identification is not presented here but is rather to be found in D.2 of this appendix.)

Question	Raw N	Weighted N	Frequency Distribution	
Generally speaking, do you usually think of yourself as a Republican, a Democrat, an Independent or what? (If Democrat or Republican), Would you call yourself a strong (R/D) or not a very strong (R/D)? (If independent, no party, other or don't know), Do you think of yourself as close to the Republican or Democratic party?	833 1,405 166 145	1,044 1,660 207 184	Strong identifiers Weak identifiers Independents Missing data	33.7% 53.7 6.7 5.9

5. *Propensity to Take Sides.* The propensity to take sides was measured by a single dichotomous item which was standardized to be comparable to other measures and indices.

Question	Raw N	Weighted N	Frequency Distribution	
In many communities there are groups that are opposed to each other. Thinking still about this community, what are the major groups that oppose each other here? (If needed), I mean, the groups that have differences of interest, or who have controversies. Do you generally consider yourself a supporter of one group or the other?	2,031 518	2,435 660	Doesn't take sides or doesn't see group conflicts Takes sides	78.7% 21.3

6. *Index of Issue Extremity.* This summary index is a product of a number of subindices that measure direction of opinion on social welfare, civil rights, and evaluation of police performance.

We will first define each of these subindices and then indicate how they were transformed and combined to obtain the summary measure of issue extremity.

There are three indices measuring attitudes toward social welfare. The first combined the following four questions, dichotomizing each so that an individual could be classified as favoring government responsibility or favoring responsibility by private groups and/or individuals. This index has a maximum score of 4 for those who thought some governmental unit had primary responsibility in each area to zero for those who maintained that either the individual, his family or private groups had the main responsibility in all four areas.

Question	Raw N	Weighted N	Frequency Distribution	
There is much talk about	1,402	1,661	Individual and family	53.7%
whose responsibility it	154	204	Local government	6.6
is to solve problems of	275	346	State government	11.2
the sort we just talked	550	678	National government	21.9
about. Which group	106	132	Private groups	4.3
should have the main	60	71	Don't know	2.3
responsibility for solv-	2	3	No one	.1
ing that problem—the				
individual and his family,				
the local government,				
the state government,				
the national government,				
or privately organized				
groups? Think of the				
first problem we men-				
tioned of financing				
medical care.				
What about looking after			Individual and	
the aged?	1,105	1,301	family	42.0%
	206	261	Local government	8.4
	464	579	State government	18.7
	663	820	National government	26.5
	49	58	Private groups	1.9
	61	75	Don't know	2.5
	1	1	No one	
What about unemploy-			Individual and	
ment problems?	796	940	family	30.4%
	548	695	Local government	22.5
	670	816	State government	26.4
	334	403	National government	12.0
	87	109	Private groups	3.5
	112	130	Don't know	4.2
	2	2	No one	.1

Question	Raw N	Weighted N	Frequency Distribution	
What about adequate housing?	882	1,018	Individual and family	32.9%
	711	896	Local government	28.9
	415	515	State government	16.6
	341	424	National government	13.7

A second index was constructed from these same items which categorized individuals in terms of the degree to which they assigned principal responsibility for such matters to the national government as opposed to local or state governments.

The third welfare index combined the following two more general welfare questions. Each of the items was standardized before being added together.

Question	Raw N	Weighted N	Frequency Distribution	
Do you think that the difference between the income of the rich and the poor in this country is much too great, somewhat too great, or as it should be?	860	1,019	As it should be	32.9%
	869	1,044	Somewhat too great	33.7
	630	804	Much too great	26.0
	190	218	Don't know	7.4
Some people say that the government should have the major responsibility for the needs of the poor people in this country. Others say that the poor should themselves have the major responsibility to do something about their problems. What do you believe?	594	770	Government should have major responsibility	24.9%
	967	1,144	Poor should have major responsibility	37.0
	928	1,107	Both should do something	35.8
	20	25	Other	.8
	40	49	Don't know	1.6

The civil rights index, which forms part of the extremity scale, was built from the following three questions:

Question	Raw N	Weighted N	Frequency Distribution	
Do you think the government should see to it that white and Negro children go to the same schools or should the government stay out of it?	1,102	1,382	Government should see to it	44.7%
	1,200	1,427	Government should stay out	46.1
	247	286	Don't know	9.2

Question	Raw N	Weighted N	Frequency Distribution	

Do you think the govern-
ment should see to it
that Negroes can pur-
chase homes without dis-
crimination or should
the government stay
out of it?
	1,072
	
	1,281
	196
		1,361
		
		1,507
		227
			Government should
			  see to it
			Government should
			  stay out
			Don't know
				44.0%
				
				48.7
				7.3

There are many attempts to improve conditions for the Negroes in Amer- ica. Do you think that those who want to im- prove the Negro's posi- tion are trying to do it too quickly, not quickly enough, or about right?	1,400 708 248 193	1,646 870 354 225	Too quickly About right Not quickly enough Don't know	53.2% 28.1 11.4 7.3

The positive or "pro" civil rights responses were summed across the three items. The average number of pro civil rights responses for the population as a whole was a mean number of 1.5 and a median of 1.4.

The final measure that entered into the issue extremity scale was built from the following two items. This index ranged from a -3 (the most negative response to both questions) to a $+3$ (the most positive). The mean for the population was 1.3.

Question	Raw N	Weighted N	Frequency Distribution	
How good a job do you think the police do in protecting the lives and the property of the people around here—a very good job, fairly good, fairly poor, or very poor?	1,170 1,053 156 120 50	1,373 1,274 219 171 58	Very good Fairly good Fairly poor Very poor Don't know	44.4% 41.2 7.1 5.5 1.9
Do you think the police here treat all citizens equally or do they give some people better treatment than others?	1,378 824 347	1,603 1,086 406	All equally Some better than others Don't know	51.8% 35.1 13.1

The Computation of the Index of Issue Extremity

Each of the five component indices was standardized. The index of extremity involved locating the individual on some metric which did not contain any of the substantive direction of the individual items or the intermediate indices but rather measured his propensity to take extreme positions. This was accomplished by scoring the respondent, not with reference to his distance from the population mean, but on the basis of how far he was from the mean within the substantive direction of his score for the intermediate index. Thus, for example, a score of $+3$ on the police services measure is as "extreme" a response as -3, although the mean of the index is $+1.3$. Operationally this involved dividing the respondent's standardized score by the range of scores within the substantive direction and squaring to remove the sign. This was done for each intermediate index. The result was summed and standardized.

7. *Civic Mindedness.* The civic contribution variable was measured by the following self-anchoring scale.

Question	Raw N	Weighted N	Frequency Distribution	
Here is a ladder. Consider that the person who did the most for the welfare of this community was at the top rung of the ladder and the person who did the least was at the bottom rung.				
Where would you be in			Top rung (does	
terms of how much you	83	105	most)	3.4%
do for the welfare of	180	219	2	7.1
the community? (If	530	621	3	20.1
needed), Near the per-	632	771	4	24.9
son who does the most	1,037	1,274	Bottom rung	41.2
or the person who does	87	105	Don't know	3.4
the least?				

D.2. THE POLITICAL ATTITUDES

The following questions, used to ascertain the respondents' attitudes toward welfare, race, and civil rights, as well as to ascertain his party identity, are employed in many sections of the book. They are used most extensively in Chapters 15 and 16. Some of these items have been combined into scales. However, since all of these scales have been used in constructing the index of issue extremity, the reader is referred to D.1, point 6, of this appendix for a description of the construction of these scales. Listed here are only the questions and their frequency distributions.

Questions	Raw N	Weighted N	Frequency Distribution	
A. *Welfare items*				
There is much talk about whose responsibility it is to solve problems of the sort we just talked about. Which group should have the main responsibility for solving that problem—the individual and his family, the local government, the state government, the national government, or privately organized groups. Think of the first problem we mentioned of financing medical care.	1,508 979 60 2	1,793 1,228 71 3	Individual, family or private group responsible Some government agency responsible Don't know No one	58.0% 39.7 2.3 .1
What about looking after the aged?	1,154 1,331 61	1,359 1,660 75	Individual, family or private group Some government agency responsible Don't know No one	43.9% 53.6 2.5 —
What about employment problems?	883 1,552 112 2	1,049 1,914 130 2	Individual, family or private group responsible Some governmental agency responsible Don't know No one	33.9% 61.9 4.2 .1
What about adequate housing?	952 1,467 125 5	1,101 1,835 152 7	Individual, family or private group responsible Some governmental agency responsible Don't know No one	35.6% 58.2 4.9 .2
Do you think that the difference between the income of the rich and the poor in this country is much too great, somewhat too great or as it should be?	860 869 630 190	1,019 1,044 804 218	As it should be Somewhat too great Much too great Don't know	32.9% 33.7 26.0 7.4

Questions	Raw N	Weighted N	Frequency Distribution	
Some people say that the government should have the major responsibility for the needs of the poor people in this country.	594	770	Government should have major responsibility	24.9%
Others say that the poor	967	1,144	Poor should have major responsibility	37.0
should themselves have			Both should do	
major responsibility to	928	1,107	something	35.8
do something about	20	25	Other	.8
their problems. What do	40	49	Don't know	1.6
you believe?				

B. *Questions on Race and Civil Rights.*

Questions	Raw N	Weighted N	Frequency Distribution	
Do you think the government should see to it	1,102	1,382	Government should see to it	44.7%
that white and Negro			Government should	
children go to the same	1,200	1,427	stay out	46.1
schools or should the	247	286	Don't know	9.2
government stay out of it?				
Do you think the government should see to it	1,072	1,361	Government should see to it	44.0%
that Negroes can purchase			Government should	
homes without discrimination or should the	1,281	1,507	stay out	48.7
	196	227	Don't know	7.3
government stay out of it?				
There are many attempts	1,400	1,646	Too quickly	53.2%
to improve conditions	708	870	About right	28.1
for the Negroes in America. Do you think that	248	354	Not quickly enough	11.4
those who want to improve the Negro's position are trying to do it too quickly, not quickly enough, or about right?	193	225	Don't know	7.3

C. *Partisan Identification.* The following standard questions developed by the Survey Research Center at the University of Michigan were used to ascertain the individual's partisan identity. Strong Democrats and strong Republicans were those who gave either the Democratic or Republican party as an answer to the first question, and claimed to be strong identifiers on the second question. The remainder Democratic and Republican categories are composed of those who said that they were either Democrats or Republicans to the first question but claimed they only weakly supported the party, and those who, when first asked, said they were independent but on the third question indicated that they leaned in one direction or the other. Those classified as independents would not associate themselves with either of the parties through the various probes.

Questions	Raw N	Weighted N	Frequency Distribution	
Generally speaking, do	528	697	Strong Democrat	22.5%
you usually think of	876	1,057	Democrat	34.2
yourself as a Republi-	166	207	Independent	6.7
can, a Democrat, an	529	603	Republican	19.5
independent or what?	305	347	Strong Republican	11.2
(If Democrat or Re-	145	184	Missing data	5.9
publican), Would you				
call yourself a strong				
(R/D) or not a very				
strong (R/D)? (If inde-				
pendent, no party, other,				
or don't know), Do you				
think of yourself as close				
to the Republican or				
Democratic party?				

Appendix E
The Structure of
Participation:
Some Validity Checks

Factor-analytic techniques—on which we lean heavily for our analysis of the structure of participation—have been criticized for a number of reasons: They are particularly sensitive to the format of the data that is entered into the technique, and their appropriateness for the kinds of ordinal measurements we have has been questioned. In this appendix we will deal with the validity of the results of our factor analysis in three ways:

1. We will discuss the format of the data in order to indicate that there is relatively little likelihood that our results are the artifacts of questionnaire design or response set.

2. We will summarize data on a replication of the analysis on independent data files in a number of other nations.

3. We will present an analysis parallel to our factor analysis using Guttman-Lingoes Smallest-Space Analysis to see whether a different method of dimensional analysis applied to the same data yields the same results.

Appendix E-3 was prepared with the assistance of Rachel Katz of the Israeli Institute of Social Research.

E.1. THE LOCATION AND FORMAT OF THE PARTICIPATION QUESTIONS AND THE ISSUE OF RESPONSE SET

In order to avoid response set, we first tried to spread participation questions throughout the hour-and-fifteen-minute interview, rather than concentrate them in one section. Furthermore, insofar as possible within the limitations of a coherent conversation with the respondent, we attempted to intermix the questions indexing different modes of activity. Finally, we attempted in several instances to include extreme variations in the format of questions which we hypothesized belonged to the same dimension of activity.

For example, note the differences in the form, location, and format of the five items that constitute the cooperative activity and social contacting factor (factor 3 in the final rotated solution): The two questions concerning initiation of contacts with government officials occur relatively early in the interview and are themselves separated by several pages of questions. The two questions aimed at determining whether the respondent had ever worked with an existing organization or formed his own group in order to solve a community problem appeared much later in the questionnaire. The remaining item included in, and highly associated with, this factor came between these two sets of questions and varied dramatically from both of them in format. This variable, the number of active memberships maintained by the individual in organizations that regularly attempt to solve community problems, was in actuality not a single question at all, but a composite index. To obtain this measure, each respondent was first asked if he currently was a member of sixteen different types of organizations and voluntary associations. For each of the types in which he claimed membership, he was then asked whether he took an active part in the organization or whether he was a passive member.

Then the interviewer returned to each organization of which the respondent was a member, and asked of each one whether it regularly attempted to solve social problems in the community. On the final index entered in the factor analysis, the respondent was given one point for every active membership he maintained in an organization that regularly attempted to solve community problems. The format of this question, then, was truly distinct from that of the other questions forming this factor. In short, there appears to be little structural reason to believe that artifact of location or similarity in question form led these five items to be more closely associated with each other than with other participtation questions included in the questionnaire.

The case against measurement artifact is also supported by what happens to the contacting items when they are separated into those with a particularized reference and those with a social one. If the generalized response set phenomenon was the factor that caused all the participation items to be positively interrelated, then those who gave affirmative answers to the contacting questions would have been equally likely to give affirmative answers to all of the other participation items, whether the referent of their contact was particularized or social. This, we have clearly demonstrated, is not the case, for contracting with an individual referent bears almost no relationship to the performance of other kinds of activity, whereas contacts with a social referent do. Since these four contacting items were created from the same two questions (the distinction being based on the substance of the contact derived from a later question), then it is both logically and empirically impossible that the differences in their relationship to the other modes of activity could be due to question location or format.

Furthermore, from the standpoint of measurement artifact, there appears to be little reason to expect that the social contacting variables would, as they do, form part of the cooperative factor rather than load on some other factor. But in contrast, there is strong reason to expect this to be the case, given our theory concerning the situation in which such contacts involve citizens and the purposes to which they may be put.

E.2. EVIDENCE FROM CROSS-NATIONAL REPLICATIONS OF THE FACTOR ANALYSIS

Our argument about the structure of participation is a quite general one, not one based on specific characteristics of American politics. It would greatly validate our distinctions applied in the American case if similar distinctions were found elsewhere. A similar factor analysis was run on data from four other countries—India, Japan, Nigeria, and Austria. The heterogeneity of the countries made for a most powerful test of the generality of the pattern. In each of the countries a quite similar set of factors was found to that reported in Chapter 4.

Furthermore, the validity of the similarity of structure found across the five nations is increased by the fact that the specific items used to tap the particular modes of participation differed somewhat from nation to nation. In Austria they were based on a quite different set of items. That one finds a similar structure using heterogeneous measures adds to one's confidence in the "reality" of the structure found. For a full report on these parallel analyses see Sidney Verba, Norman H. Nie and Jae-on Kim, *The Modes of Democratic Participation: A Cross-National Comparison* (Beverly Hills, Cal.: Sage Publications, 1971).

E.3. A SMALLEST-SPACE ANALYSIS OF THE STRUCTURE OF PARTICIPATION BEHAVIOR

Factor analysis involves a number of assumptions and computations that have made it the subject of some debate as a tool of dimensional analysis. We subjected the participatory acts to an alternate technique of spatial analysis— Guttman-Lingoes Smallest-Space Analysis[1]—in order to see if this method (which makes assumptions different from those of factor analysis and is

---

[1] The specific technique used is SSA-I, the first of a series of computer programs for smallest-space analysis, based on nonmetric relative distance models for the analysis of data matrices. It is meant for the analysis of *symmetric* matrices of similarity or dissimilarity coefficients. For more detailed recent discussions see L. Guttman, "A General Nonmetric Technique for Finding the Smallest Coordinate Space for a Configuration of Points," *Psychometrika*, vol. 33 (month 1968), pp. 469-506; J. C. Lingoes, "A General Survey of the Guttman-Lingoes Nonmetric Program Series," mimeographed (1969); and "A General Nonparametric Model for Representing Objects and Attributes in a Joint Metric Space," in J. C. Gardin, ed., *Archéologie et Calculateurs* (Marseilles: Centre National de la Recherche Scientifique, 1970), pp. 277-298; and J. C. Lingoes and E. Roskam, "A Mathematical and Empirical Study of Two Multidimensional Scaling Algorithms," *Michigan Math. Psych. Program Technical Report MMPP 71-1*, mimeographed (1971).

computationally distinct) yields the same basic structure of participation.

If Smallest-Space Analysis revealed the same basic patterns of political activity, it would provide important validation that the distinctions and patterns we report in Chapter 4 are real and not simply artifacts of our factor analysis.[2]

There are several important differences between factor analysis and Smallest-Space Analysis.

1. Where factor analysis treats the magnitude of distances between elements in the correlation matrix as absolute "interval" differences, Smallest-Space Analysis utilizes only their *ordinal rank-order*. The latter therefore places less weight on the absolute values of correlations, but gives more weight to their simple relative differences.[3]

2. No estimates of communalities are attempted in Smallest-Space Analysis, and because it treats the matrix as an ordinal ranking, modification of the diagonal elements is not required.

3. Because of the emphasis on the nonmetric rank ordering and since there are no attempts to estimate communalities, the thrust in factor analysis to determine the precise relationship of each variable to each factor (the factor loadings) is subordinated to the search for the most direct configuration or pattern of the variables. Subordinating the value of communalities and deemphasizing the precise relationship among coordinates (axes), eliminates the problem of the number of factors to be extracted and simplifies the quest for the best rotational method.[4]

Each approach has its advantages and disadvantages and each emphasizes different features of the dimensional space. Precisely because they are somewhat different approaches, they become most useful for our purposes here—if the basic structure of participation is clear and strong it should be made visible by both methods.[5]

Chapter 4 presented two rotated factor solutions—one of the original thirteen participation variables and one of the fifteen variables created when contacting is split into two types. We will present a replication of each of these

---

[2] A social reality of course affected by our selection of acts from the potential universe of content, format of questions, and response set.

[3] The program tries in an iterative process to plot the variables under consideration as points in a geometric space such that the rank order of the relations between them is preserved: if variable *i* correlates more with variable *j* than variable *k* with variable *l*, then the plotted distance between the points representing variables *i* and *j* should become smaller than the distance between points *k* and *l*. Diagonal coefficients are excluded from the computations. The method shares with factor analysis the restrictions of monotonicity preservation and the search for a solution in the smallest possible space. However, smallest-space analysis eliminates the further restriction of factor analysis for reproducing the observed correlations from the interpoint distances by a metric formula, which corrects for communality. See Guttman, "A General Nonmetric Technique for Finding the Smallest Coordinate Space for a Configuration of Points"; Lingoes, "Recent Computational Advances in Nonmetric Methodology for the Behavioral Sciences," *Proceedings of the International Symposium: Mathematical and Computational Methods in Social Sciences,* (Rome: International Computation Center, 1966), pp. 1-38, and "A General Nonparametric Model for Representing Objects and Attributes in a Joint Metric Space"; and L. Guttman and I. M. Schlesinger, "Smallest-Space Analysis of Intelligence and Achievement Tests, *Psychological Bulletin,* vol. 71, (month 1969), pp. 95-100.

[4] Even among proponents of factor analysis, the areas of largest contention and ambiguity involve the problems of how to modify the communalities during the extraction phase and how to best rotate the factors in the rotation phase.

[5] For an empirical comparison of both methods see Schlesinger and Guttman, "Smallest-Space Analysis of Intelligence and Achievement Tests."

analyses using Smallest-Space Analysis. Let us first look at an SSA[6] of the thirteen original participation variables and then turn to our refinement of particularized contacting. Figure E-1 presents a two-dimensional plot of the thirteen participation variables as produced by smallest-space analysis.

The resulting structure of activity is highly consistent with the findings of our first factor analysis. The pattern in Figure E-1 is virtually identical in substance to the rotated factor solution in Table 4-3 (p. 65). Each of the four modes of activity occupy distinctive "regions" of the smallest two-space and each of the individual items within the modes are clearly locatable within their appropriate regions. The smallest-space analysis criteria of fit also indicate that this is a very clean and strong solution.[7]

The subtleties in the SSA diagram also concur with the findings from the various parts of our factor analysis. First, voting is clearly the most distinctive mode of activity: All three measures of voting, while in close proximity to each other, are at quite a distance from all three other modes. The relative distance separating voting from the other three modes is much greater than the distances between any of the other three modes.

Second, the ambiguous position of citizen-initiated contacts is also once again apparent—while contacting forms a region of its own, these two activities are very close to the cooperative acts, being as close or closer to each of them than they are to each other.[8]

Third, the pattern is consistent with our earlier arguments and findings about the kinds of characteristics which separate the modes of participation. The left-right continuum in Figure E-1 appears to differentiate among the modes according to the *degree of initiative required*. And even within each of the modes, left-right position appears to differentiate among the items on this dimension. In this aspect the pattern is clearer with SSA than with factor analysis. The left-right continuum roughly corresponds to the prime activity dimension.[9]

[6] Abbreviation for Smallest-Space Analysis.

[7] The degree of "fit" of the solution—the adequateness with which the data matrix is represented by the plot—is evaluated by the Guttman-Lingoes normalized phi-coefficient, which measures the amount of error—the "loss-function." Usually, however, it is expressed in a derival from the phi-coefficient—the "coefficient of alienation." It ranges from zero to 1 in such a way that the better the fit between the data matrix and the plot, the closer to zero the coefficient (Schlesinger and Guttman, "Smallest-Space Analysis of Intelligence and Achievement Tests"; and Lingoes, "A General Nonparametric Model for Representing Objects and Attributes in a Joint Metric Space").

[8] The ambiguity in the location of active memberships in community problem-solving organizations parallels the ambiguities in its placement in the factor analysis. This variable, which loads most strongly on the cooperative activity factor, is nevertheless one of the only variables that split its loading among other factors. Its bridge position between campaign activity and contacting is also revealed by its position in the SSA diagram.

[9] The "simplical" order found in Table E-1 gives clear evidence of this activity continuum [for an elaboration of the idea of simplical and other orders see Guttman, "A New Approach to Factor Analysis: The Radex," in P. F. Lazarsfeld, ed., *Mathematical Thinking in the Social Sciences* (New York: Free Press, 1954), pp. 258-348, and "Order Analysis of Correlation Matrices," in R.B. Cattell, ed., *Handbook of Multivariate Experimental Psychology* (Chicago: Rand McNally, 1966); and M. B. Jones, *Molar Correlational Analysis*, Pensacola, Fla.: U.S. Naval School of Aviation Medicine, monograph, 1960]. The order in this matrix, which is an accompanying feature of the smallest-space analysis, corresponds to the horizontal continuum in the diagram: The strongest correlations are found along the diagonal; moving away from the diagonal toward the upper-right or lower-left corner they taper off in size. It is interesting to note that a number of substitute variables could have been used without in any way affecting the basic continuum. Variable 6 could have been replaced by variable 5, variable 10 by variable 9, and either 11 or 13 could substitute for 12. All indicate the *degree* of activism dimension differing only in their vertical position. Table E-1 gives the complete correlation matrix arranged concordant with SSA, while Tables E-2 and E-3 reflect the horizontal and vertical dimensions. Tables are at end of Appendix E.

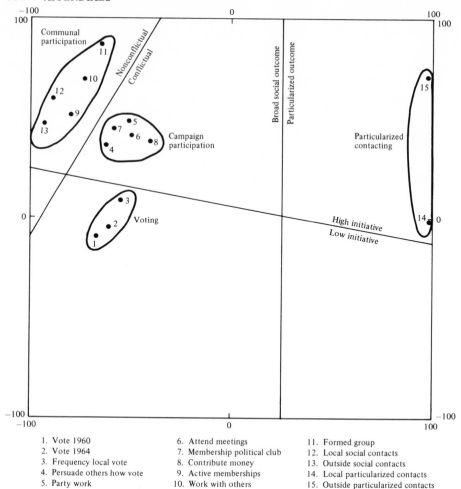

1. Vote 1960
2. Vote 1964
3. Frequency local vote
4. Persuade others how vote
5. Party work
6. Attend meetings
7. Membership political club
8. Contribute money
9. Active memberships
10. Work with others
11. Formed group
12. Local social contacts
13. Outside social contacts
14. Local particularized contacts
15. Outside particularized contacts

Figure E-1. SSA Diagram of the Thirteen Participation Variables (coefficient of alienation = .160)

The vertical direction separating some of the variables suggests another type of differentiating factor.[10] This dimension distinguishes campaign activity from cooperative participation. That is, not only do the cooperative acts appear to require more initiative, being further right on the diagram (a pattern consistent with our arguments), but the campaign activities tend to be located in the upper part of the diagram while the cooperative activities occupy the lower portion of the figure. Thus, just as in the factor analysis we can see that these two modes of participation appear quite distinct.

The SSA diagram then clearly shows the regional segregation of the four modes of activity. It highlights the uniqueness of voting. The smallest-space analysis makes clear the distinctions in degree of activism highly related to our

[10] See Table E-3.

theoretical initiative dimension and empirically similar to the prime activity factor. Finally, the diagram suggests the importance of the conflict dimension. Only our third dimension—the scope of the outcome—is not apparent in the diagram. However, this dimension was also hidden in our factor analysis until we separated citizen-initiated contacts according to the scope of the outcome to which they pertain. We will now repeat the smallest-space analysis, after separating these two forms of contacting just as we did in our second factor analysis.

A Smallest-Space Analysis of the Fifteen Participatory Acts Including Both Forms of Contacting

Figure E-2 presents a second SSA solution including the first eleven acts and replacing the two original contact variables with the four transformed

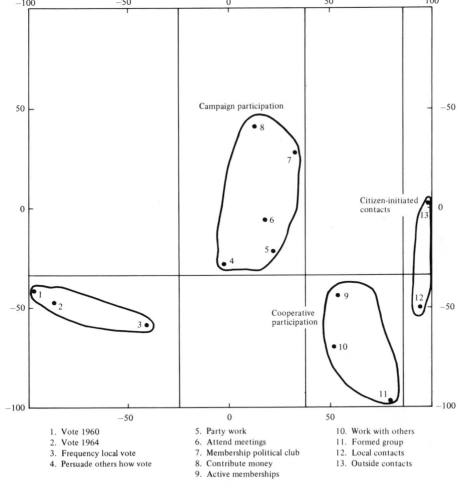

1. Vote 1960
2. Vote 1964
3. Frequency local vote
4. Persuade others how vote

5. Party work
6. Attend meetings
7. Membership political club
8. Contribute money
9. Active memberships

10. Work with others
11. Formed group
12. Local contacts
13. Outside contacts

Figure E-2. SSA Diagram of the Fifteen Participation Variables, Including Both Forms of Contacting (coefficient of alienation = .107)

contact variables which control for the scope of outcome of the contact. Once again the resulting configuration closely parallels that located by the final rotated factor solution reported in Table 4-5 (p. 72). The substance of the patterns can be most clearly understood by the "partitions" (the straight lines) of the two-space and the intersections of these partitions.

We begin with the vertical partition which segments the left portion of the diagram from the right portion. It separates personalized contacting from all other modes of participation and seems therefore to correspond to our theoretical dimension of the scope of the outcome. The distance separating particularized contacts from all other modes suggests how complete the separation is and how prominent this dimension is in the overall structure. The SSA and out factor analyses are both very clear on this point.

The second main partition bisects the figure into upper and lower portions and appears to correspond closely to the degree of activism or initiative. The measures of voting are below the partitioning, all the other acts are above it. Though the regions are somewhat compacted when compared to the previous solution, the general pattern is quite clear. The position of only one variable—particularized contacts in the local community—deviates slightly from what our theory would predict. However, its position and the compaction of the initiative dimension are a function of the extremely low correlations between the personalized contacting measures and between them and the other modes of activity. Their low correlations with the other modes do, we believe, reflect reality, but distort the configuration. Their low correlations with each other are artifacts of the way these two variables were measured and tend to distort both the diagram and the social reality it attempts to present.

Though we once again find that the regions are somewhat compressed by the relative distance of particularized contacting, the conflict dimension nevertheless remains visible as the third partition of the space, with voting and campaign activity falling below and to the right of the line of partition, and the communal acts—now composed of contacts with a social referent—and the cooperative acts falling above and to the left of the line. So again it appears that each of the modes of activity occupies a separate region in the two-space. Considering the three partitions simultaneously, the region of voting is delimited by broad social goals, by low initiative and by the presence of some conflict. Campaign activity can be characterized in a similar way except of course that it lies well into the region of high initiative. The region for communal activity is also in the public as opposed to the private sphere and on average ranks even higher as to the amount of initiative involved. Communal activity is further delimited in that it falls on the negative side of the conflict dimension. The region occupied by particularized contacts lies at the furthest possible extreme on the particularized side of the scope-of-outcome dimension. It falls on the high side of the initiative line though the placement of the partition here appears directed as much by our theory as by the empirical placement of the acts.

CONCLUSION

Whereas the imagery, language, and thrust of smallest-space analysis differs from factor analysis and thus leads us to slightly different kinds of descriptions, the central features in the pattern and structure of participation strongly support our earlier interpretations. The picture of participation remains essentially unaltered. However, one additional note of caution should be introduced. While SSA and factor analysis differ in a number of important ways, they are both based on the same simple correlation matrix. From this point on the SSA is an independent validation of the factor analysis. Whether or not the basic matrix has built-in biases or distortions that would affect both outcomes, remains unknown. However, the fact that smallest-space analysis uses only the rank-order magnitude of the coefficients would seem to offset such problems. Establishing further validity of the structure would appear much more dependent on improving our measurements of the various kinds of activity than on alternative methods of spatial analysis.

Table E-1

Pearson r Simple Correlation Matrix (x 100) Among Thirteen Political Activities
(arrangement in agreement with the smallest-space analysis)

Participation variable	Voting			Campaign					Cooperate			Initiate	
	1	2	3	4	5	6	7	8	9	10	11	12	13
1 Vote 1960	–	71	60	19	19	18	13	17	18	17	09	11	12
2 Vote 1964	71	–	64	21	19	20	14	17	18	18	10	13	14
3 Frequency local vote	60	64	–	24	26	25	18	20	23	22	14	17	18
4 Persuade others how vote	19	21	24	–	47	35	27	27	22	24	23	24	22
5 Party work	19	19	26	47	–	50	46	36	27	31	24	26	22
6 Attend meetings	18	20	25	35	50	–	45	37	30	23	24	25	21
7 Membership in political club	13	14	18	27	46	45	–	36	20	22	22	17	19
8 Contribute money	17	17	20	27	36	37	36	–	24	21	12	19	20
9 Active memberships	18	18	23	22	27	30	29	24	–	34	28	26	27
10 Work with others	17	18	22	24	31	23	22	21	34	–	38	29	23
11 Formed group	09	10	14	23	24	24	22	12	28	38	–	22	19
12 Contacted local	11	13	17	24	26	25	17	19	26	29	22	–	23
13 Contacted outside	12	14	18	22	22	21	19	20	27	23	19	23	–

Table E-2

Pearson *r* Simple Correlation (x 100) Matrix Among Eight Political Activities
on Horizontal Continuum in Space Diagram

Participation variable		1	2	3	4	5	9	12	(13)
Vote 1960	1	—	71	60	19	19	18	11	(12)
Vote 1964	2	71	—	64	21	19	18	13	(14)
Frequency local vote	3	60	64	—	24	26	23	17	(18)
Persuade others how vote	4	19	21	24	—	47	22	24	(22)
Party work	5	19	19	26	47	—	27	26	(22)
Active memberships	9	18	18	23	22	27	—	26	(27)
Contacted local	12	11	13	17	24	26	26	—	
(Contacted outside)	(13	12	14	18	22	22	27		—)

Table E-3

Pearson *r* Simple Correlation (x 100) Matrix Among Six Political
Activities on Vertical Continuum in Space Diagram

Participation variable		8	7	6	5	10	11
Contribute money	8	—	36	37	36	21	12
Membership in political club	7	36	—	45	46	22	22
Attend meetings	6	37	45	—	50	23	24
Party work	5	36	46	50	—	31	24
Work with others	10	21	22	23	31	—	38
Formed group	11	12	22	24	24	38	—

Appendix F
Types of Participators:
A Cluster Analysis

Cluster analysis is an empirical means of typologizing. Given a population with a set of independently measured characteristics—in our case the amount of activity within each of the four modes of participation—cluster analysis is a search technique for locating groups of individuals who have a similar pattern across all the characteristics. The first step is to compute distances among individuals in a multidimensional space formed by their scores on the four modes of activity. On the basis of these distances the cluster technique determines which individuals should be assigned to which clusters and informs us as to how much clustering there is. "Good" clustering exists if most of the population can be assigned to relatively few distinct clusters and if those within each cluster are quite similar to each other. For instance, a cluster analysis would confirm our particular expectations if most citizens could be grouped into clusters resembling the patterns anticipated in Table 4-8 (p. 78), and if the clusters were internally homogeneous—i.e., if the activity patterns of those in each cluster were truly similar. Like factor analysis, cluster analysis is a highly empirical technique. It becomes most useful therefore, when one has, as we do, clear prior expectations of what is to be found.

What we attempt to do in this analysis can be seen in Figure F-1. There we present a visual representation of a hypothetical clustering of participants. We use only three of the four modes of participation because three dimensions are all we can represent graphically. Voting is represented by the width of the cube, campaign activity by the depth, and communal participation by the height. Each dot represents an individual citizen whose position within the cube reflects his score on all three dimensions.

The basics of cluster analysis are easily comprehended from this figure. Such analysis is simply a search for clusters or "swarms" of individuals who have similar scores on each of the variables in question and thus neighbor each other in multidimensional space. The hypothetical distribution in Figure F-1 has "good" clustering in that most citizens fall into one or another of a limited number of clusters and there is a great deal of homogeneity within the clusters. And the particular set we have presented is consistent with our expectations as to the specific clusters we would find. The clusters represent—using the numbers in the figure—the inactives (1), the complete activists (2), the voting specialists (3), the communalists (4), and the campaigners(5).

The specific technique of cluster analysis that we use is called *hierarchical clustering*.[1] The most distinctive feature of this particular clustering method (and that which distinguishes it from classical clustering techniques) is that once individuals are placed into initial clusters, the *individual* distances separating them from each other and from others outside of the cluster are no longer directly employed in determining the composition of clusters on subsequent rounds. Once an individual is placed into a cluster his position in multidimensional space (and hence his distance from others) becomes that of the *centroid* or average position of the cluster to which he belongs. (The cluster centroids were represented by the heavy dark point of the approximate center of each of the clusters displayed in Figure F-1.) The values of the centroid are then used in calculating what further combinations are to be made. In this way, later rounds of clustering build on earlier ones. Thus the term *hierarchical clustering*. This technique is less exact then the classical methods of clustering (which preserve and utilize all of the individual distance comparisons at each round) but is the only method of clustering that is feasible with a sample the size of ours.[2]

---

[1] The most thorough treatment of cluster analysis is found in Robert C. Tryon and Daniel E. Bailey, *Cluster Analysis* (New York: McGraw-Hill, 1970). Hierarchical clustering is discussed in J. H. Ward Jr., "Hierarchical Grouping to Optimize an Objective Function," *American Statistical Association Journal* 58 (1963), pp. 236-244. For simple computer programming of the hierarchical clustering, see Donald J. Veldman, *Fortran Programming for the Behavioral Sciences* (New York: Holt, Rinehart and Winston, 1967), pp. 308-317.

[2] Because hierarchical clustering substitutes the cluster centroid or average, once individuals are placed into clusters it drastically reduces the number of distance comparisons that must be made and stored after the first few rounds of clustering have been made. It should be noted, however, that even with the vast reduction in computation and storage requirements obtained by the use of the hierarchical technique cluster analysis of any types is exceedingly costly and can only be performed on survey samples like ours if a very large and very inexpensive computer is available. The specific analysis reported below, for example, took over twenty minutes of CPU time on an IBM 360 model 75 computer. Furthermore, the task was reduced down to these barely manageable dimensions only by tailor-made programming and a complex yet efficient preclustering method that combined all cases with identical scores and created new weighted records from these. In this way actual clustering was required on only about 1,200 weighted cases rather than on the 2,549 cases actually in our file.

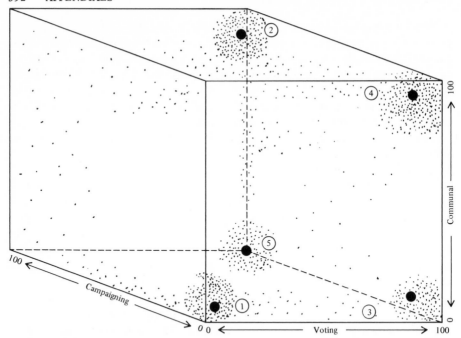

Figure F-1. A Pictoral Representation of a Hypothetical Cluster Analysis of Three of the Partipation Variables

The variables we employed in the cluster analysis were the factor scales of the four modes of participation (discussed in Appendix B.2). However, in order to achieve greater comparability in the computation of spatial distances, these scales have been transformed so that each ranges from zero to 100.[3] In the distance calculation phase of the clustering, two of the four scales have also been assigned differential weights. Distances between individuals and clusters on the campaign and communal activity have been assigned their full weights, while the weight for voting distances has been slightly reduced, and

[3] The cluster analysis was based on the four standardized participation factor scales that were introduced in Chapter 4 and described in greater detail in Appendix B.2. However, these scales were modified slightly in order to make them more amenable to cluster analysis and to the computation of spatial distances, which is the central portion of the clustering process. The transformation of the factor scales utilized attempts to make the measures better suited for clustering by removing extreme or outlying values, preserving the metric distances of the original measures (an important requirement of cluster analysis) while giving them a common range and scale, and trading identical means and standard deviations with differing ranges for variable means and standard deviations with identical ranges. This latter modification makes the individual score more reflective of the absolute amount of activity indicated by each of the modes.

There were two steps in the adjustment of the scales: (1) The extreme tails of the scale were truncated so that at least 10 percent of the total sample was assigned a value equal to the one containing the 10th or 90th percentile. For voting this meant that a few cases with extremely low values were moved up. For campaign and communal activity and particularized contacting, which are even more skewed but in the opposite direction, the upper 10 percent were reassigned values equal to those actually maintained by those in the 90th percentile. The truncation of the extremities in these scales were performed so that the extreme cases had a reasonable chance to combine with more significant segments of the population. (2) After the truncation of extreme values, the scales were transformed by the following formula so that each would have scales with identical ranges:

$$\text{T value} = (100/R_i) \cdot (V_{ij} - O_i)$$

that for particularized contacting substantially reduced.[4] Voting, and to a greater extent particularized contacting, therefore play a somewhat smaller role in determining which individuals will be grouped into the same cluster and which clusters will be combined into larger ones. The weights for these two modes of participation have been reduced because our previous analysis indicated that they are not very strongly related to the performance of other acts and are therefore likely to have a greater amount of unpatterned scatter. Furthermore, both modes are less central participatory characteristics in defining the more active types of participators and we did not want relatively random and theoretically unimportant variations in these variables to prevent those with otherwise highly similar patterns of participation from being clustered together.[5]

where:

R_i = the range of the ith participation variable (i.e., the maximum minus the minimum value of the oblique factor indices of voting, communal, and campaign activity after truncation of extreme values)

O_i = the origin or minimum value of the ith participation variable after truncation

AV_{ij} = the actual value ot the jth case on the ith participation variable after truncation

The division of $(100/R_i)$ produces a number equal to the worth of a unit of the ith participation variable as measured by the factor scale if that scale were to be given values ranging from zero to 100. The product of the multiplication of this factor times the number of units the individual is above the origin provides each respondent with a score within the zero to 100 range.

The following four sets of measures of central tendency and distribution describe the measures more precisely. A comparison of the means, medians, and direction of skew of the scales provides additional insight into the reasons for the emergent clusterings.

	Mean	Median	Standard Deviation	Skewness
Vote	76	87	36	−1.22
Campaign	29	13	35	1.02
Communal	28	14	37	.80
ParCon	14±			

±Because the transformation of particularized contacting results in a dichotomous variable, most statistics are inapplicable.

[4] If equal weighting were utilized, the distances would be calculated so that a ten-point difference between particularized contacting scores and a ten-point difference between campaign activity scores for two individuals would each contribute equally to the sum of the distances separating the two respondents. However, under our revised weighting scheme, these two individuals would be somewhat closer together (i.e., the sum of the distance would be smaller) and their distance from each other on particularized contacting would be less than that separating them on the campaign variable. The actual weights employed set the square of the distances separating particularized contacting at .50 of their original value, those for voting at .75, and those for campaign and communal were given full weights of 1.0.

[5] This problem is particularly significant for personalized contacts, first because of the almost total lack of correlation between this measure and the other modes of participation, and second, because of the way particularized contacting was measured. The reader will recall that the empirical distinction between particularized contacting and contacting on broader social issues was a totally *ex post facto* one made only after we discovered a number of clues as to the analysis. Further, while the resultant created measure appeared quite adequate for dimensional analysis, which requires only patterns of simple covariation, such a measure is not very well suited to the demands of cluster analysis. The factor scale score for particularized contacting is totally composed of two dichotomous items that were themselves split off from two more general questions about initiating contacts with public officials only at the coding stage. The result is that on this factor scale individuals can have only one of three values no matter how the scale is transformed. The majority of citizens, who by this crude measurement report no particularized contacts, have the lowest possible score. Those who have made one such contact have an intermediate score, and those few citizens who report two such contacts have the highest possible score. The truncation and transformation procedure then further reduced these to two scores. The 85 percent of the population who report no such contacts all have a score of zero, while the 15 percent making one or more such contact have a score of 100. The 3 percent who had made two such contacts were placed with the other 12 percent in order to eliminate the effects of extreme values. This procedure was used for all of the scales. (See footnote 3.)

We assigned a minimum size for an acceptable cluster: it must comprise at least 3 percent of the sample—an arbitrary but reasonable definition of a significant and analyzable segment of the population. And we established a criterion of internal homogeneity—i.e., the maximum average distance that can separate individuals in the same cluster.[6]

Within these two constraints the clustering attempted to place as many respondents as possible into the smallest number of acceptable clusters on the basis of their weighted distances from each other. Our preliminary attempt resulted in a set of clusters of sufficient size and sufficient internal homogeneity to meet our two criteria, plus a residual set of unacceptable clusters that did not. The questions we asked were, What proportion of the citizenry can be satisfactorally typologized by the clustering criteria, and how do these types compare to the six we expected to find as outlined in Table 4-8, p. 78?

The answer is that 83 percent of the sample were successfully classified into nine clusters meeting the size and homogeneity criteria. Six of these nine clusters display patterns of participation that closely match our predictions. Furthermore, the additional three acceptable clusters are not new and unexpected types of activists but rather "shadow" or variant groups of several of the six types we expected to find. The data are reported in Table F-1. The table presents the nine acceptable clusters and their patterns of political activity. For each of the clusters or types, the table presents its mean level of activity on the four participation modes and the percentage of the total sample falling into the cluster. The first six clusters correspond to those we predicted we would find in Table F-1 and are labeled accordingly. The last three are the "variant" clusters. We can consider them briefly.

1. *The Inactives (14%):* The first cluster, of those we predicted, consists of 14 percent of the sample and clearly contains the inactives. These citizens engage in virtually no political activity, and have means at or near zero on all four modes of activity.

2. *The Voting Specialists (21%):* Those in this cluster vote quite regularly, but engage in no other form of participation. This is the single largest cluster comprising 21 percent of the sample and matching the voting specialist profile predicted by our analysis.

3. *The Parochial Participants (3%):* This is the smallest cluster, containing a little less than 3.5 percent of the sample. But it has a unique activity profile. Each respondent in this cluster has initiated at least one particularized contact but none engaged in any significant amount of campaign or communal

---

[6] The measure of homogeneity is the mean distance of the individuals from the cluster centroid and is termed the *mean error*. Unfortunately there are few agreed-upon guidelines for determining the amount of acceptable error. The size of the error is, of course, affected not only by the relative distance but also by the scale of the variables. It was for this reason that we standardized the scales so that all ranged from zero to 100. Ultimately we set the mean error criteria at 22 units. This is the maximum permissible average sum of the distance of cases from the cluster centroid. The point was chosen by executing experimental clusters on small numbers of cases and assessing their degree of homogeneity under various mean error criteria. The 22-unit criterion appeared to produce quite homogeneous clusters yet was generous enough so that a significant proportion of the cases was likely to cluster.

Table F-1

Cluster Analysis of the Modes of Participation: Initial Clusterings (Acceptable clusters only)^{ab}

	Participation profile				Percentage of total sample
Cluster type	Voting	Campaign activity	Communal activity	Particularized contacting	
1. Inactive	7	11	3	00	14.5
2. Voting specialists	95	5	3	0	21
3. Parochial activists	81	13	4	100	3
4. Communalists	95	20	89	0	9
5. Campaigners	97	92	25	0	6
6. Complete activists	97	92	93	0	9
7. Inactives with occasional voting	51	7	2	0	7
8. Shadow communalists	93	10	47	0	8
9. Shadow campaigners	93	46	3	0	6
Remainder from un- acceptable clusters					16.5
Total population means	76	28	29	13	100%

Predicted clusters: (clusters 1–6)
Other acceptable clusters: (clusters 7–9)

^{a}Full reports on mean error for all clusters are reported in Tables F-3 and F-4, at the end of this appendix.
^{b}These means include unclassified as well as classified factors of the population.

activity. (Their scores on these two scales are just as low as those found among the totally inactive citizens.) The frequency of voting among this group is about average for the population as a whole, which is also consistent with our predictions.

4. *The Communalists (9%):* As expected, the most striking characteristic of the communalists is the contrast between their unusually high level of communal participation and their low level of campaign activity. They also vote with considerable frequency.

5. *The Campaigners (6%):* The campaigners grouped in this cluster display a pattern of participation that is the mirror image of that of the communalists—a high rate of campaign activity and a low level of communal involvement. Like the communalists, these citizens are very regular voters.

6. *The Complete Activists (9%):* The last of the predicted types is the group of complete activists. Those clustered here vote, participate in campaigns, and engage in communal activity—and do all three with exceptional frequency. The only type of activity they do not perform is particularized contacting, and here we made no predictions.

The first six types of participators match our predictions almost perfectly. A detailed examination of the cluster characteristics of these groups indicate that they have a great deal of internal homogeneity.[7] The six groups together constitute over 60 percent of the total sample and almost 80 percent of those who were successfully classified by the cluster criteria.

We now turn to the three remaining (nonpredicted) clusters to see how they relate to the expected set.

7. *The Occasionally Voting Inactivists (7%):* The citizens grouped here are in many ways similar to the inactives: They engage in negligible amounts of campaign activity, communal activity, and particularized contacting. However, this group differs from the inactives in that they sometimes vote. They are, however, far from regular voters. They score, on the average, 51 on the voting scale. This is about twenty-five points below the mean for the population as a whole. Such a score would be obtained by a citizen who perhaps voted in one Presidential election (but only one) and never in local elections; or perhaps voted occasionally at the local level but missed both Presidential elections about which we asked.[8] In short, these citizens may best be characterized as inactives who occasionally show up at the polls. It would appear to do little damage to either our typology or to social reality if this group were to be combined with the inactives (cluster 1). This we have done in all our subsequent analyses.

[7] A complete report on the cluster analysis excluding levels of mean error for acceptable and nonacceptable clusters is in Tables F-3 and F-4.

[8] Though the voting mean of this group appears to place them almost exactly between the inactives and the voting specialists, the numbers are, in this case, a bit deceiving for their frequency of voting is in reality much closer to that of the inactives. The voting scale is strongly skewed in the positive direction—the mean for the population is 76 and the median is 85. Almost 45 percent of the population score the maximum possible on the voting scale of 100, while only 10 percent have scores of zero. A score of 51 corresponds to the 20th percentile of the voting scale.

8. *The "Shadow" Communalists (8%):* The respondents grouped into this cluster display a pattern of participatory involvement much like that of the communal activists. Like the communalists, they vote regularly, and their most salient characteristic is the large discrepancy between their levels of communal and campaign activity. The main difference between this group and the earlier cluster of communalists is that the level of activity for this group is much lower.

However, the communalists and the shadow communalists are not quite as different as the numbers might suggest. First, the shadow communalists engage in much more communal activity than a mean of 47 (on a scale ranging from zero to 100) might appear to indicate. The population average on that scale is 27, thus this group scores twenty points above the average for the population. Most of this group perform at least two or the five relatively difficult communal acts.[9] Second, while the shadow communalists have lower scores on the communal index than do the true communalists (cluster 4), their level of campaign participation is also much lower—thus the contrast which is the central feature of both groups remains strong.

9. *The Shadow Campaigners (6%):* The relationship of those in this last cluster to the campaigners of cluster 5 closely parallels the relationship between the two types of communalists. Both clusters of campaigners have similarly high voting frequencies and both engage in a considerable amount of campaign activity in comparison to their low rate of communal participation. At the same time, the shadow campaigners perform less of both types of activity than do those in the original cluster of campaigners. Every argument we made about the essential similarity of the two communalist groups could be made here. The shadow campaigners also engage in much more campaign participation than the average citizen does, and the contrast between the level of campaign and communal activity is, if anything, even sharper here.

The nine types of participators located through the cluster analysis present us with a more refined typology of political activists than the six types we originally expected. No doubt there is some difference between a totally inactive citizen and one who occasionally votes. There is probably an even more significant difference between a campaigner or communalist who performs four to five difficult acts and one who engages in only two such activities. Nevertheless, each of the three additional types clearly reflects one of the basic patterns of political activism that we expected to find. Given this

---

[9] The observant reader at this point might ask why is it that a score of 51 on the voting scale reflects very low frequencies of voting while a score of 47 on the communal activity scale is said to stand for a considerable amount of activity. The answer lies in the way social reality gets translated into our measures. Most people vote with considerable regularity and thus the mean voting rate is 76. Fewer people are highly active in the more difficult acts of communal participation and this is reflected in its population mean of 28. Communal activity and voting are, in reality and in our measures, skewed in the opposite directions. This skew means that less than a third of the sample have a communal activity score of greater than 40 while over 80 percent of the sample have this score or greater on the voting index. Had we reported medians rather than means, the shadow communalists would have looked much more active when compared to the population as a whole, and the occasionally voting inactives would have appeared much closer to the inactives than to the voting specialists.

fact, we have, in our analysis, combined the citizens who fell into clusters 7 through 9 with the clusters they most nearly resemble among the original six. In doing this, we blur some distinctions. Nevertheless, the groups we combine are sufficiently similar, the combined types sufficiently distinct, and the gains to be obtained by simplifying the typology substantial enough that we feel justified in making these combinations.

RECLUSTERING ON PARTICULARIZED CONTACTING: A NECESSARY REFINEMENT

There is one glaring anomaly in the patterns of clustering reported in Table F-1 that is not totally consistent with our expectations. With the exception of the parochial activists who concentrate on particularized contacting, none of the respondents in any of the other clusters report making such contacts. The total absence of individuals making particularized contacts among the communalists, campaigners, and complete activists is particularly puzzling given their high level of participation on other equally demanding modes of activity. An examination of the residual groupings that failed to meet the minimal cluster criteria quickly revealed what happened during the clustering to those who combined personalized contacts with other modes of participation.

For each type of activist in our typology (with the exception of the inactives and the voting specialists) there is a parallel residual grouping that displays an almost identical pattern of political activity except for the fact that the citizens in those clusters report making particularized contacts. But the distance between those who make such contacts and those who do not was too great for them to be grouped into the same clusters despite the fact that they had virtually identical scores on the other three modes of activity, and despite the fact that particularized contacting was underweighted in the calculation in an attempt to prevent this from happening.[10]

Part of the explanation has to do with the way particularized contacting was measured.[11] But more important is the almost total lack of relationship between particularized contacting and the other modes of activity. Because it has a random relationship to the performance of other acts, any type of participator might or might not make such contacts. And this is, of course, consistent with the specific contingent problems that are the subject of such contacts—problems that can affect any type of citizen. The way we measured particularized contacting exacerbated this tendency and made the reduction in

---

[10] All of the residual clusters involving those who have made particularized contacts are reported in the table below. There are several interesting findings in this table. The clusters are strikingly similar to those reported in Table F-2. Only two of the eight clusters contain patterns that are not virtually identical to those in Table F-2 and one of these has only eight cases in it. The fact that the particularized contactors from the same patterns of activity as the noncontactors testifies to the soundness of the solution. It is almost like breaking the sample into separate parts and replicating the analysis—an often-recommended statistical procedure, and one in this case that yields a similar solution. Also, these clusters constitute half of all of the unclustered portion of the sample even though particularized contacts are made by less than 15 percent of the sample.

[11] See footnote 5 for a discussion of the measurement of particularized contacting.

weighting inadequate to overcome the more or less random spread of particularized contacting among those who engage in other forms of activity.

We made no prediction about the rate of particularized contacting (in Table F-1) for those participators who were active in the other demanding modes of participation—i.e., for the communalists, campaigners, and complete activists—because we felt it made no difference. Particularized contacting defines a citizen's participatory pattern only when he performs this relatively difficult act but does nothing else except perhaps vote intermittently. This pattern defines the parochial participant. His exclusive involvement with the government as a provider of particularized benefits makes him an interesting and unique type of participant. As for those citizens who participate actively *vis-à-vis* broad social outcomes, some may also make particularized demands

Table F-2
Participatory Profiles of the American Citizenry

		Scores on participation scales for		
	Voting	Campaign activity	Communal activity	Particularized contacting
1. Inactives	37	9	3	0
2. Voting specialists	94	5	3	0
3. Parochial participants	73	13	3	100
4. Communalists	92	16	69	12
5. Campaigners	95	70	16	13
6. Complete activists	98	93	92	15
Unclassifiable population $\overline{X}$	76	29	28	14

Participation Profiles of All Nonacceptable Clusters Involving Particularized Contactors

		Participation Profile			
Cluster type	Voting	Campaign activity	Communal activity	Particularized contacting	Percentage of sample
1. Complete activist	99	98	89	100	1.4
2. Campaigner I	100	93	36	100	.5
3. Campaigner II	91	82	5	100	1.1
4. Communalist I	89	22	95	100	1.2
5. Communalist II	88	7	46	100	1.4
6. Low-vote parochial participants	44	17	5	100	1.2
7. ?	2	5	57	100	.2 (8 cases)
8. ?	94	36	41	100	.9
					7.9

Table F-3

Cluster Analysis of the Modes of Participation: Acceptable and Unacceptable Clusters

		Participation profile				
Cluster type	Voting	Campaign activity	Communal activity	Particularized contacting	Percentage of total sample	Mean error of cluster
Predicted clusters						
1. Inactive	7	11	3	0	14	21
2. Voting specialists	95	5	3	0	21	12
3. Parochial activists	81	13	4	100	3	20
4. Communalists	95	20	89	0	9	22
5. Campaigners	97	92	25	0	6	22
6. Complete activists	97	92	93	0	9	16
Other acceptable clusters						
7. Inactives with occasional voting	51	7	2	0	7	16
8. Shadow communalists	93	10	47	0	8	16
9. Shadow campaigners	93	46	3	0	6	17
Unacceptable clusters						
10. Error too big and size too small						
Complete activist (with particularized contacting)	99	98	89	100	1.4	13
Campaigner (part. con.)[a]	100	93	36	100	.5	13
Campaigner (part. con.)	91	82	5	100	1.1	24
Communalist (part. con.)	89	22	95	100	1.2	18
Communalist (part. con.)	88	7	46	100	1.4	21
Low-vote parochial "	44	17	5	100	1.2	24
a. ???	2	5	57	0	.2	30
b. ???	94	36	41	0	.9	20
c. ???	54	7	62	0	1.1	27
d. ???	9	2	64	0	.9	27
e. ???	50	16	40	0	1.5	31
f. ???	2	5	40	0	1.4	36
Total population means[b]	76	28	29	13	95.8%	

[a]"Part. con.": i.e., who engages in particularized contacts.
[b]These means include unclassified as well as classified portions of the population.

Table F-4

Participatory Profiles of the American Citizenry

	Scores on participation scales for					
	Voting	Campaign activity	Communal activity	Particularized contacting	Percentage of sample in type	Mean error of cluster
1. Voting specialists	94	5	3	0	21	11
2. Parochial participants	73	13	3	100	4	15
3. Communalists	95	19	89	11	11	20
4. Shadow communalists	92	10	47	13	9	17
5. Campaigners	97	93	28	15	8	21
6. Shadow campaigners	94	48	6	11	7	18
7. Inactives	7	11	4	0	14	20
8. Occasionally voting inactives	55	7	4	0	8	15
9. Complete activists	98	93	92	15	11	16
Unclassifiable					93 7 100%	

and some may not. Whether they do or not is, at most, an ancillary characteristic of their participatory behavior.

For these reasons it would have been an error to delete from the typology those cases that had not been classified simply because they combine particularized contacting with other definable pattern of participation. We therefore reclustered all residual cases to determine if they would have been placed into existing clusters were it not for the fact that they engaged in some particularized contacting. The method we used is called *seed clustering* because existing clusters become the seeds around which additional clustering can take place.[12] In this clustering we ignored rates of particularized contacting (i.e., gave their distances weights of zero) for all clusters except for the two inactivist groups (clusters 1 and 7 in Table F-1).[13] However, we permit additional cases to fall into existing clusters only if they do not appreciably raise the total mean error of the clusters to which they are being assigned.[14] This second round of clustering allowed us to place about half of the 16 percent that had been unassigned into one or another cluster.

THE FINAL CLUSTER RESULT

In summary, our cluster analysis went through several stages: the initial clustering that produced nine main groups plus a miscellany of additional groups, the reassignment of the occasional voters and the "shadow" communalists and campaigners, and the reassignment of the activists who also engaged in particularized contacting. The result is our refined typology of political actors reported in Table 4-9, p. 80. Table F-2 gives the mean scores for these final groupings on the participation scales. Table F-3 reports on the original hierarchical clustering solution that went into the seed clustering. Table F-4 reports on the seed clustering results.

[12] For different uses of the "seed" method, see Tryon and Bailey, *op. cit.*, chapter 8. The seed method usually is used as a trial value when the expected pattern of cluster is otherwise known or as the final criterion of the core clusters if there are good theoretical grounds to specify them.

[13] In the seed clustering we also enable the occasionally voting parochial participants (cluster 6 in the table in footnote 11) to combine with the other parochial activists (9n cluster 4 of Table F-2). We do this because the frequency of voting is not a central defining characteristic of the parochial activists.

[14] In actual calculation the assignment of cases to the seed clusters is on the basis of their distance from the existing cluster centroid. The mean error of the cluster is recomputed after each case is added to make sure that cases added by this method do not reduce the homogeneity of the cluster as originally constituted. Of course those variables that are not weighted are not counted in the calculation of distance or error. All the nonclassified cases were reclustered regardless of whether or not they involved particularized contacts. Supplementing a hierarchical cluster analysis with a seed clustering is generally a good idea for one of the few drawbacks of the hierarchical method is that once placed into clusters, individuals never have a chance to recombine with other clusters even though latter rounds of clustering may produce clusters that are closer to its profile than the original cluster in which it was placed. The seed clustering then permits these "misassigned" cases to be grouped with the appropriate cluster so long as they are sufficiently near the cluster centroid not to introduce any new error.

Appendix G
Some Methodological Notes on Our Use of Parametric Statistics

G.1. GENERAL COMMENTS ON USING PARAMETRIC STATISTICS WITH ORDINAL SURVEY DATA

In many parts of this book we use linear and parametric statistics (such as means, Pearson correlation coefficients, factor analysis, and multiple regressions) to describe relationships among variables. In view of the continuing controversy over the appropriateness of the use of parametric statistics with ordinal data, some comments and justifications are in order. These comments address themselves to two issues. First, why use such statistical techniques instead of others whose assumptions are more justified given the measurement level of our variables? Second, what are the probable effects (distortions, biases, etc.), if any, that result from the use of such techniques?

There are three factors that have led us to rely upon linear and parametric statistics. First, our dependent variables are strong multiple-item indexes based on ordinal survey items. Through factor analysis we create standardized participation scales that have good ability to differentiate and provide a useful metric. Furthermore, these standard participation scales are the product of comparatively "hard" survey data—they are reports of behavior rather than attitudes or opinions. These characteristics of our scales allow us to employ strong and sensitive measures of variation and covariation, and keep us from losing information by a gross classification of respondents as high, medium, and low participants.

Second, we felt we needed summary measures in order to display our many relationships in a concise and easily understandable format. In order to present our relationships in cross-tabular format, we would have been forced either to dichotomize our participation measures, or to present tables with a large number of difficult-to-read cells.

Third and most important, many of the most interesting and significant relationships examined in this book involve a relatively large number of variables, and there are simply no manageable nonparametric statistical techniques for such tasks. For example, there is no well-developed ordinal or nonparametric counterpart for factor or cluster analysis—at least as usable techniques. To deal with the question of the empirical structure of participation in a systematic way implies, almost by definition, the use of parametric techniques.

Furthermore, our attempts to unblock the complex package of forces that lead to participation also led us to parametric statistical techniques. Though there are a number of bivariate ordinal measures of association, the many limitations of these ordinal statistics are well known. They do not lend themselves to easy interpretation or to easy manipulation, and most important, few if any can be used in multivariate situations.[1]

Without the use of linear statistics, even those investigations involving three or four variables, such as the analysis of age and participation in Chapter 9, would have been virtually impossible.

The important question is what effects, if any, such procedures are likely to have had on our interpretation of the causes and consequences of participation and what types of precautions one can take to guard against such effects. Since Stevens' classic proscriptions[2] on the appropriateness of various statistics

---

[1] Recent developments in this area include: James A. Davis, "A Partial Coefficient for Goodman and Kruskal's Gamma," *Journal of the American Statistical Association* 62 (January 1967), pp. 187-190; Leo A. Goodman and William H. Kruskal, "Measures of Association for Cross-classifications," Journal of the *American Statistical Association* 49 (July 1954), pp. 732-764, and "Measures of Association for Cross-classifications. III. Approximate Sampling Theory," *Journal of the American Statistical Association* 58 (April 1963), pp. 310-364; Ronald K. Hawkes, "The Multivariate Analysis of Ordinal Data," *American Journal of Sociology* 76 (March 1971), pp. 908-926; Maurice G. Kendall, *Rank Correlation Methods.* 2d ed. (London: Griffin, 1959); Jae-On Kim, "Predictive Measures of Ordinal Association," *American Journal of Sociology* 76 (March 1971), pp. 891-907; Raymond N. Morris, "Multiple Correlation and Ordinally Scaled Data," *Social Forces* 48 (March 1970), pp. 299-311. Robert H. Somers, "A New Asymmetric Measure of Association for Ordinal Variables," *American Sociological Review* 27 (December 1962), pp. 799-811, and "An Approach to the Multivariate Analysis of Ordinal Data," *American Sociological Review* 33 (December 1968), pp. 971-977. Ordinal statistics presented in these papers are still a long way from providing us with good or comparable multivariate capacity.

[2] S. S. Stevens, "On the Theory of Scales of Measurement," *Science* 103 (June 1946), pp. 677-680. He presents the now well-known four levels of measurements—nominal, ordinal, interval, and ratio scales, with appropriate statistics.

for different scales of measurement, most social researchers and many statistics texts, particularly those designed for social scientists, have followed his lead.[3] In the last few years however, the extent to which these cautions should be followed absolutely has been questioned.[4] The strongest case for using parametric statistics on ordinal data is based on a number of practical experiments that compare relationships among variables using both parametric and nonparametric measures. Their general conclusions tend to support what many nonstatisticians in the data analysis field have suspected for some time—that the use of parametric or "strong statistics" on ordinal or rank data usually effects neither the description of the general magnitude of relationships, nor levels of statistical significance when compared with what is found with parallel nonparametric or ordinal measures.[5] In short, some evidence suggests that there is nothing inappropriate about using interval measures of association on scales of ordinal measurement, provided that the resultant interpretation or application of the statistics is congruent with the level of measurement of the given data.

Even if one accepts these general guidelines, as we do, there exist a number of dangers in applying linear statistics. There are the issues of curvilinearity and interaction. Linear statistics, whether used on interval or ordinal data, assume linear relationships or at least strongly monotonic ones. Whenever there exists curvilinearity, contingent relationships, or interaction terms, linear correlation or any multivariate extensions thereof (e.g., multiple regression factor analysis) will produce incorrect estimates of the nature and magnitude of the relationship. Given our heavy reliance on linear association, we have tried to be as careful as possible in this regard, consistently checking for nonlinear relationships, interaction terms, and contingent relationships.

Through the course of our analysis we have uncovered a number of relationships of each sort—findings that themselves speak to the importance of remaining sensitive to these issues. We uncovered a curvilinear relationship between age and participation,[6] and in Chapter 18 between levels of commu-

[3] Two of the well known texts are Hubert M. Blalock Jr., *Social Statistics* (New York: McGraw-Hill, 1960) and Sidney Siegel, *Nonparametric Statistics for the Behavioral Sciences* (New York: McGraw-Hill, 1956).

[4] Examples are found in B. O. Baker, C. F. Hardyck, and L. F. Petrinovich, "Weak Measurements vs. Strong Statistics," *Educational and Psychological Measurement* 26 (1966), also in B. Lieberman (ed.) *Contemporary Problems in Statistics* (Oxford University Press, 1971), pp. 370-381; Sanford Labovitz, "Some Observations on Measurement and Statistics," *Social Forces* 46 (December 1967), pp. 151-160, and "The Assignment of Numbers to Rank Order Categories," *American Sociological Review* 35 (June 1970), pp. 515-525. But the controversy is by no means completely resolved by these studies. For continuing discussion, see comments by Lawrence S. Mayer, Sybil and Donal Schweitzers, Louis G. Vargo, as well as Labovitz replies in *American Sociological Review* 36 (June 1971), pp. 517-522.

[5] See F. M. Lord, "On the Statistical Treatment of Football Numbers," *American Psychologist* 8 (1953), pp. 750-751.

[6] Since the middle aged group tends to be more active than the others, age was divided into six categories and was represented by five dummy variables to account for the resulting curvilinearity. For the discussion of the uses of dummy variables, see J. Fennessey, "The General Linear Model: A New Perspective on Some Familiar Topics," *American Journal of Sociology* 74 (July 1968), pp. 1-27; D. B. Suits, "The Uses of Dummy Variables in Regression Equations," *Journal of the American Statistical Association* 52 (December 1957), pp. 548-551.

nity participation and degree of leader concurrence. We located and described a number of contingent relationships (such as that between participation and ideology that appear to operate for Republicans but not for Democrats). We dealt with contingent relationships between participation and leader concurrence in consensual vs. nonconsensual communities—where the relationships often ran in opposite directions.

Finally, in a number of places we located interaction effects. An example is our analysis of the relationship between participation and some of the characteristics of organizational involvement. In short, the reliance on linear statistics is not incompatible with the location of nonlinear relationships as long as care is taken to make sure that relationships described in linear terms are indeed linear.

Perhaps the only actual problem entailed in using parametric statistics involves the estimation of population parameters when the measures upon which correlations and regression weights are computed are ordinal rather than interval in scale. Hence, for example, the standard procedure of squaring Pearson's r to obtain the amount of variance in variable X, which can be accounted for by variable Y, becomes much more tenuous when the variables involved are of ordinal rather than interval scales. In this regard we have tried wherever possible to avoid such interpretations, which involve estimating population parameters, though in a few instances we do come close to such interpretations. In those few places where we do make such statements we tend to deal with the relationship among our standard participation scales or between those scales and some independent variable that itself approaches interval measurement. Because the standardized participation scales are interval in "form" (having standard units of participation stemming from the factor analysis) and because we interpret the relationships in terms of the increases and decreases in "our" standardized participation units and not in terms of more global participation measures or even other measures, we do not feel that our interpretations are a significant violation of the statistical guidelines. More often, our interpretations of the parametric statistics simply compare differences among groups or subpopulations, and in these, by far the most numerous applications, there is no attempt to estimate population parameters.

G.2. LINEAR CORRECTIONS THROUGH REGRESSION RESIDUALS

We use linear adjustments as a method of control in many parts of this book, especially when more than one control variable is involved. We use this method in order to isolate the effect of some independent variable while controlling for either the prior or the confounding effects of other characteris-. tics. By such techniques, for example, we are able to examine the relationship between race and participation, controlling for the different class compositions of blacks and whites. We are able to deal with the effects of institutional involvements such as participation in voluntary associations while controlling for many of the demographic factors that account for the differential rates of involvement in organizations. We use statistical linear controls rather than actual or cross-tabular ones for several related reasons to which we alluded earlier. First, we use them because of the problem of disappearing Ns that is involved even when large samples are utilized. Only one, or at most two, control variables can be used in cross-tabular analysis before some cells have virtually no cases left in them. For this reason it is impossible even to think of dealing with three or more cross-tabulated control variables. Second, even if our sample was of an unlimited size it would be impossible to display or interpret data involving more than one or two control variables using cross-tabular techniques.

The basic mechanism of control we use takes out all the "linear" effects of the control variable or variables from the dependent variable. The rationale is that the observed relationship between the independent and the residual dependent variable is the result of "additional" impact of the independent variable (independent, that is, of all of the confounding effects of the control variables). The actual control is accomplished through multiple regression using the b's, or regression weights, as the best estimate of the independent linear impact of each of the control variables. The residual or corrected variable is what is left after the regression prediction has been made.

To be more concrete, let us consider the following example. Each of our respondents has a score on the overall participation index. In order to give him a new score, corrected for his characteristics of life position, including his age, sex, race, and social status, we obtain a multiple regression prediction equation, which gives an estimate of his predicted score given his particular set of social characteristics. We then subtract this predicted score from his actual score. This new variable is then his corrected measure of participation once we have accounted for his social characteristics. If a respondent's predicted and actual score are the same, it can be said that he participates at a rate expected from his social characteristics. If his predicted score is greater than his actual score, he can be said to participate less than one would expect given his characteristics; and finally, if his actual score is greater than his predicted score, he can be said to be an overparticipator.

This new, or corrected, measure can then be related to some other characteristic such as level of organizational involvement, strength of identification with political parties, or type of community in which one lives. In each of these instances we can ask what type and how much additional impact such variables have, after one has corrected for the prior, or confounding, effects of social characteristics. A fuller discussion on how those residual measures are to be read and interpreted is presented in Chapter 9.

Three problems must be faced, however, when employing this type of linear correction. First, the relationships among the control variables themselves and the relationships between each of the control variables and the dependent variable must be linear. However, nonlinear relationships can be handled by breaking the variables at their points of nonlinearity and thereby converting the variable into a series of dummy variables. Such dummy variables were created and used, for example, for the curvilinear relationship between age and participation.[7] If all the relationships involved in the regression correction are approximately linear, or if the nonlinear relationships have been correctly handled through the dummy variable technique, the correction should be quite sound and unbiased.

The second problem, that of potential interaction effects, is related to the first problem, but it is an independent one, and more difficult to handle. Interaction between two control variables and the dependent variable means that some joint set of values of the two predictor variables has a nonadditive effect on the dependent variable. For example, the relationship between income and education can be linear, as can the relationship between each of the variables and participation. But if having both high income and high education give one an inordinate boost in rate of participation (i.e., a more than additive increase), then there is significant interaction. Interaction is a difficult problem because it is hard to locate. It may only occur, for example, for those who share a particular combination of values of three variables. Obviously, all of the combinations and permutations can never be fully checked. Once discovered, such interaction terms can be quite easily incorporated into the general linear model by dummy variables. Although we tried to be careful to examine relationships for interaction wherever they seemed likely, it was impossible to conduct a full-scale test for interaction in every situation.

The third issue that deserves consideration in this discussion of the analysis of regression residuals lies outside of the biases or distortions in the regression equation itself. It pertains to the consequences of correlation between the independent variable and the control variable. If one or more of the control variables is associated with the independent variable—which is true most of the time and in fact is the *raison d'être* of the control technique—we are likely to be taking out too much by taking out all the linear effects of this control variable. In fact, whenever there is association we will be taking out some of the effects for which the control variables and the independent variable are jointly responsible. Therefore the strategy of analysis implied by the use of linear adjustment is a conservative one.

For this reason the control procedure used here makes best sense if there is clear hierarchical structure among the control and independent variables. For instance, if we are willing to examine the impact of organizational involvement after giving all the credit to social-status variables, we do not lose anything by taking out all the impact of social-status variables from the dependent variable. The resultant relationship between the residual dependent variable and organizational involvement will tell us about the "additional" impact of organizational activity. We are therefore not trying to estimate the total "independent" impact of organizational involvement; we merely want to

[7] See footnote 6, p. 405.

ascertain whether some significant additional effect exists. One may consider this method of control as a compromise solution to a full-fledged analysis of covariance.

Given the options and methods of control, we think on balance that this method is a particularly good one. Though the method is more conservative than is desirable, the residuals are quite easy to construct and to work with, and far easier to communicate than the only reasonable alternative, full analysis of covariance.

Appendix H
Description of the Sample of Local Community Leaders

In each of our sixty-four target communities, seven leaders were interviewed. They were selected on the basis of position, and an attempt was made to cover the widest number of sectors and institutions as possible within the limitations of our seven interviews, which were distributed in the following way:

1. Highest local elected official. Most often, this was the mayor. Occasionally it was the president of some local governing council. In the several places without any elected leadership, it was the highest elected official in the county who had special responsibilities for the locality.

2. The highest elected official of the county in which the community is located. When there was no elected official within the community, two county officials were interviewed, i.e., the head plus a second elected official or if necessary an appointed official with some special responsibility for the community or area of the county in which the community was located.

3-4. The heads or presidents of the largest local Democratic and/or Republican organizations or clubs. If there were no Democratic and/or

Republican organizations within the community, the head(s) of the county party organization(s) was interviewed about the locality.

5. Business leader. The president of the local chamber of commerce was interviewed. However, when there was no local chamber of commerce the proprietor of the largest commercial or manufacturing establishment was interviewed.

6. The resident editor or publisher of the largest local newspaper. The following selection rules were used: If both were residents of the community, the publisher was interviewed; if the publisher was a nonresident, the editor was interviewed. When there was more than one daily newspaper, the head of the largest was interviewed. If there was no daily paper, the head of the largest weekly was selected. If there were no local newspapers at all, we checked on radio stations and interviewed the appropriate head. If this search process still yielded no meaningful head of local media, the head of the nearest daily was asked to give us the name of the most knowledgeable local newsman. If this produced no meaningful name, no interview was attempted.

7. The head of the local school board. The highest more or less full-time working official was interviewed. If there was no appropriate head of the school board, the principal of the largest secondary school was interviewed. If the school district was county wide or a consolidated one serving more than one community the highest official responsible for education in the target community was selected. If the target community was served by more than one district, one of the following procedures was followed: The head of the district serving the largest portion of the community was interviewed if all but a small section of the community was served by it; if both districts served a sizable portion of the community, interviews were conducted with heads of both; if the community was served by more than two districts, the heads or most responsible officials of the two numerically most important districts were interviewed.

Each of these leaders was treated identically in the calculation of the concurrence scores (see Appendix I). When elites were used as informants about various community characteristics, their responses were either aggregated and averaged or the information was obtained from the appropriate leaders' interviews depending on whether or not the information was general or within their special domain. For example, when obtaining information on the variety of organiztions within the community, the responses of all the elites were utilized. On the other hand, when attempting to ascertain the activity levels of the local party organizations, the party leaders were relied on as the sole informants.

Appendix I
The Computation of Citizen Elite Concurrence Scores

CONCURRENCE ON COMMUNITY PRIORITIES

Citizens were asked the following question in the cross-section interview: What is the most important problem facing this community?

The local leadership sample was asked the following three questions: (1) What is the most important problem facing this community? (2) We have been talking about what you think are the local problems—now what does the average person around here think are *his* problems and needs? (3) I would like to know if there are some community problems that you have been particularly active in trying to solve—which are the two problems to which you have given most time and effort?

Two answers were recorded to the questions asked of the citizens; three to each of the questions asked of the leaders. The questions were coded by using the same open-end code. This code contained several hundred specific categories of answers. These categories were broken down into twenty-five categories of problems that still remain rather specific in their referent. Well over 90 percent of the answers could be placed in these twenty-five categories.

The number of responses that fell in each of the categories was summed for the set of leaders in each community. This was done separately for the leaders' answers to each of the three questions they were asked. A concurrence score was then computed for each of the cross-section respondents based on how closely the set of leader responses matched his own. This is equal to the number of times the citizens' chosen problems appear among the members of the leadership sample in the community, divided by the number of elites in the elite sample in the community. This number is then multiplied by 100, making it equal to a percentage of the leaders who concur with the citizens' community priority schedule.

The concurrence score for each respondent in the cross-section sample was computed separately for the match between the respondent's mention of community problems and the leadership sample's mention of problems that they *thought* the community faced, that they *thought the citizens thought* the community faced, and that they reported they *were working on*. These were then averaged, and each individual was given an overall concurrence score. Separate analyses of the three measures of concurrence—concurrence between citizen attitudes on the one hand, and the leaders' own attitudes, perception of citizen attitudes, and activity—indicated that although there were differences among them, they were similar enough to be combined into a single measure. In addition, a concurrence score for the community as a whole was computed. It is simply the average of the concurrence scores of all the citizens in the sample in each community.

The notion of concurrence can be understood by a simple example. Suppose a citizen said that the main problem facing the community was traffic. If all the leaders in our sample for that community had said they thought traffic was a problem, the citizen's concurrence score would be 100—indicating that 100 percent of the community leaders agreed with him. If half had mentioned traffic, his score would be 50; if no leader mentioned traffic, the citizen would get a score of zero. This would be the concurrence between citizen views of problems and leaders' own views. A similar score would be computed for the proportion of times a problem mentioned by a citizen turned out to be that on which a leader was working and the proportion of times it turned out to be that which a leader perceived as the views of the citizens. The average of these three scores formed the overall concurrence score for the citizen. Average that for the community, and one has community level concurrence score. In short, the concurrence score for a community can be thought of as a measure of the relative frequency with which the problems reported by the citizens of a community are also reported by the leaders.

One complication involved the fact that some respondents gave no valid answers to the question on community problems (they said they did not know, or had just moved to town, or they gave vague and uncodeable answers), other respondents gave one codeable answer, and others gave two codeable answers. The number of valid answers given, of course, affects the concurrence score. To give no answer means that leaders could not agree; to give two answers means that one's chance of receiving agreement from leaders is greater than if

Table I-1

Example of Computation of Concurrence Score for Individual Respondent

Categories of community problems	X Number of times mentioned by leadership sample in community	Y Respondent's answers: 0 = not mentioned 1 = mentioned	Q
1	5	0	
2	3	1	3
3	0	0	
4	2	0	
5	2	0	
6	0	1^a	
7	1	0	Q = the largest
.	.	.	number in column
.	.	.	X that is paralleled
.	.	.	by a 1 in column
25	0	0	Y.

Q = 3
N = number of elite respondents = 9
Concurrence = Q/N 100 = 33.3

^{a}If one or two leaders had mentioned problem 6, this would not have affected the respondent's score, since we assign him a matching score on the problem where he receives the most agreement. If four leaders had mentioned problem 6 we would assign him that score and ignore the agreement on problem 2. If three leaders mentioned 6, he would get a score of 3—it would not matter for which.

one gave one answer. This, we felt, was not unwarranted from a substantive point of view. The citizen who can not articulate a problem is unlikely to receive concurrence, and the citizen who is very articulate is more likely to receive concurrence. But it did leave the gnawing problem that our concurrence measure might really be measuring articulateness.

Our solution was to score those who could mention no problem as having a concurrence score of zero. They were few and we felt that the substantive argument outweighed the methodological concern. However, the citizens who mentioned more than one problem were larger in number—about half the sample. They were not given a concurrence score equal to that received on both problems mentioned, but equal to that received on the problem where concurrence was greatest. This gives them a bonus for being articulate, but not as great as it would be if we computed concurrence for both problems.

Last, to check on the possible contaminating effect of articulateness, we reran the basic relationships reported in Chapters 18 and 19, controlling for articulateness—i.e., for the average number of valid answers given by respondents in each community. The control had no effect on the pattern of relationships.

See Table I-1 for an example of the computation of an individual's concurrence score.

Index

72 73 74 75 10 9 8 7 6 5 4 3 2 1